I0831119

HOME FOR CHRISTMAS

Decorating for the Holiday Season

teNeues

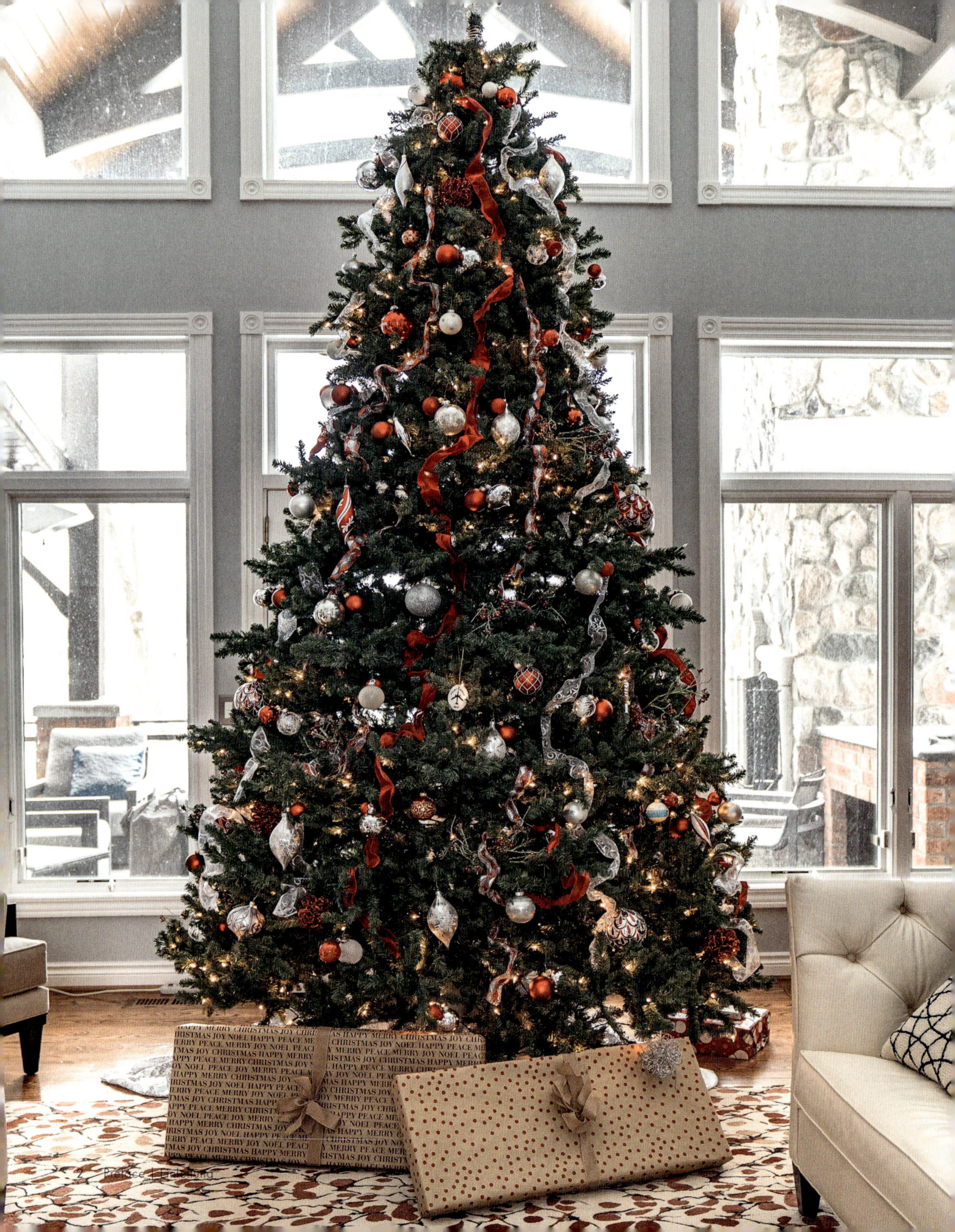

Contents

FESTIVE, FUN AND FABULOUS

by Claire Bingham

But give me holly, bold and jolly,
Honest, prickly, shining holly;
Pluck me holly leaf and berry
For the day when I make merry

From Holly by Christina Rossetti

How do you decorate your home for Christmas? By plunging into classic red and white for a scheme that feels fresh and inviting, or nestling down amongst nature's bounty in a state of cozy hibernation? Wherever you sit on the festive spectrum, the whisper of Christmas gets all our creative juices flowing, be we practical or celebratory. The art of decorating the home for Christmas can be tinsel-strewn or subtle—we lean towards the artisan as much as the sparkle—and inside this book, we show you how. To help with the preparations, here, you'll find lots of inspiration for decorating the home at Christmas, and plenty more besides.

PREPARING THE HOME

The excitement for Christmas can begin any time past July. December is a calendar opposite to the heat of summer, where thoughts of curling up in front of a fire, wearing cozy sweaters and celebrating with friends under twinkling lights is an extension of the holiday mood; yet instead of basking at the beach, we're wrapped up and sparkling. The run-up to Christmas is part of the ritual, contributing to the rhythm of the year. However, before we determine how we fill our homes and what style of bauble we hang on the tree, there is planning. As with any celebratory occasion: having an idea of colors, mood, and itinerary are helpful to embrace the season with aplomb. It also brings cheer and focus to what may otherwise be a dreary time of year.

During autumn, think about gathering natural foliage and foraged blooms to create handmade garlands, Christmas cards and wreaths. Now more than ever, workshops offer a place in our lives for creative inspiration and enrichment. For example, a wreath-making workshop hosted by expert florists can guide you in creating an exquisite decoration for your front door. Also important to consider is how to consciously select a sustainable and ethical tree, one that is grown locally, in a responsibly managed way. All of this is important. If we plan, we can give more of ourselves—and when Christmas Eve arrives, we are able to bask in love and candlelight (because that table setting has been considered and looks divine). Anticipation really is the best bit.

CHRISTMAS COMES ALIVE

For anyone with a love of Christmas, decorating the house is central to the magic. The gathering of green-

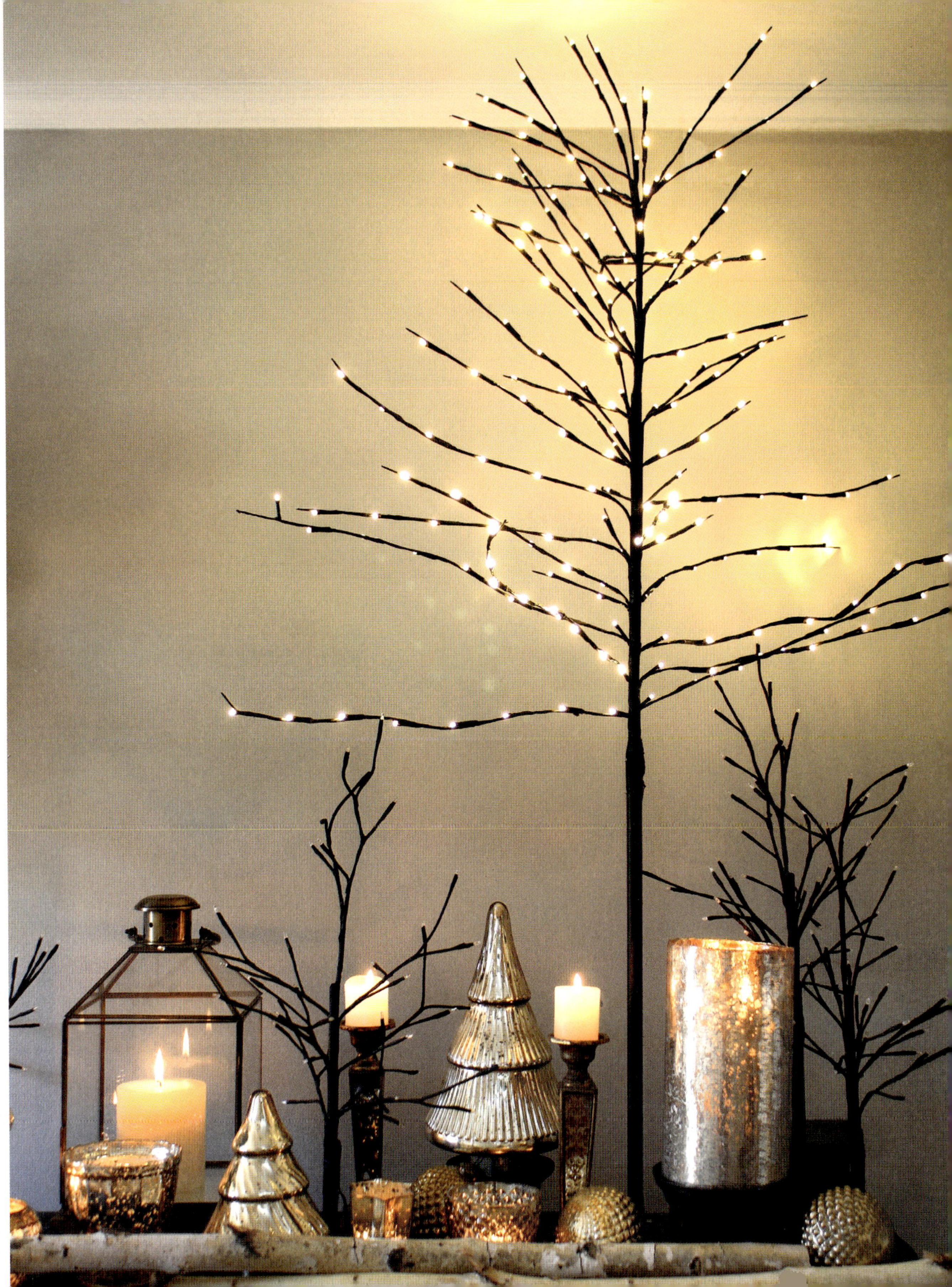

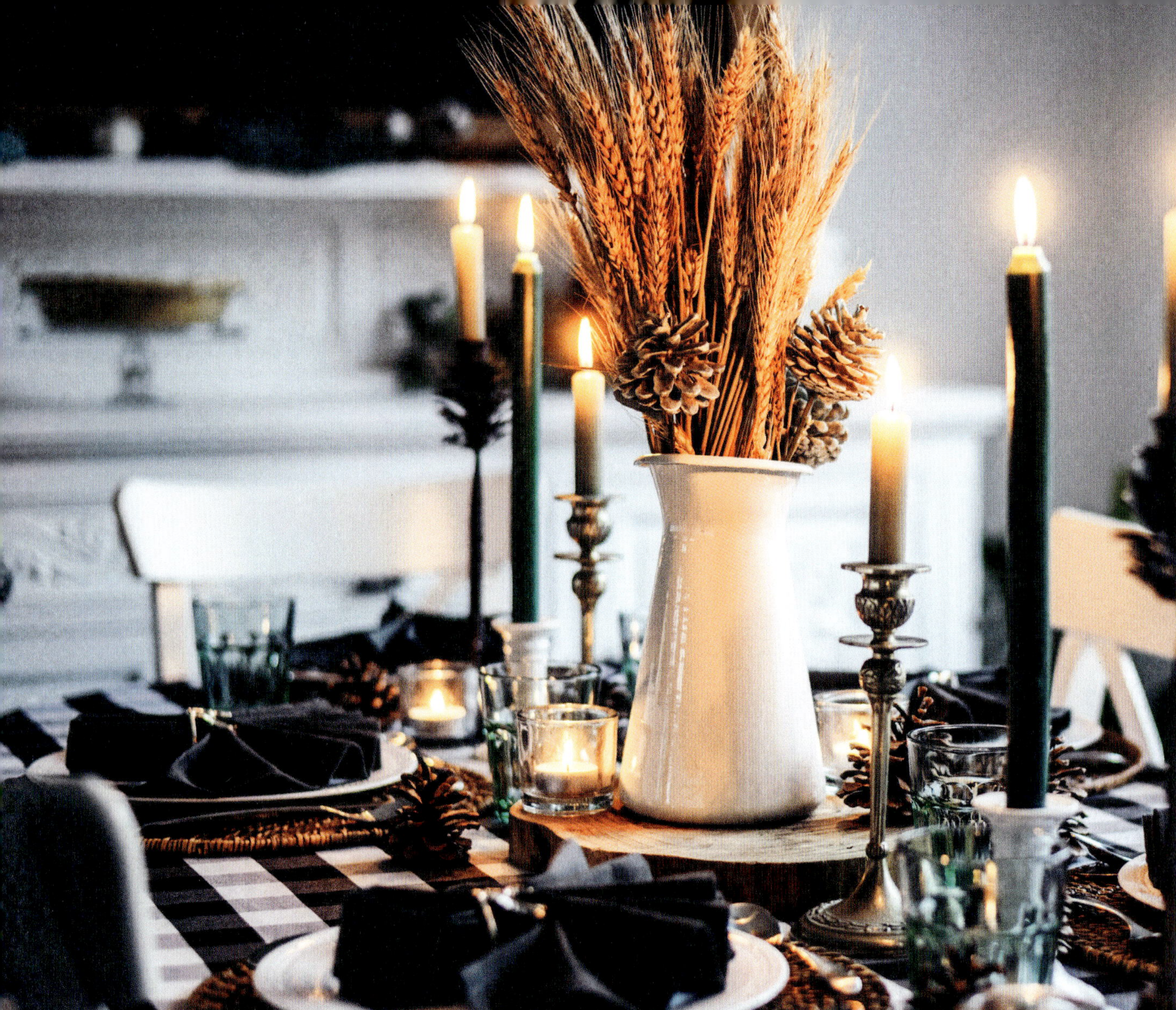

ery and berries, creating arrangements and unwrapping treasured baubles all spark joy and are good for the soul. But what style do you go for? Traditional or modern? Natural or bright? Do you wish to evoke visions of candy canes and nostalgia with classic red and green, or opt for the glimmer of gold that's both heartwarming and chic? Throughout this book, we show all manner of festive decorating styles—from merry and bright to palettes of rich greens that feel understated and abundant at the same time. There are no wrongs.

For some homes, less is more, with pared-back displays inspired by the natural world and a simple color scheme. Other homes make merry with a riot of color ramping up the drama and excitement. Color stands out amazingly against a white backdrop. Other homes embrace the old-world charm of vintage

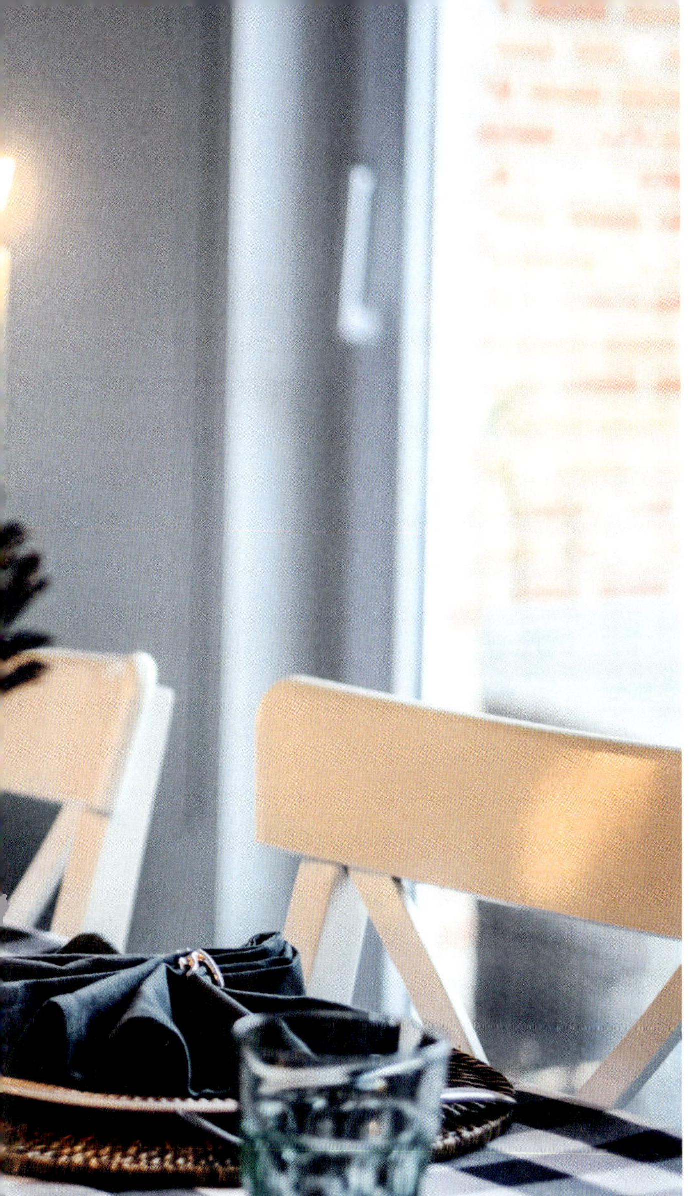

silver and snowy pinecones. The joy of rustic style is that it needn't be perfect to be charming. Traditional or with a twist, you'll thrill to the possibilities this time of year holds.

SET THE TABLE

The finishing touch to any Christmas home is the table. Creating a dining table with ambience and atmosphere is a pleasure and a big player in the rituals of Christmas Day. It starts small with a tray made for breakfast with hot chocolate and panettone and concludes with a dining table dressed for gathering and bonhomie. The best festivities revolve around loved ones bonding over food and drink—so cutlery, glassware and centerpieces are all part of the story for any party set to sparkle.

In any given situation, candlelight is key. There are two camps. One is to go for a candelabra where the light is placed high. Vintage silver looks beautiful on a modern or traditional table. The alternative is to go low, with pretty tea lights dotted around the table in cut-glass holders that are unobtrusive and easy to move around. Tablecloths are a conundrum. Plain linen is always a winner; however, pattern is a great way to add more color to the table. A good mix of stripes and Chinoiserie feels festive—and the patterns help hide spills. Delving into detail, add a personal touch with British Christmas crackers made using pretty napkins and oversized ribbons. Match these to a wide ribbon tied in a bow at the back of each chair. For as with all Christmas decorations—from the tree to beautifully gift-wrapped presents—when in doubt, add a ribbon.

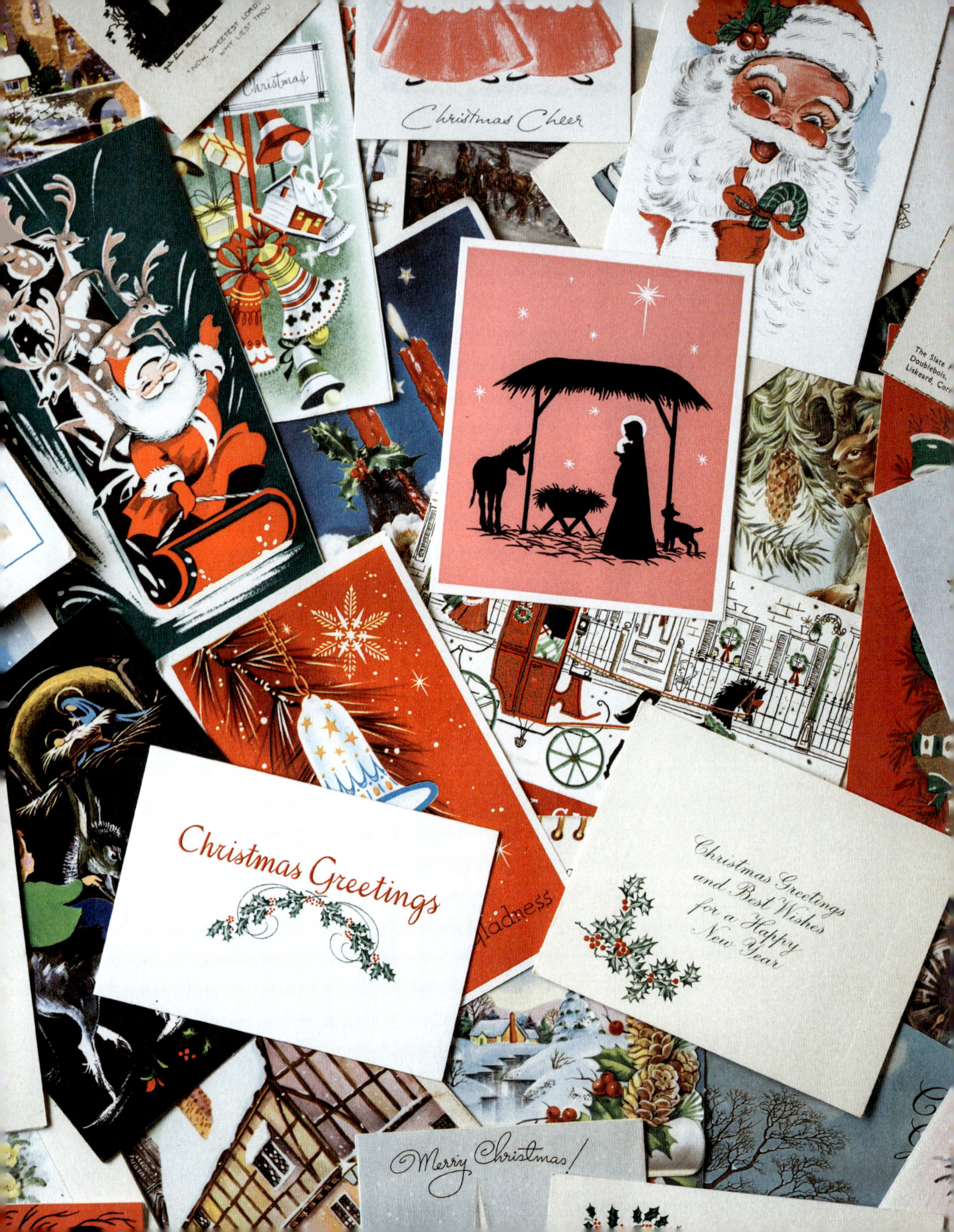

Christmas
Christmas Cheer
Christmas Greetings
Christmas Greetings and Best Wishes for a Happy New Year
Merry Christmas!

Countdown
to
Christmas

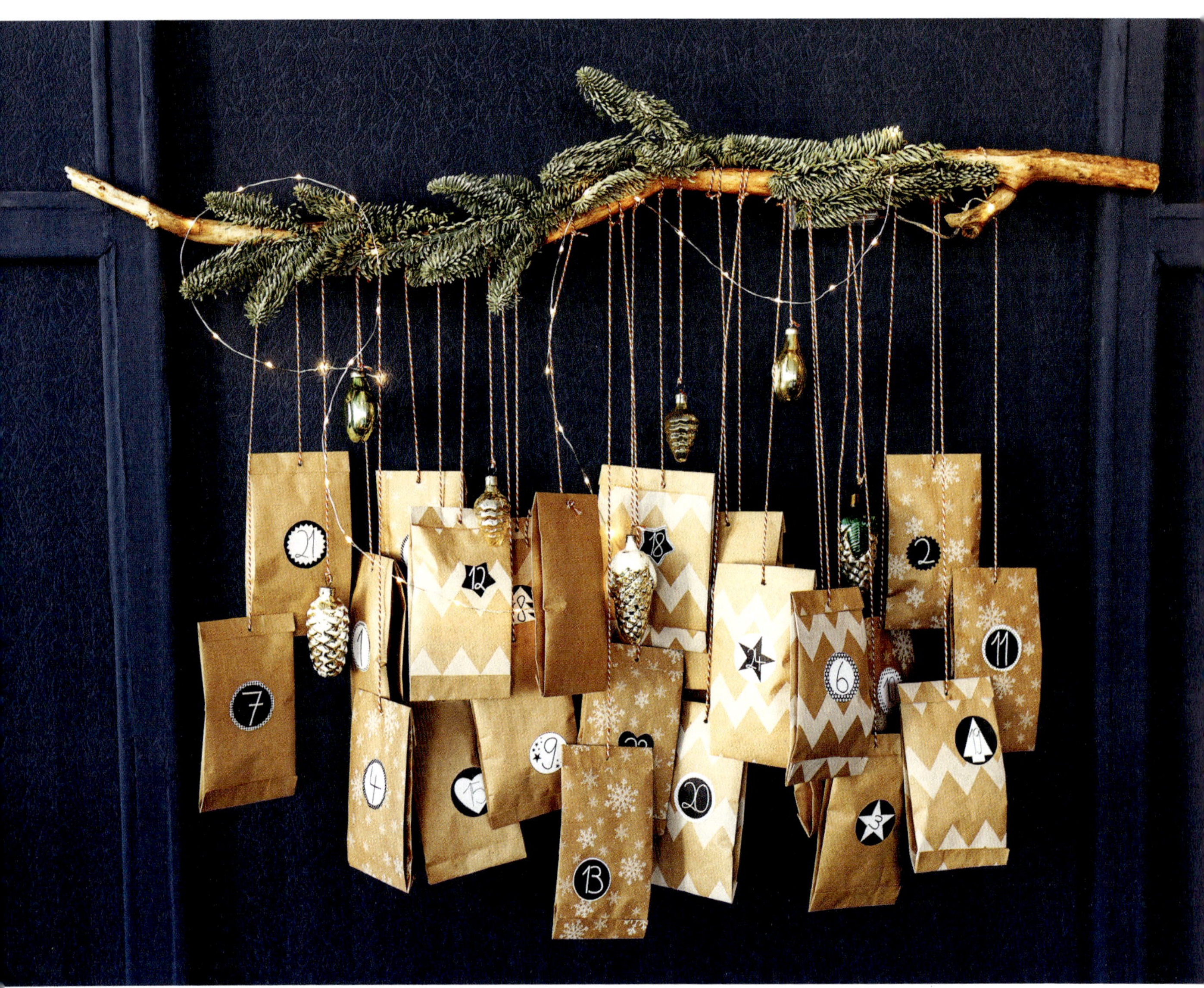

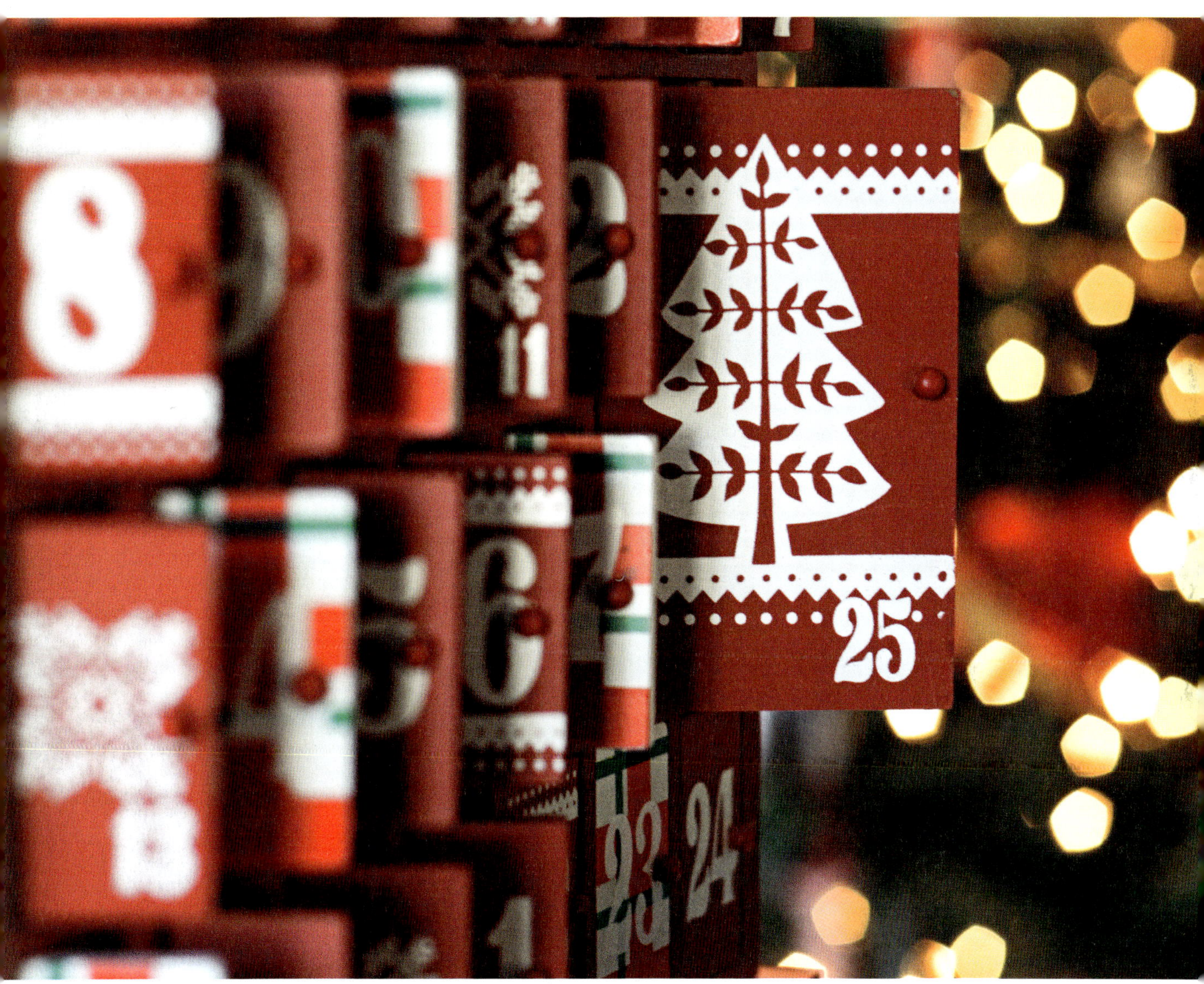
8
11
6
25
24

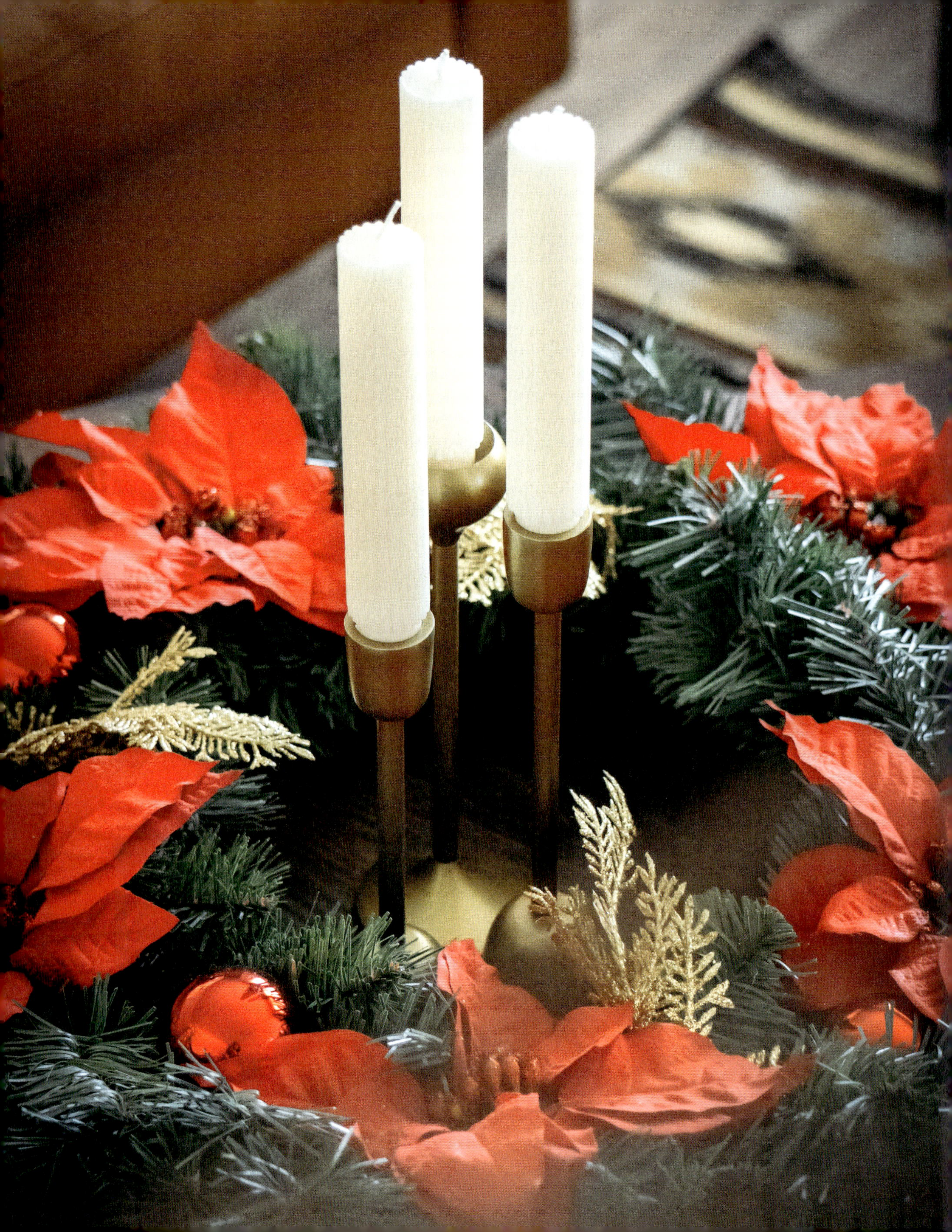

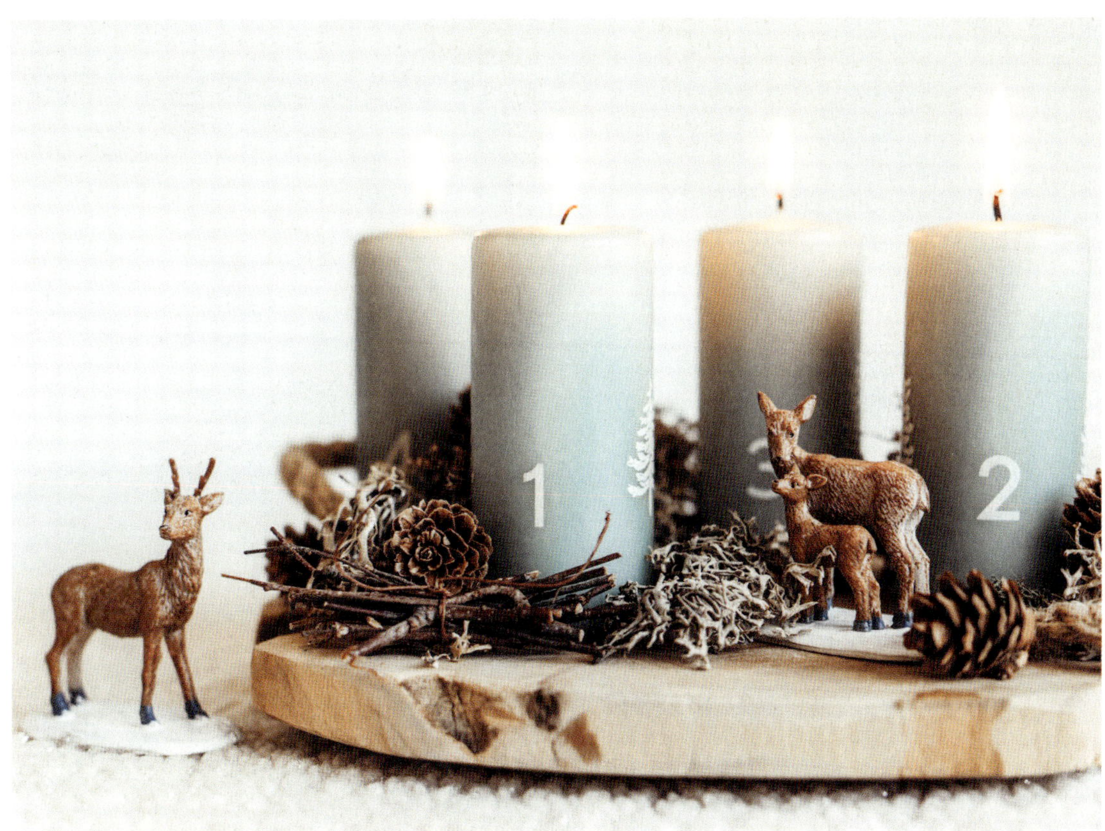

Entering a beautifully prepared home filled with festive touches never fails to spark joy. And this begins with Advent. A key ritual of Christmas, a rustic dish or wreath centerpiece of red poinsettia with spiced candles at the center is as heartwarming as it is striking. Forest animals and pine cones add rustic charm to the situation and a grown-up advent calendar never fails to induce an excited homecoming smile. Pop chocolates into small paper envelopes, each labelled with numbers 1-24, and hang from a branch with string.

Fun fact: The traditional German advent wreath (usually a horizontal circle of greenery with 4 candles) dates back to 1839. It was meant to shorten the time until Christmas. Every Sunday before Christmas another candle is lit.

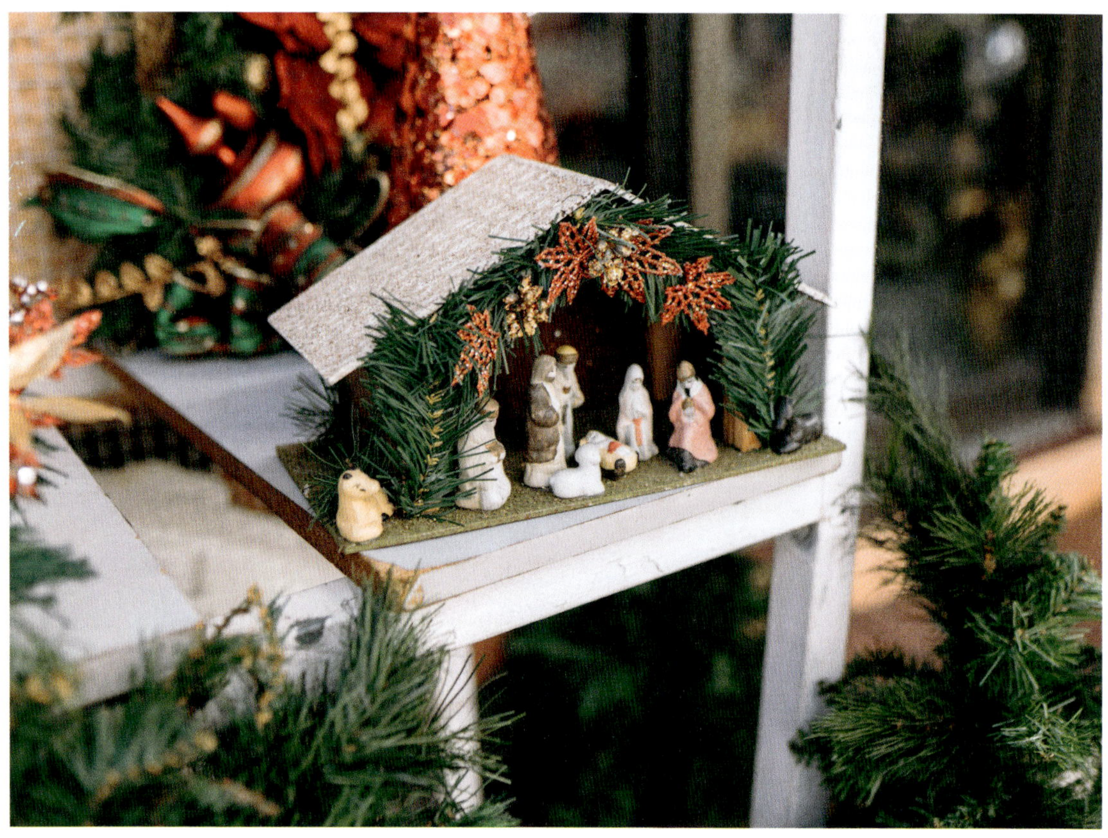

A nativity scene captures the spirit of the season and is a cherished tradition that celebrates the true meaning of Christmas. Throughout December, it is a focal point for the family to enjoy, but it is the putting together of these Christmas displays that make magical memories. Gingerbread homes and cookies fall into this category; aromas and memories are intertwined with the baking and decorating. Certain scents such as ginger, cinnamon and orange all help prepare for the festive period.

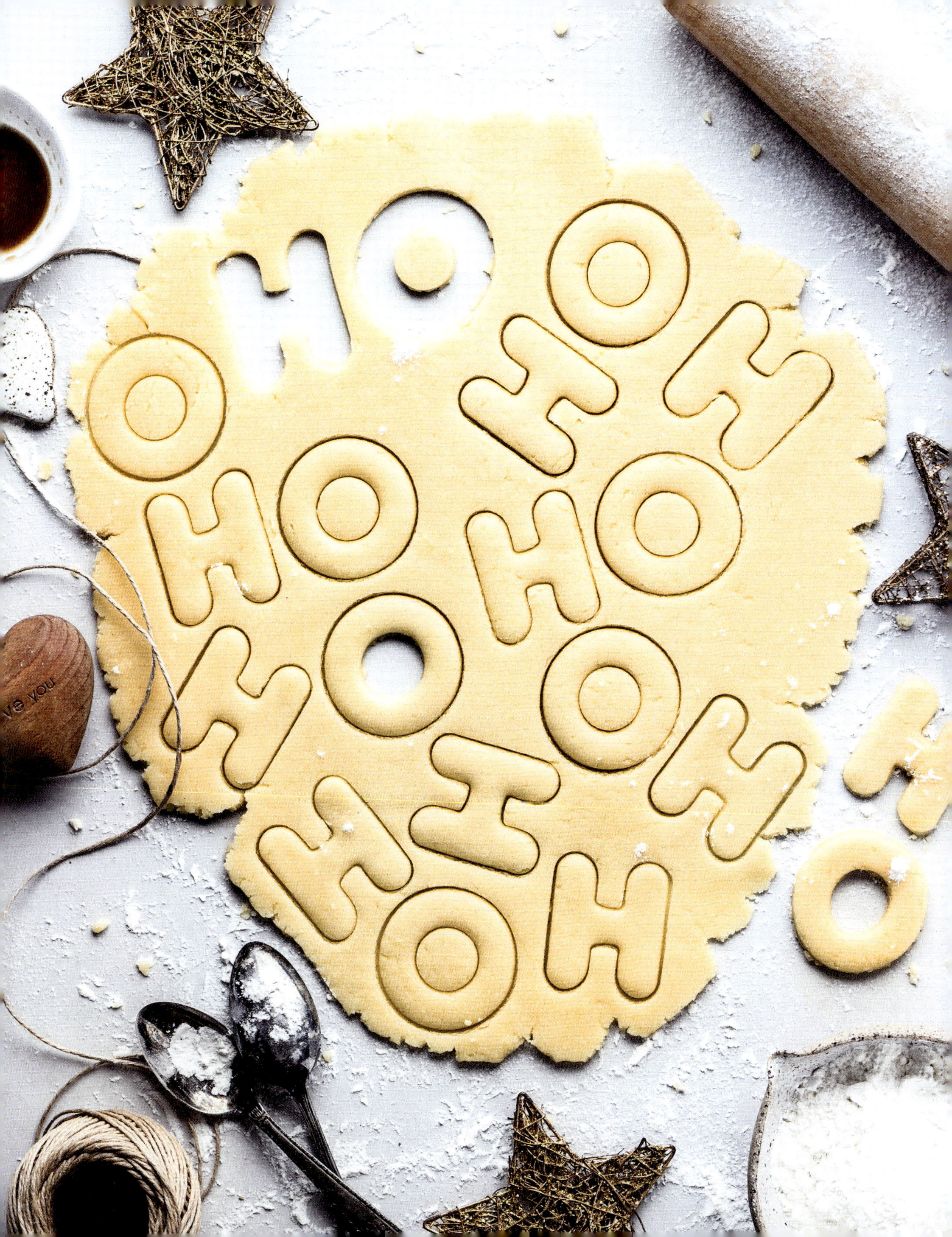

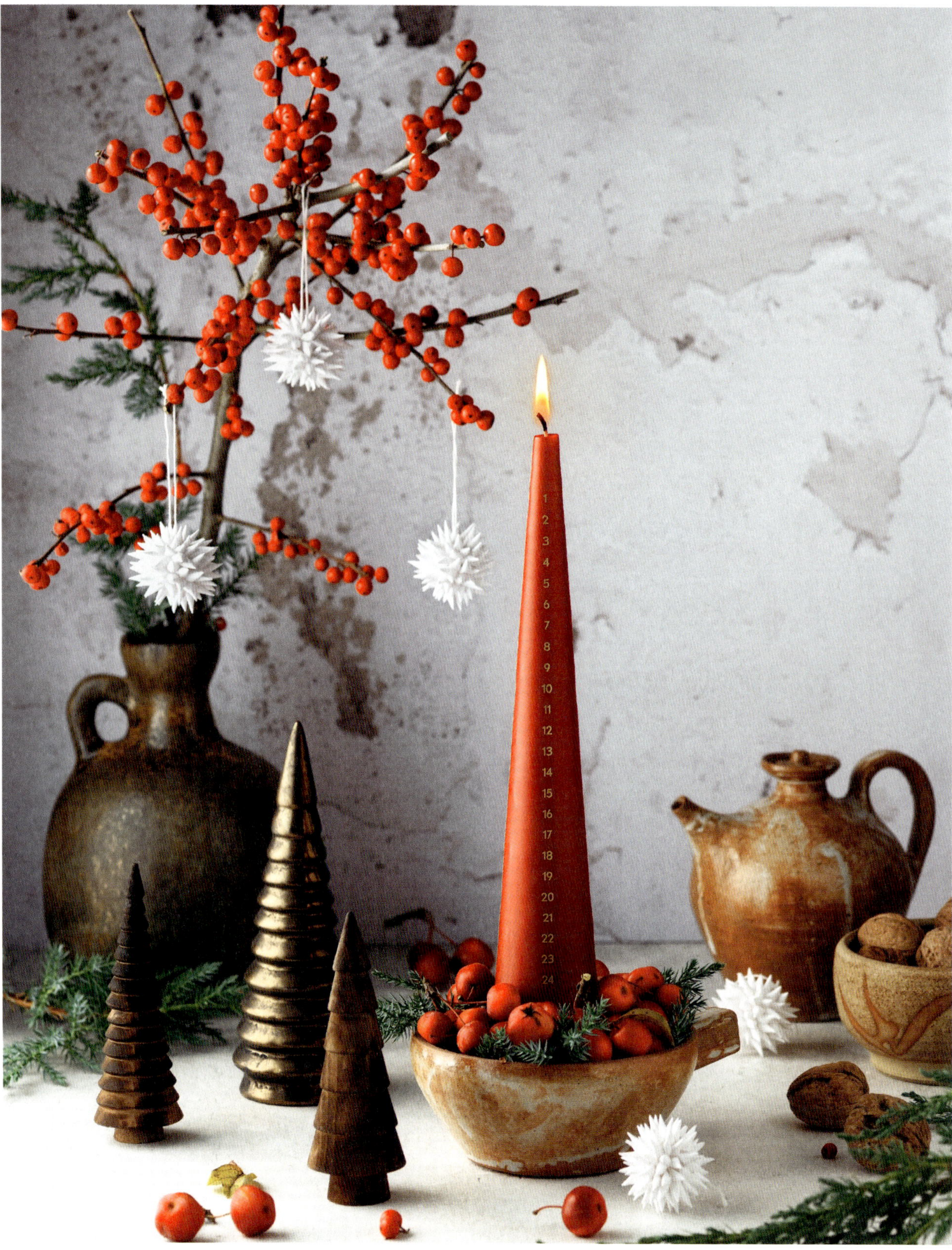
1
2
3
4
5
6
7
8
9
10
11
12
13
14
15
16
17
18
19
20
21
22
23
24

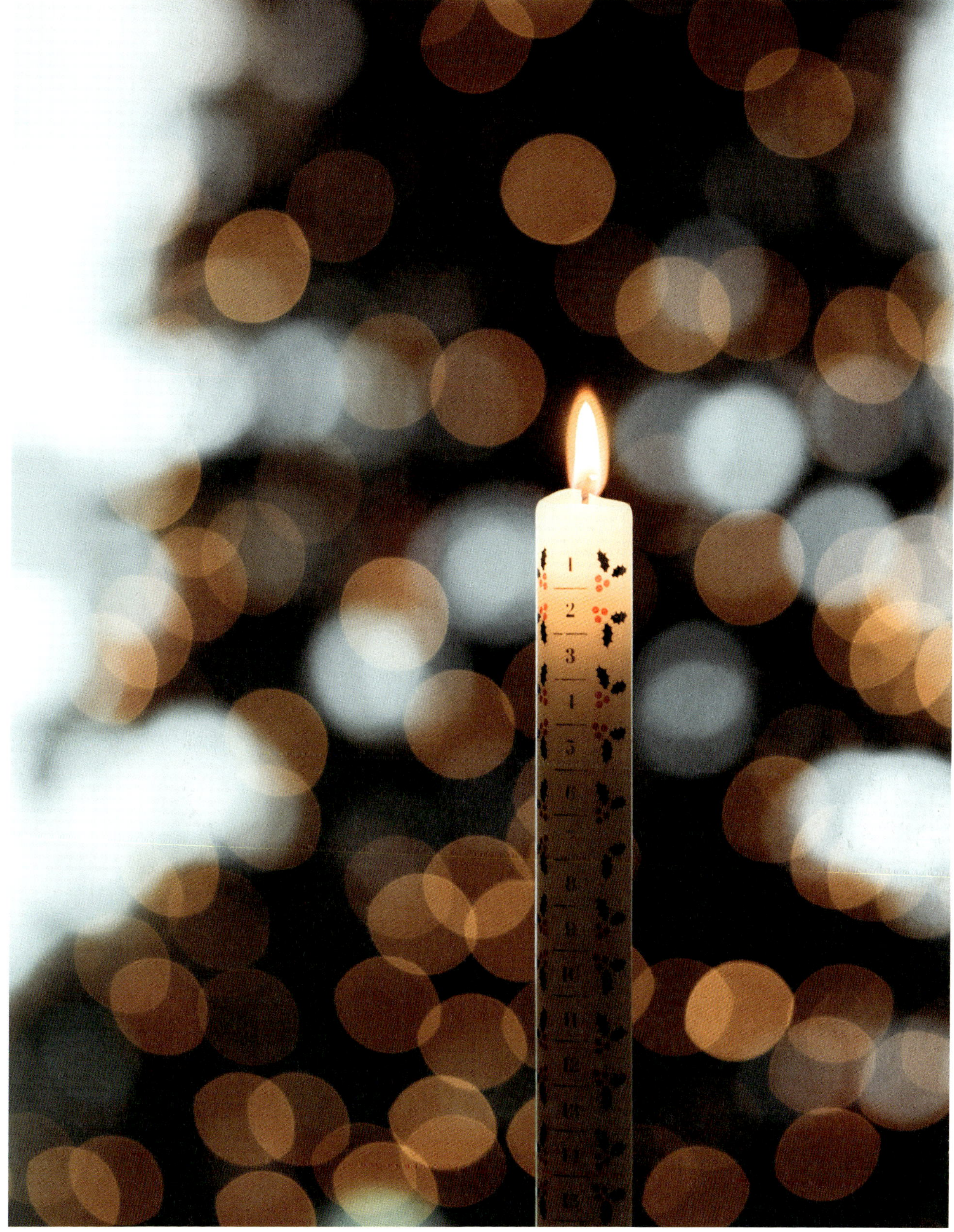
1
2
3
4
5

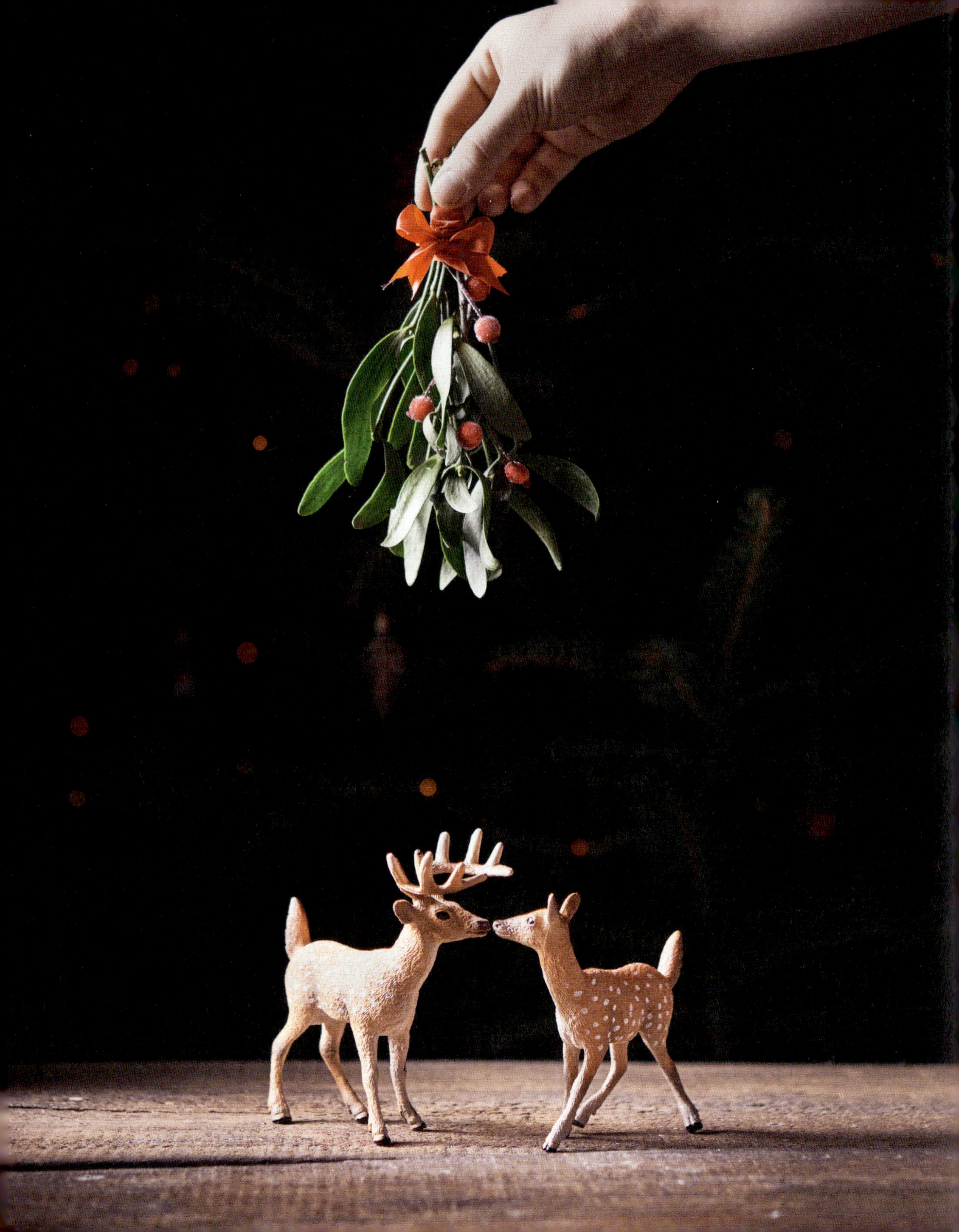

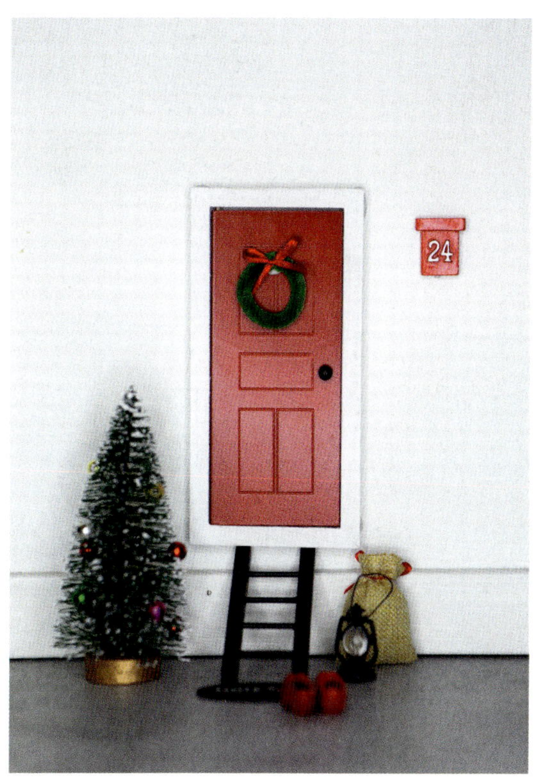

Cast a spell with a sprig of mistletoe hanging from your door finished with a ribbon at the end; if fairy dust is more your speed, a miniature door for a gnome is cute and will delight all children. Use candy canes as decorations and dollhouse furniture to bring the magic to life.

The origins of kissing under the mistletoe go back to Norse mythology—introduced as a Christmas tradition and symbol of love during the 18th century in England.

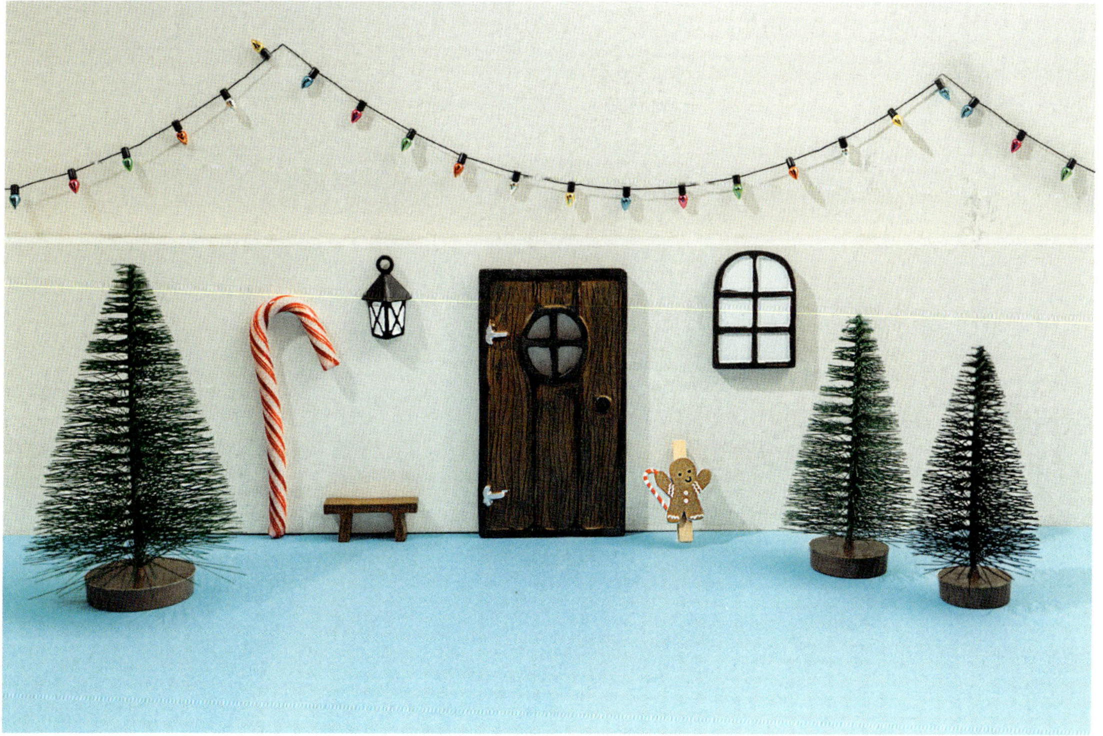

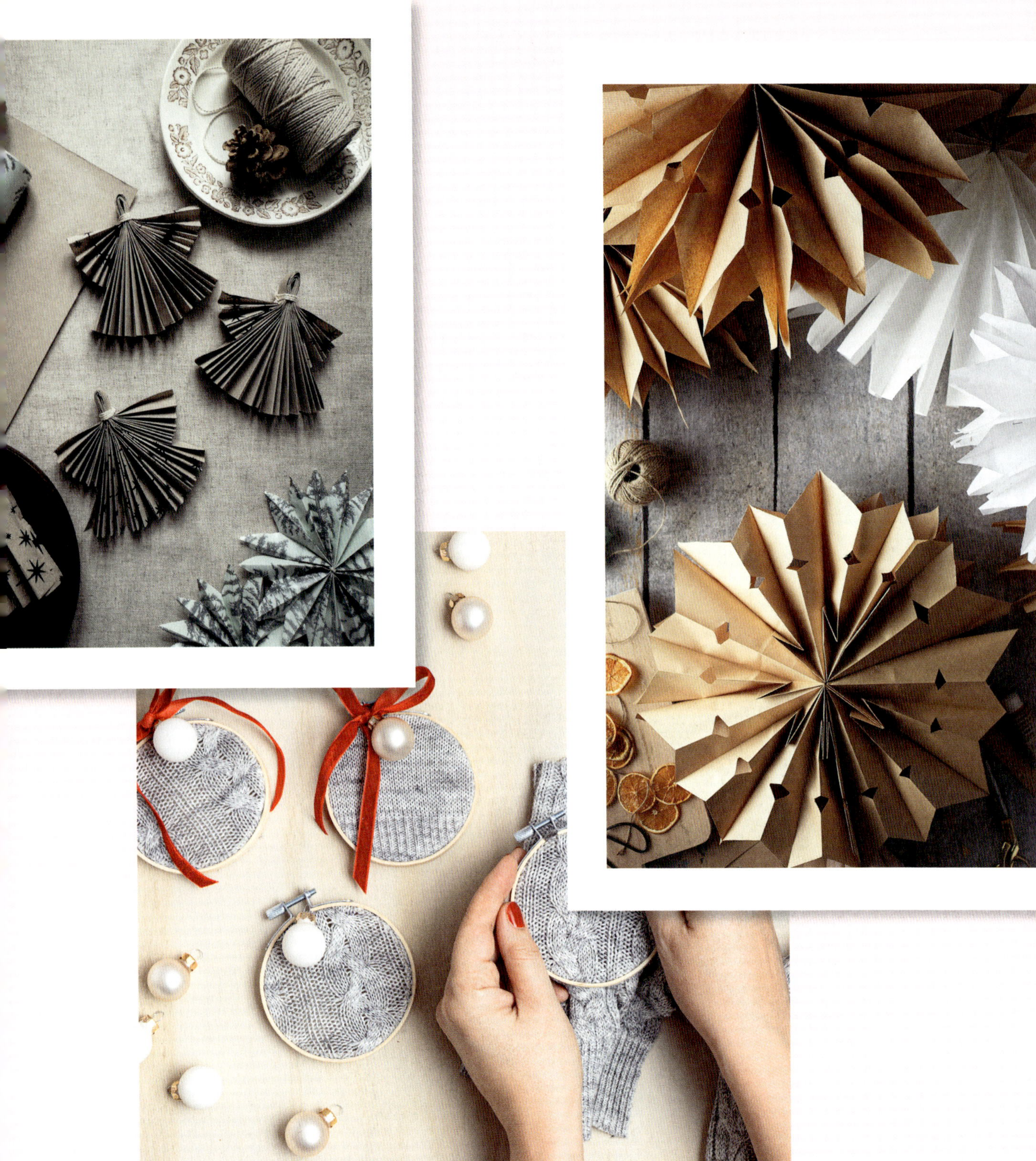

DIY

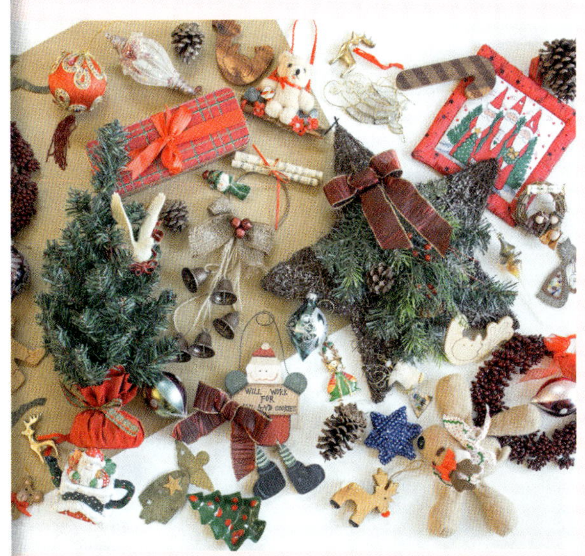

CRAFTING BEAUTIFUL DECORATIONS

There is nothing like handmade touches to make a family Christmas feel special. Craft a creative moment by making origami paper decorations—it is a great way to reuse wrapping or parcel paper. Add pretty ribbons so they are ready to hang up. Crochet and knits are a tactile alternative to baubles. Reuse old socks and mittens with the wool held in place with embroidery frames, dressed up with vintage pearls and ribbons. Or introduce macrame wreaths and stars for a touch of wonderful old-world charm.

If there was ever a time to get creative, Christmas is it. DIY-ing your décor ensures you can craft a unique look while saving money.

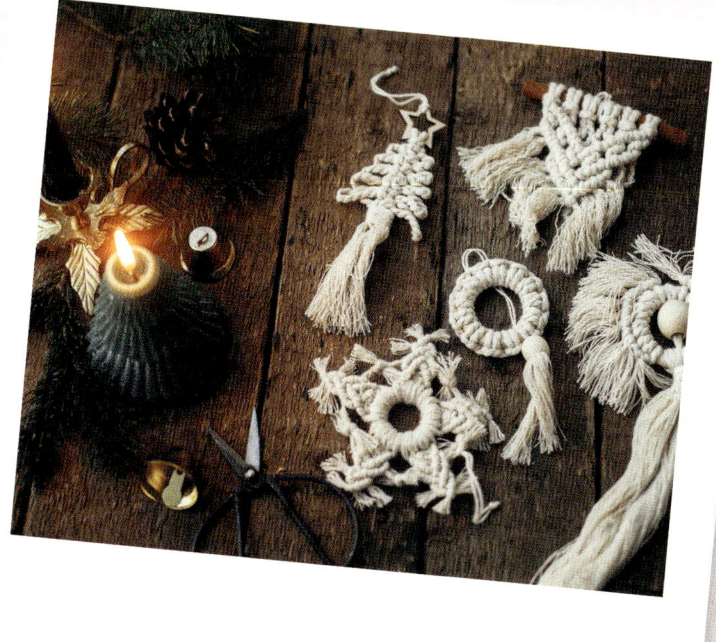

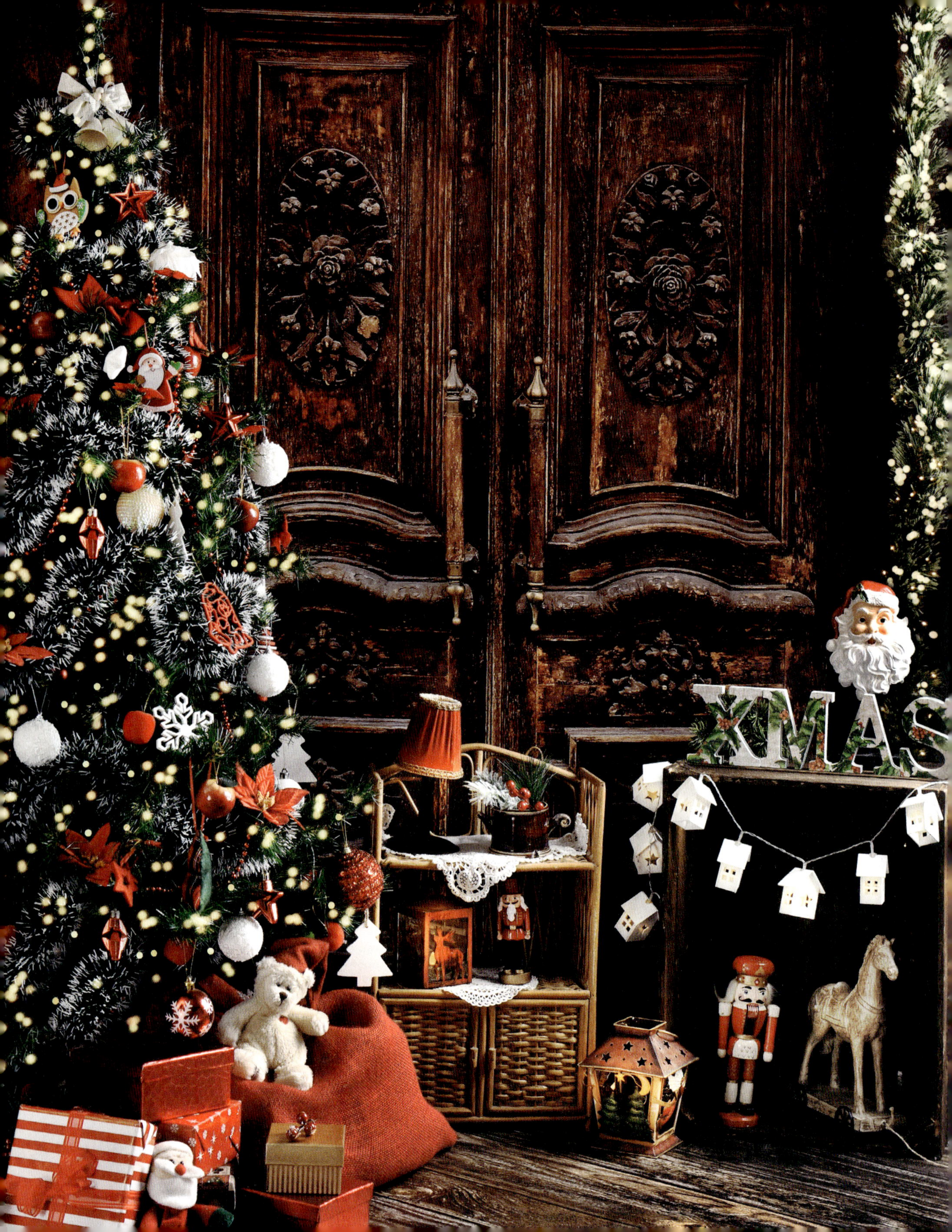
XMAS

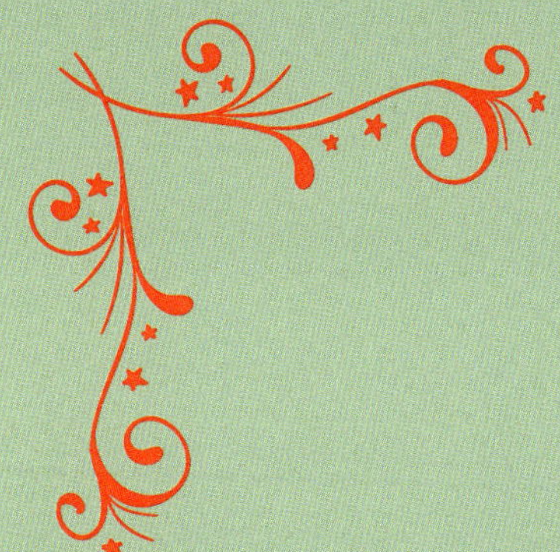

Style inspiration

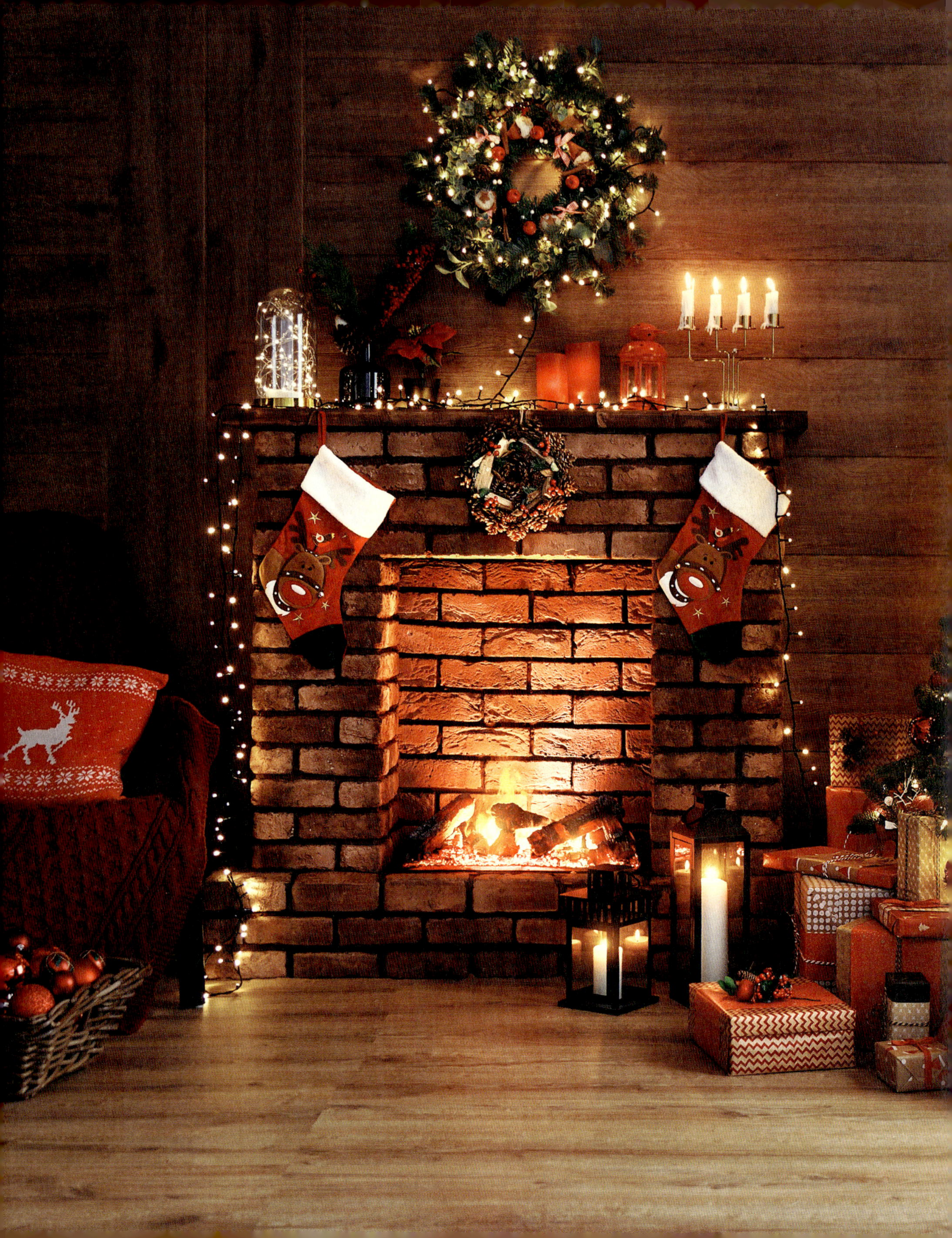

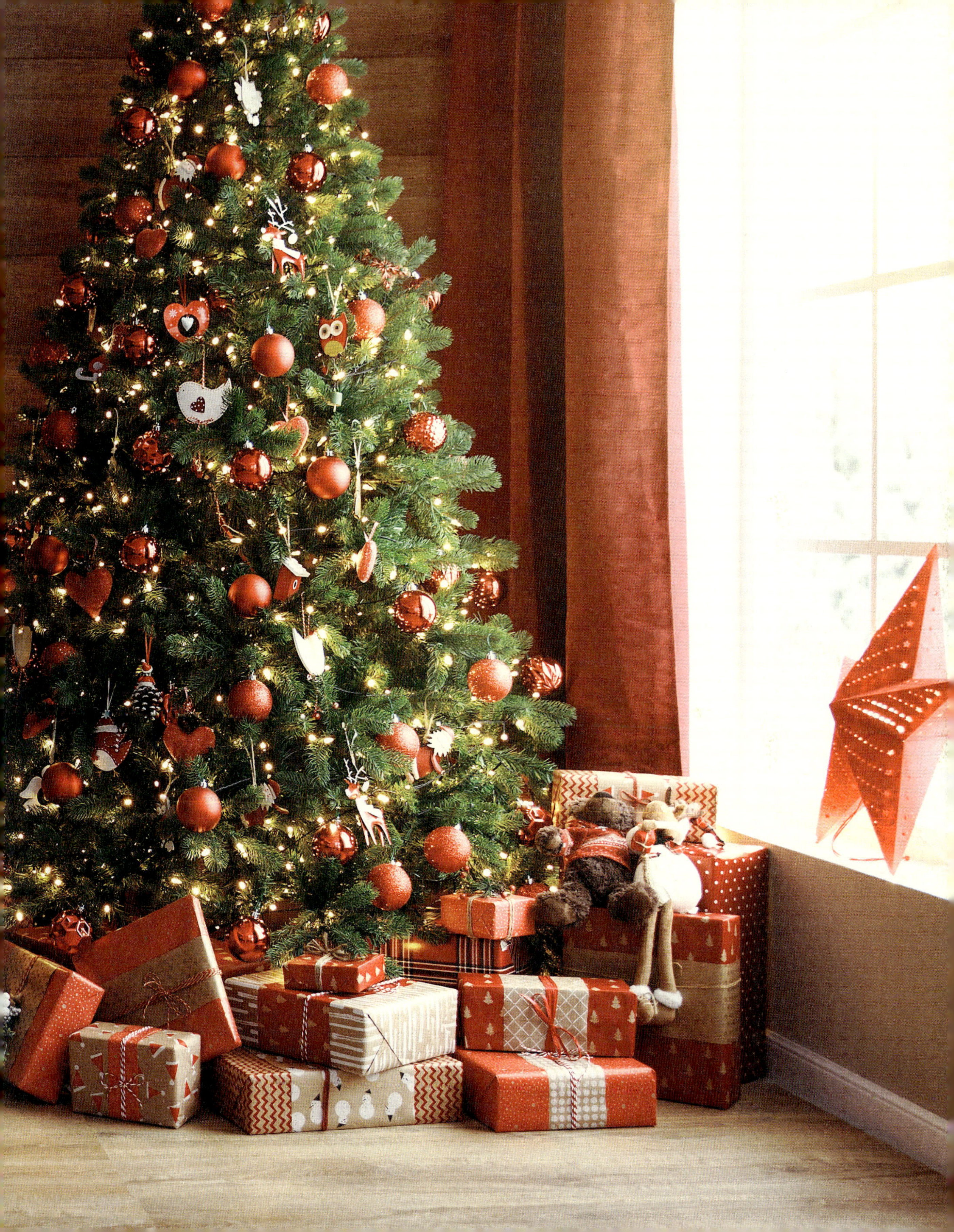

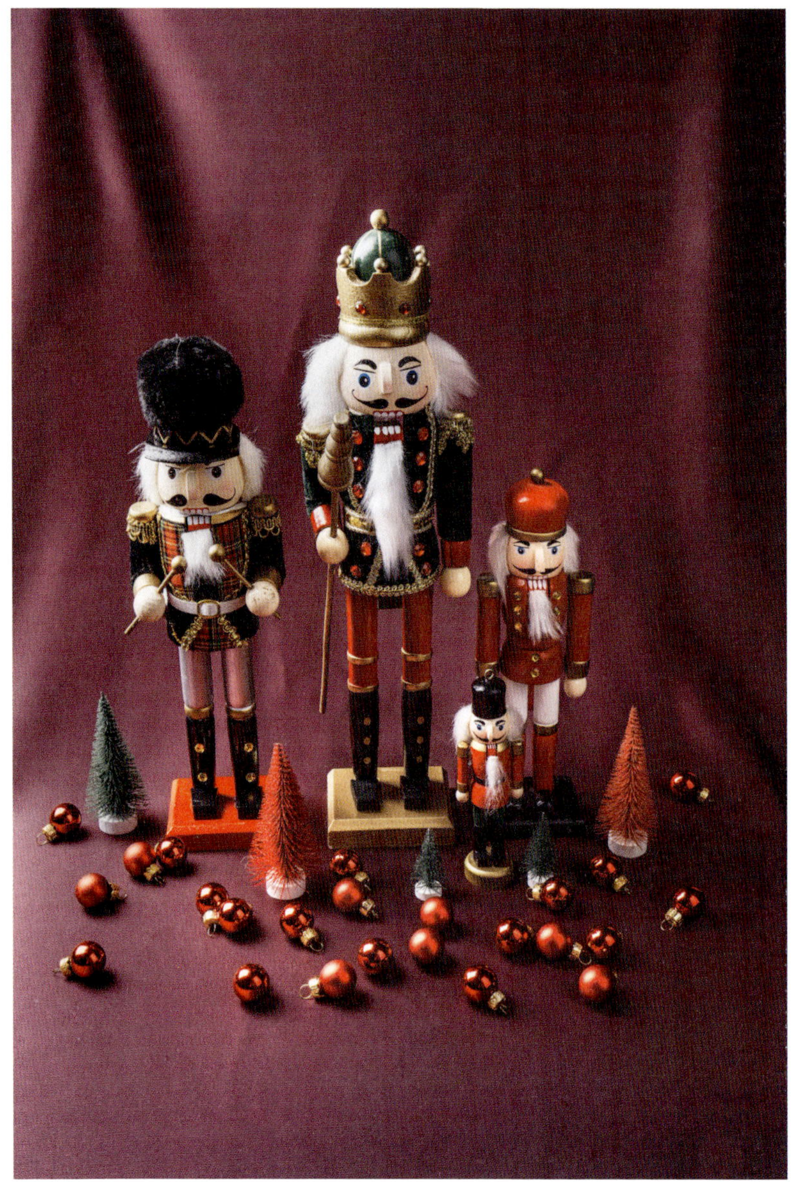

ROOTED IN TRADITION

Is there anything warmer and more welcoming than pops of red and green against a neutral palette? A traditional pine forest and berry color scheme reflects the shades of nature at Christmas—and it thrives on the contrast between shiny gold, red and dark green branches.

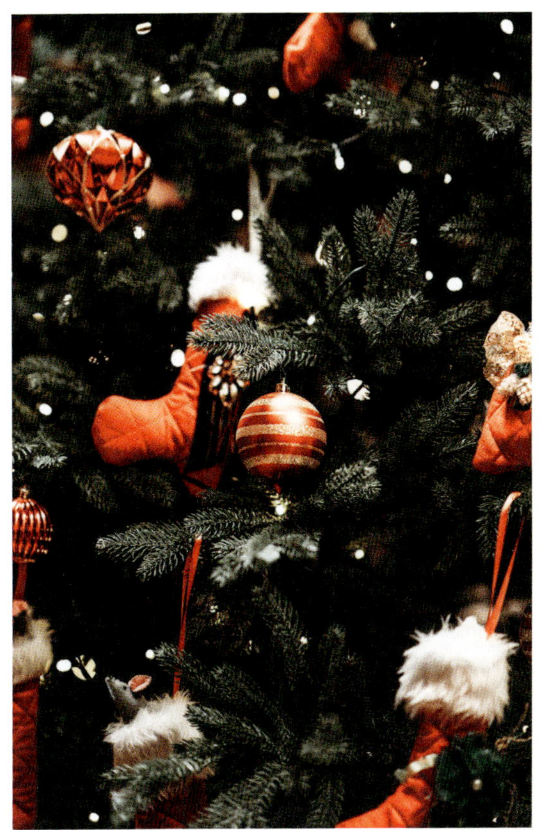

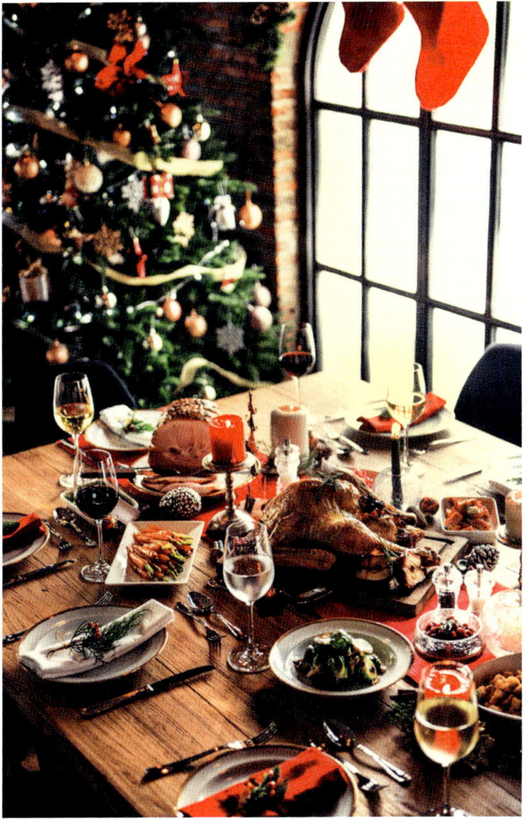

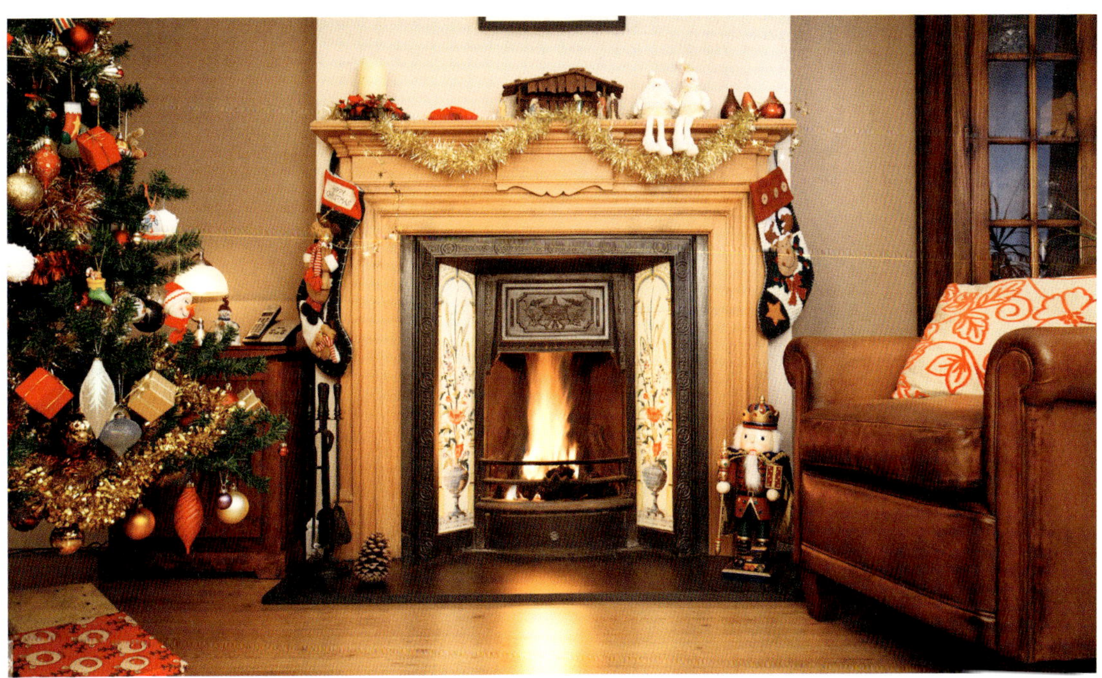

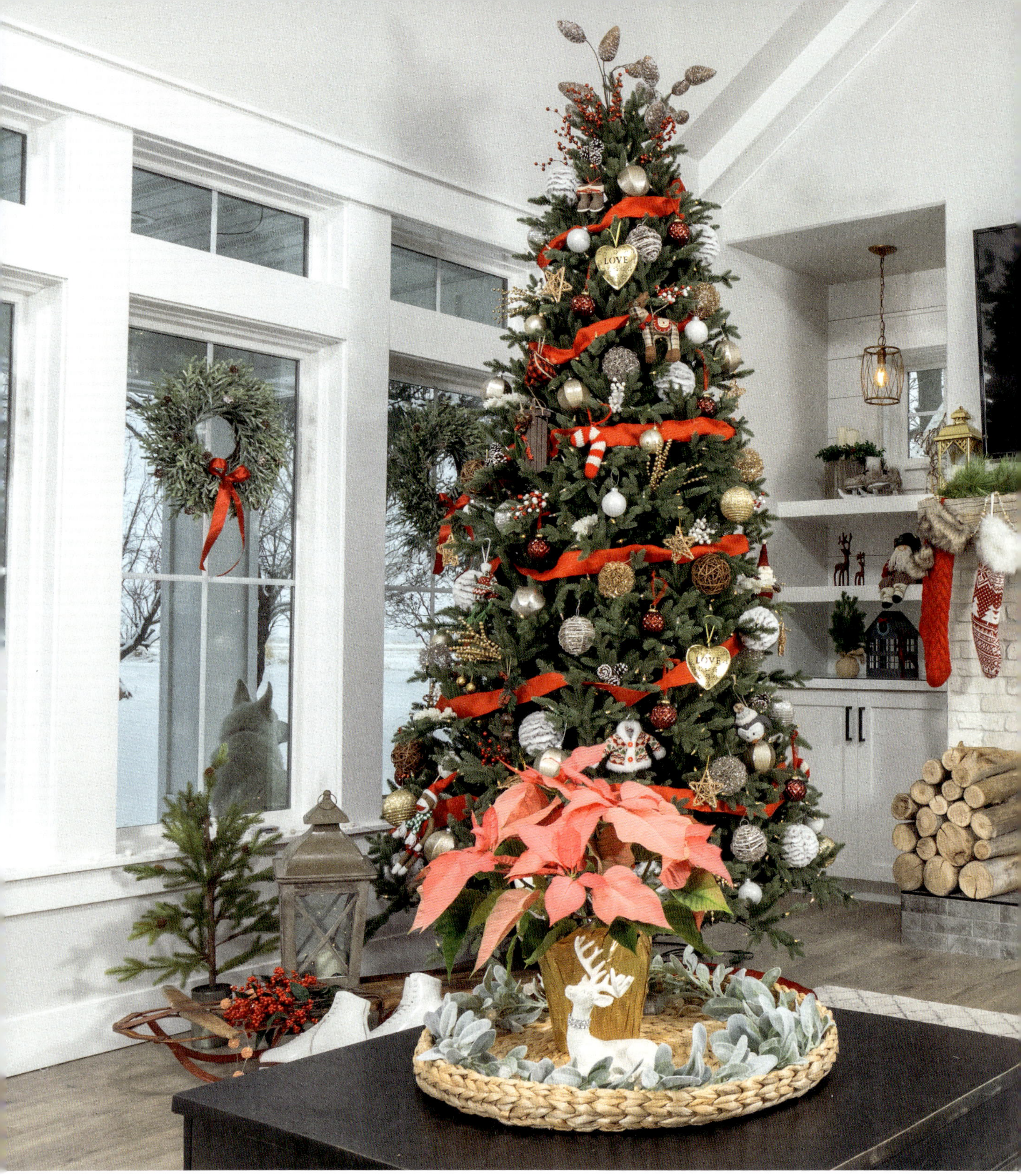
LOVE
LOVE

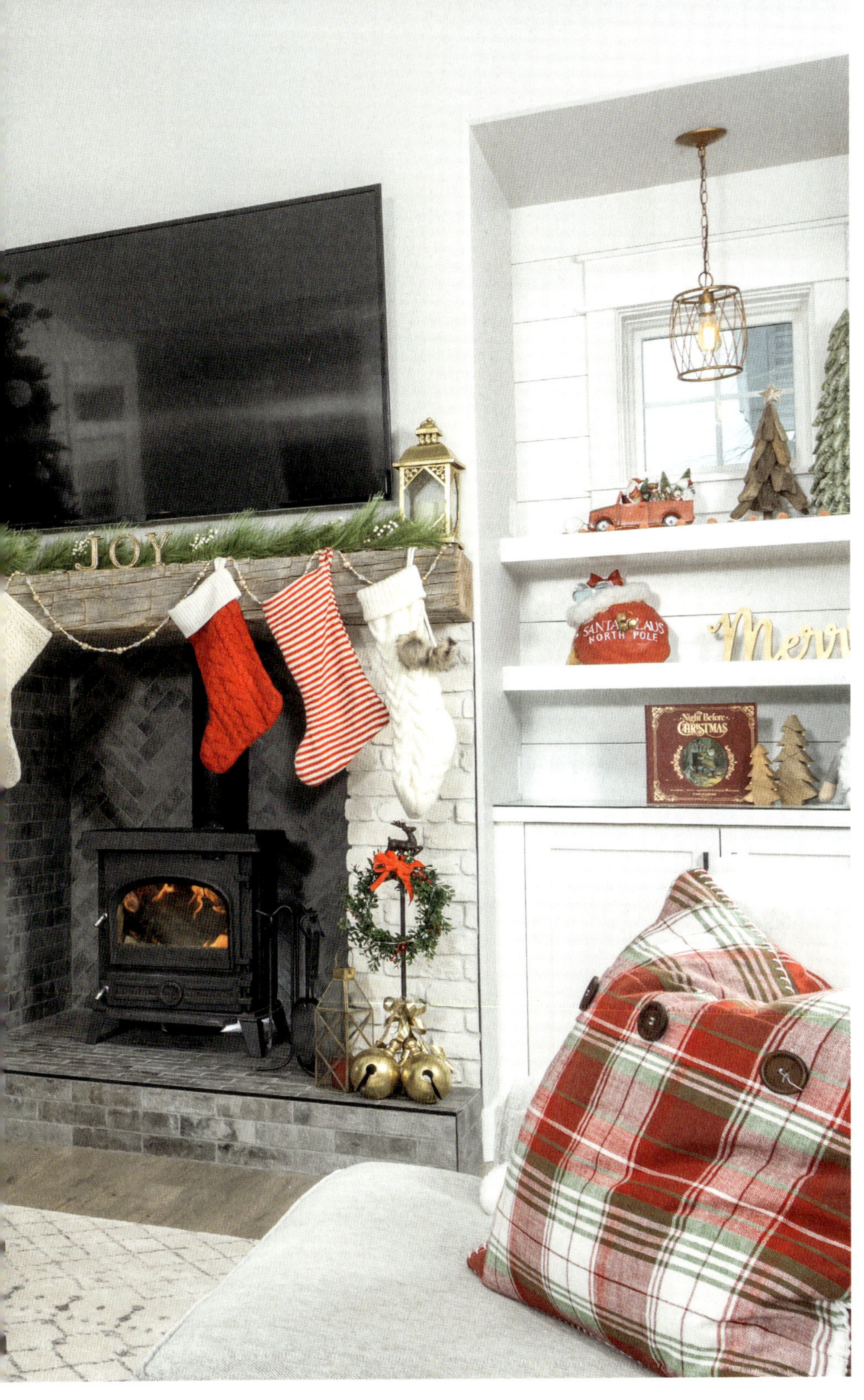
JOY
NORTH POLE
Night Before
CHRISTMAS

FEATURE

CHRISTMAS AT CARLTON TOWERS

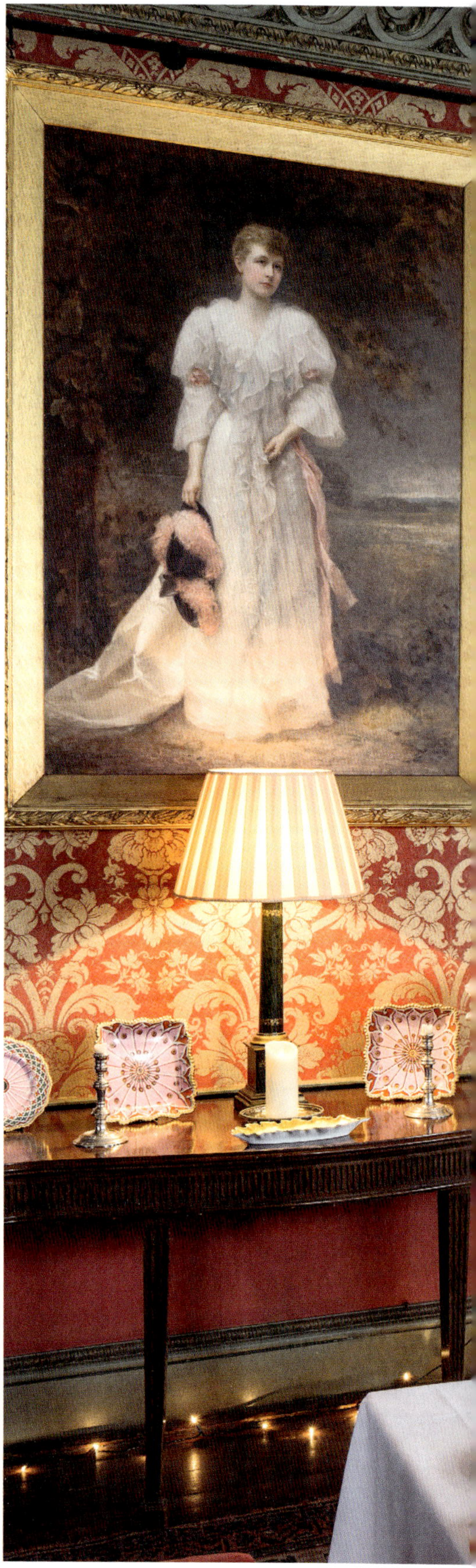

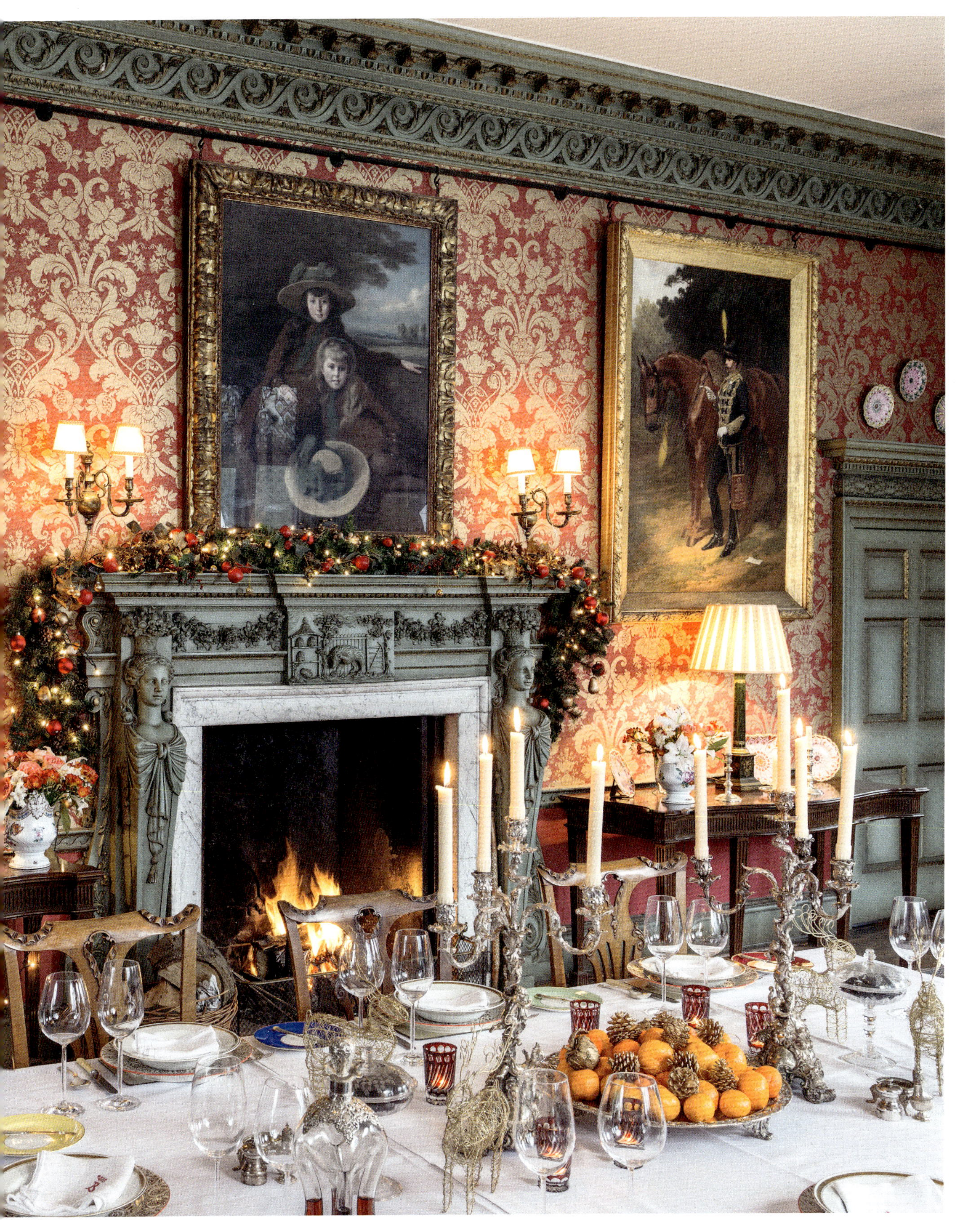

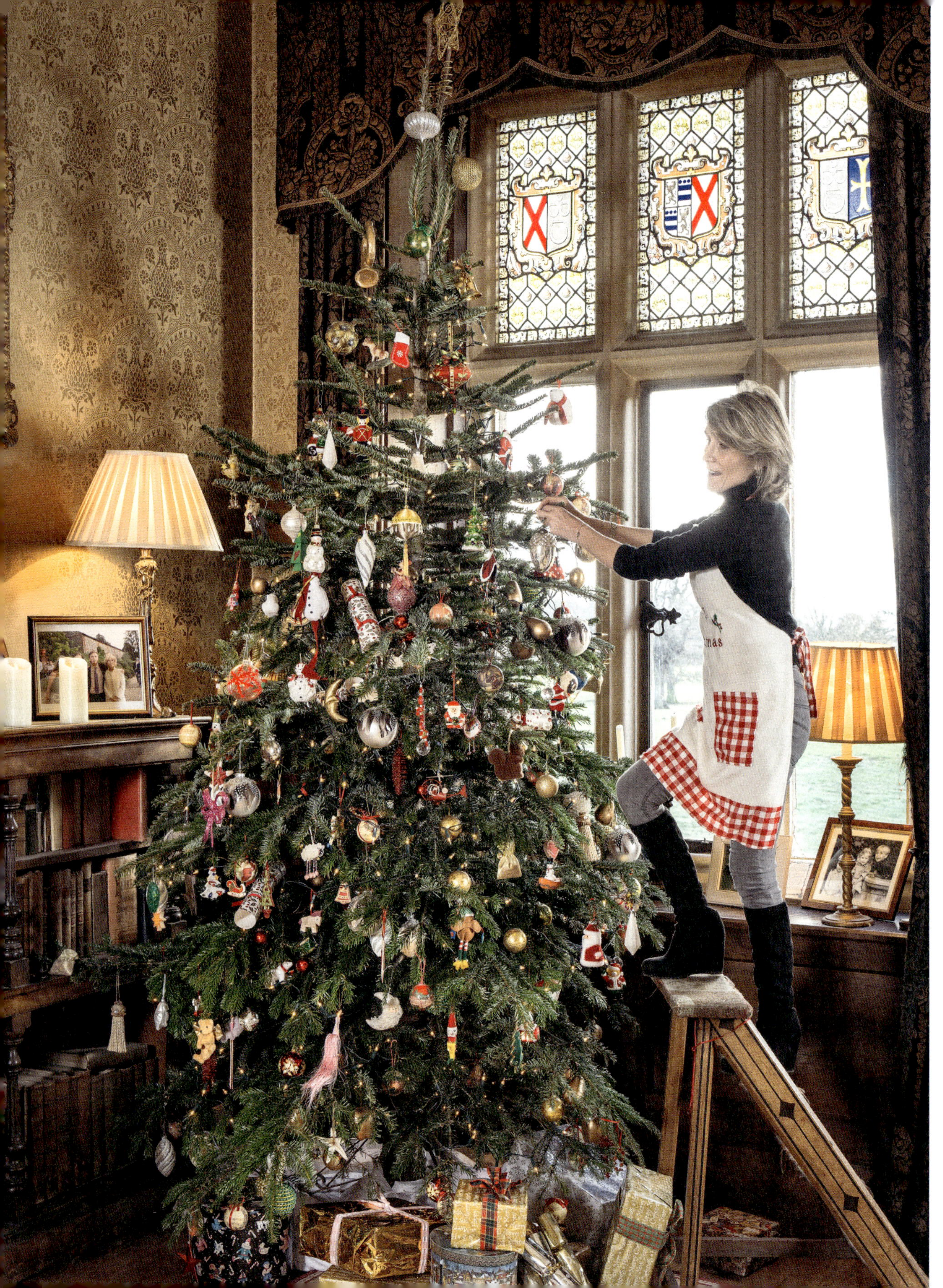

Lady Emma Fitzalan-Howard decorates the 10-foot tree herself.

Christmas Magic with History

Carlton Towers in Yorkshire is the home of Lady Gerald Fitzalan-Howard (she prefers to be called Emma), her husband Gerald and their three children, Arthur, Florence and Grace. "The estate, which encompasses over 3000 acres, has been in Gerald's family for centuries," says Lady Emma. "In the late 18th century, the long east wing was added by Thomas Stapleton, and it incorporated a neo-classical chapel. In due course, the house passed to his great-nephew, who put his own mark on the house by converting the chapel into an enfilade of state rooms with a series of service rooms behind." It is those vast, lavishly embellished rooms that are now highly sought after as a venue for parties, weddings, and corporate events. Emma explains, "There is scarcely a weekend in the year when there isn't a function of some sort taking place at Carlton. Gerald and I held our own wedding reception here twenty-five years ago in December, and it was the most magical setting."

The couple's mission has been to make Carlton Towers earn its keep as well as being the family home, requiring it to be updated for the 21st century. But instead of adding another wing, they concentrated on modernizing what was already there. Although Emma had no professional experience in interior design, she learned on the job.

As the Chair of the Selby branch of Action Research, the Doncaster branch of the NSPCC, and 'Selby Hands of Hope,' run by the indefatigable Wendy Singh, children are her prime concern. "Every year for Action Research, we host a big 'Winter Warmer' carol concert sung by the choristers of Selby Abbey. When I hear those voices waft through the Venetian Drawing Room, I feel Christmas has really begun."

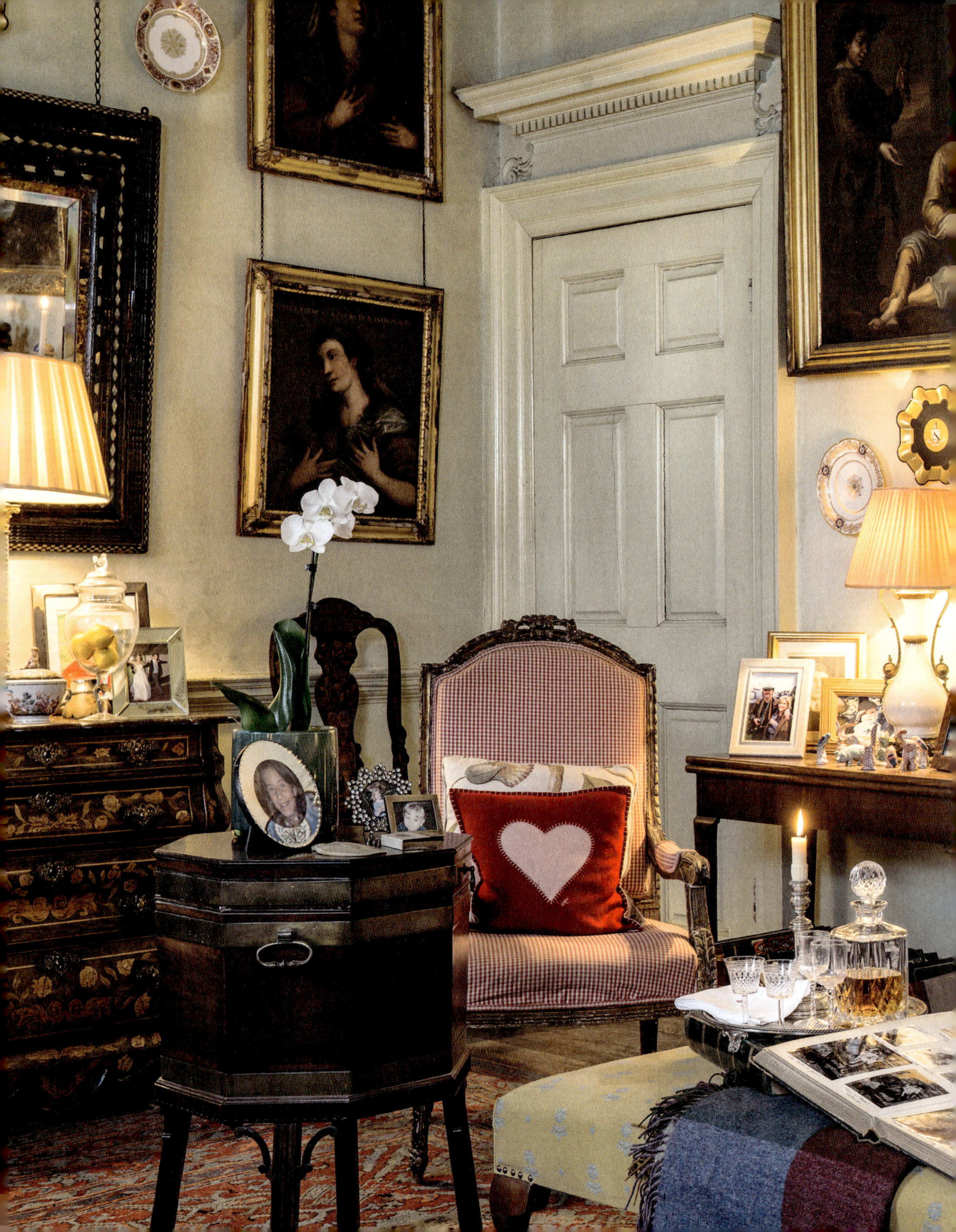

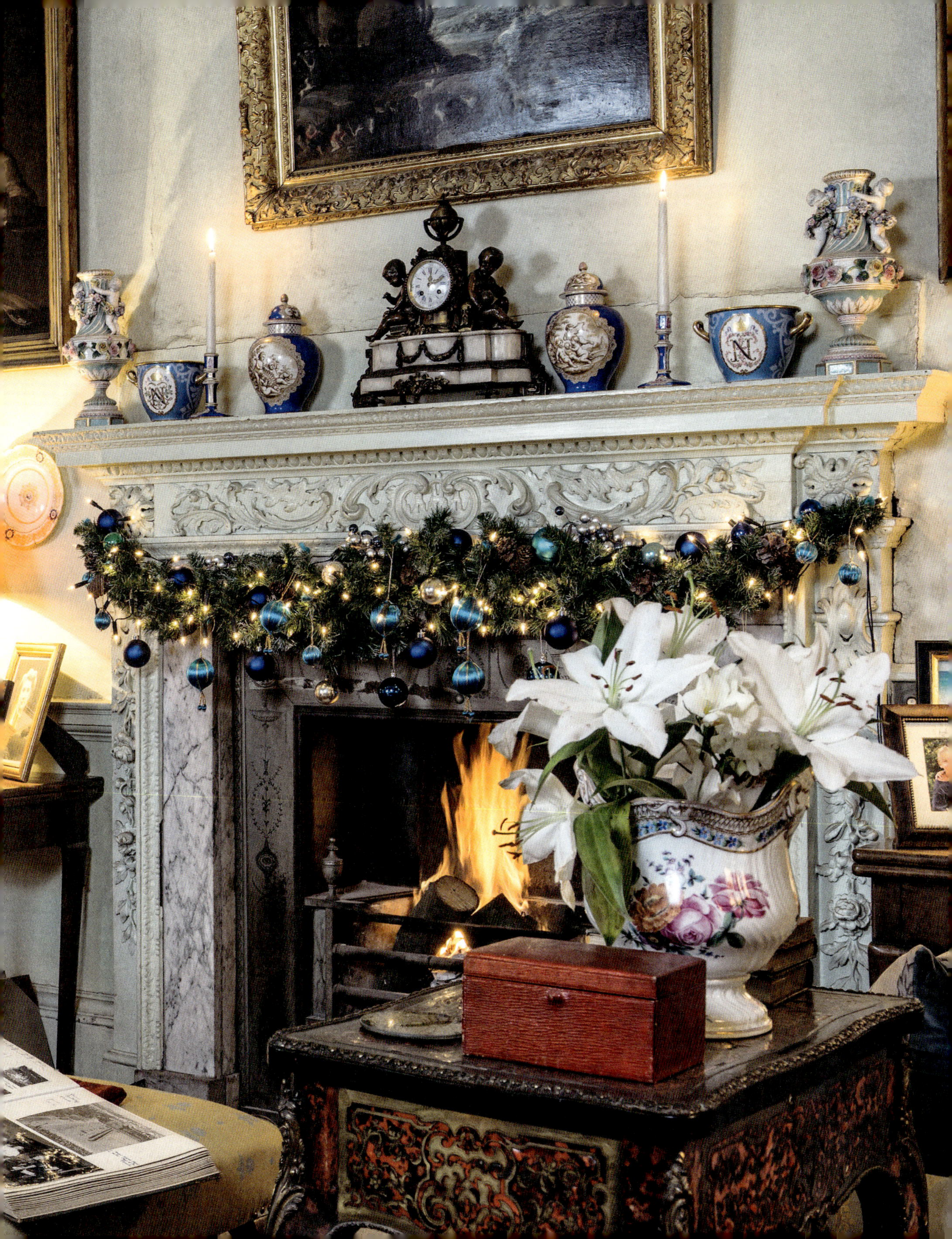

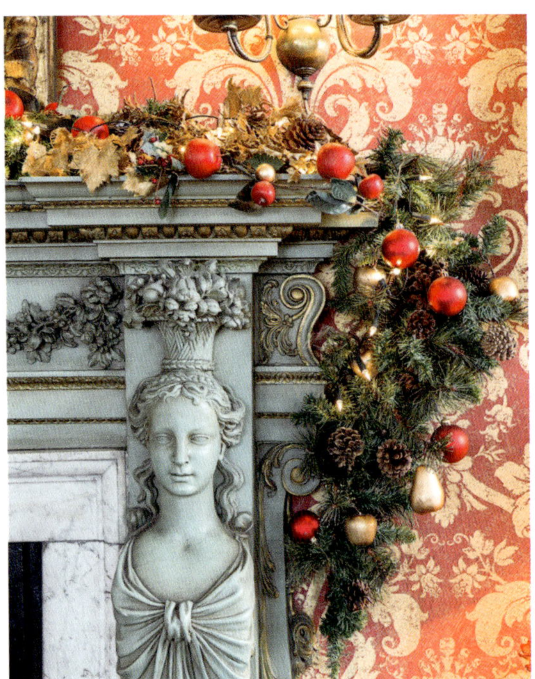

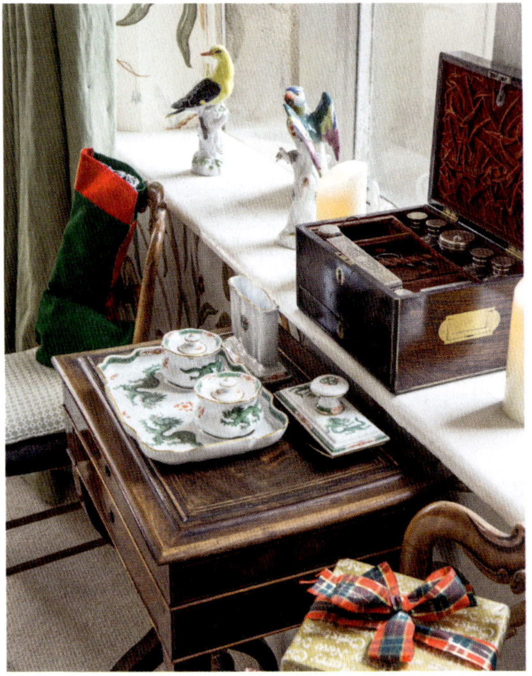

Carlton Towers hosts several Christmas-themed events in November and December, including a festive indoor market in the staterooms, wreath-making workshops, afternoon teas and guided tours as well as Christmas concerts.

Because the family loves cooking and fine foods, they host multiple Christmas-themed meals, including Santa Brunch, Sunday Lunch and Christmas Party Nights.

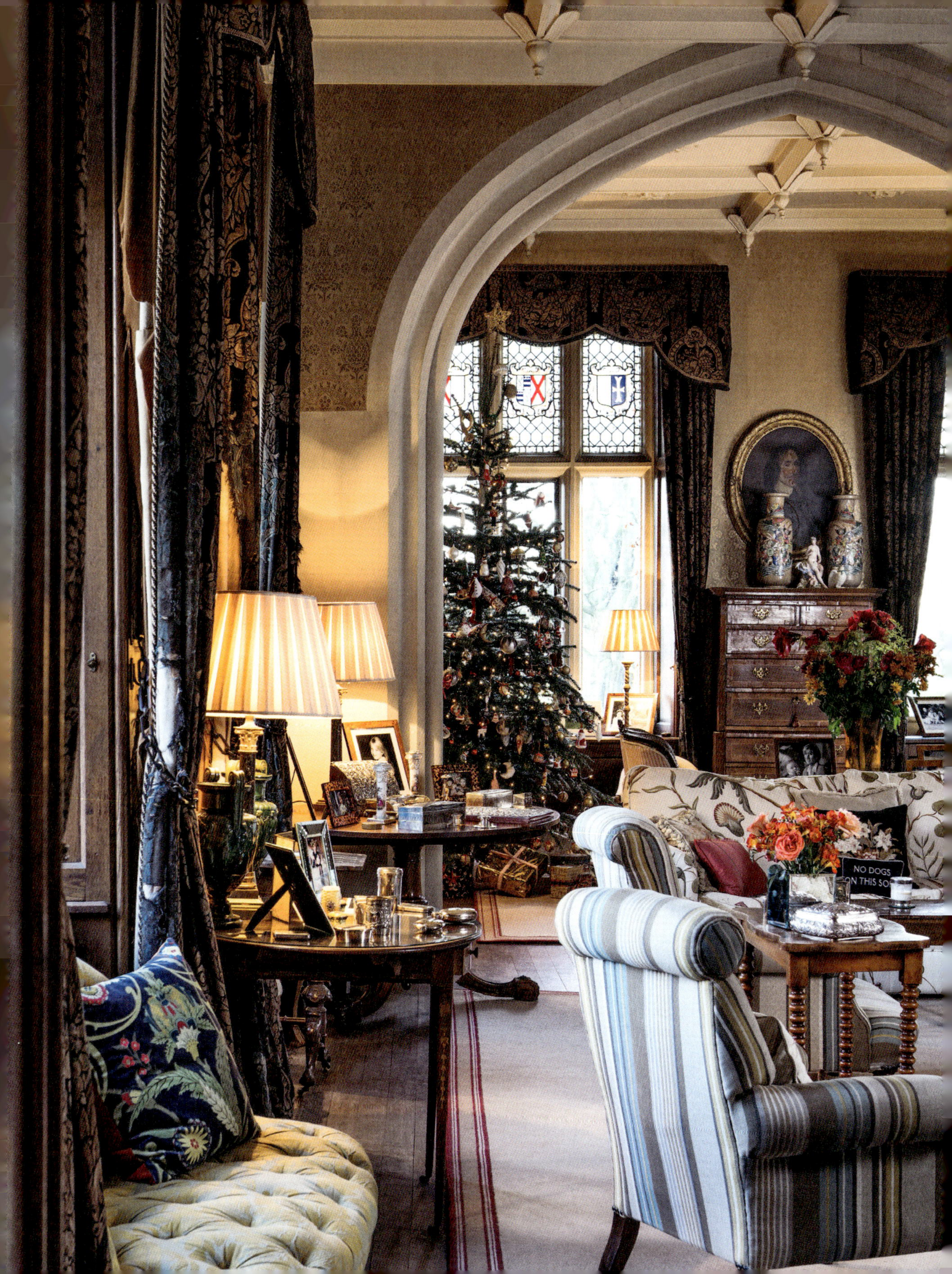
NO DOGS

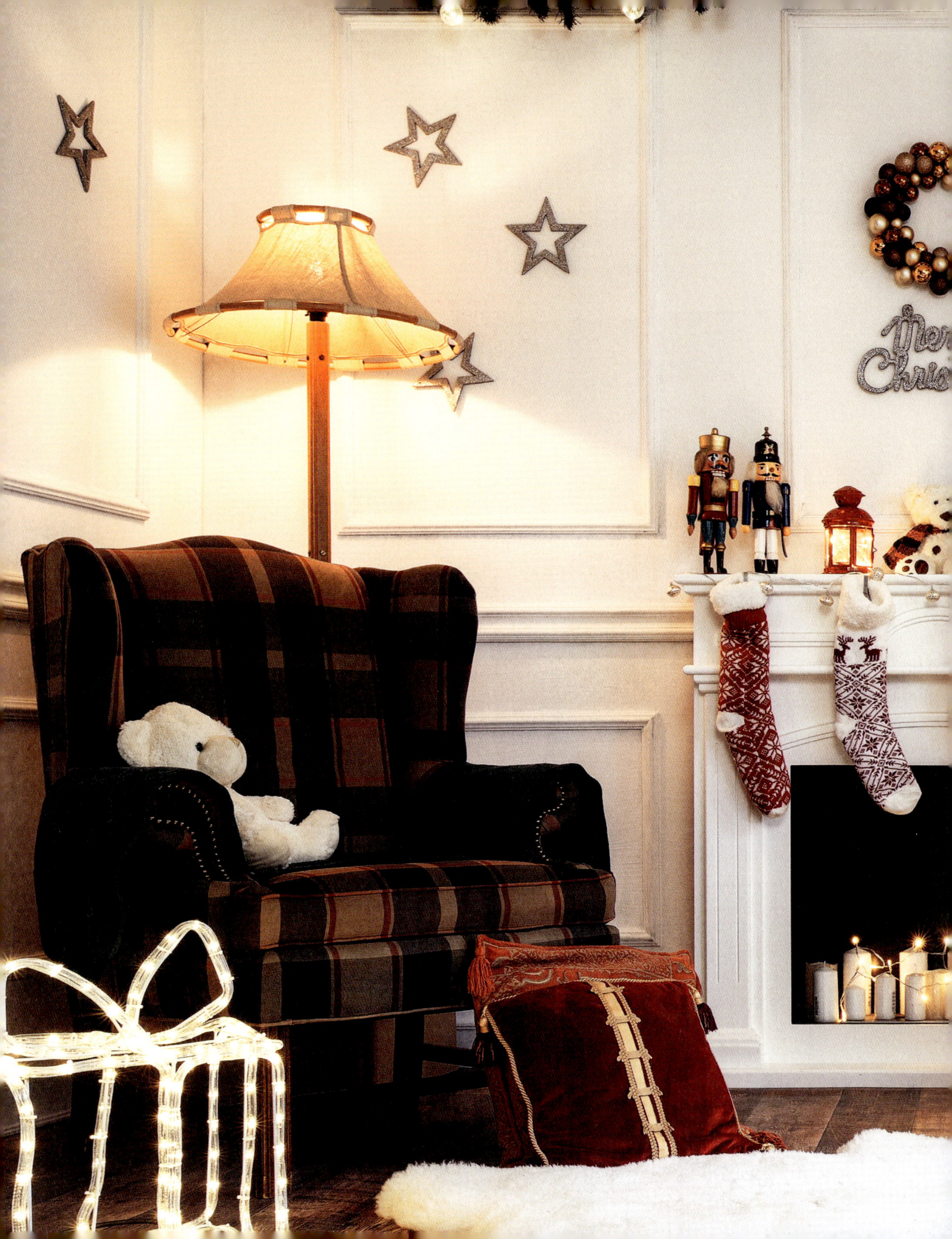

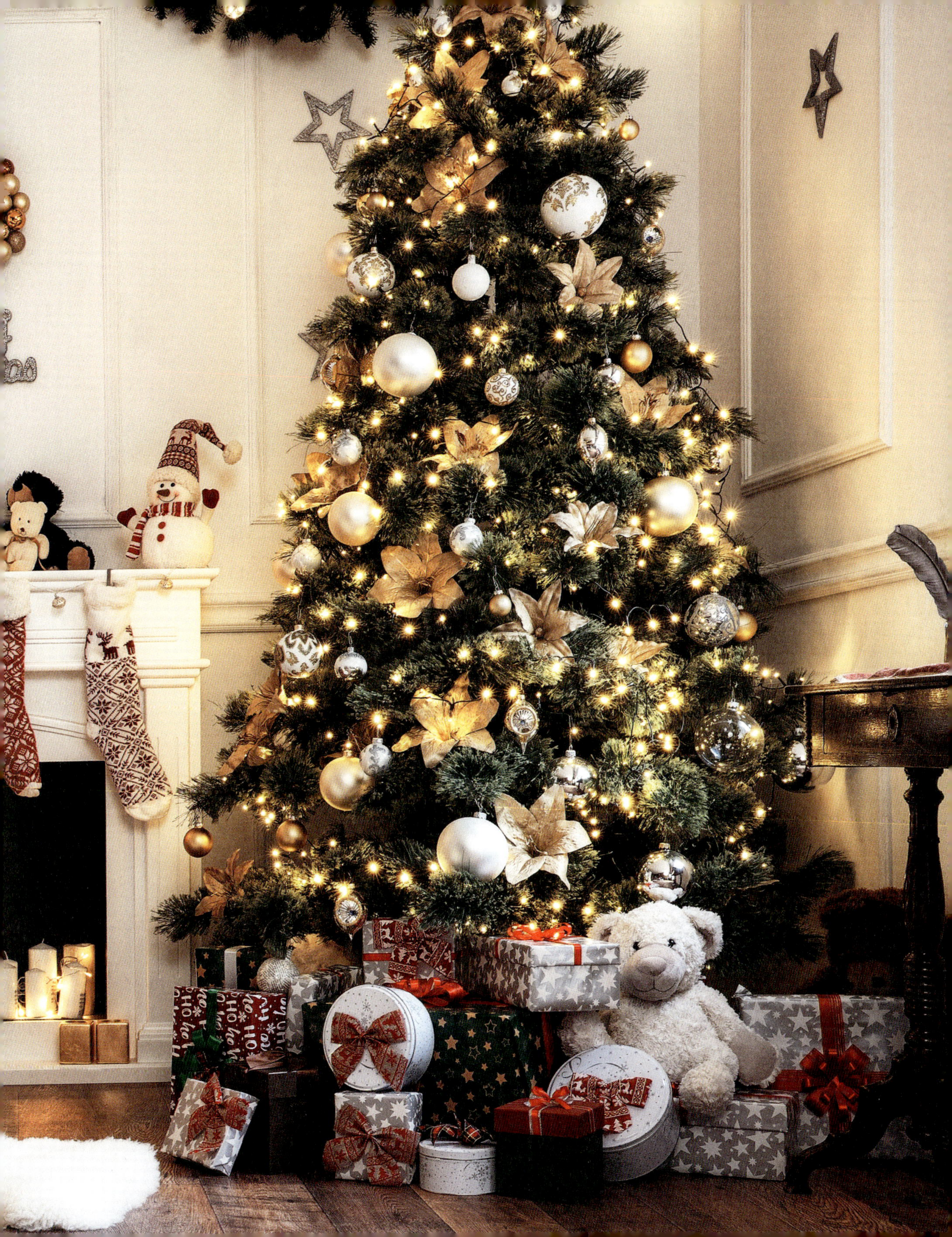

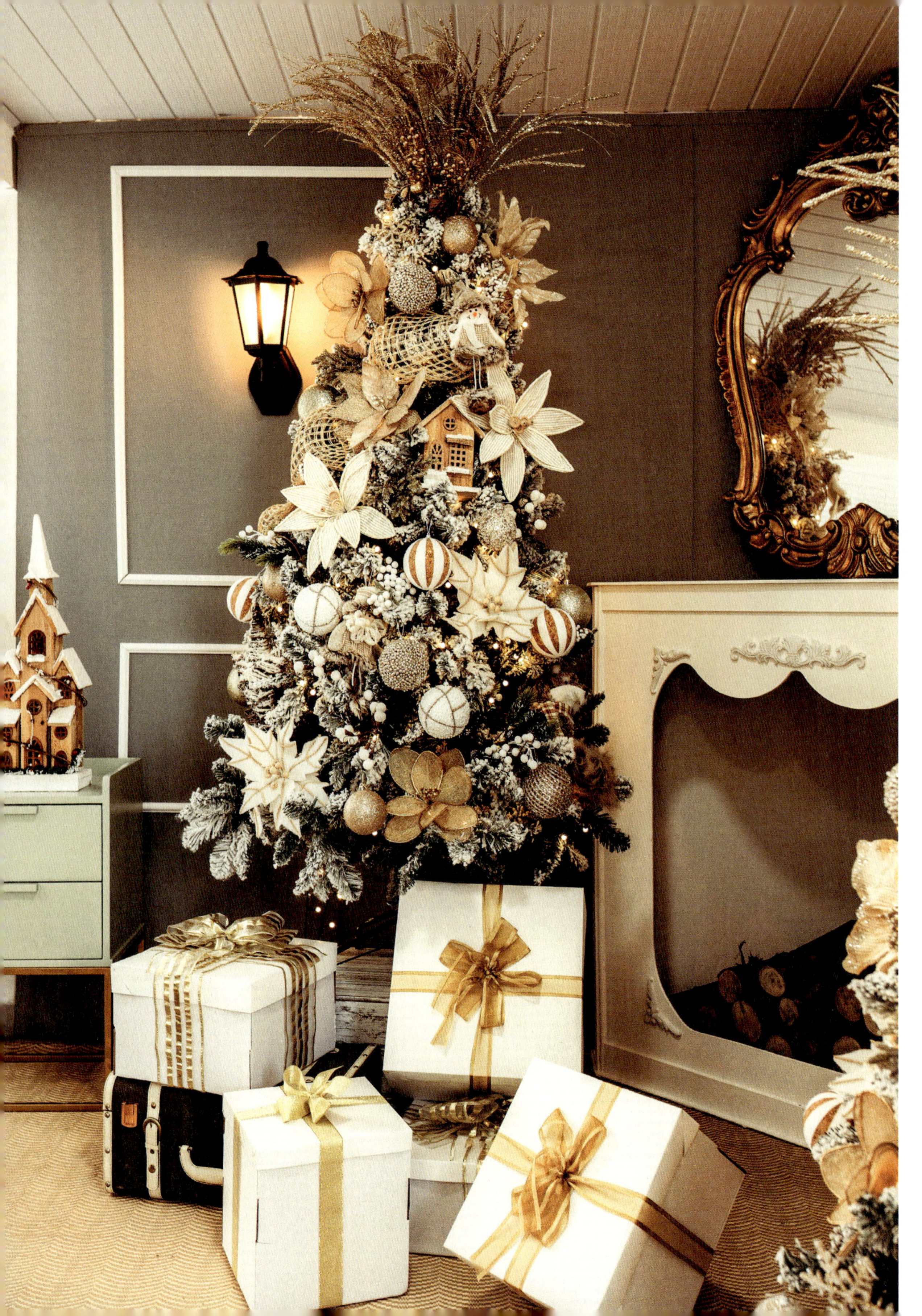

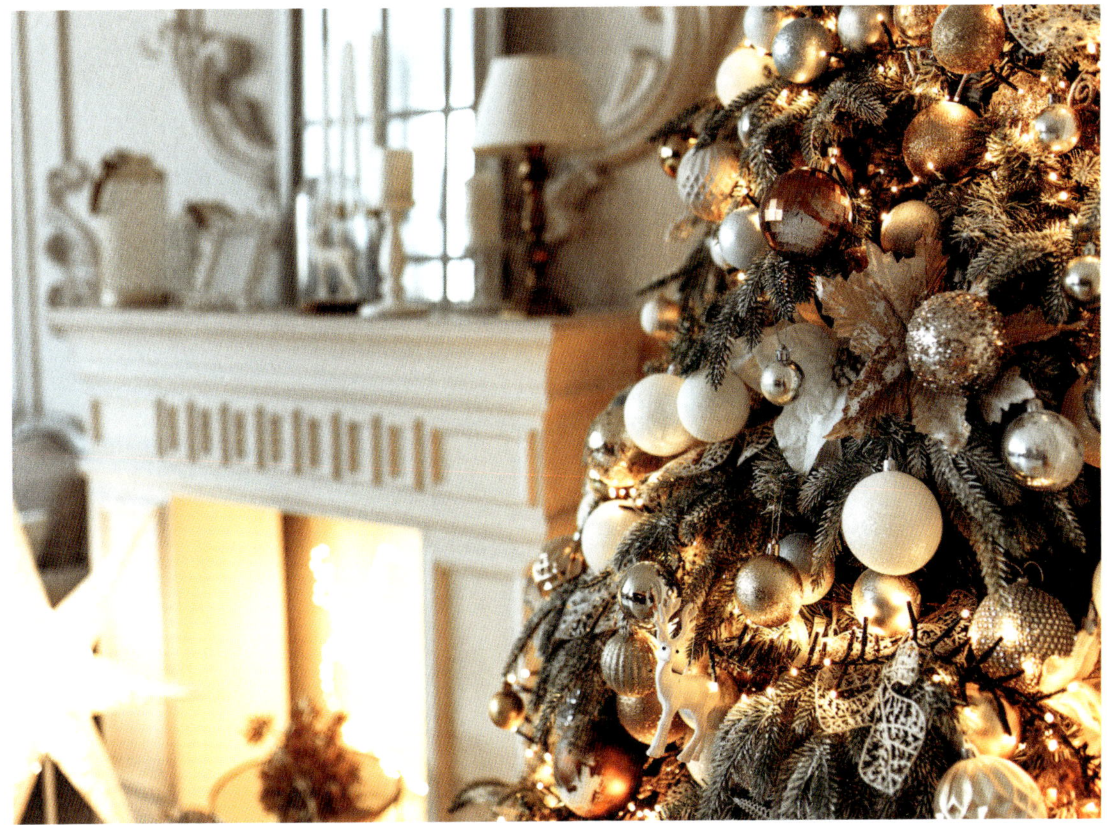

ALL THAT GLISTENS

A controlled color palette will elevate a room. This opulent scheme is grounded in white, gold and earth tones. The tree branches are frosted, and the presents tied with ribbon. As part of the Christmas preparations, create a wrapping station at home and see who can make the most beautifully wrapped gift.

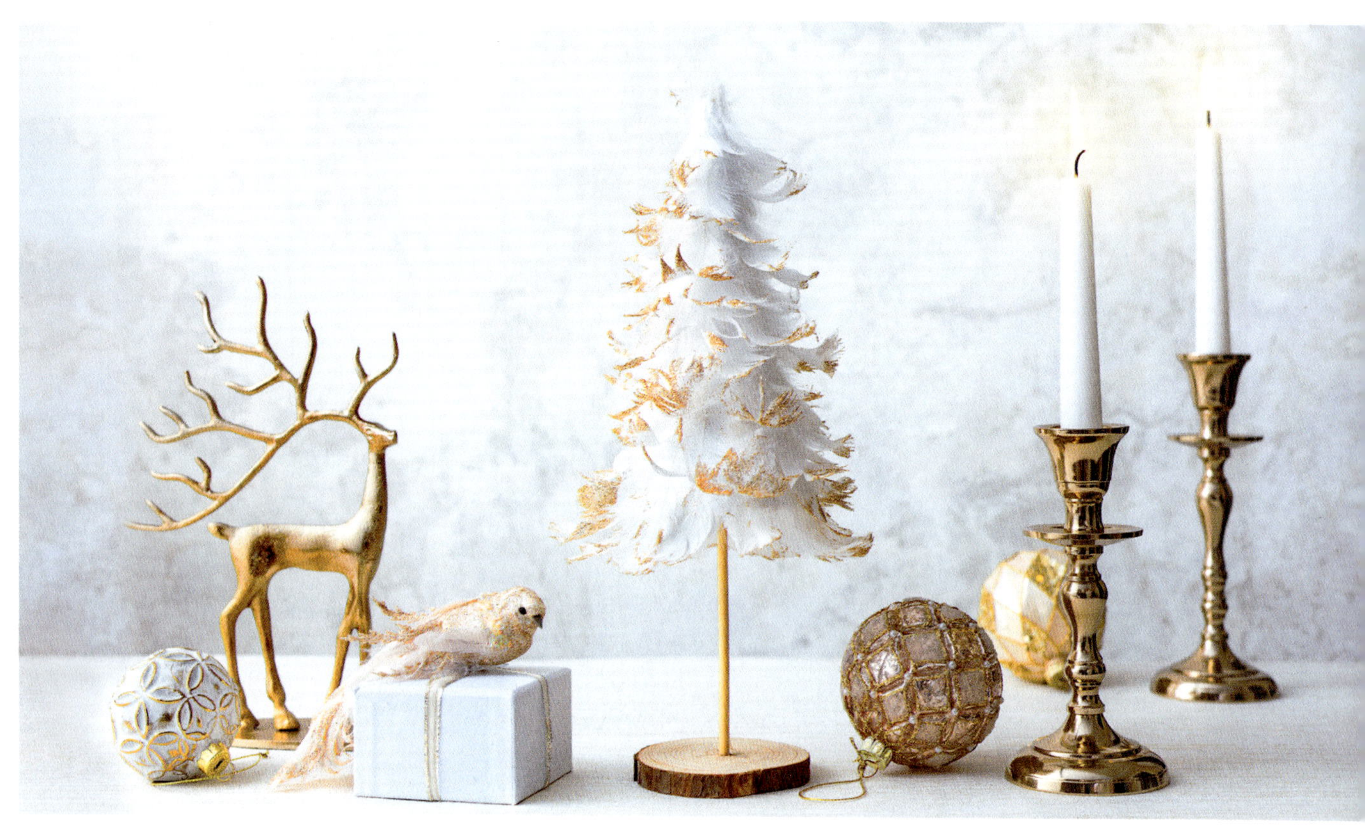

EASY DOES IT

Decorate the house in phases, starting in the first week of December. This snow cloud bedroom in grey and white features a knitted blanket at the end of the bed, fairy lights surrounding the canopy and an all-white Christmas tree decorated with gold accents. These make an elegant contrast with the natural wood of the bench.

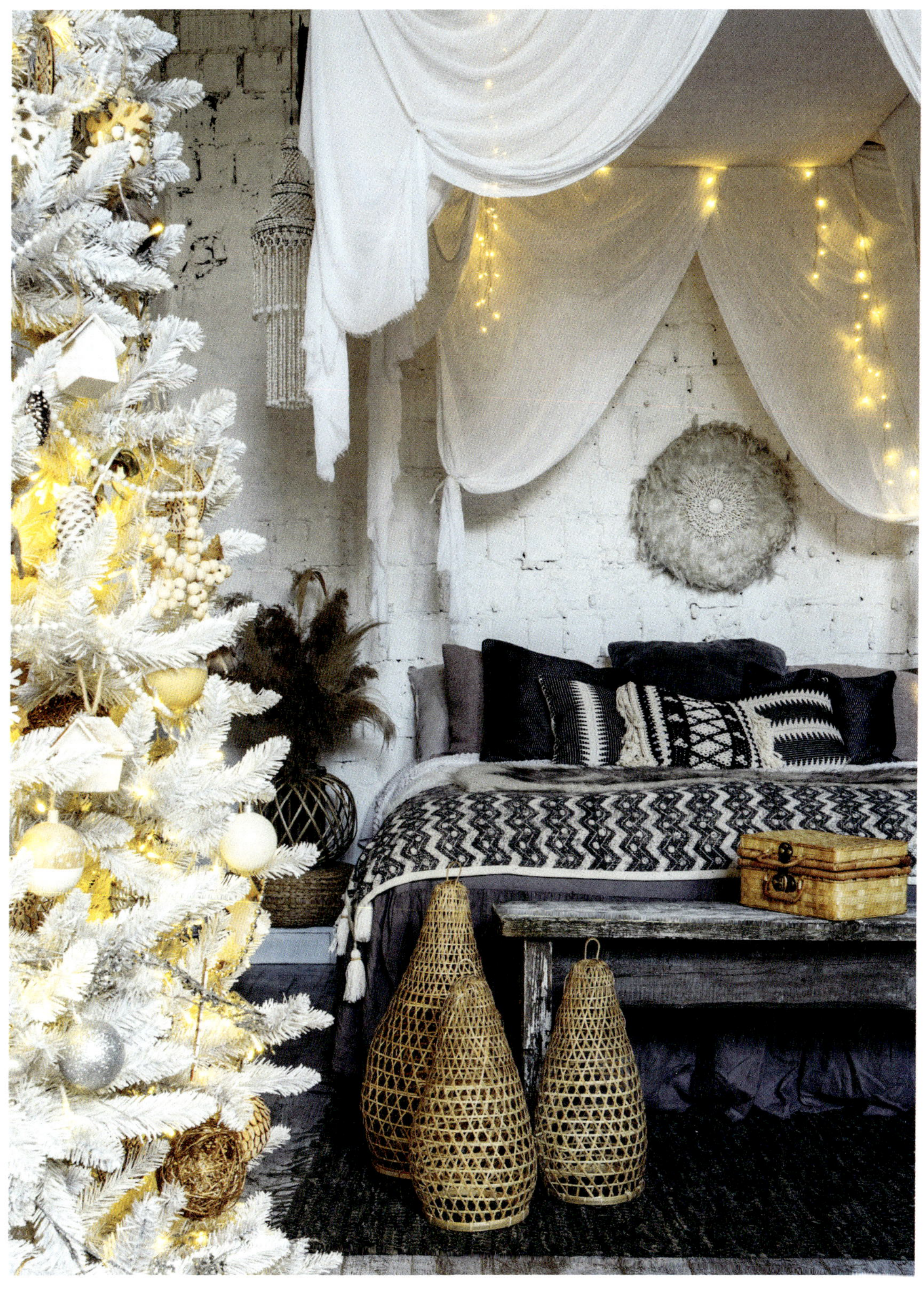

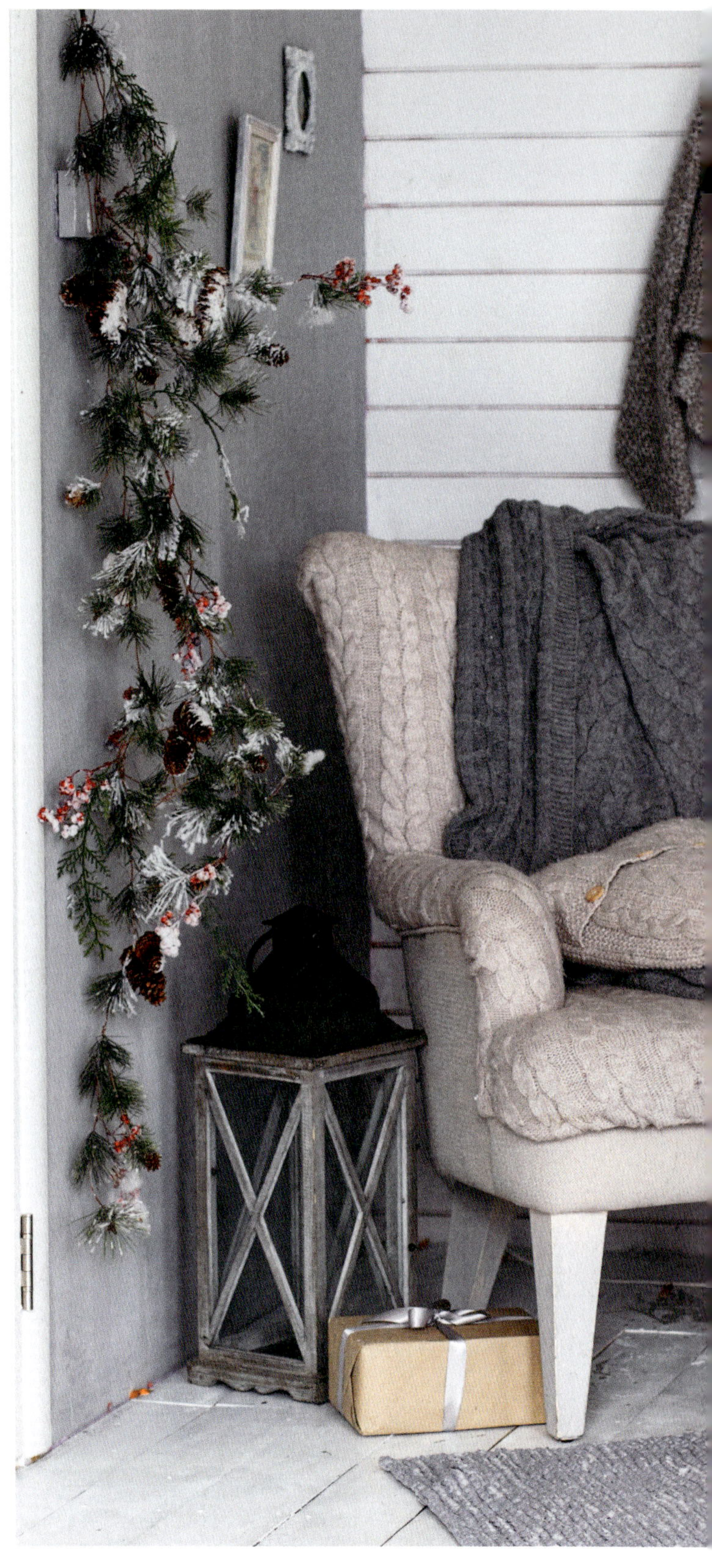

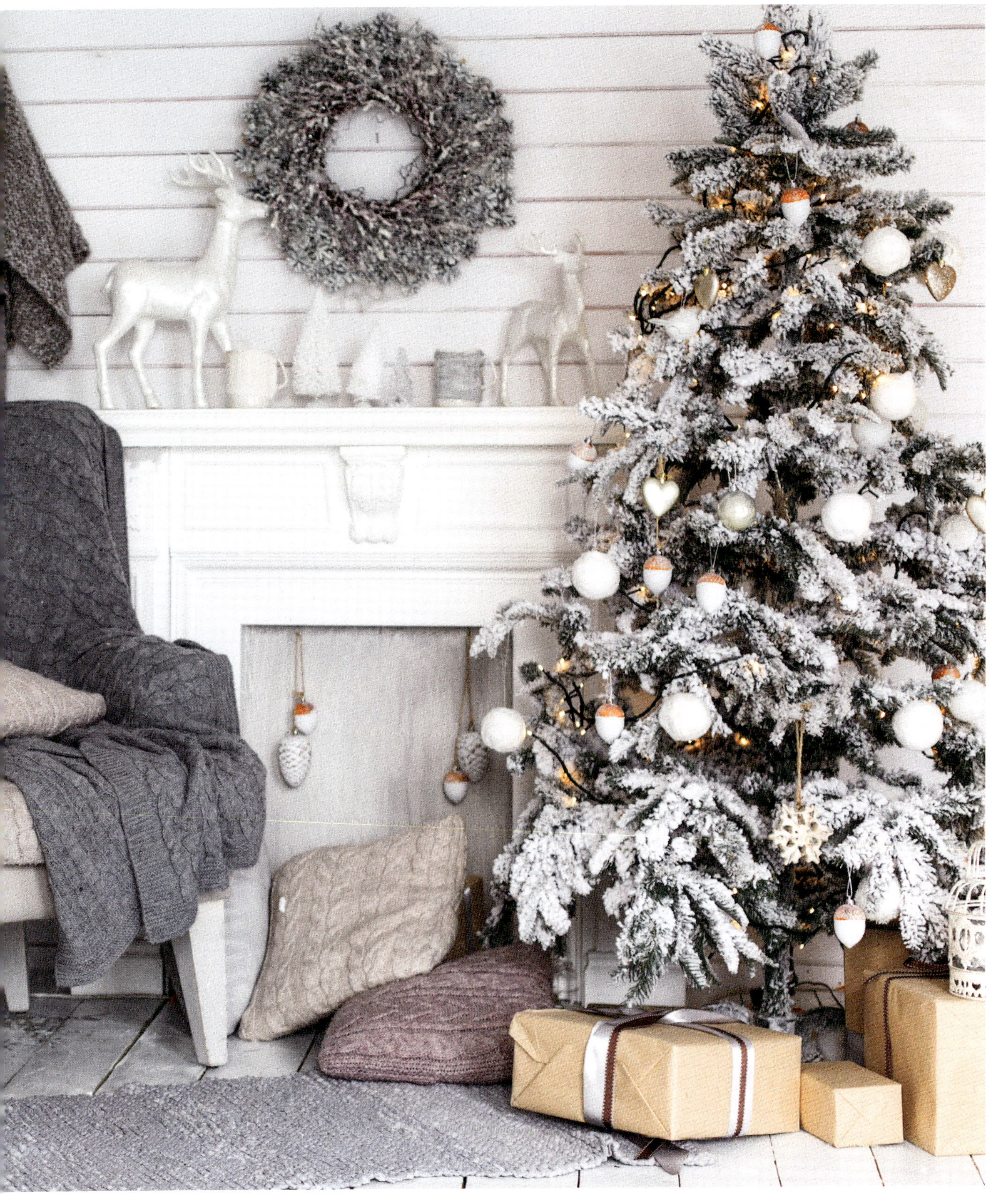

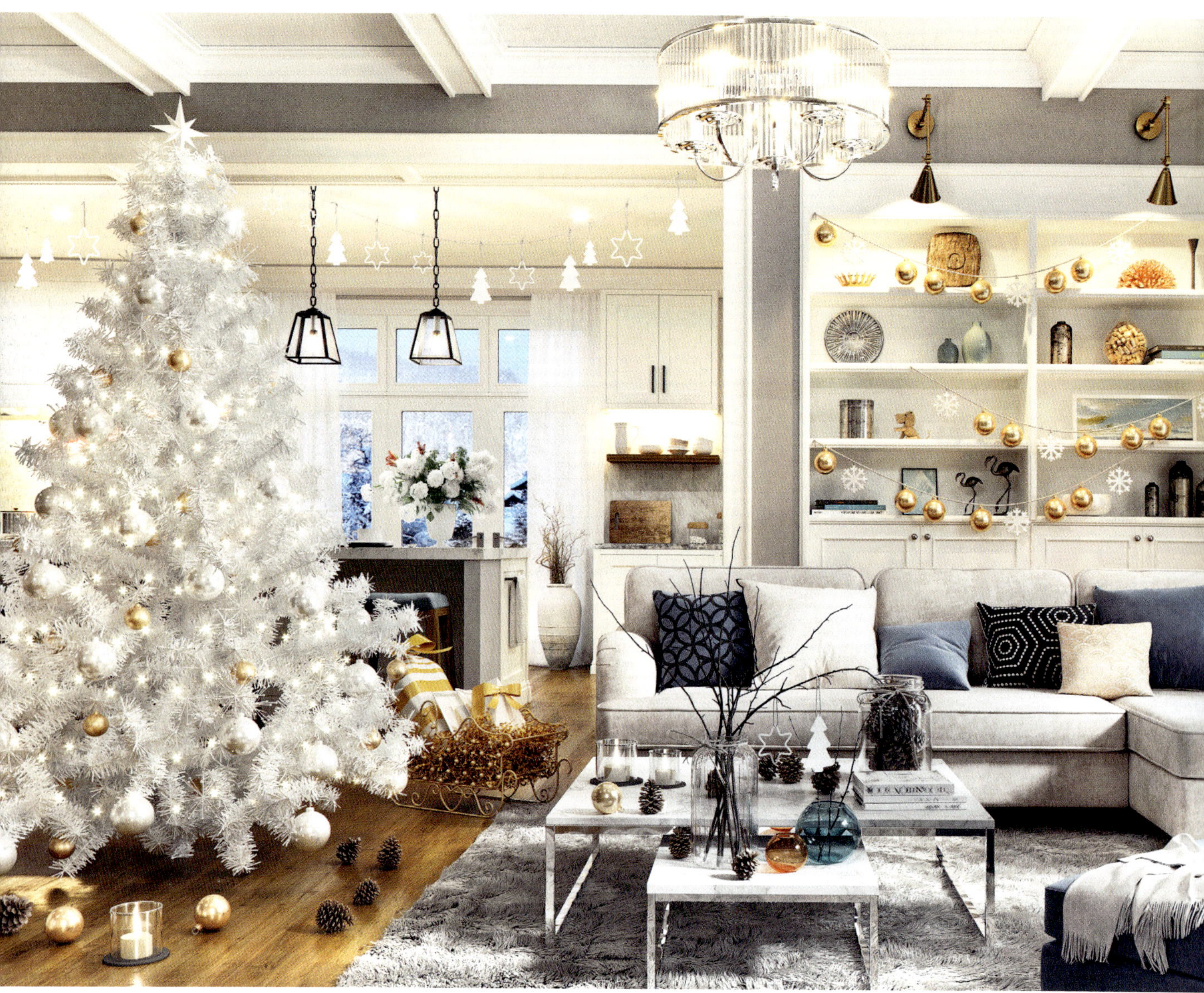

CHRISTMAS COOL

A controlled color palette where everything is mostly cream, black, or white brings lightness to a space. Throughout the home, texture is everywhere—the monochrome scheme gives a clean canvas to arrange layers of textiles and trimmings.

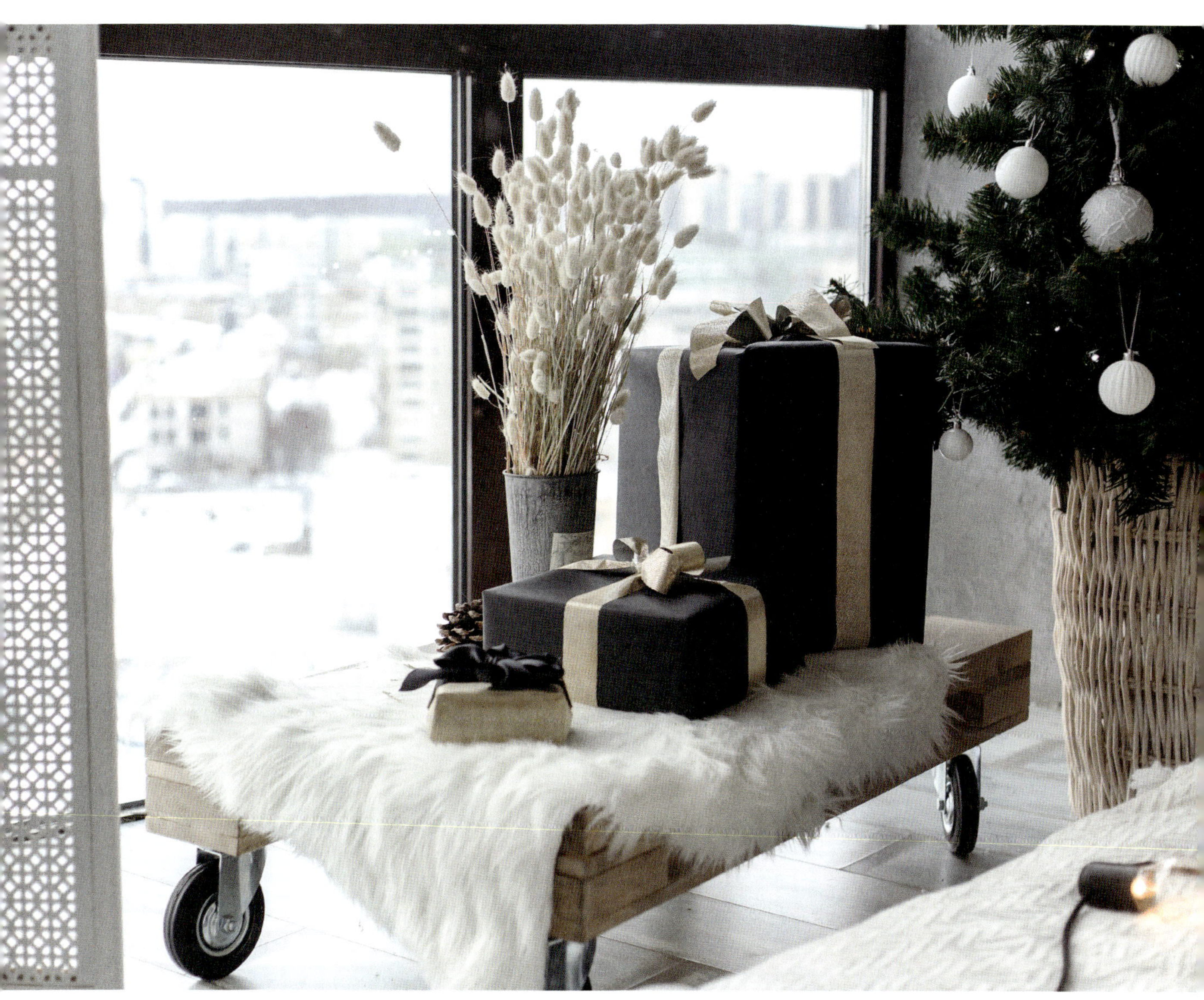

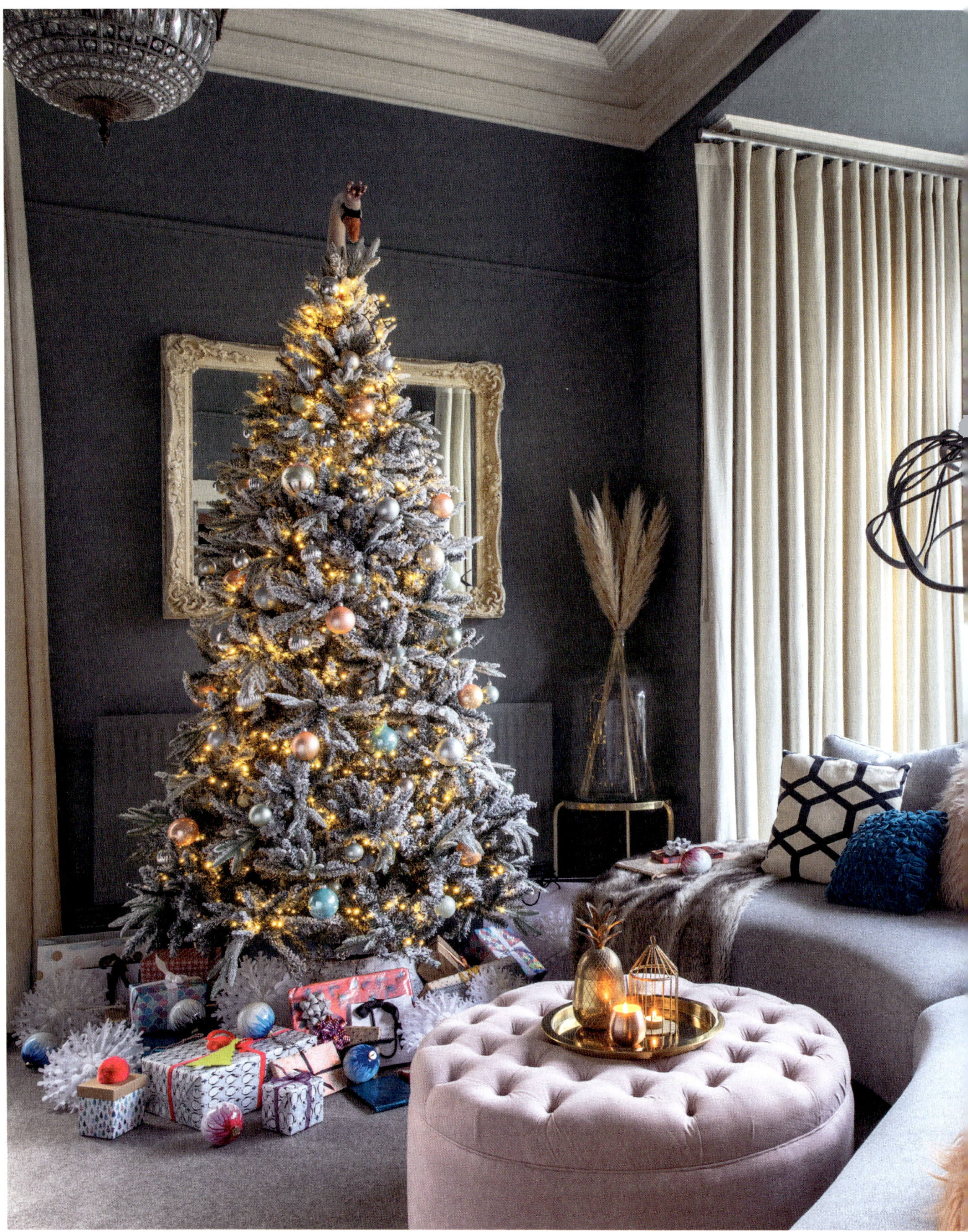

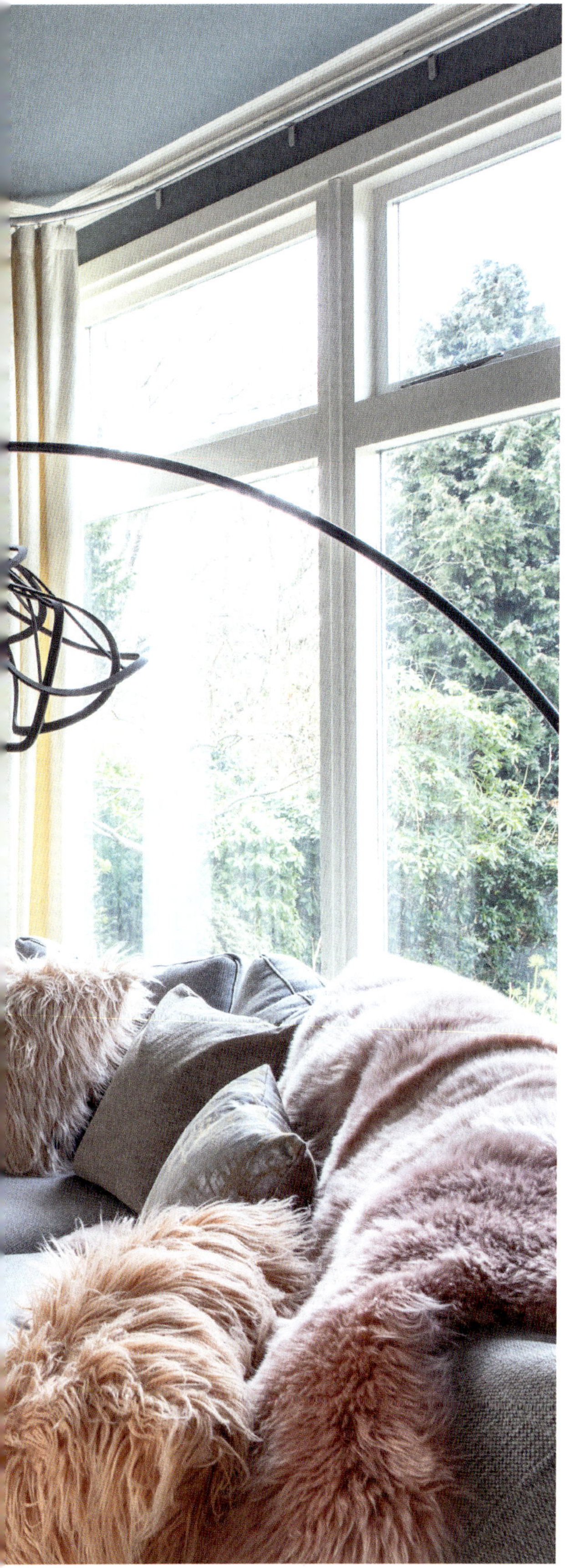

FEATURE

COLORFUL CHRISTMAS

Celebrating Individuality

A frosted tree adorned with pastel baubles that match the room's décor, while flashes of neon on decorations under the tree catch your eye. This Victorian villa in West Yorkshire showcases a blend of elegant and whimsical holiday decorations, restored period features, and thoughtfully selected fixtures, making the care and consideration behind its enhancements apparent. "Upon moving in 2005, I brightened our initially dark home with 'Antique White' by Leyland, creating a light and inviting blank slate," shares Claire Price, a children's poet and storyteller. "The original tiled floor in the entryway inspired the color palette for each room, serving as a cohesive element that ties the house together."

Claire and her husband Richard, a financial advisor, have gradually introduced more colors onto walls, furniture, and art as their budget allowed. "Sometimes, financial constraints can act as a beneficial brake on the decorating process," Claire, mother to teenagers George and Charlie, reflects. "The project's scale made it challenging to decide on decorations while raising a family. As the boys grew, and we became more familiar with the house, I grew bolder in my decorating choices."

Recent renovations transformed the ground floor into a sociable open-plan living space, ideal for holiday gatherings, and an entrance hall resembling that of a grand country estate. "The house deserved more than the narrow corridor that originally greeted guests, and we've finally achieved that," Claire states. The renovation process was messy and financially taxing, but Claire believes significant changes come from personalizing your space with meaningful items. She finds wisdom in Frank Lloyd Wright's words: "The reality of the building is not the four walls and the roof, but the space within to be lived in." Claire sees homes as sanctuaries reflecting one's passions.

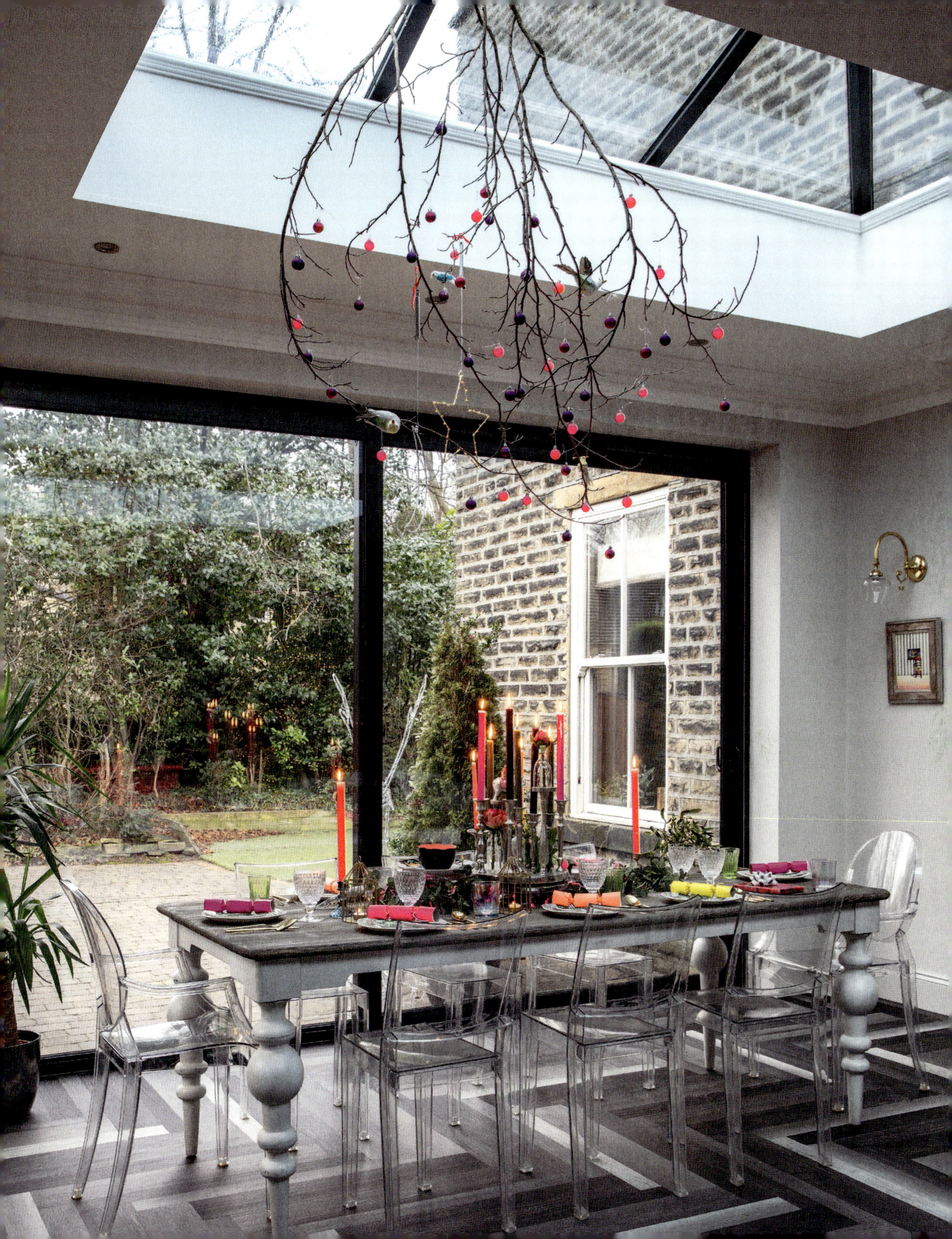

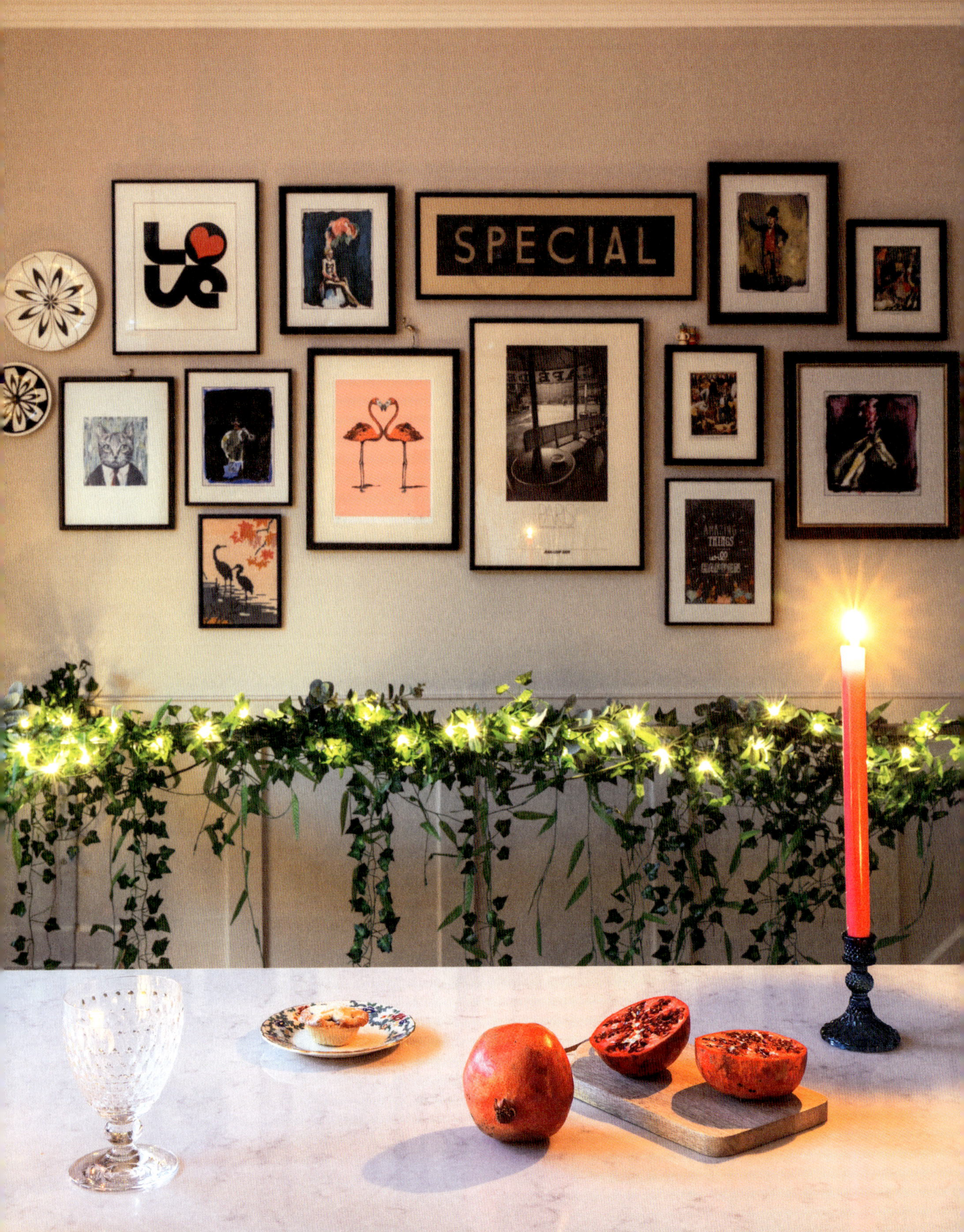
SPECIAL

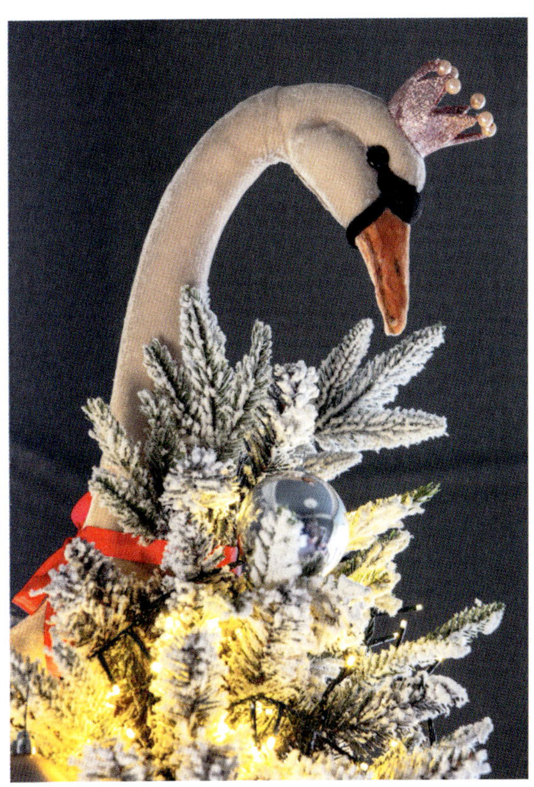

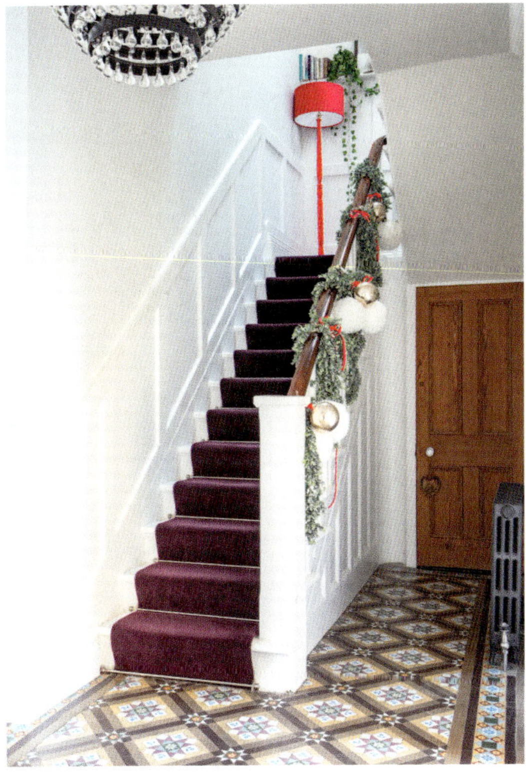

CLAIRE'S DECORATING TIPS: "If you love it, don't second-guess based on others' opinions. A swan princess atop the Christmas tree? Absolutely!"

"Giving old things new purpose, celebrating imperfections, and performing simple acts that foster a calming environment or inject fun into mundane spaces... these are my ways of imbuing my space with soul."

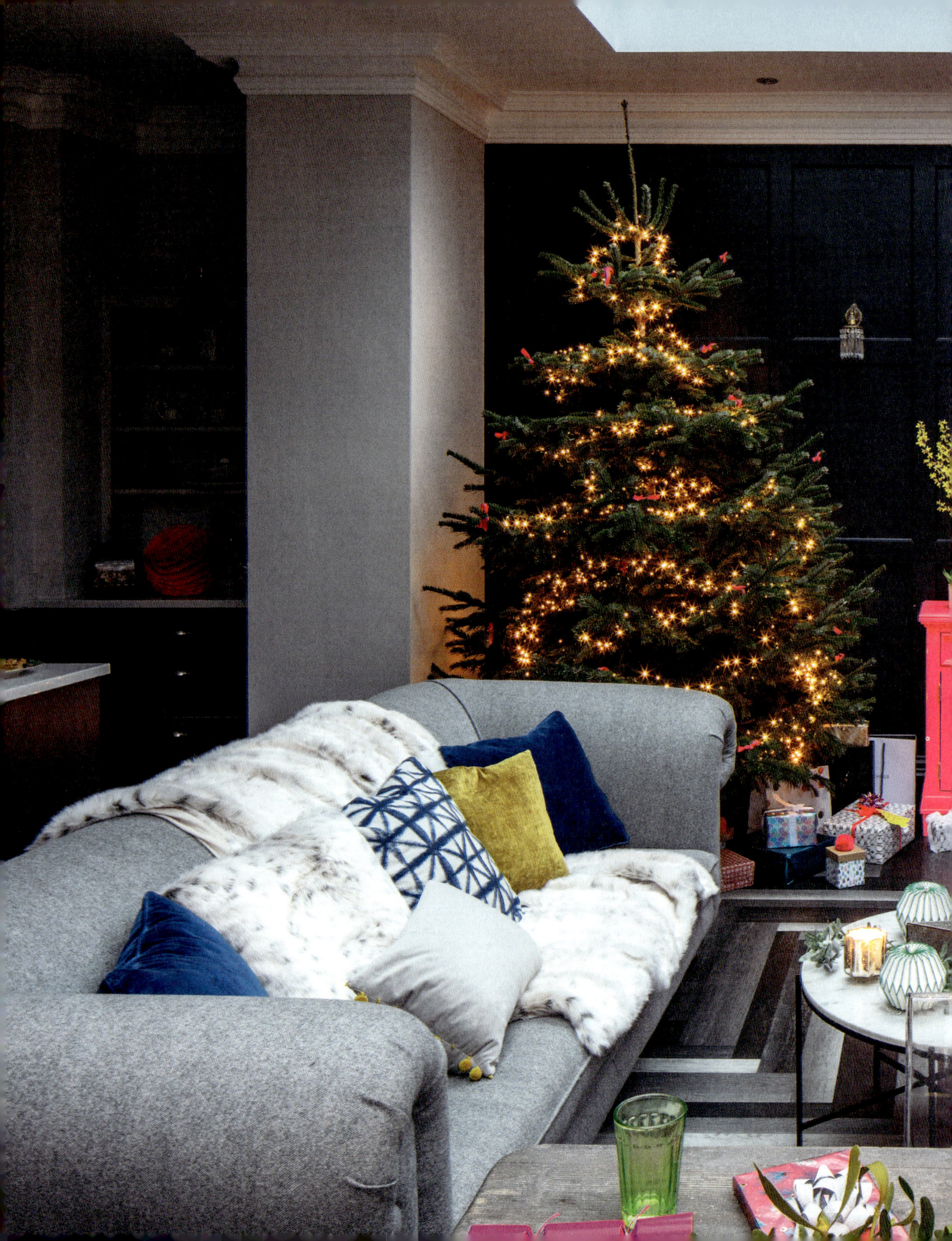

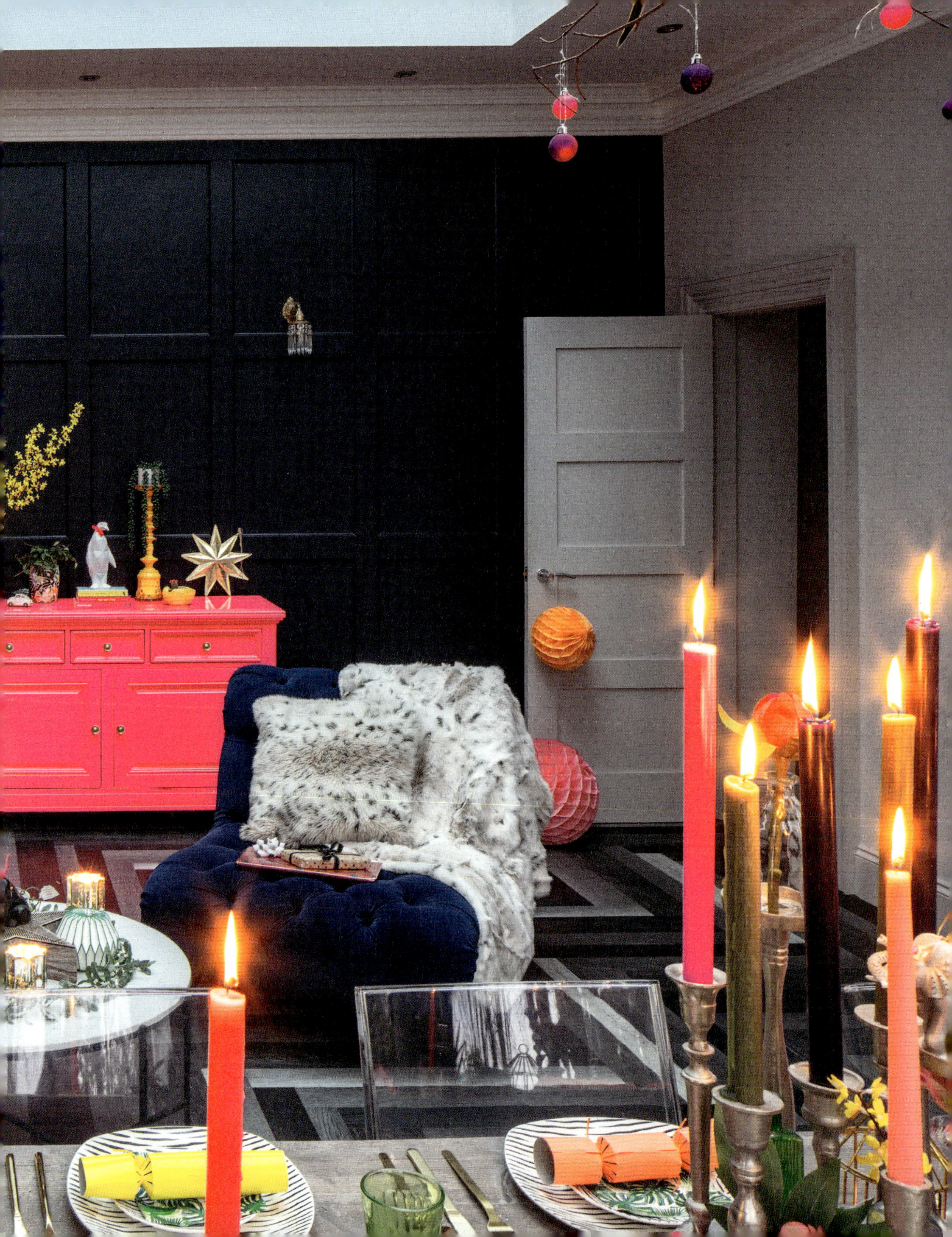

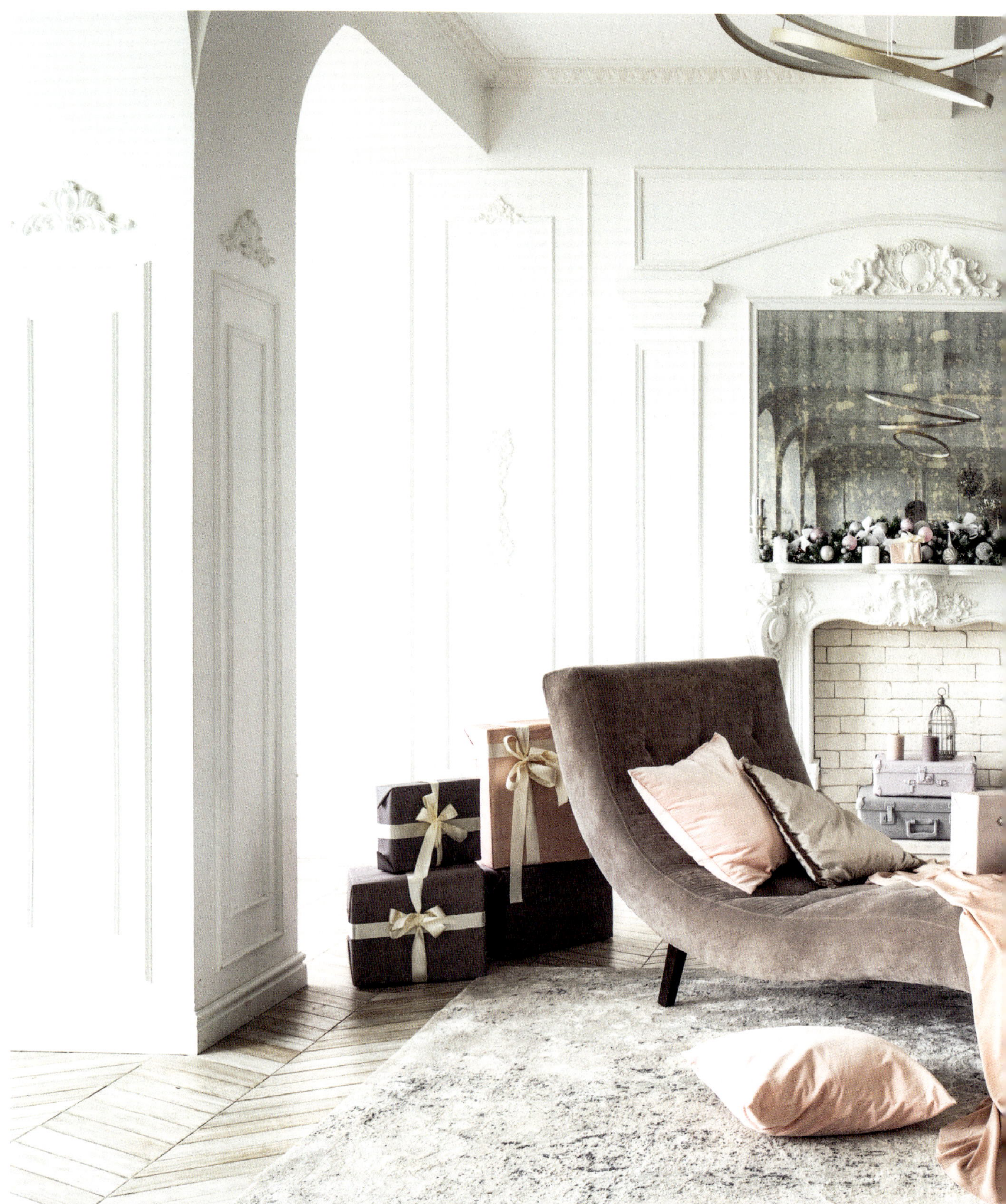

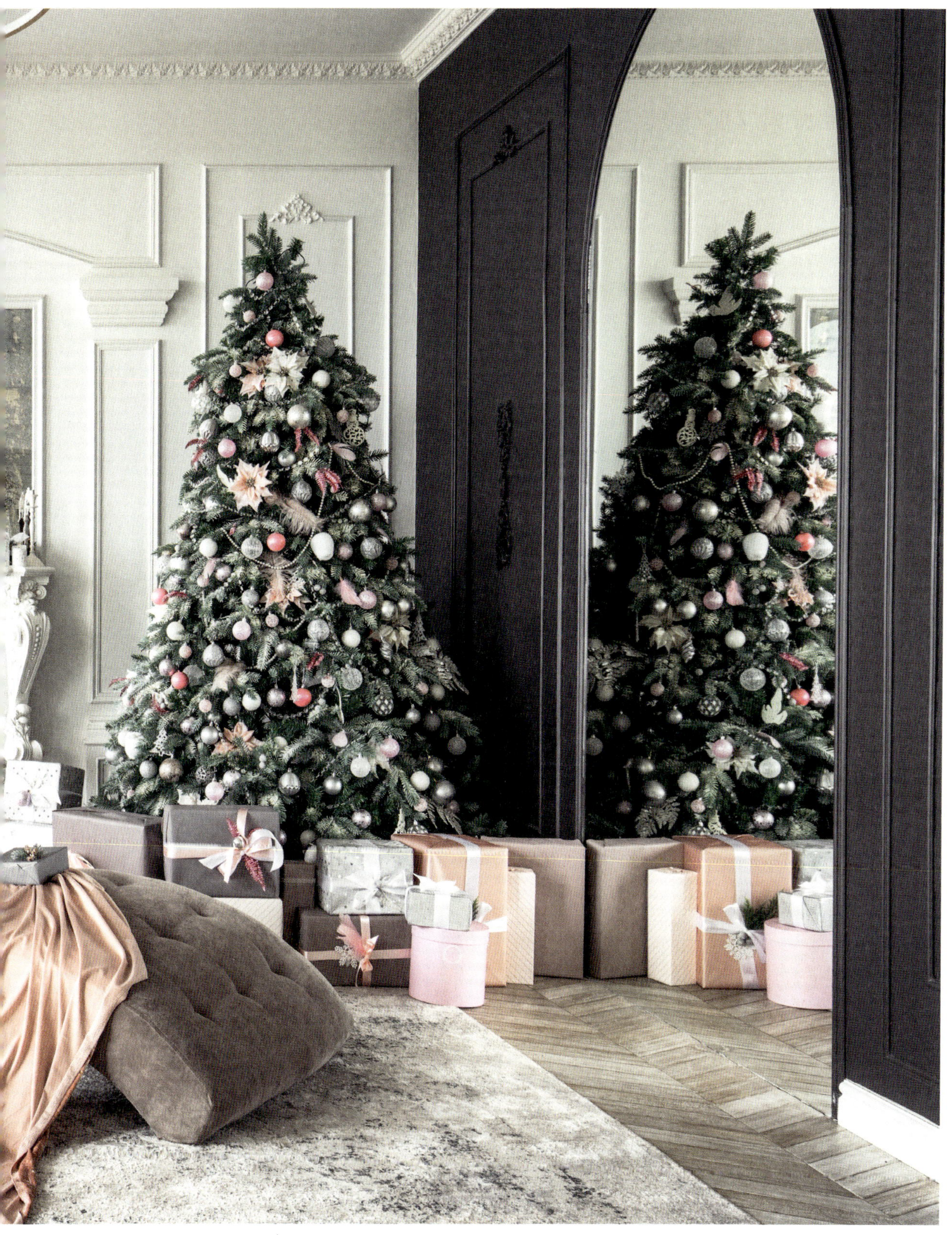

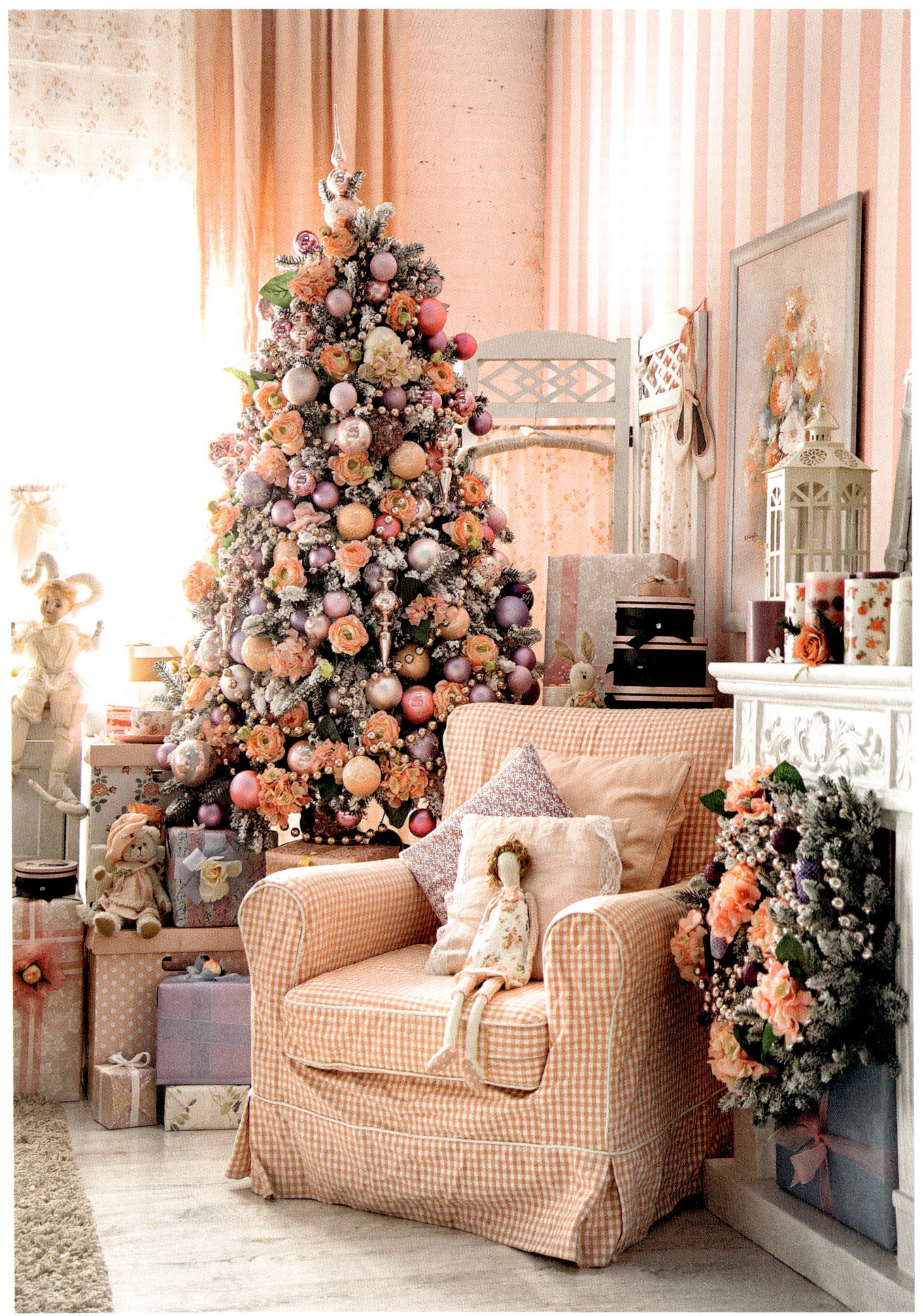

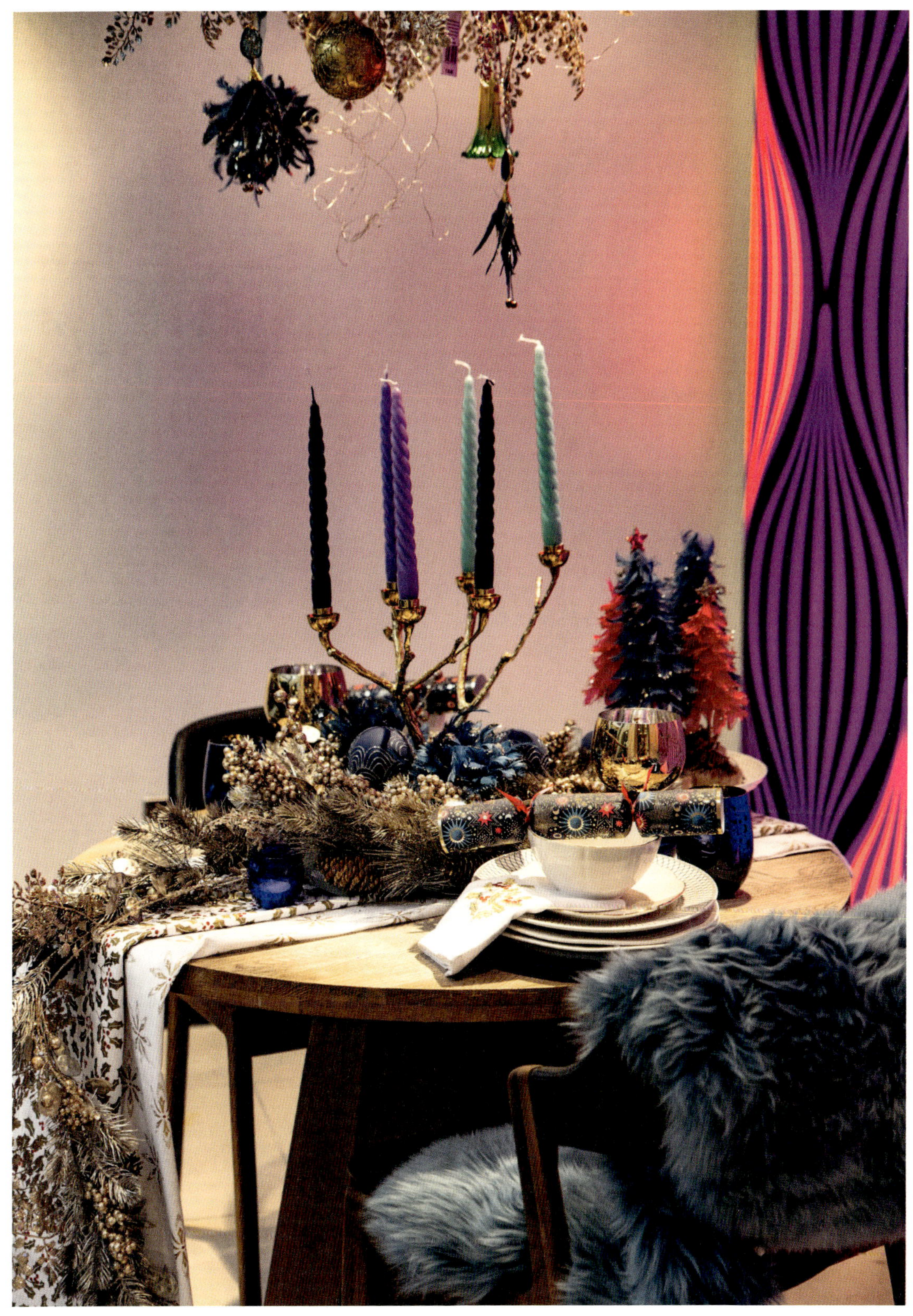

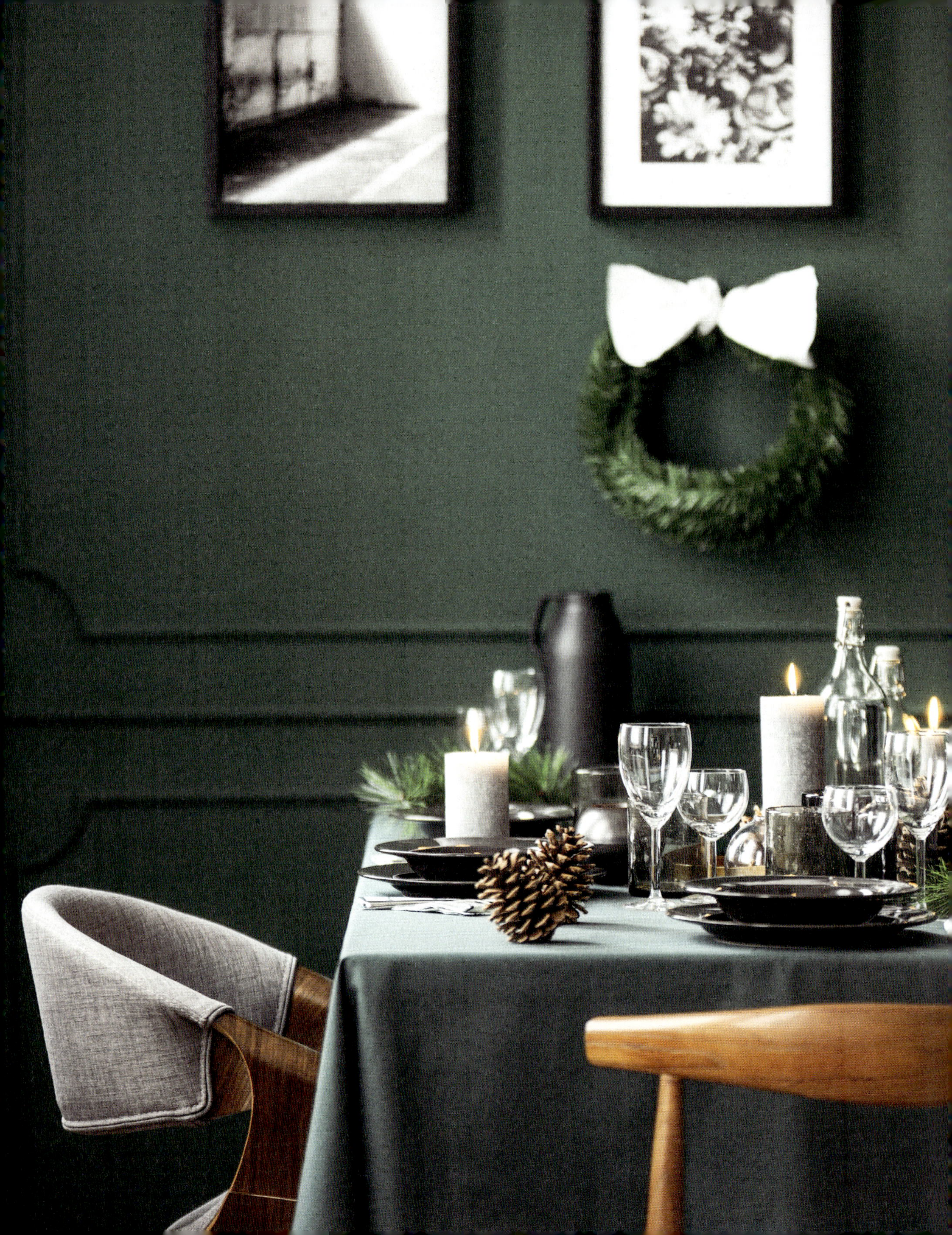

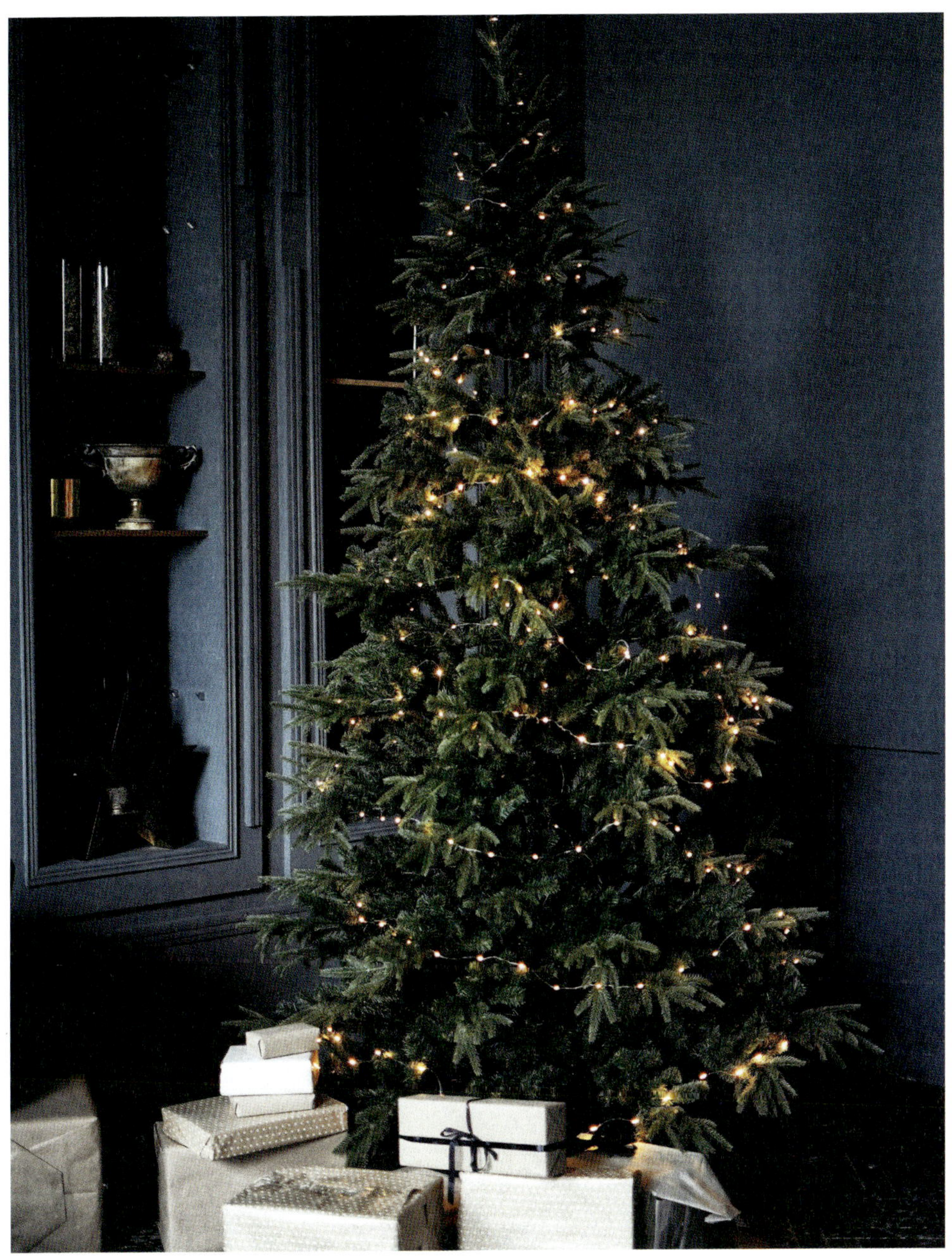

DARK AND HANDSOME

When fires burn in the living room and foliage—not flowers—decorate the home, a palette of green coupled with inky blue works across all seasons. Stick to simple glassware and mid-century furniture to keep the look feeling modern.

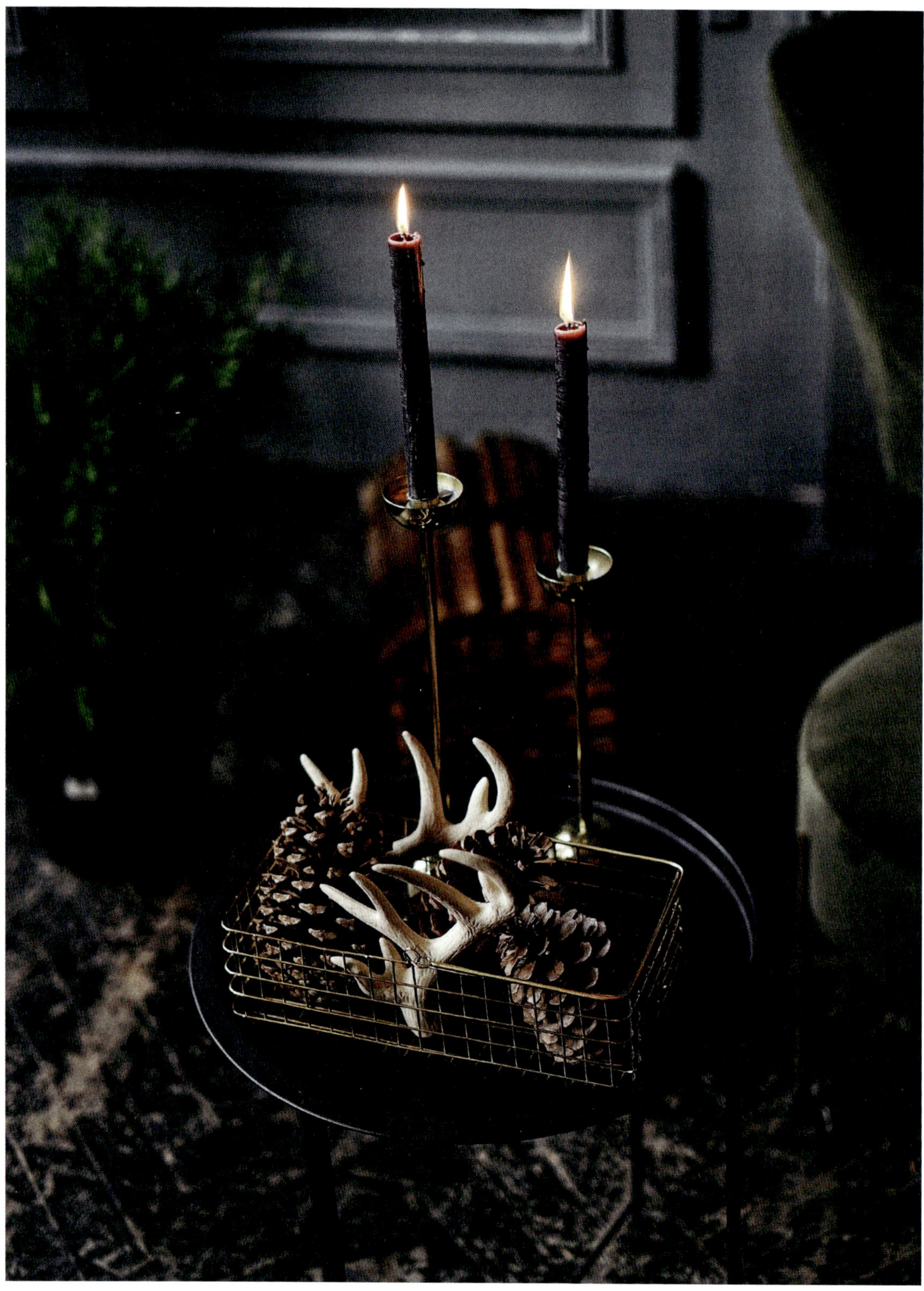

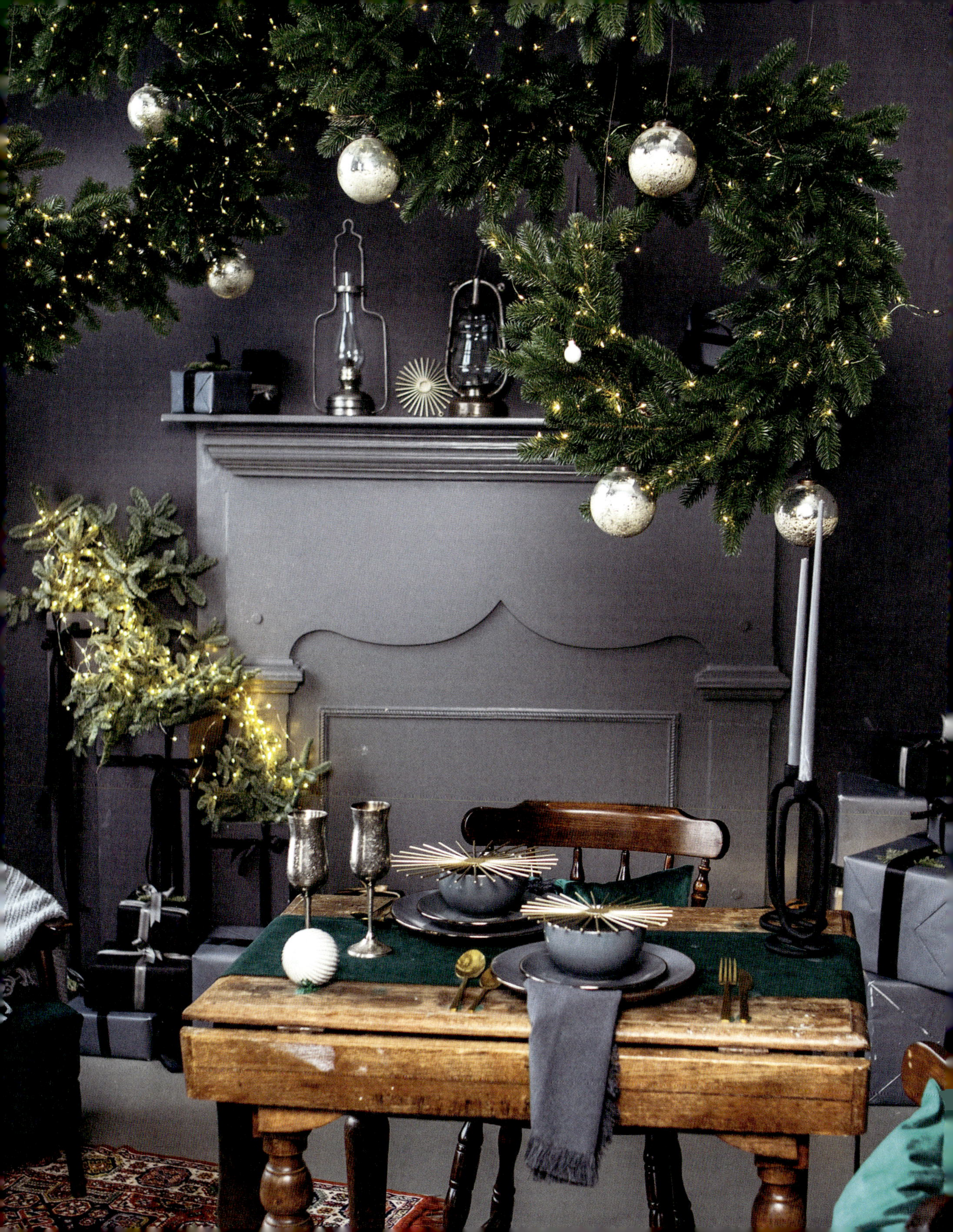

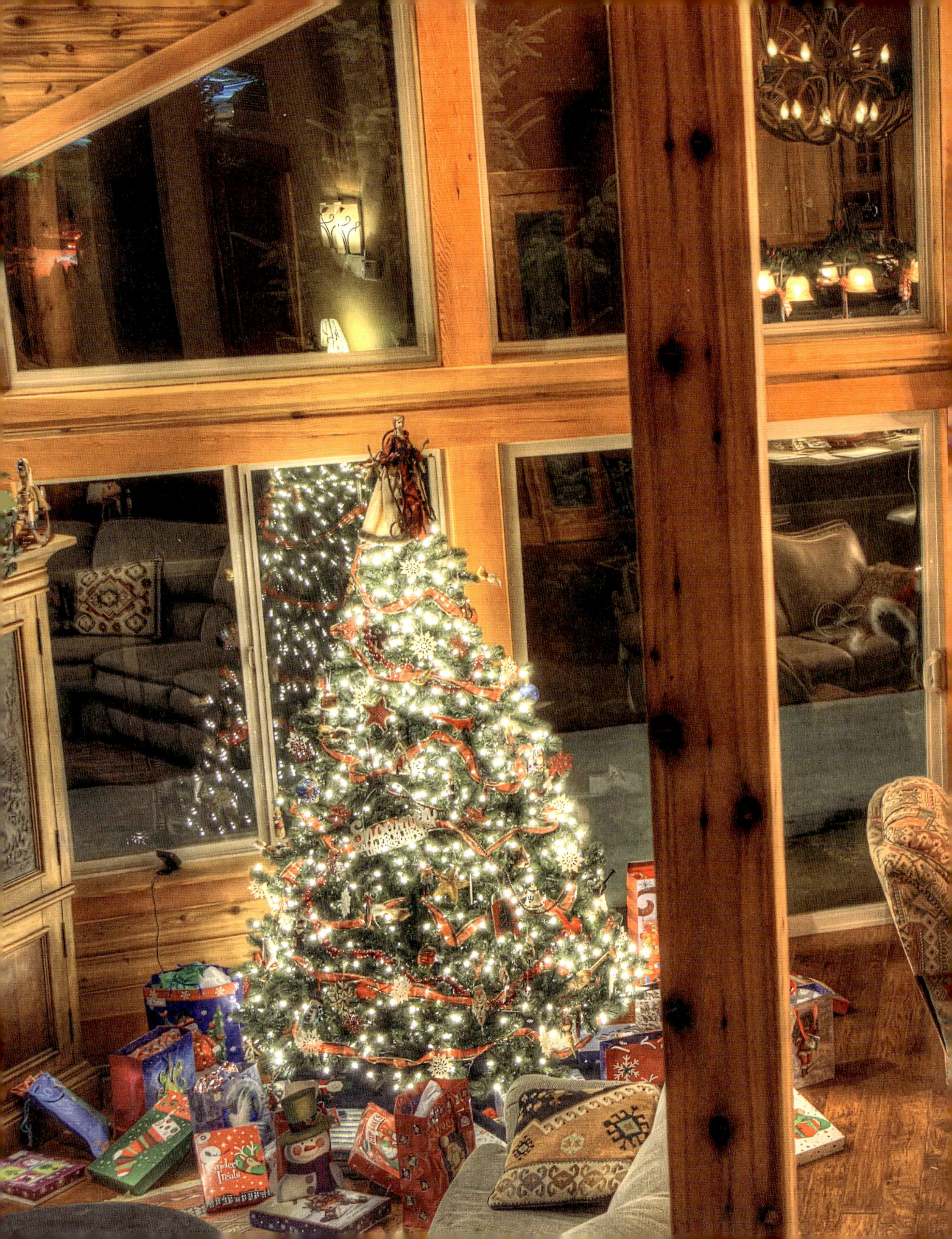

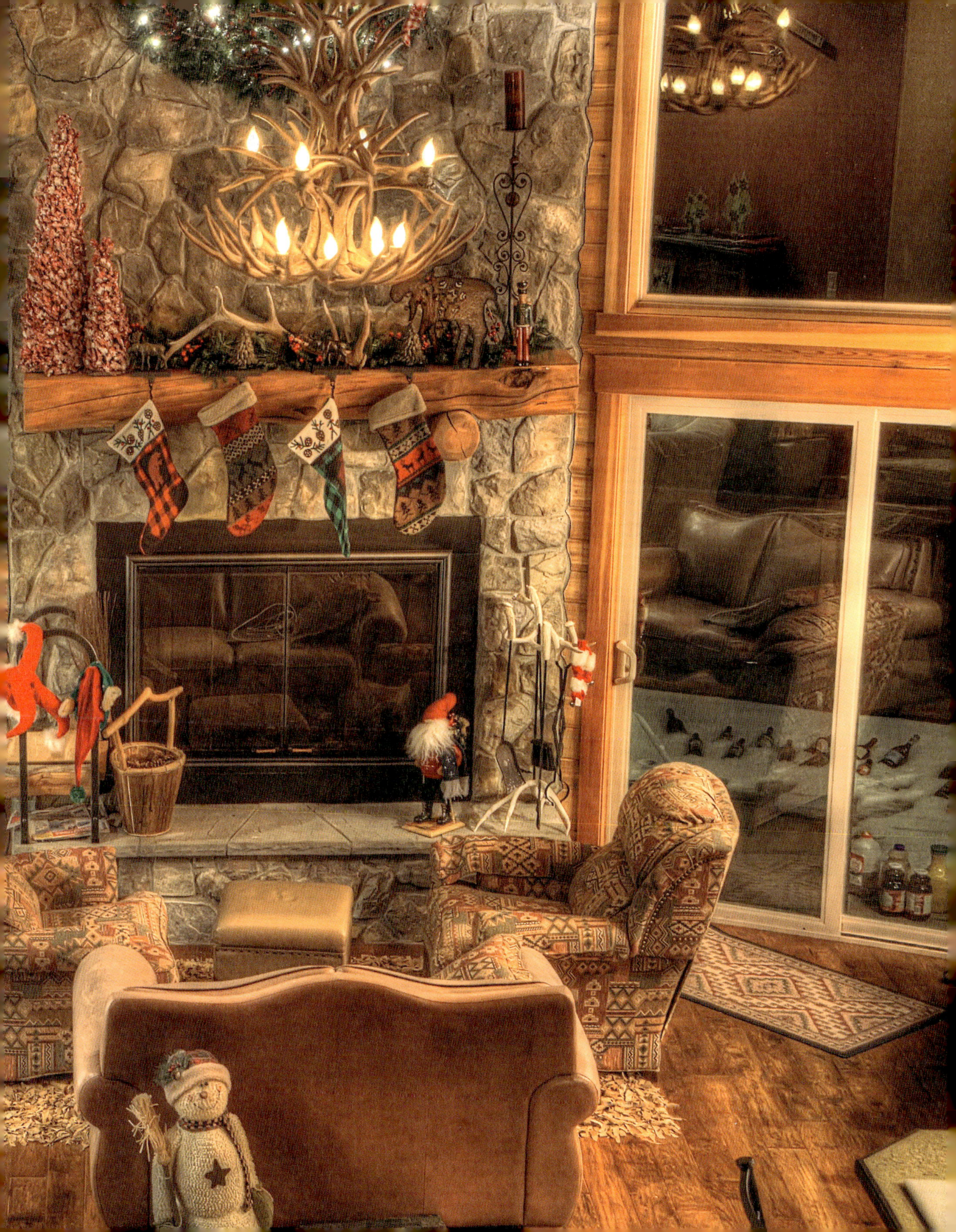

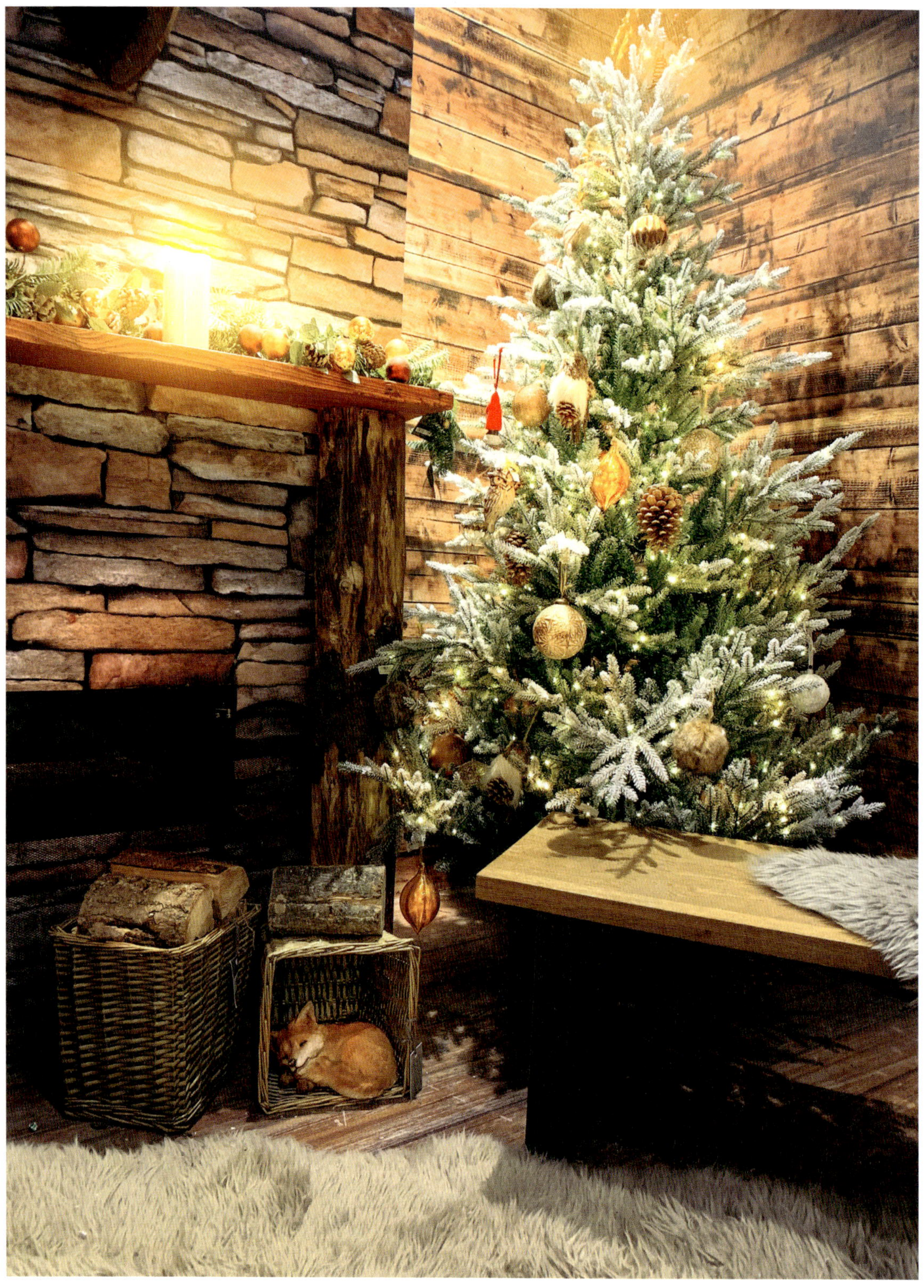

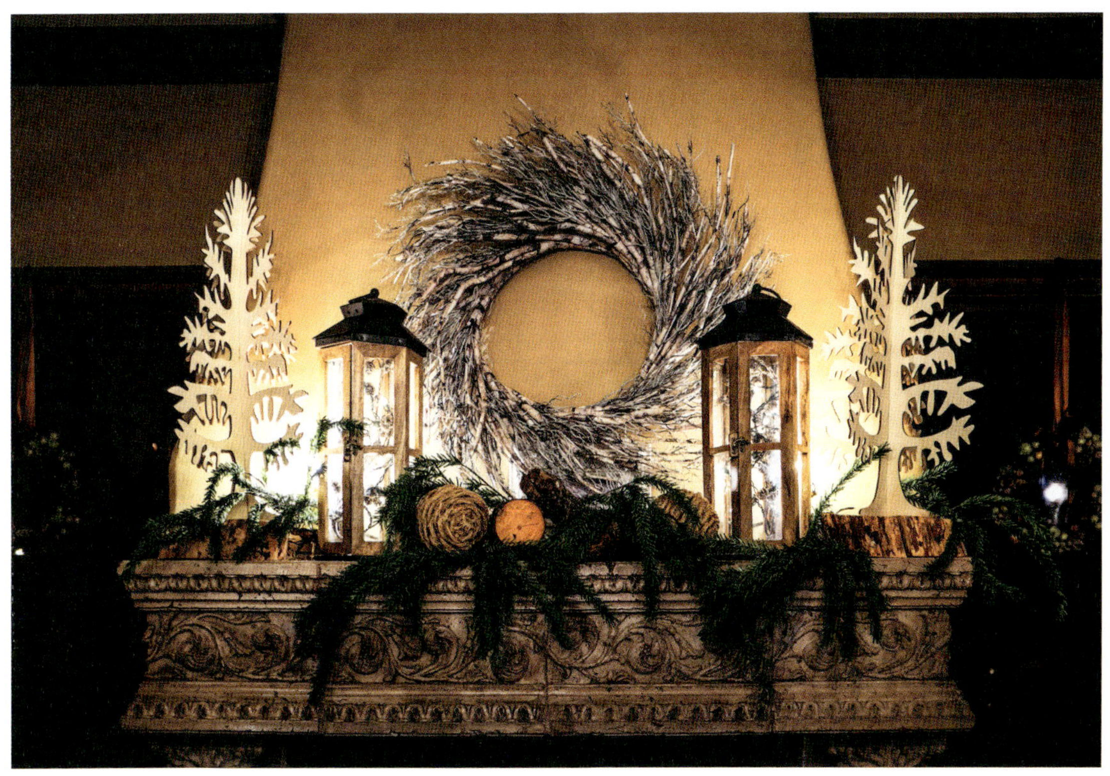

NATURAL SELECTION

The natural feel of this space, with its use of timber and stone, speaks to the outside. Sheepskin and flokati rugs deliver cozy comfort, and a fir garland on the mantelpiece is the focal point above the fire.

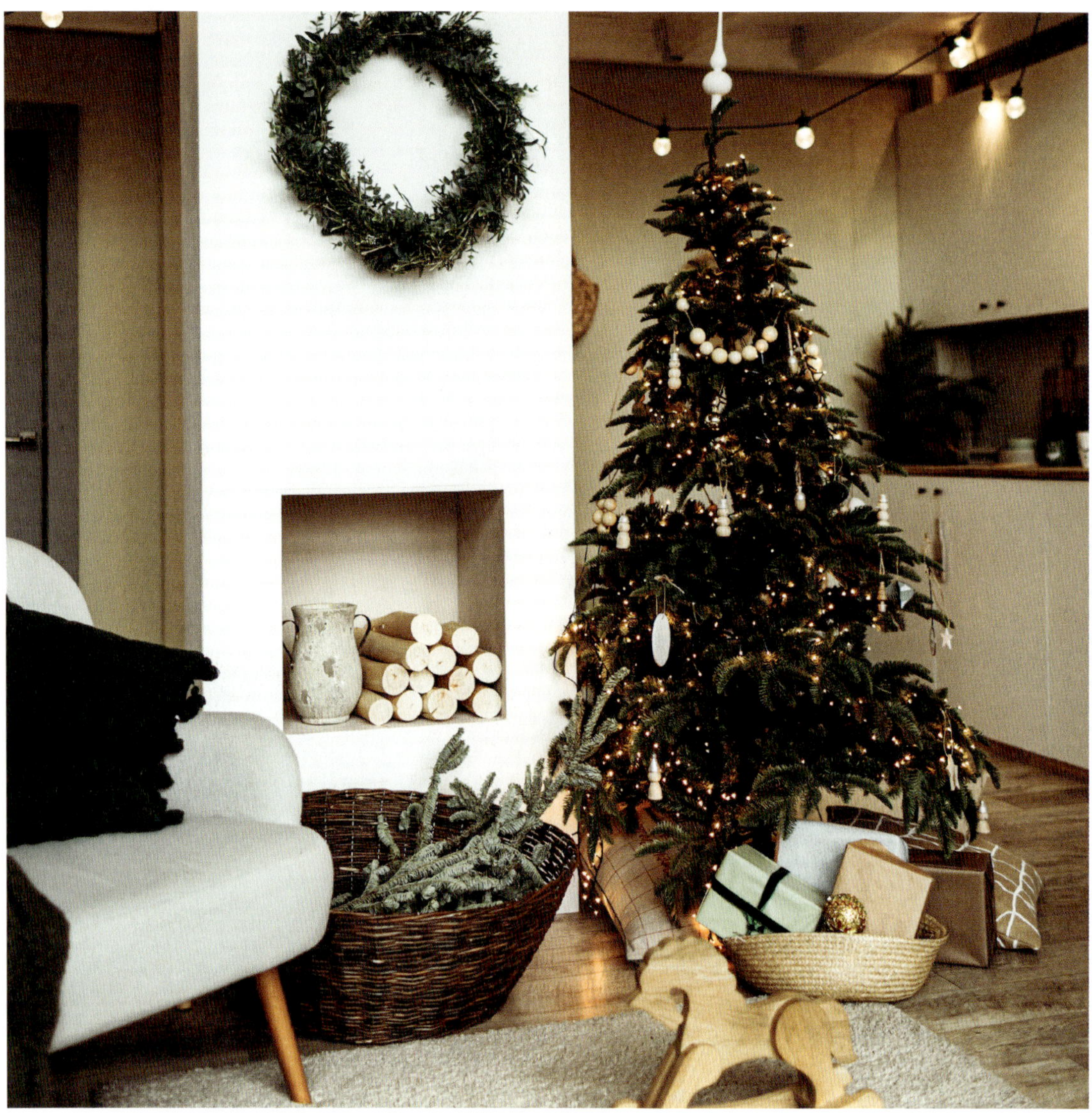

Garland lighting is strung, and wreaths are made. To recreate this simple, natural scheme, bring in branches and sprigs of fir to use for decoration in baskets and hung from the wall. Slices of oranges are dried and used to decorate a miniature tree in the bedroom.

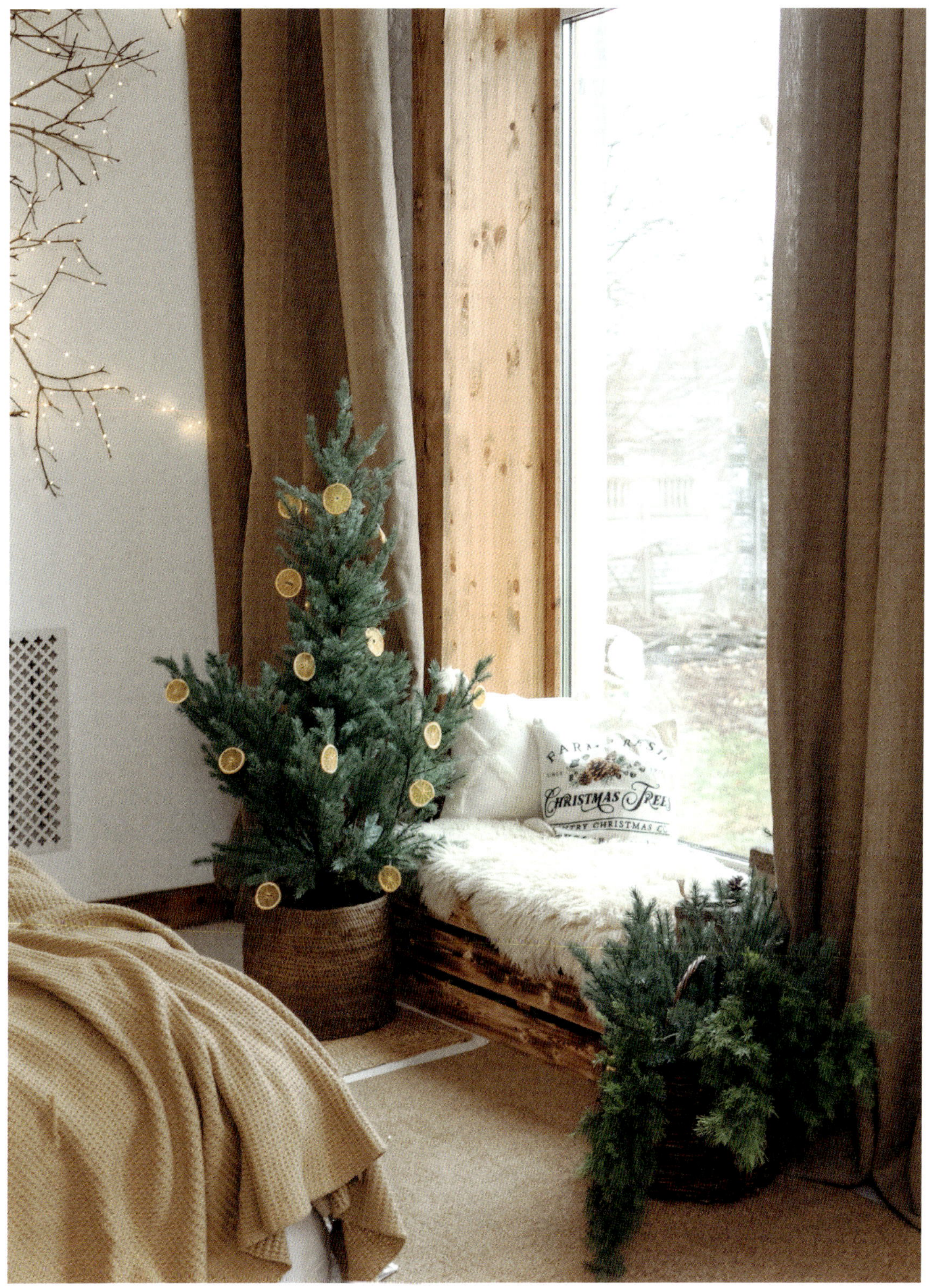
CHRISTMAS

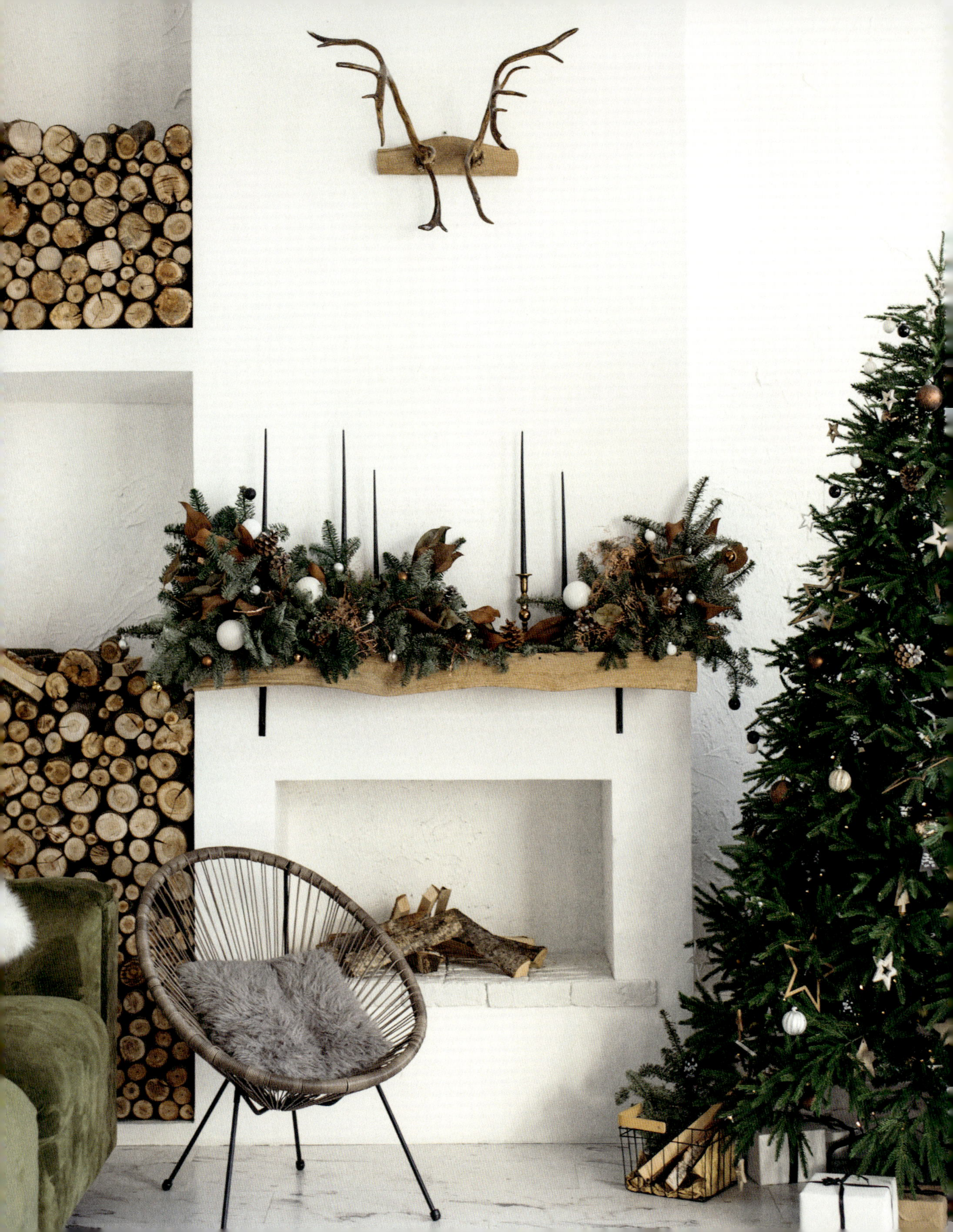

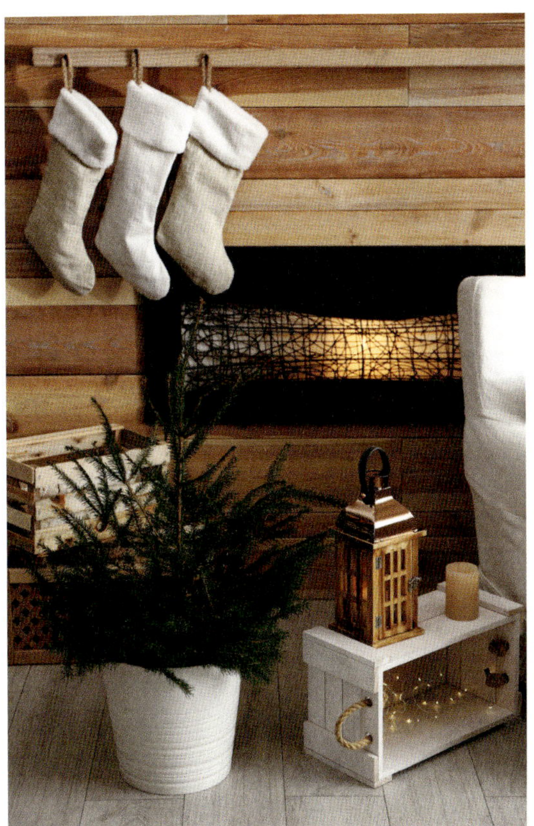

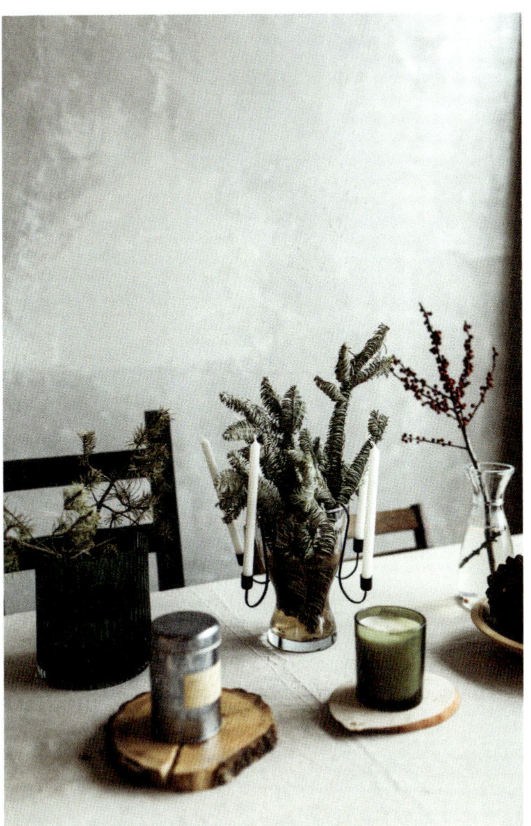

Prepare a neatly stacked alcove of logs as both part of the wintering process and as an early Christmas decoration. Authentic materials are key to this look, and incorporating stone, linen, wood, and leather means a house is calm and an ode to craftsmanship.

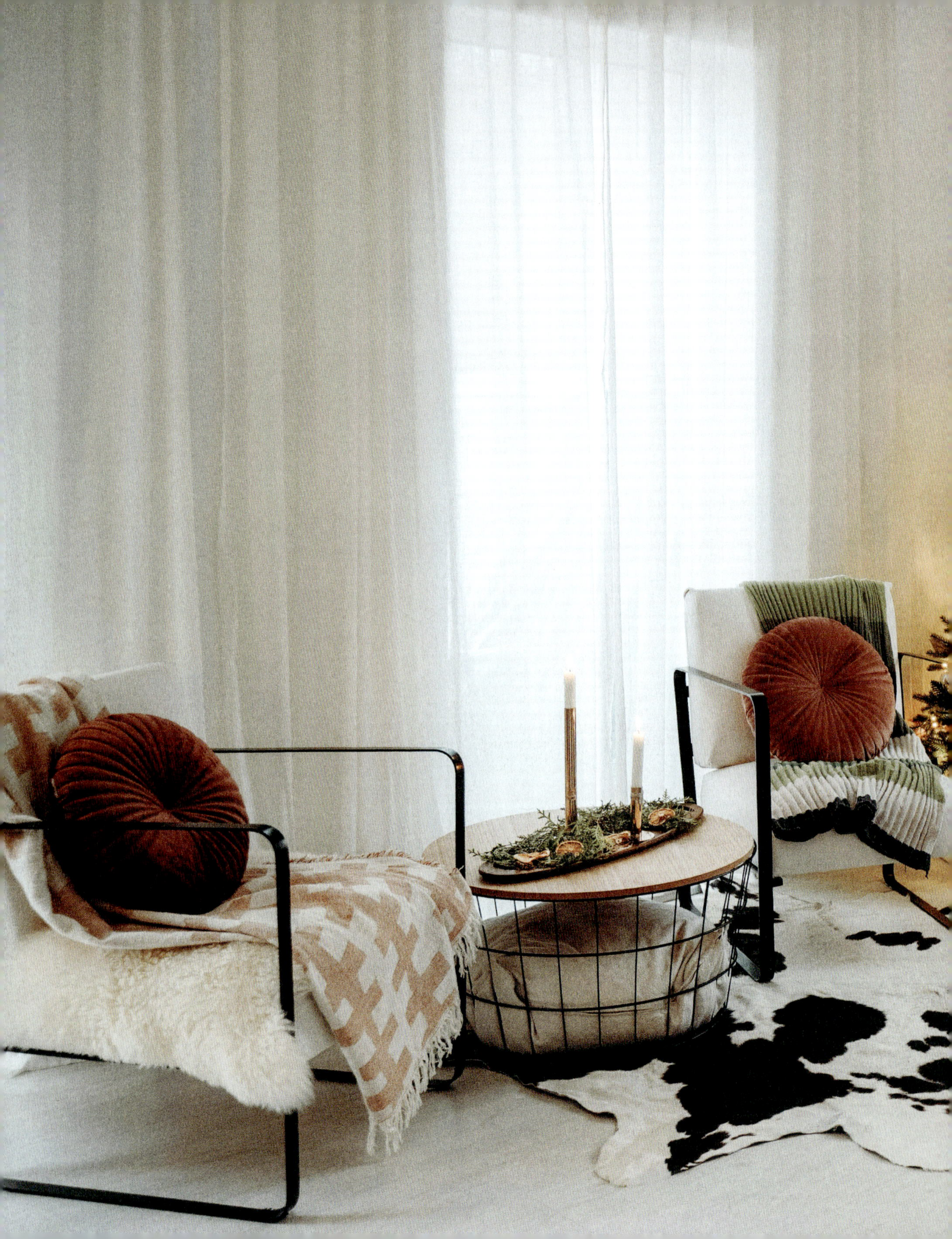

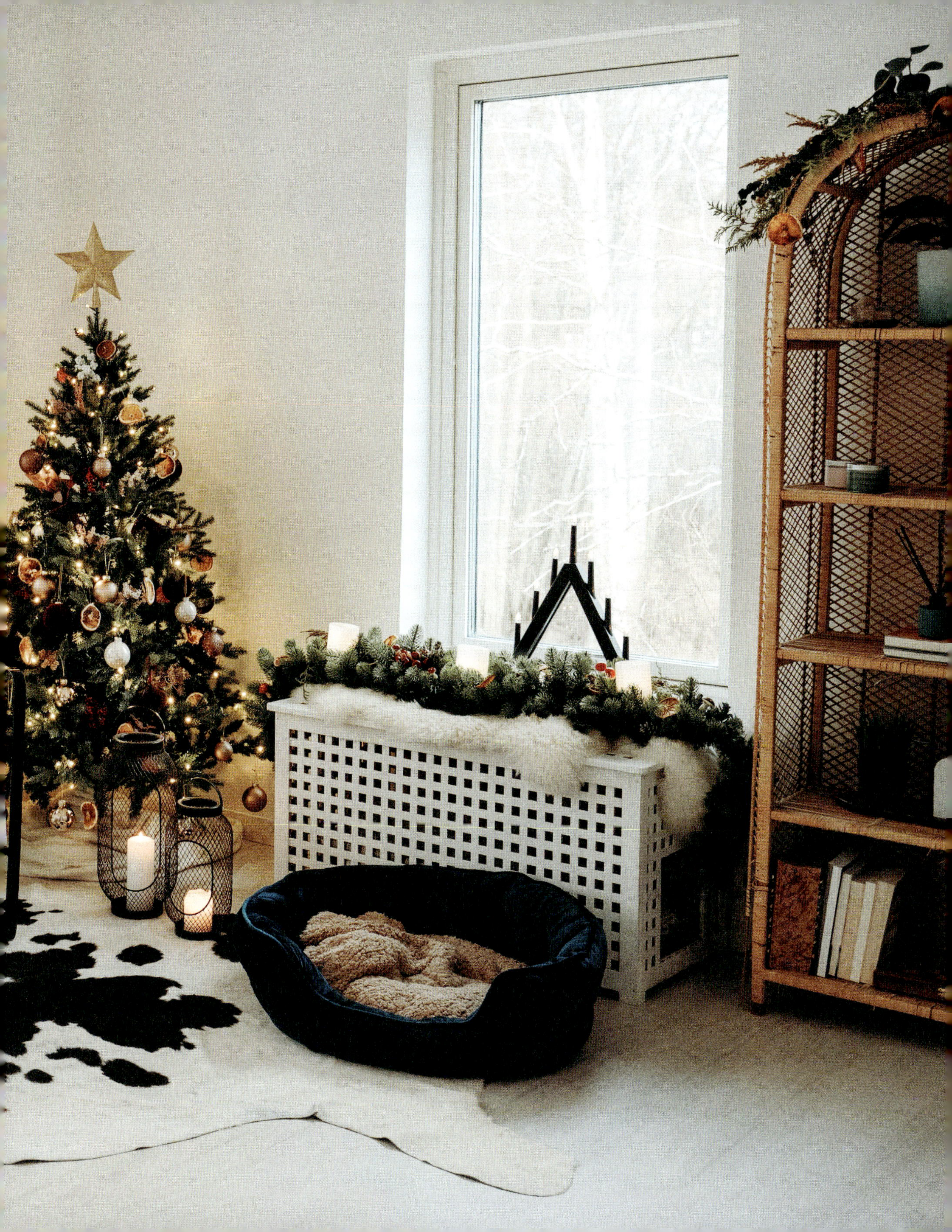

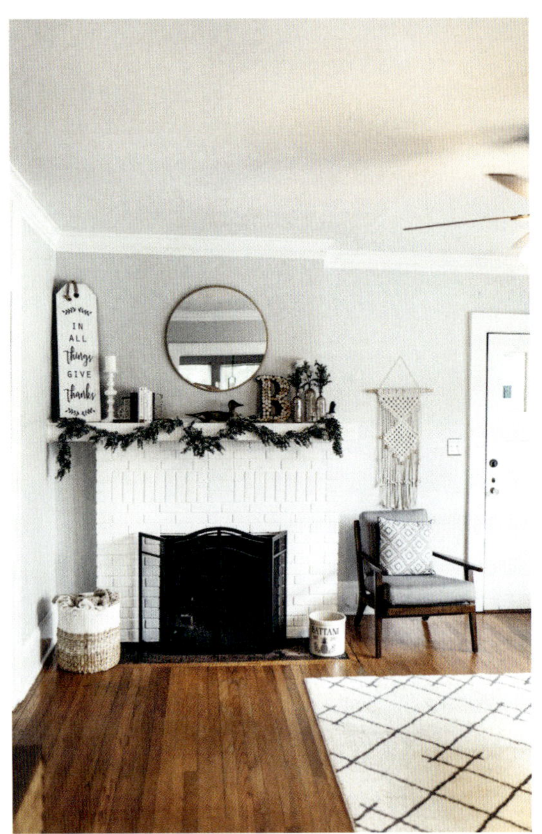

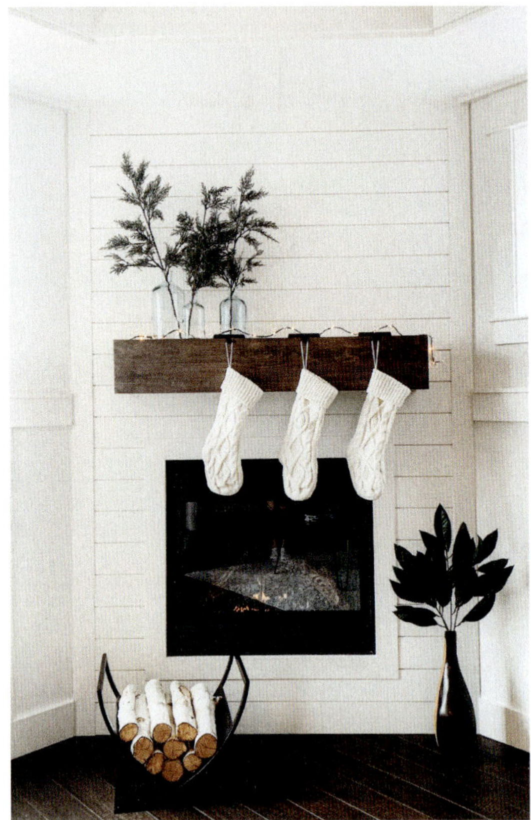

SCANDI STYLE

It's the small things that matter in this scheme; the glint of the tree's pearlescent baubles, drawn out by the otherwise unadorned branches and dark green. This is a general approach to Scandi style: a white backdrop, natural foliage and accents of glass and metallic glimmer. If you're going for a minimalist Scandi look, avoid overcrowding the tree with too many decorations—and keep the tinsel away.

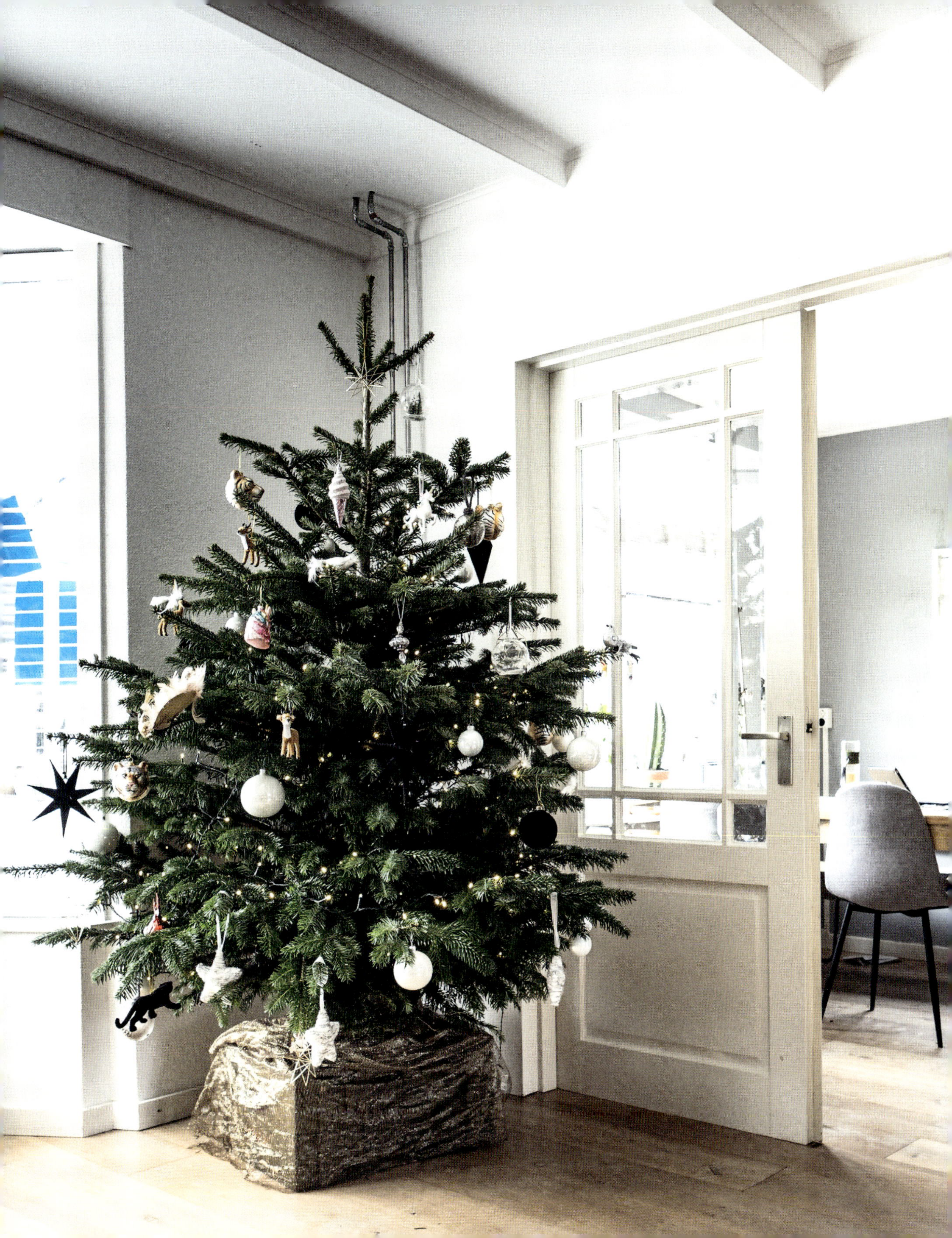

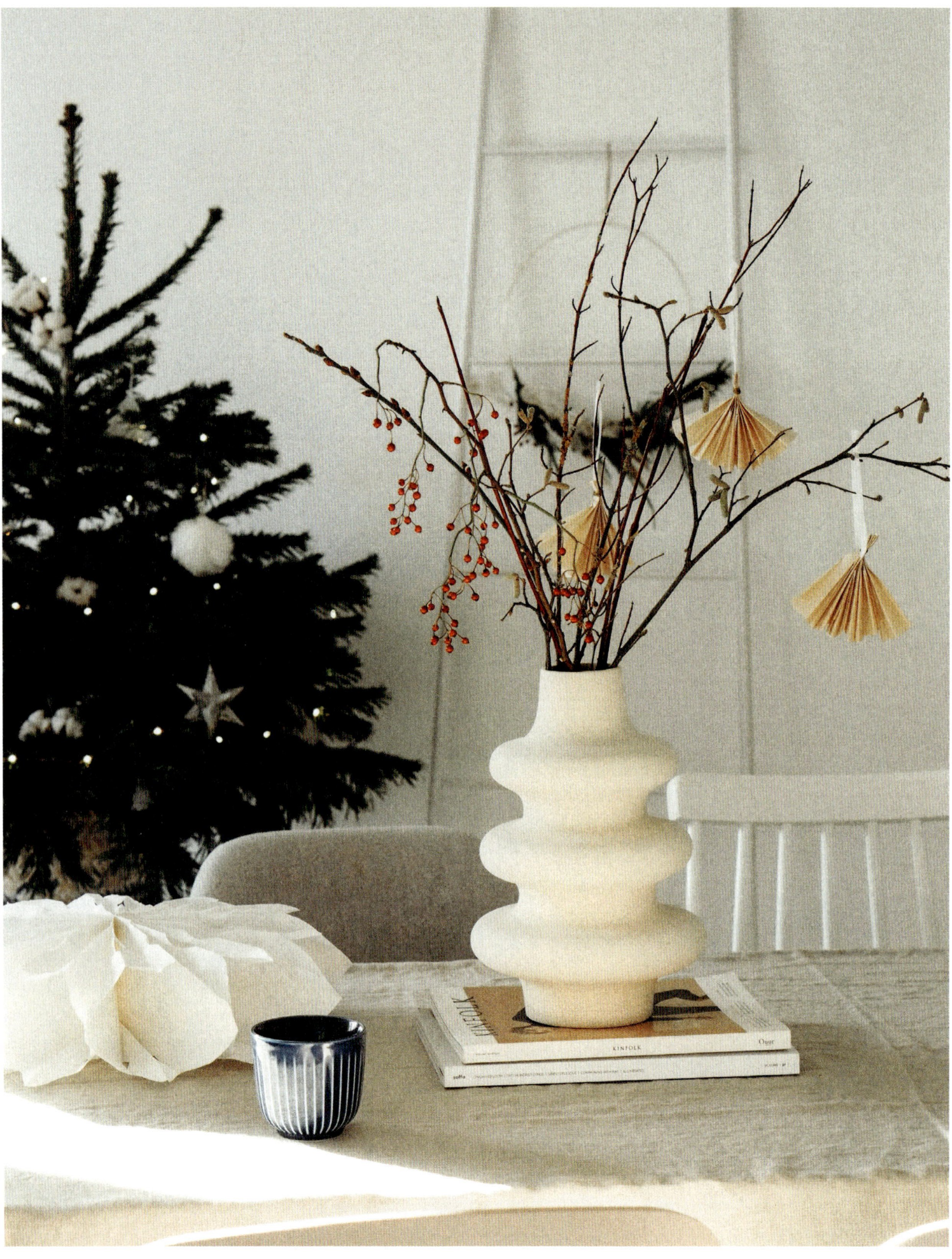
KINFOLK

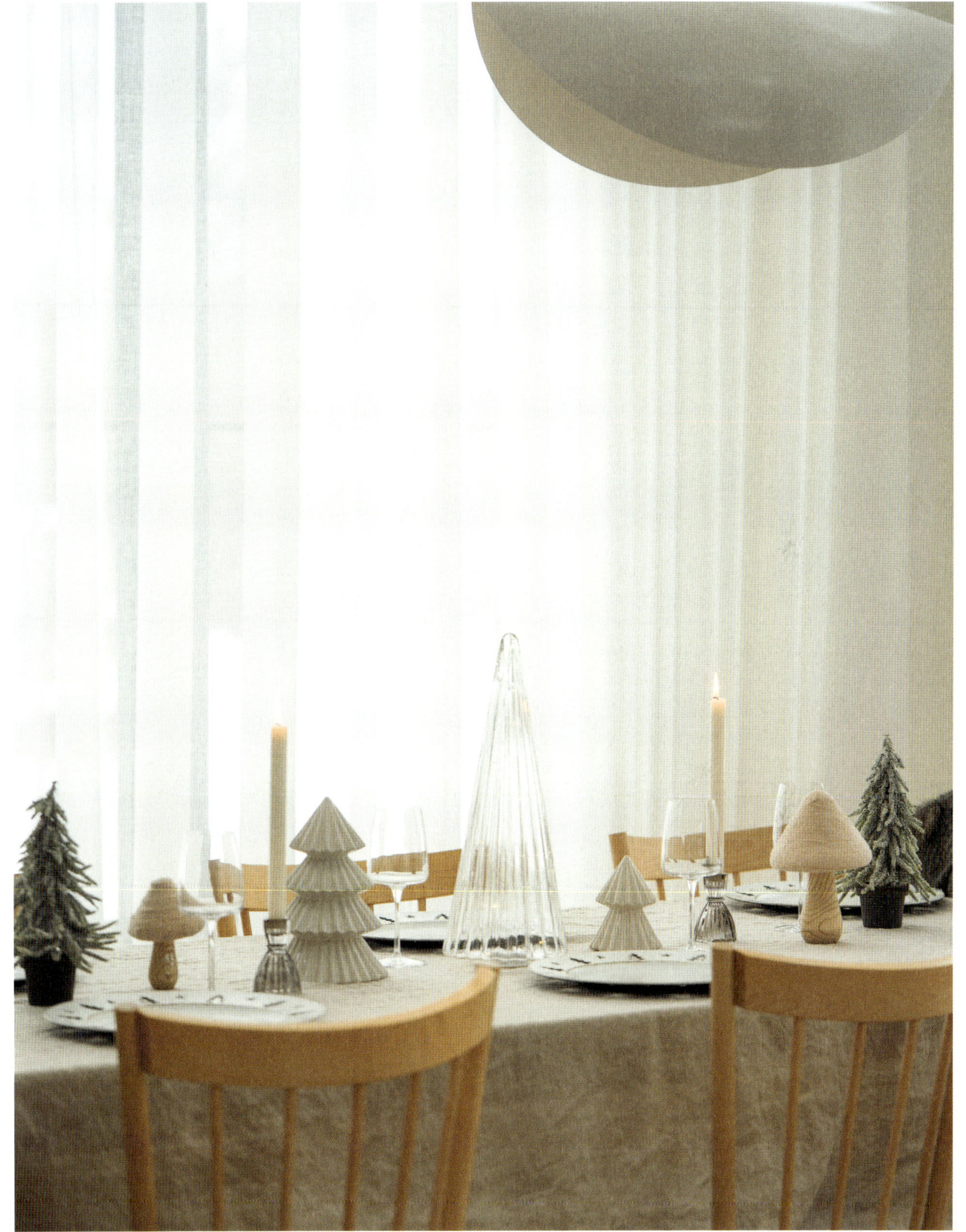

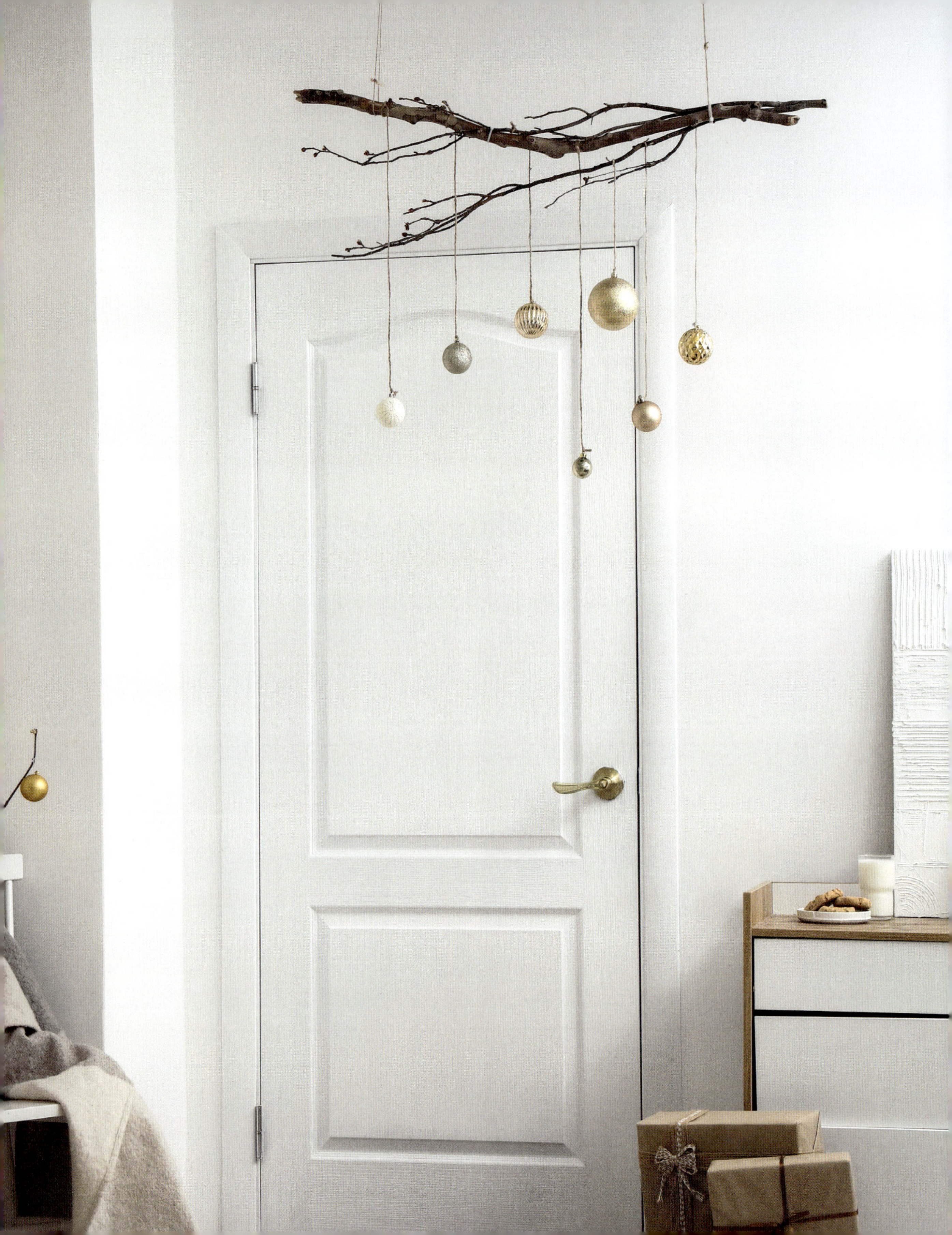

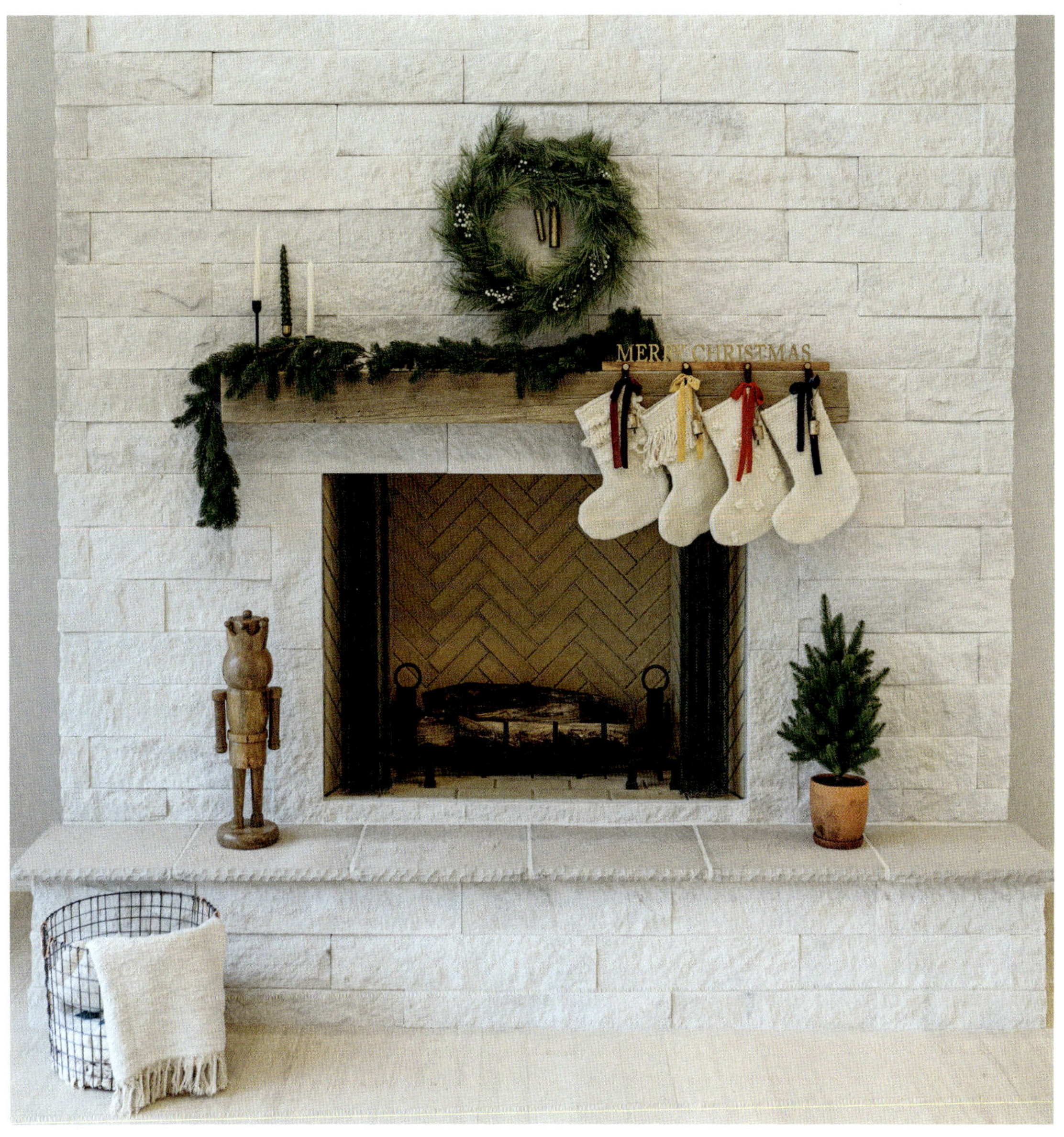

Wood is always a focal point in a white room. Hang a branch adorned with golden baubles or decorate with a wreath, tapered candles and chunky knit stockings hung from the mantel.

FEATURE
CHRISTMAS IN THE SUN

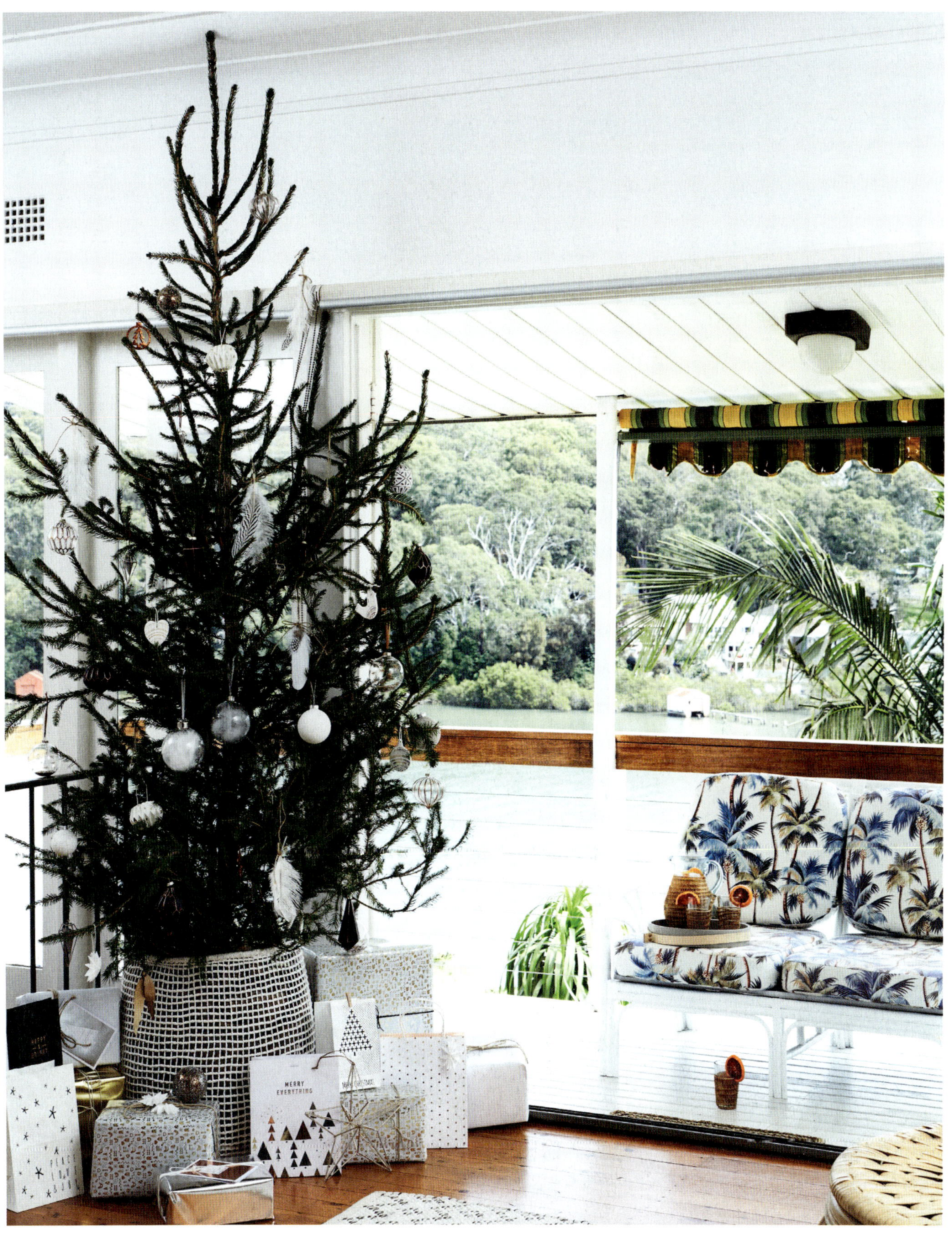
MERRY
EVERYTHING
PEACE
LOVE

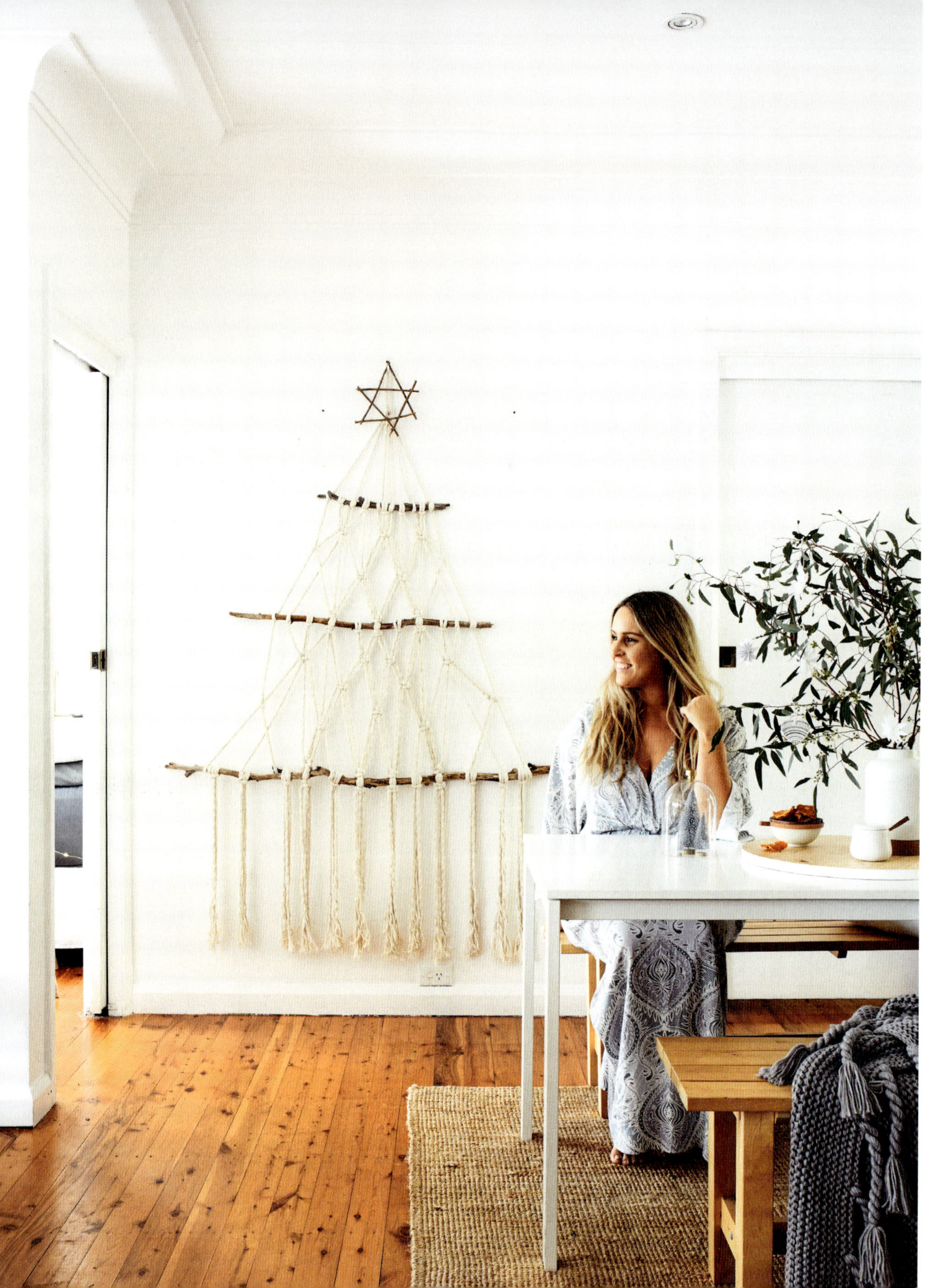

HANGING TREE: Tight on space? Why not make a macramé tree wall hanging that gives a coastal feel by using driftwood sticks to divide the levels. "I make custom pieces all the time to suit people's tastes and requirements, including this macramé tree. It's a one-of-a-kind piece due to its organic elements. The tree hanging was made using chunky natural cotton rope and driftwood sticks collected from the beach. I'm not the traditional red-and-green decoration type, so I opted to create a feature that made an impact, but was still my style."

A Bohemian Oasis at Christmas

This gorgeous waterfront cottage situated on the Georges River in Sydney, Australia, is home to the talented interior stylist and macramé artist Jessi Deakin and her partner Adam. Jessi instantly saw the potential in this light-filled, three-bedroom home, but Adam wasn't so sure. "It took a bit of convincing him, but eventually I won," Jessi says. Many of Jessi's macramé pieces are displayed throughout their home, creating an eclectic mix of coastal and bohemian vibes. Their rental cottage is situated in a quiet cul-de-sac and is surrounded by luscious green gardens and native Eucalyptus trees. The backyard slopes steeply downward through "the jungle," as Jessi calls it. "It is honestly the most peaceful area in Sydney! Sometimes when we sit out on our balcony in the evening, we find ourselves whispering because we feel bad disturbing the silence!"

The garden was so overgrown when they moved in that the pair literally had to beat down a path to the river so they could access the water and make use of the outdoor space. Since completing the landscaping, the couple now has numerous outdoor areas to enjoy year-round, including two balconies that run the length of the house, a covered patio out front, a spot by the river with a barbeque built into the stone wall, and several grassy areas that are perfect for picnics. So deciding where to host Christmas this year was an easy choice! "Decorating is always fun, and having it mostly outside freed us up a lot in terms of space," Jessi says. "We just kept it relaxed, like us."

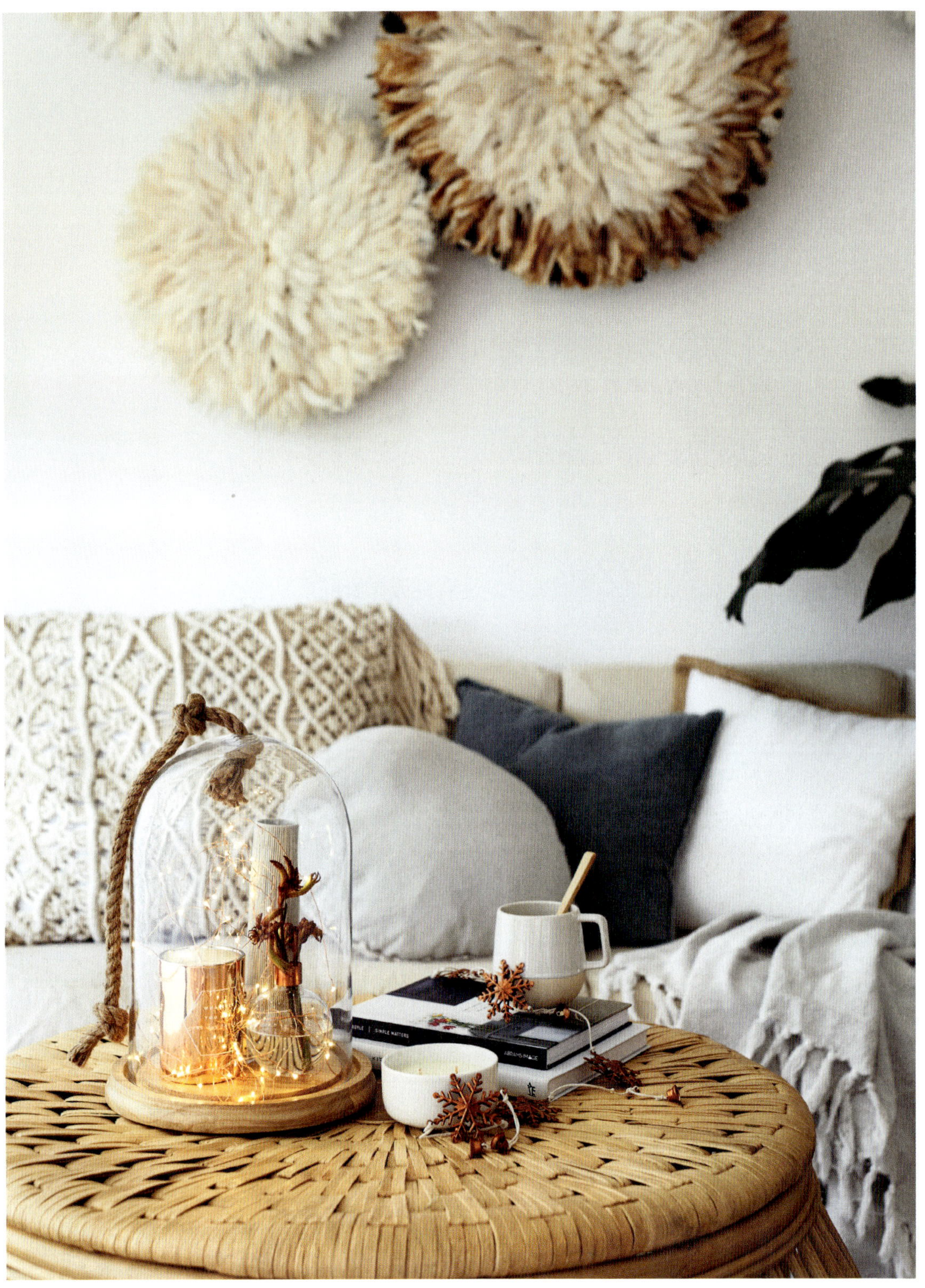

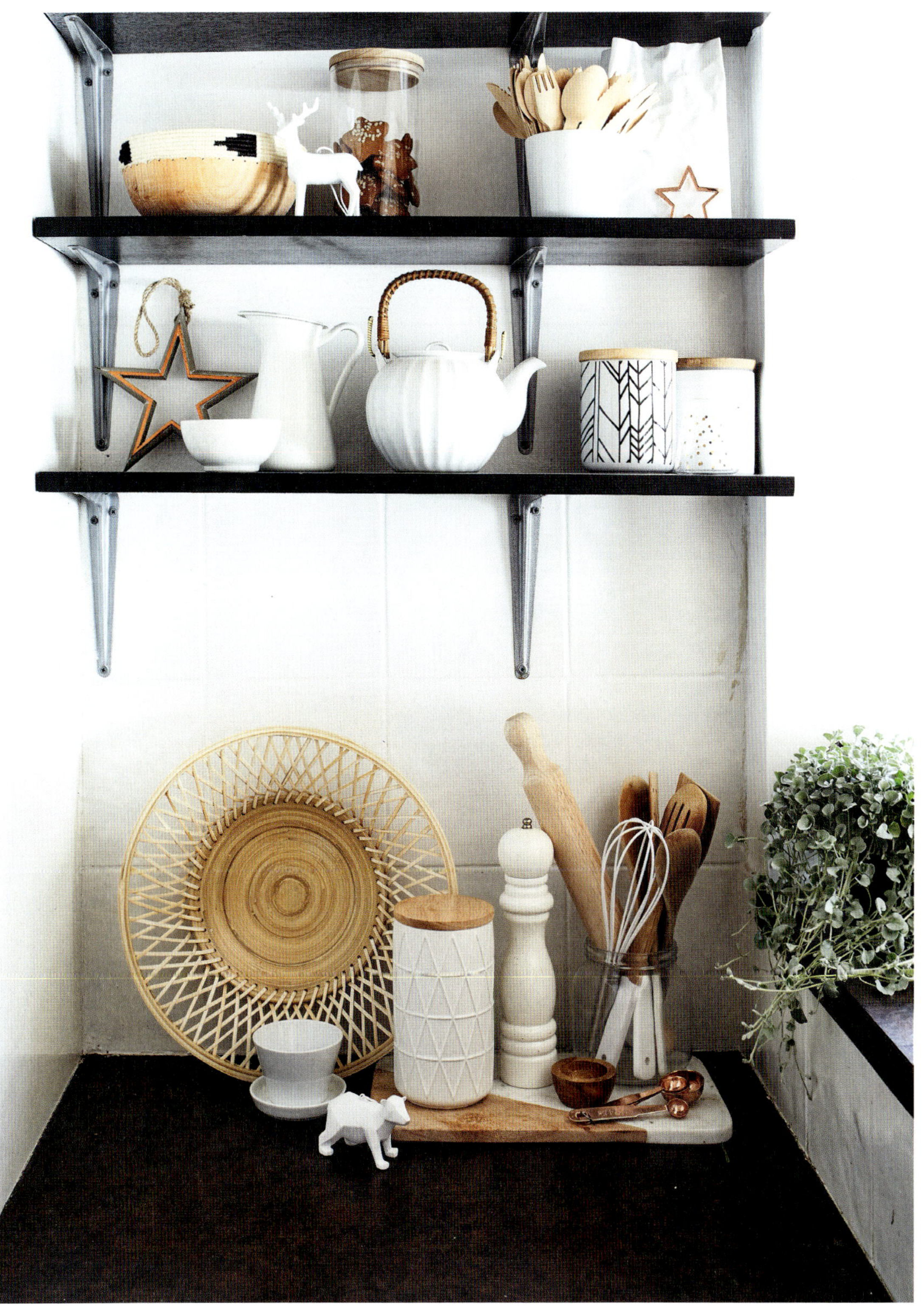

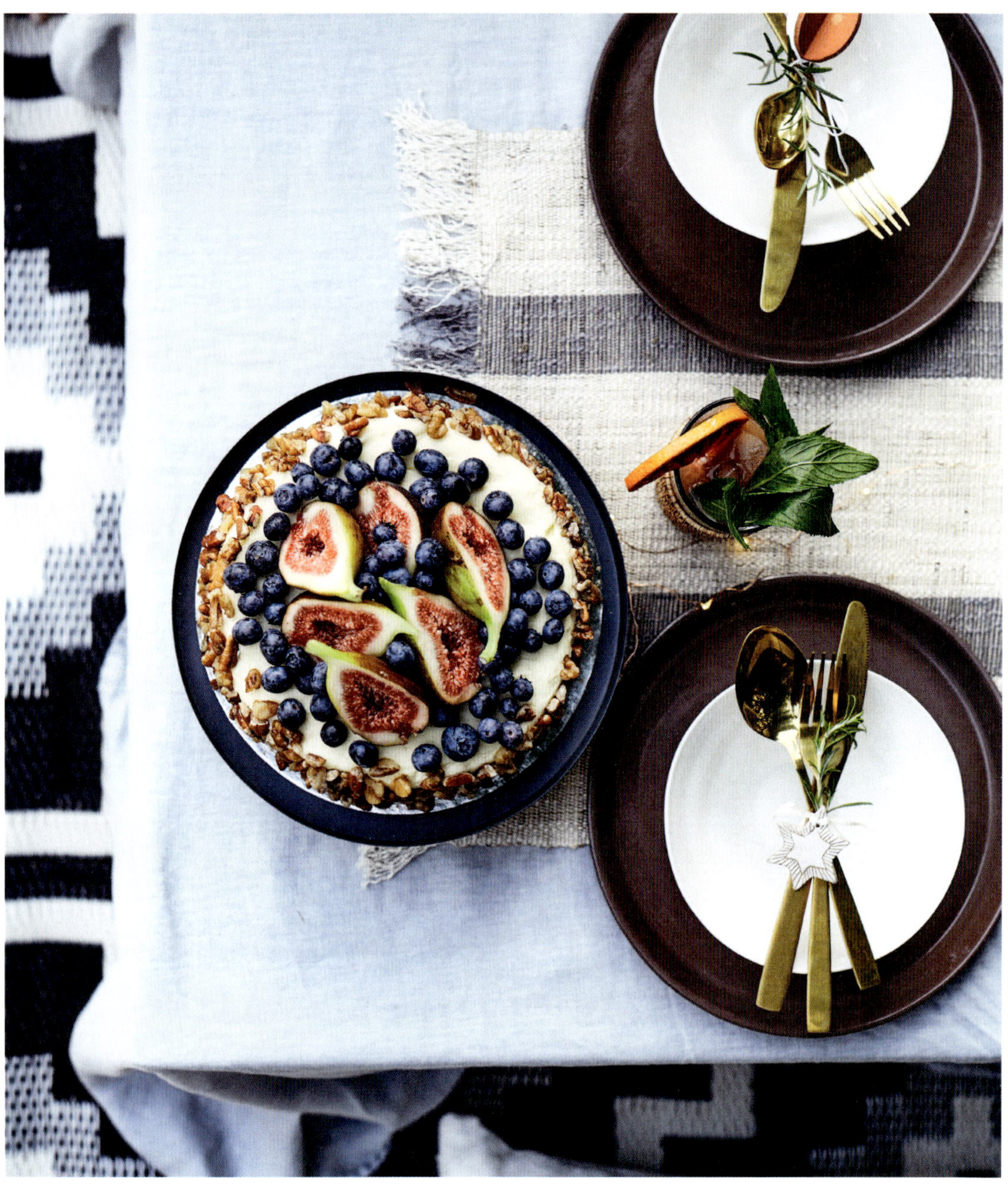

"As we don't get to experience a white Christmas in Australia, we might as well embrace the warm weather and take it outdoors," Jessi says. "It's brilliant having everyone together and in such good spirits."

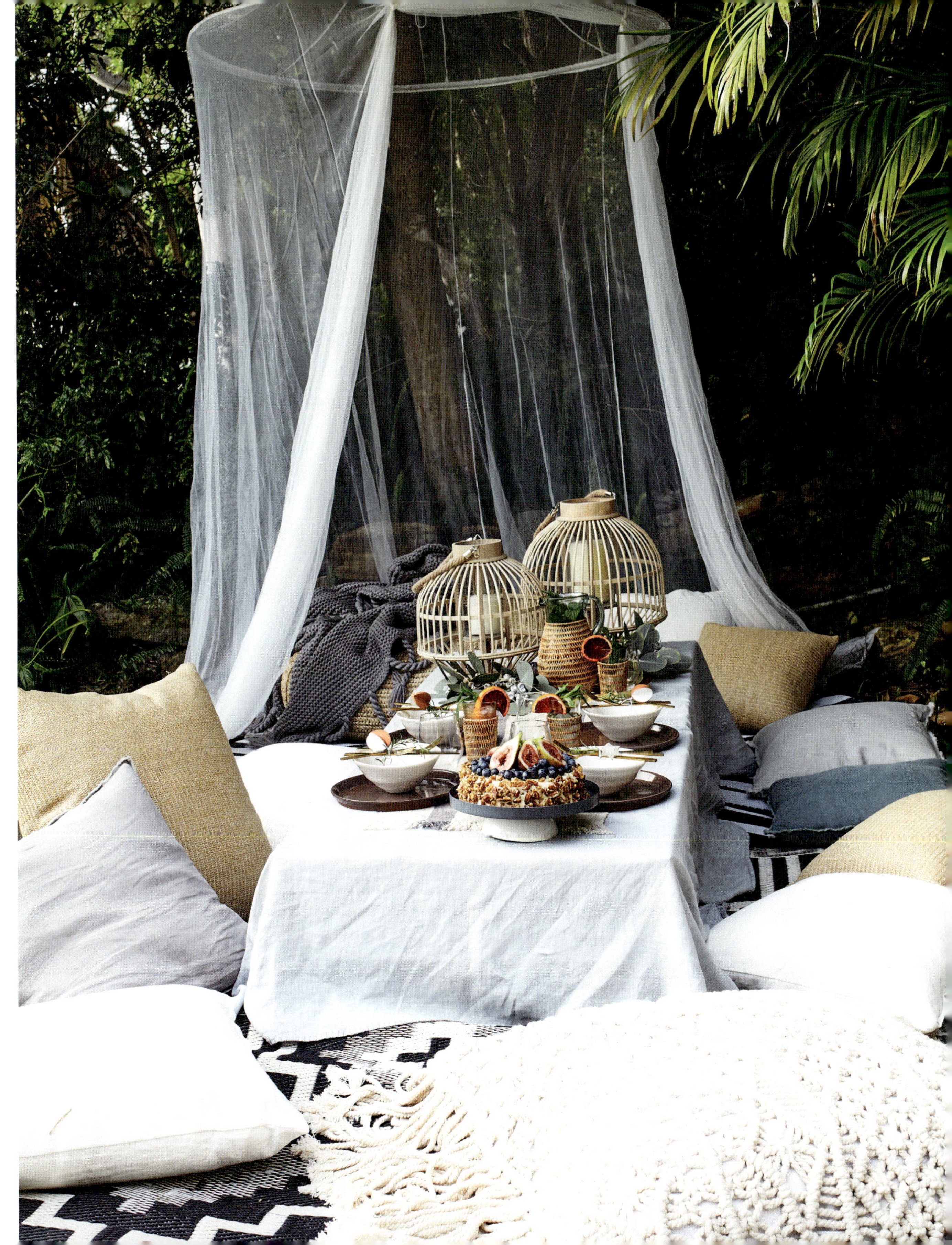

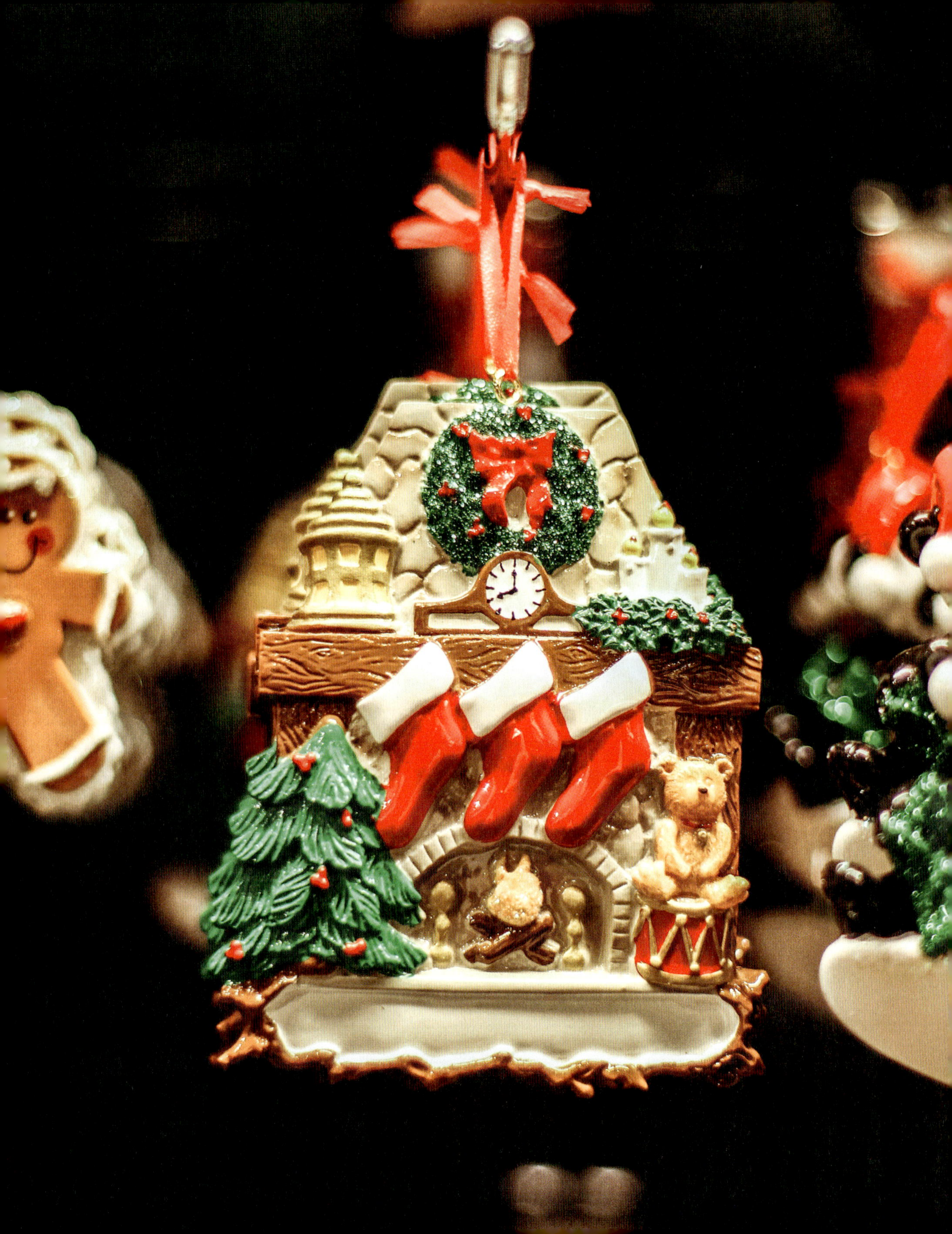

Design & decorate

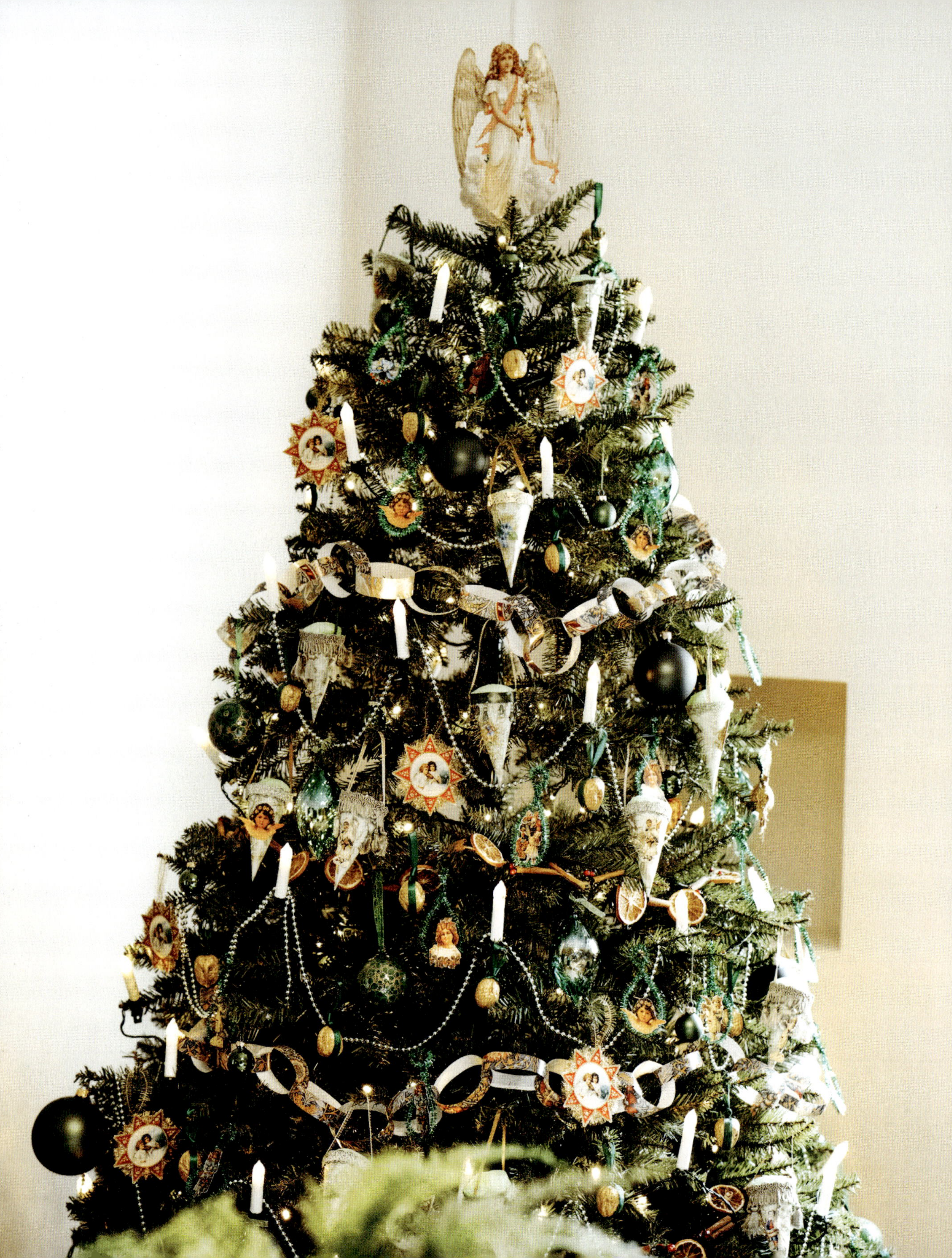

Dazzling Decs

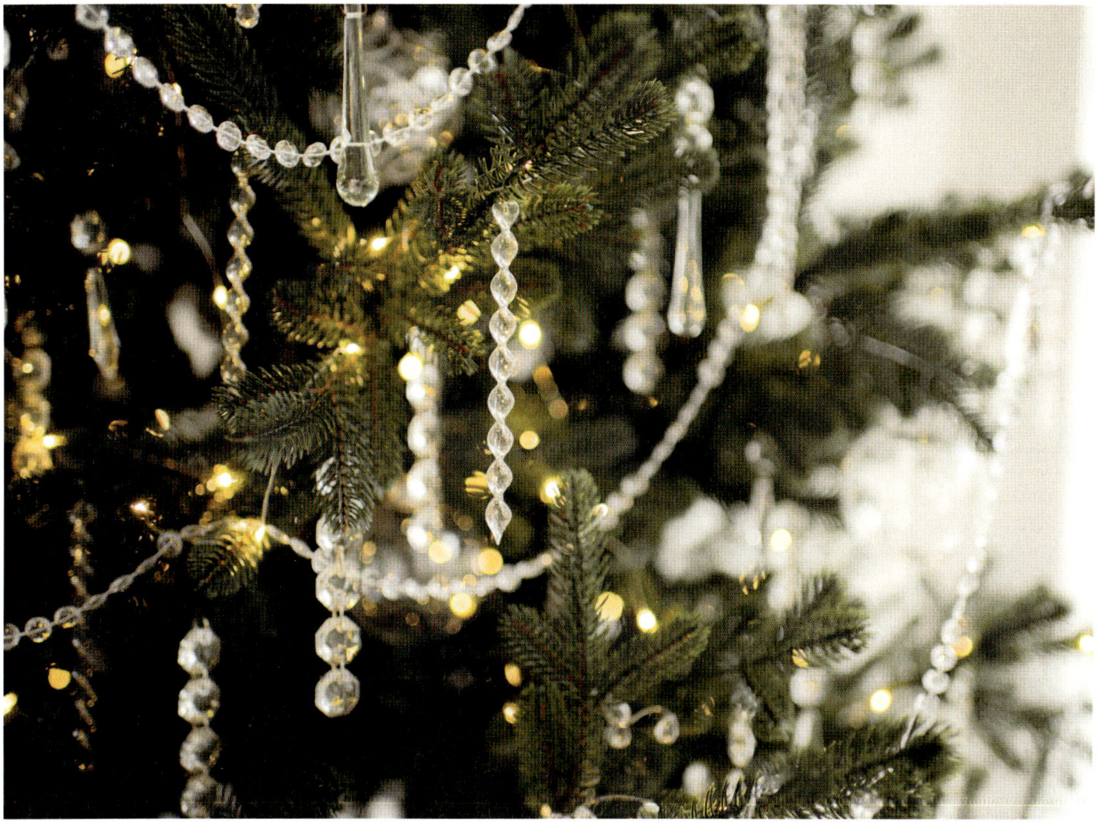

Festive décor can harmonize with the everyday pieces in your home. For many, that means neutrals. Neutral on neutrals and texture on texture means a tree is rich and layered—and allows for any brighter elements to stand out. Metallic accents as tree ornaments always look expensive, as does glass. From icicles to raindrop adornments on the tree, glass ornaments are the key to unlocking your chicest tree ever. These pieces glisten in the light and capture the imagination.

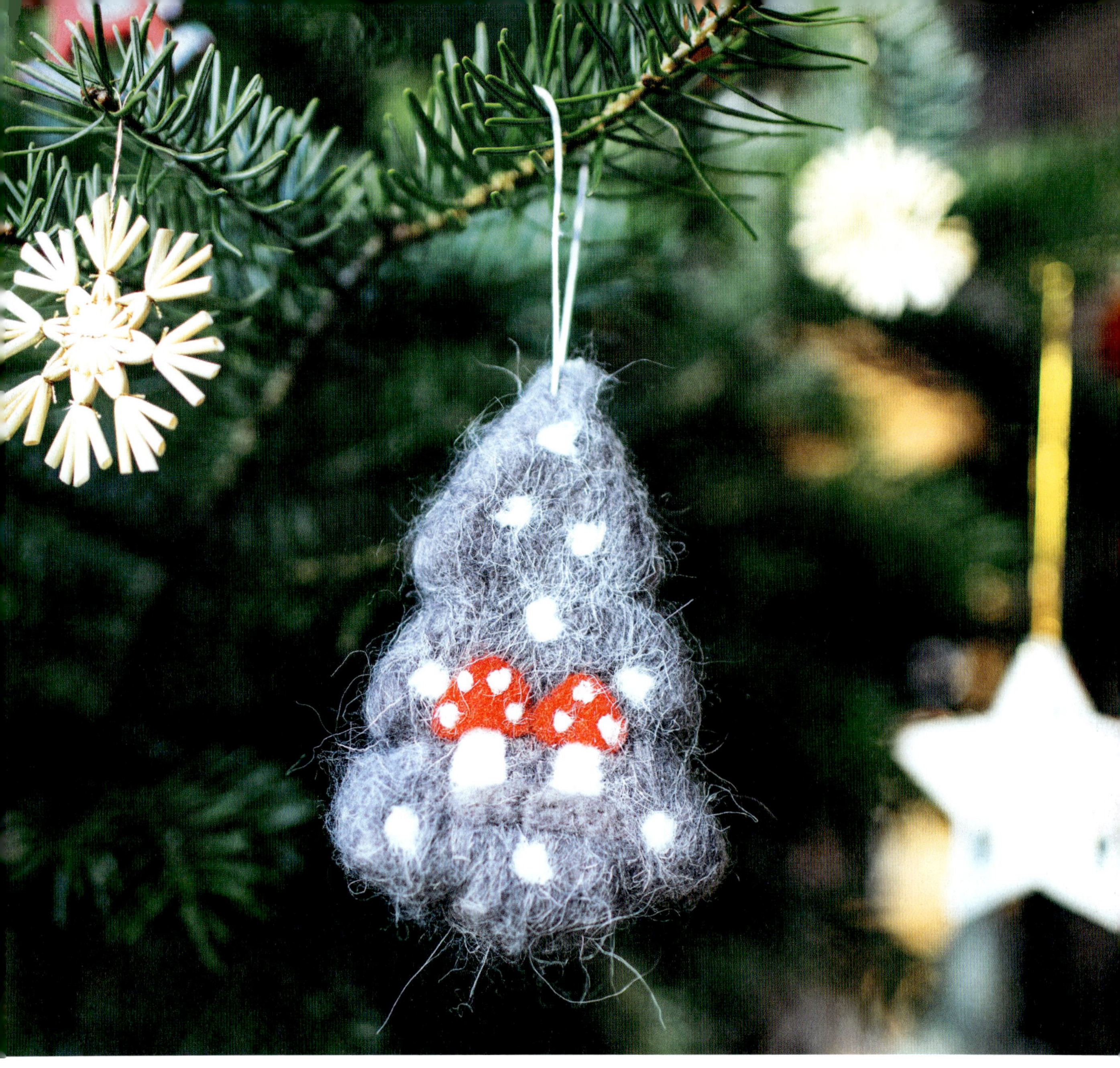

Handmade ornaments such as this felted tree with appliqué toadstools add a nostalgic touch and make a beautiful present that will always be cherished.

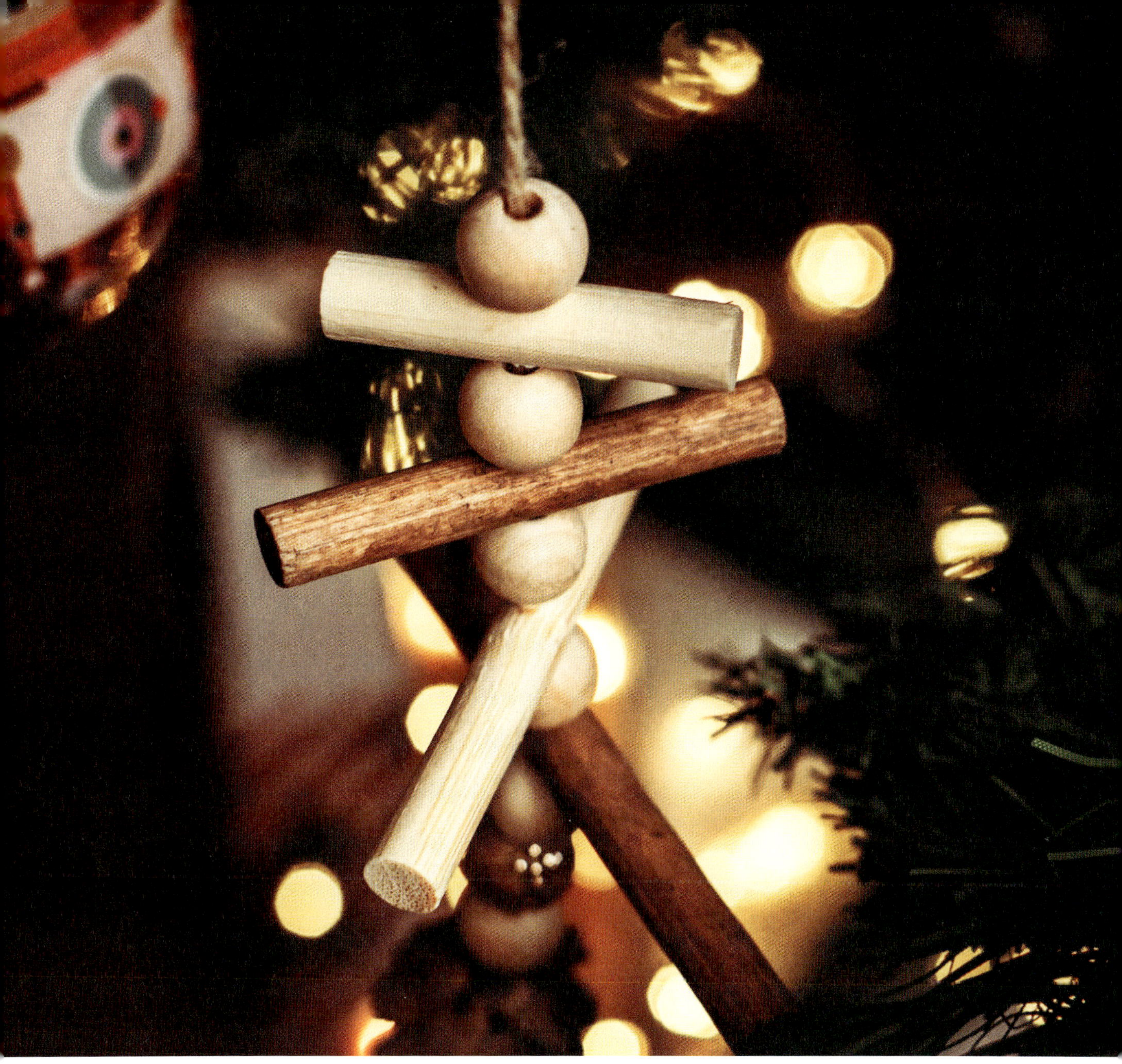

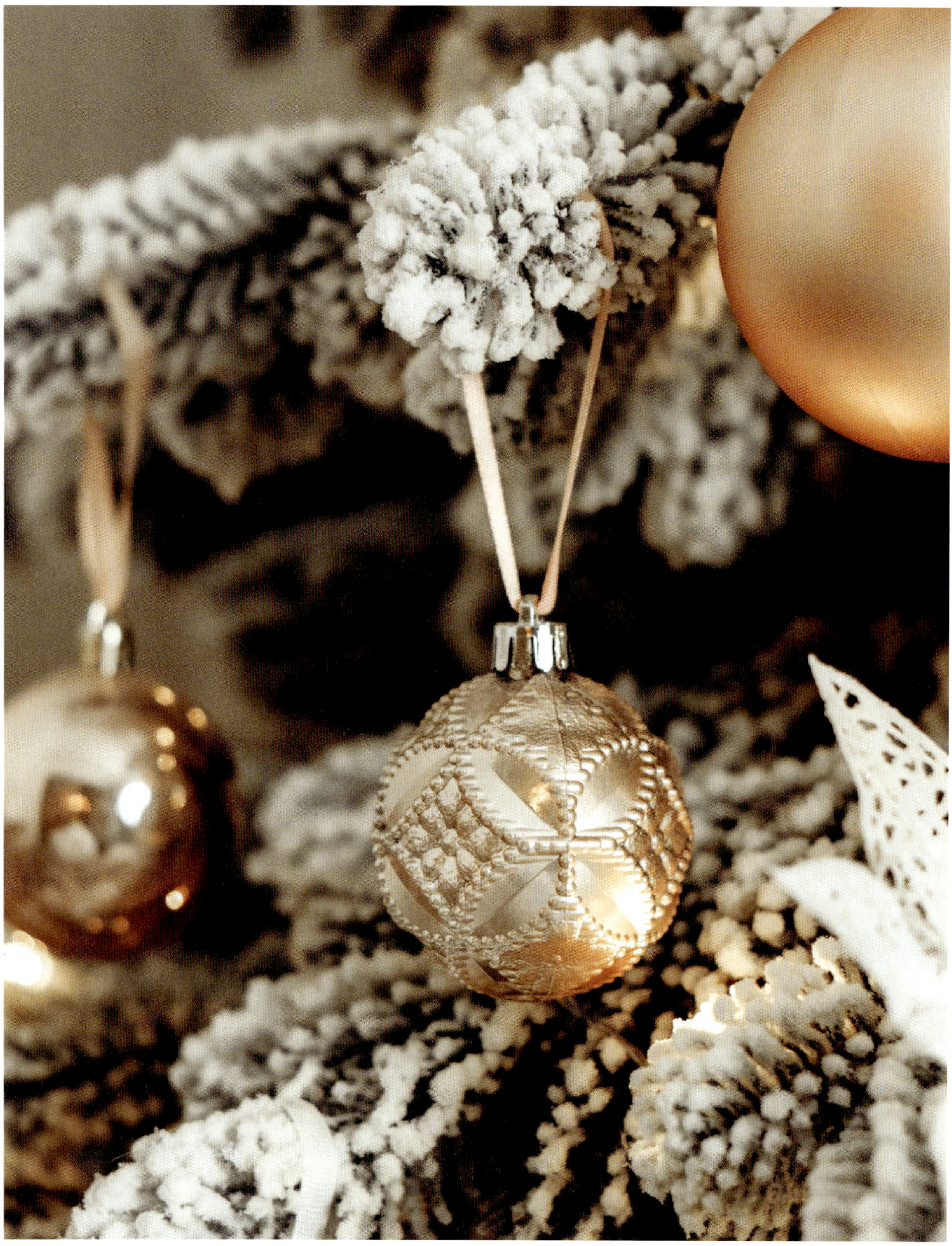

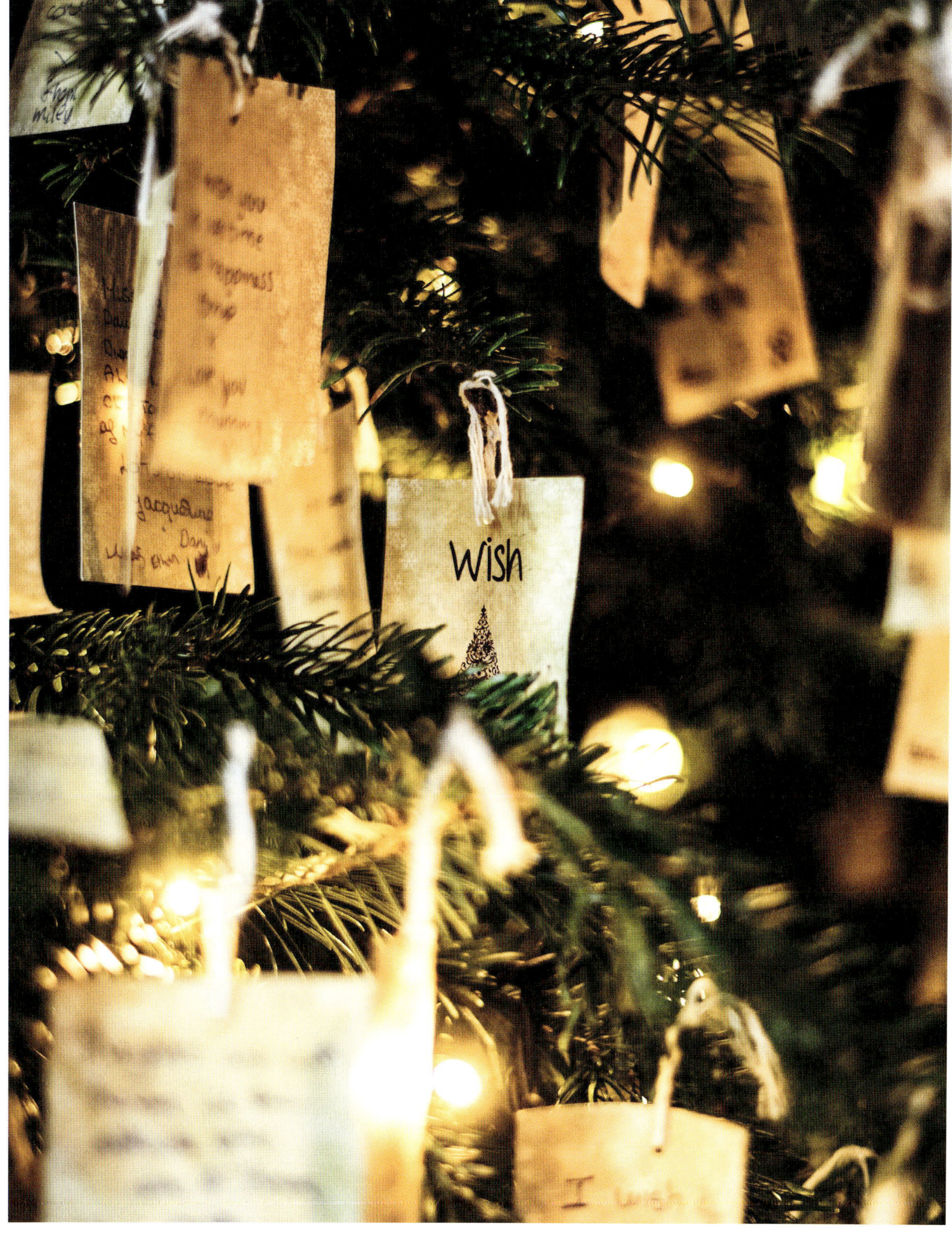
Wish

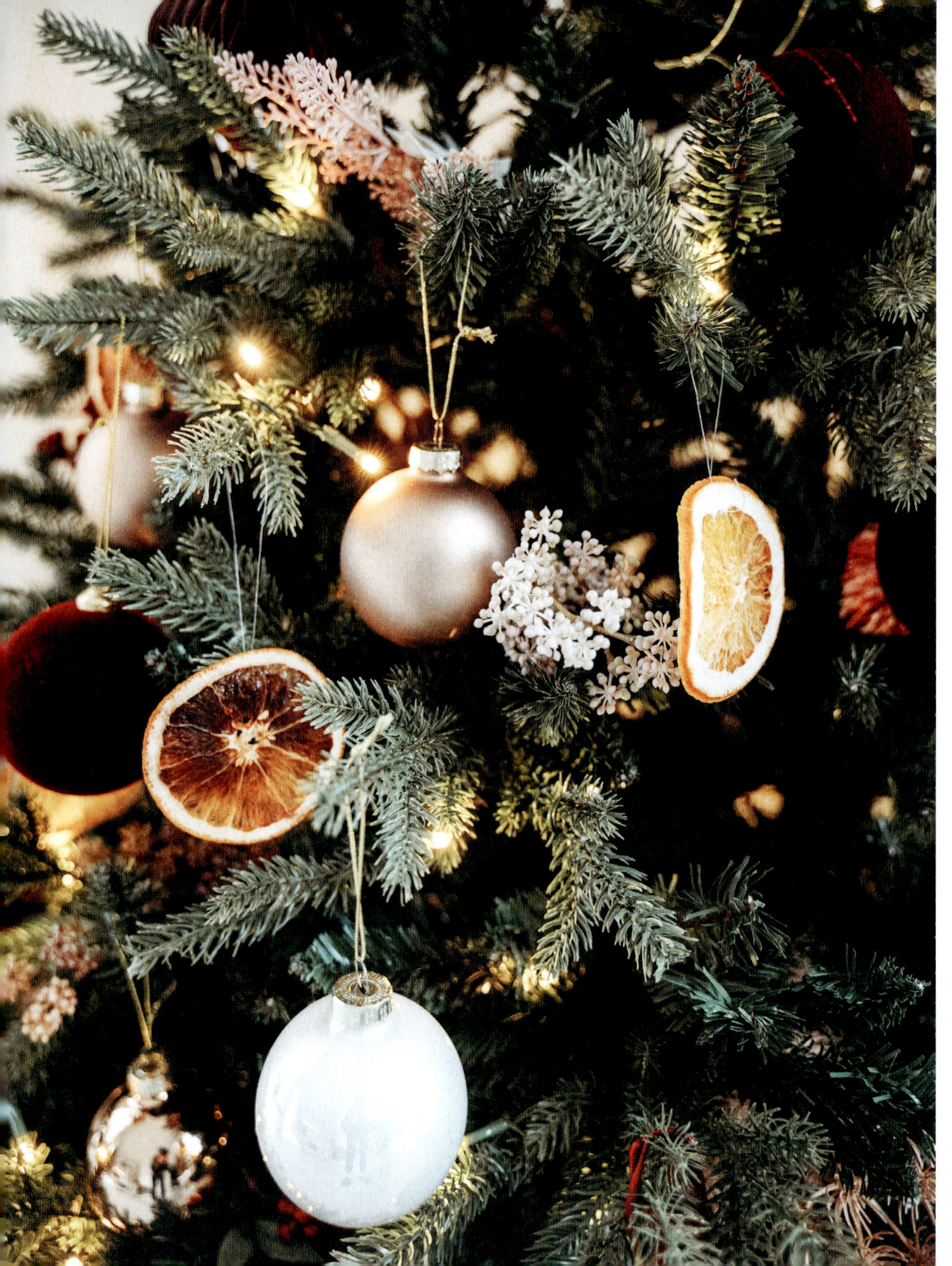

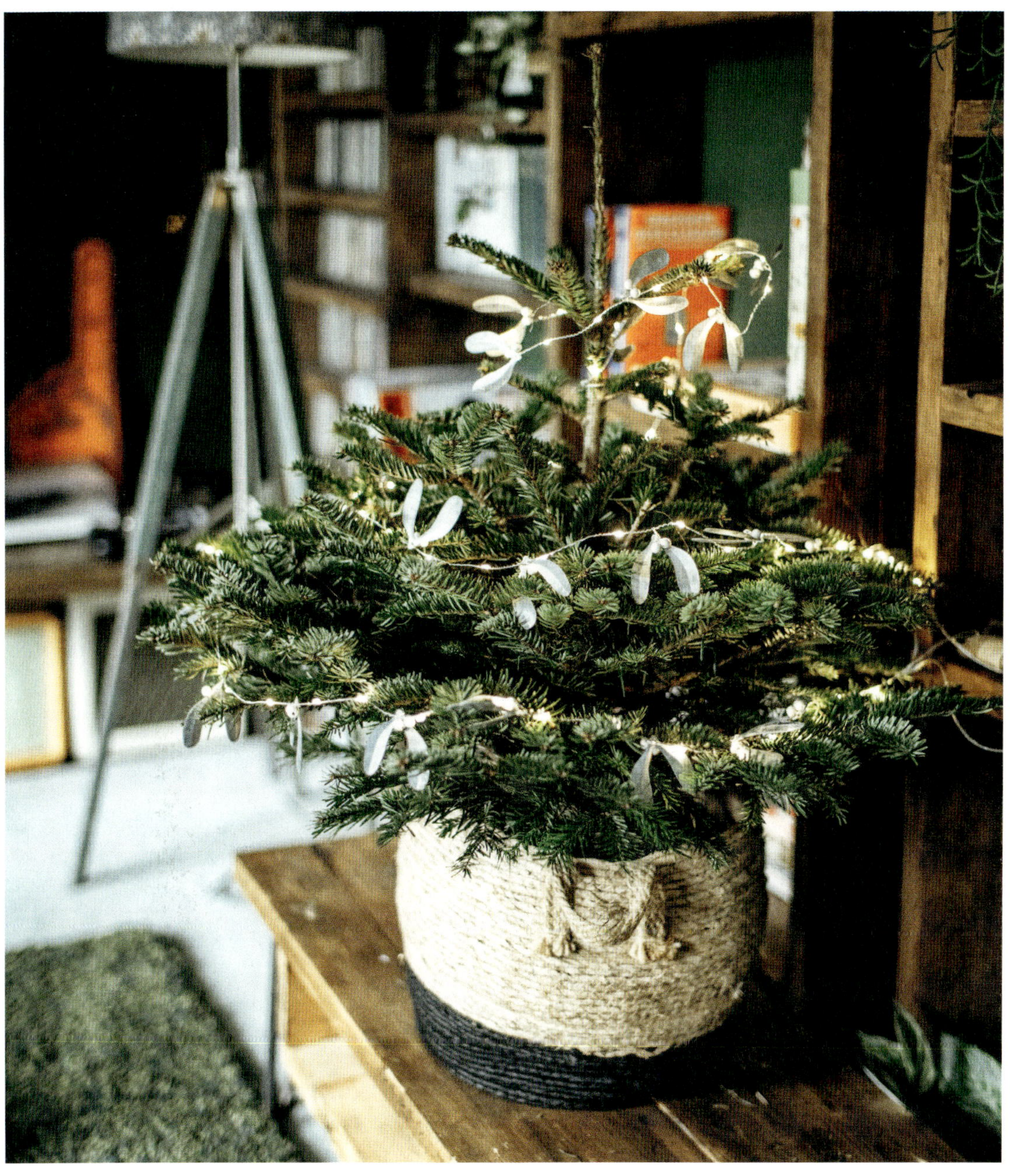

For small spaces, a miniature tree on a bench looks delightful in a basket, decorated with bows and mistletoe garlands, as well as dried oranges scented with cloves.

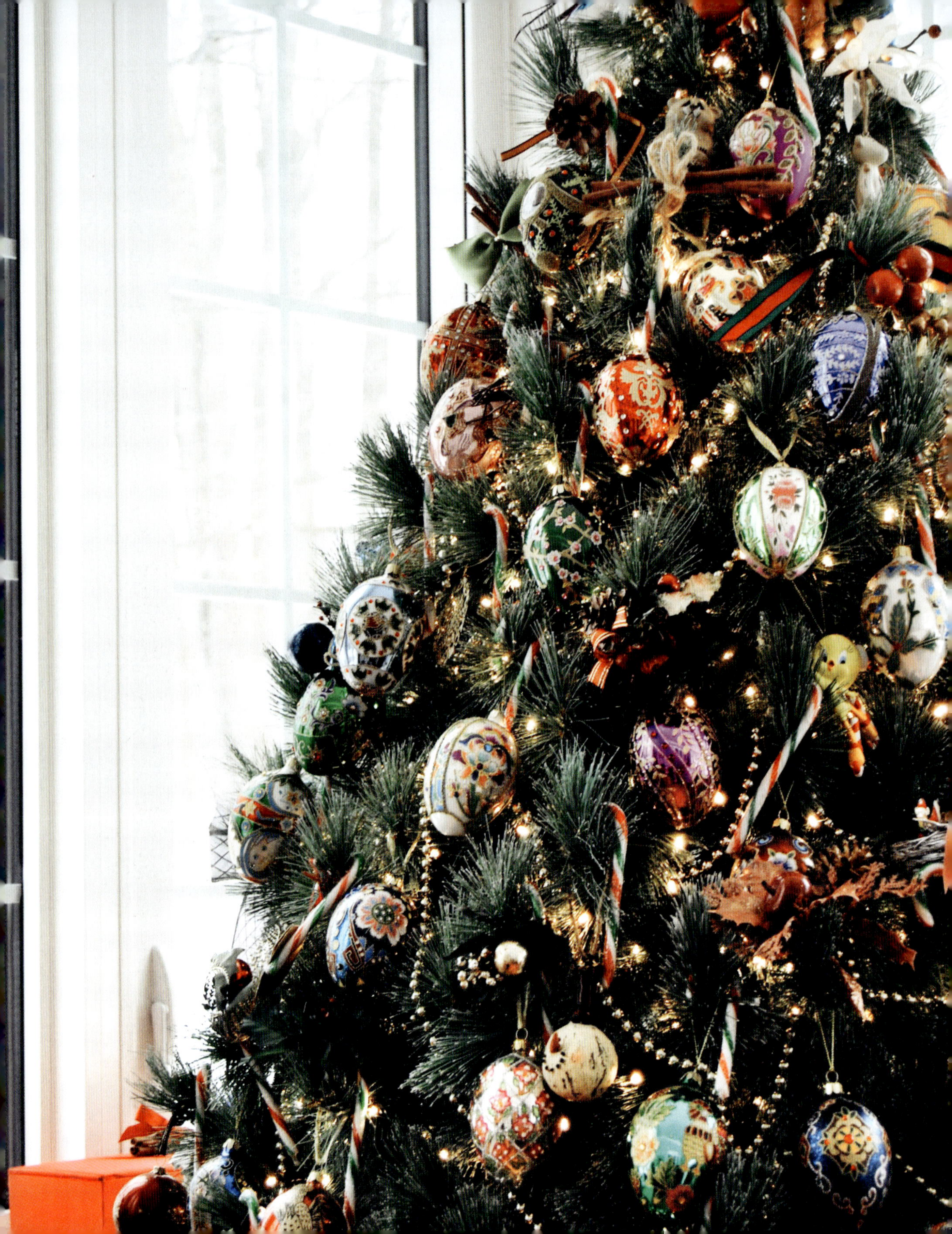

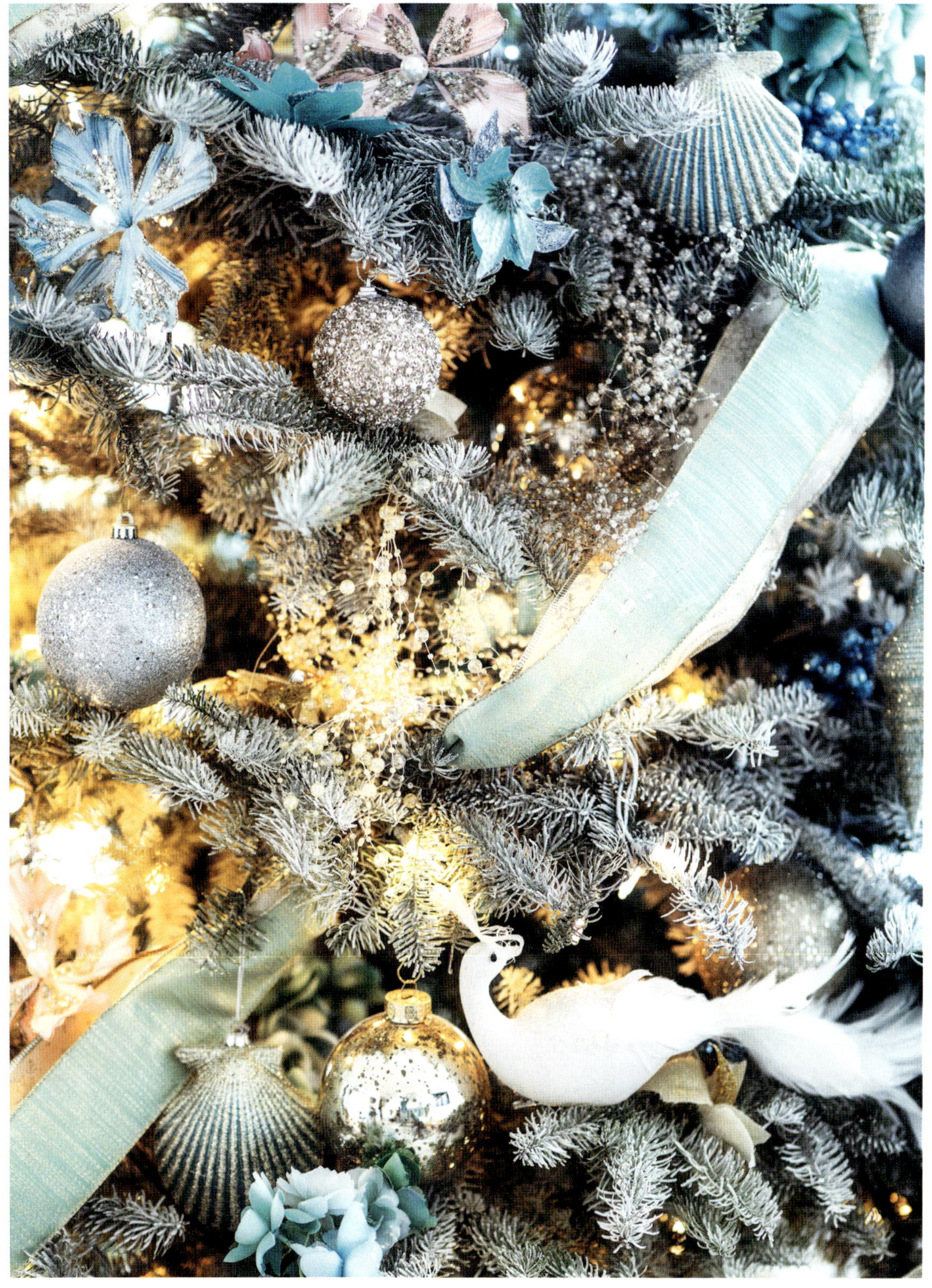

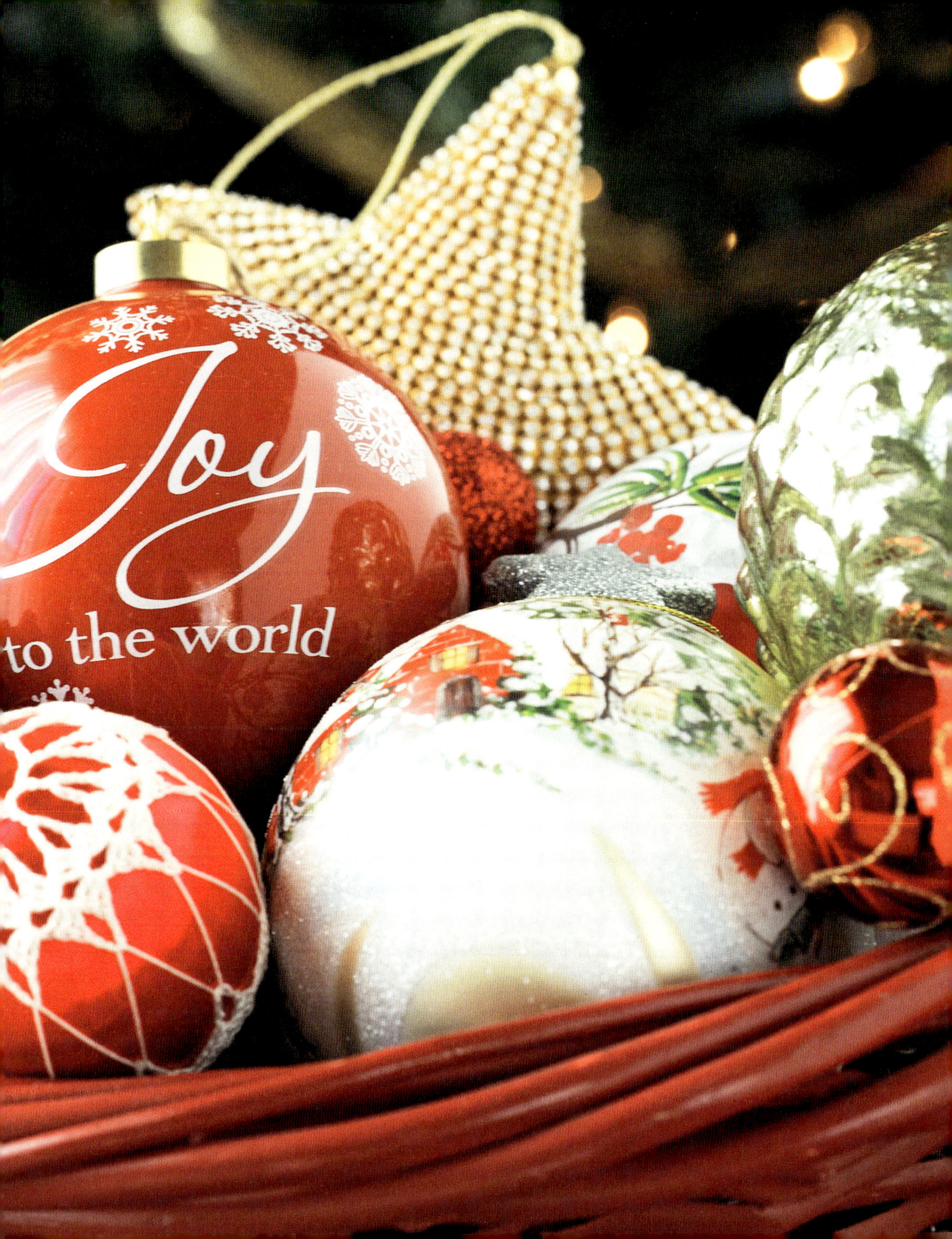
Joy
to the world

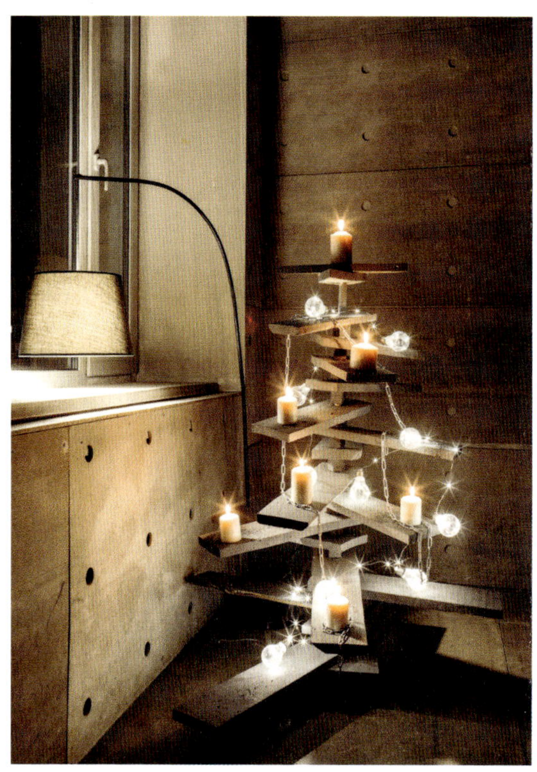

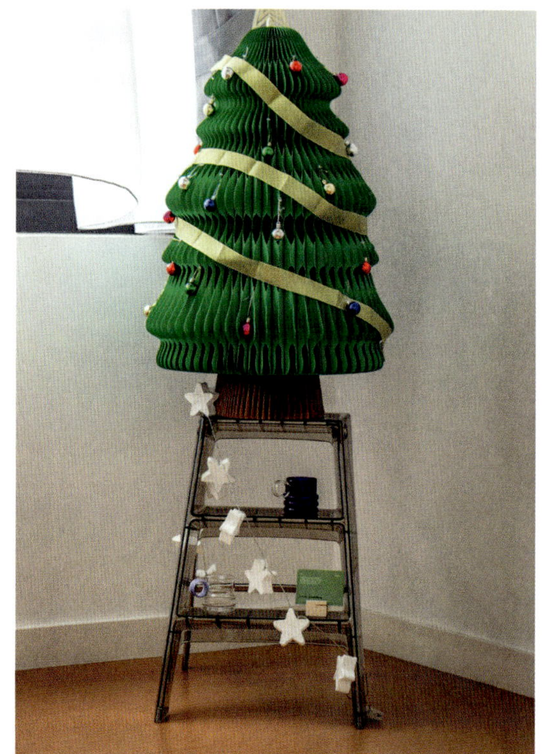

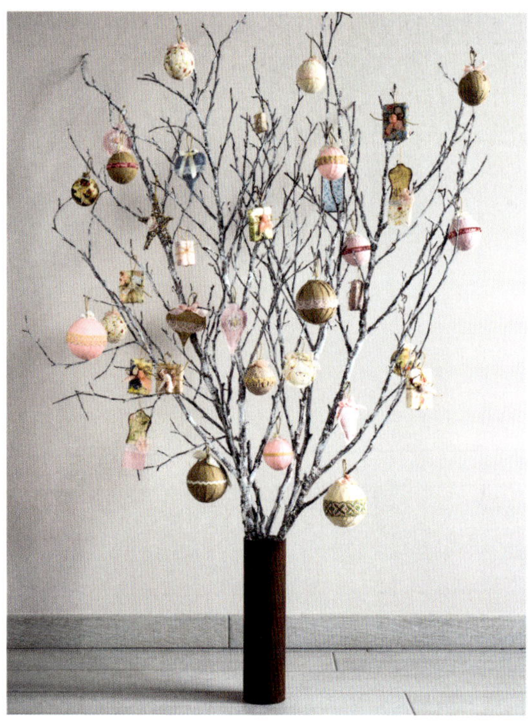

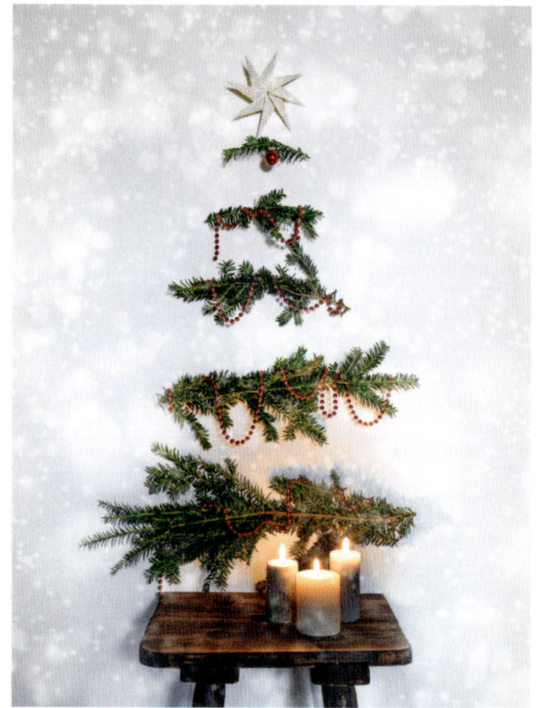

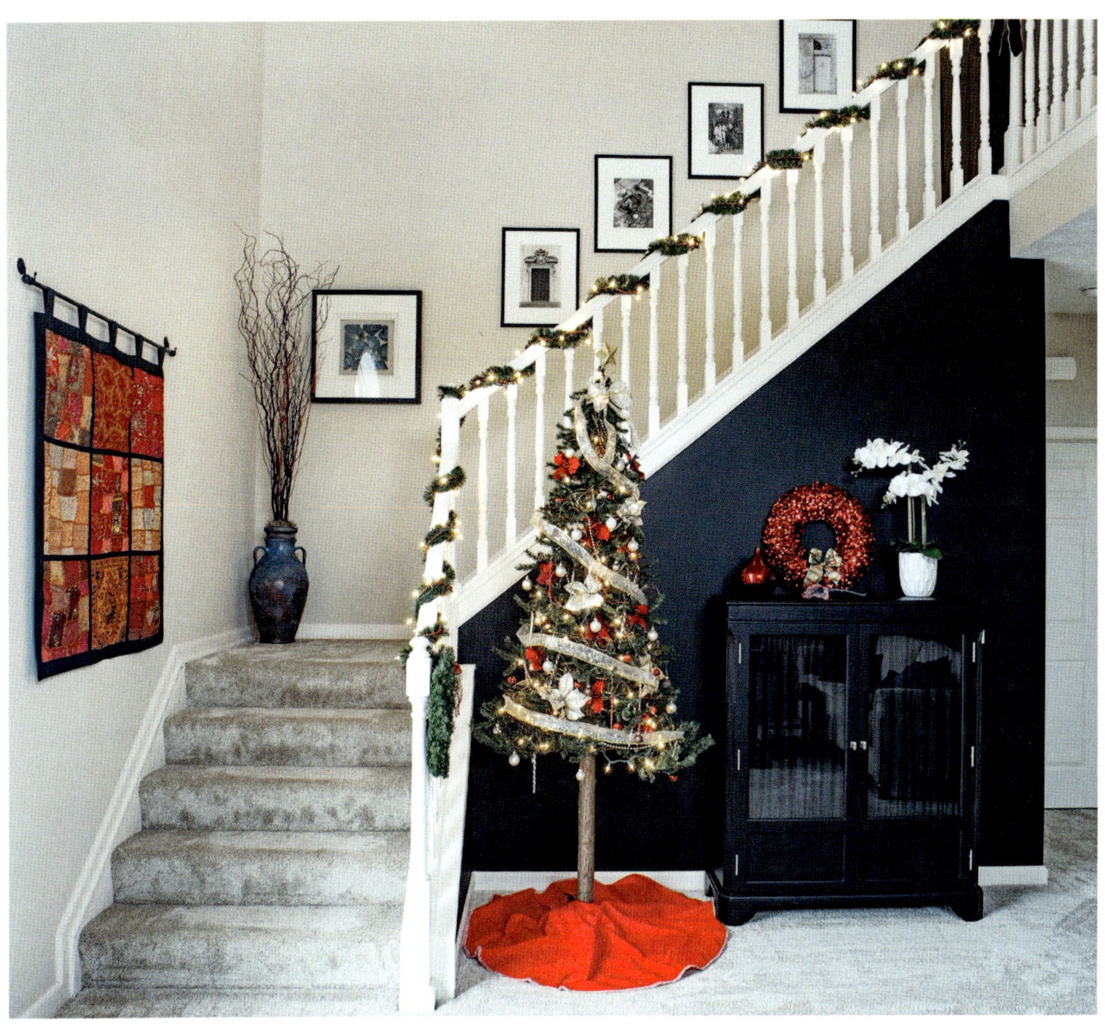

There is no reason to stick with a traditional tree. Minimalist versions made of wood or origami paper can be a modern, sustainable, and fun alternative.

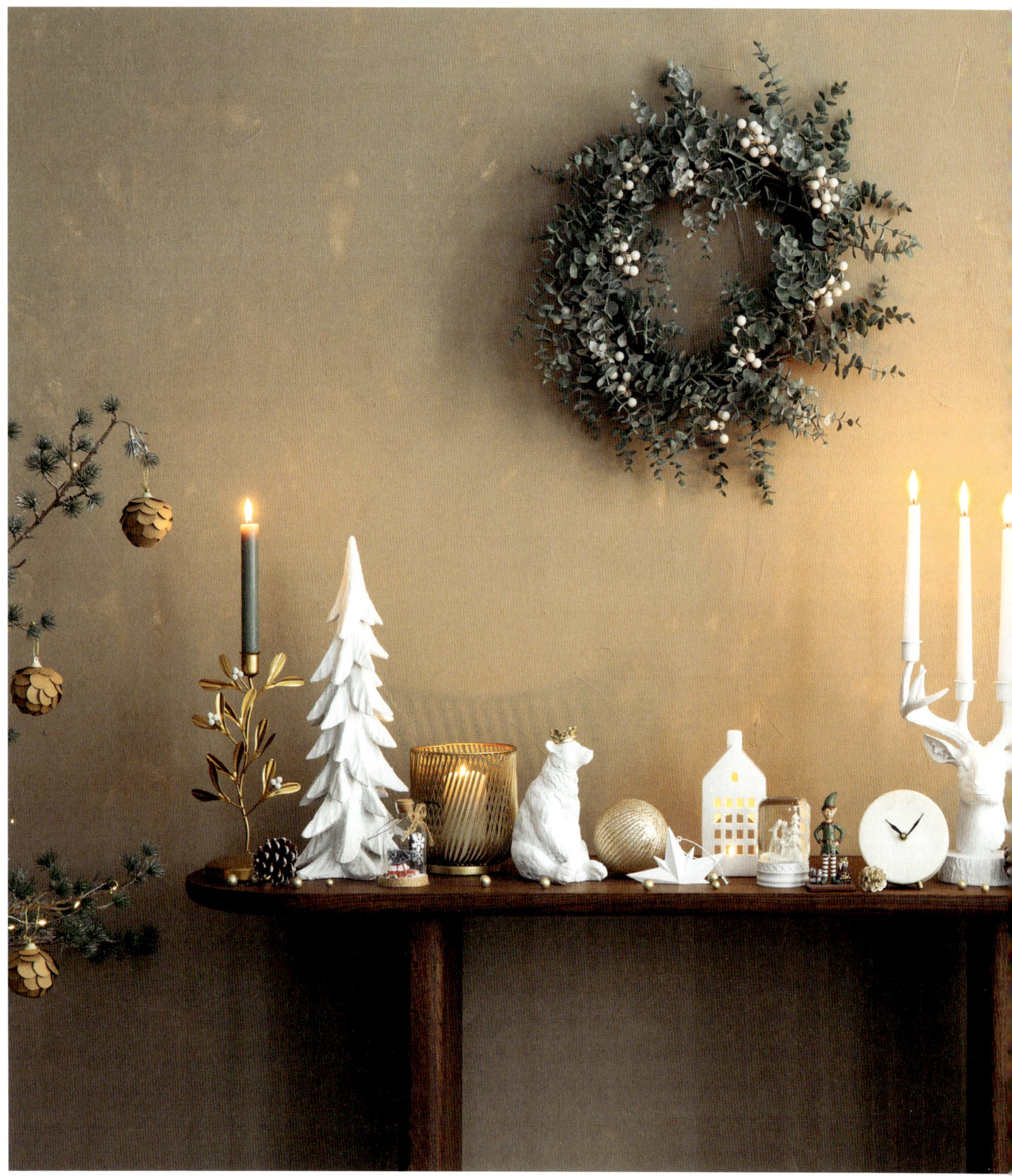

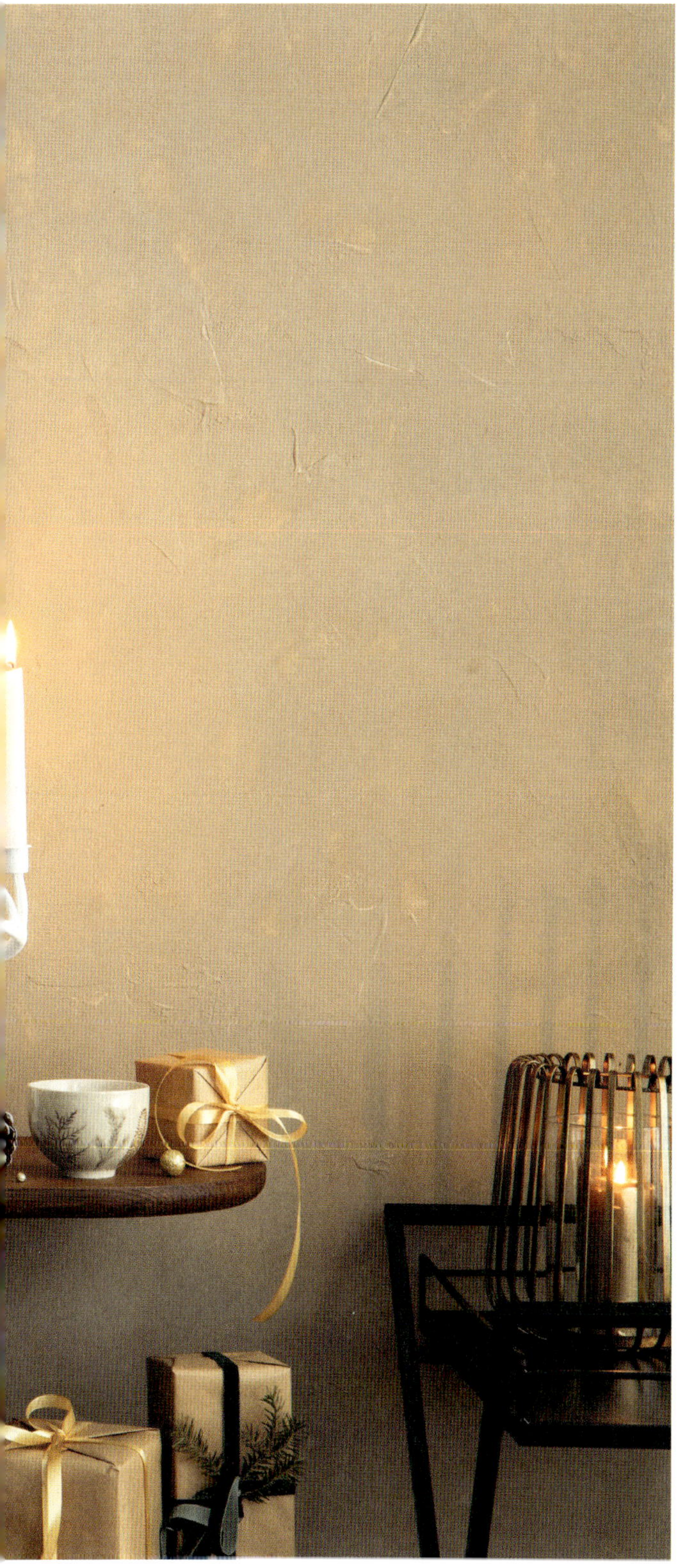

Setting a festive mood

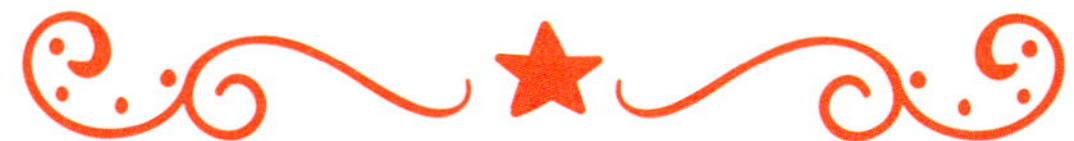

To make a space feel Christmassy and fun, extend the decorations beyond the living room with accents around the house. A console table is an opportunity to bring a sense of occasion to the hallway with candles and ornaments layered with different shapes and sizes—unified by the color scheme. A wreath hung on the wall makes for a wonderful triangular shape that draws the eye.

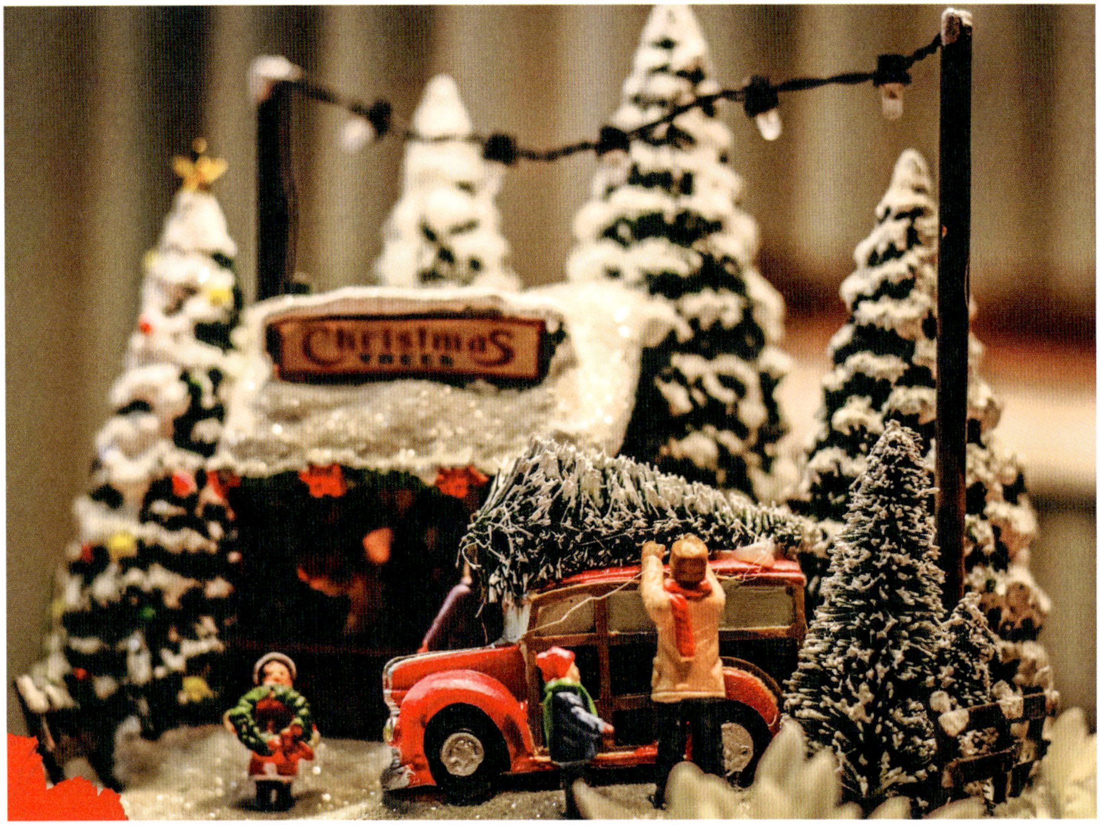

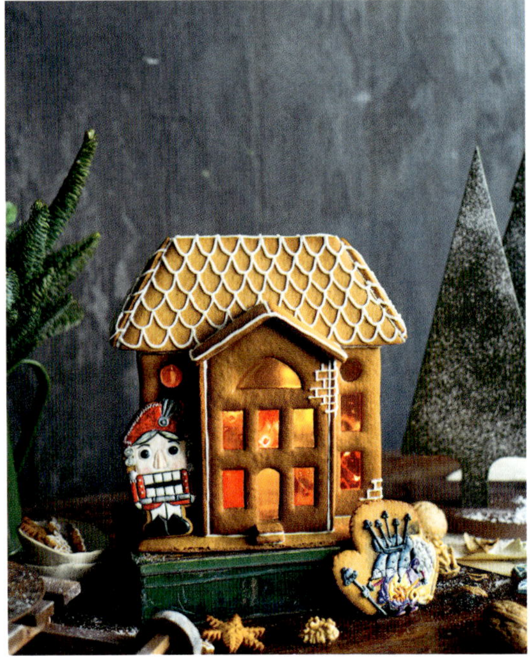

Christmas is about loved ones, so why not spend some time together? Create miniature Christmas scenes or dioramas and showcase them throughout the home.

Frosted gingerbread cookies, pastel macarons and meringues add a pretty, sweet touch that feels decadent.

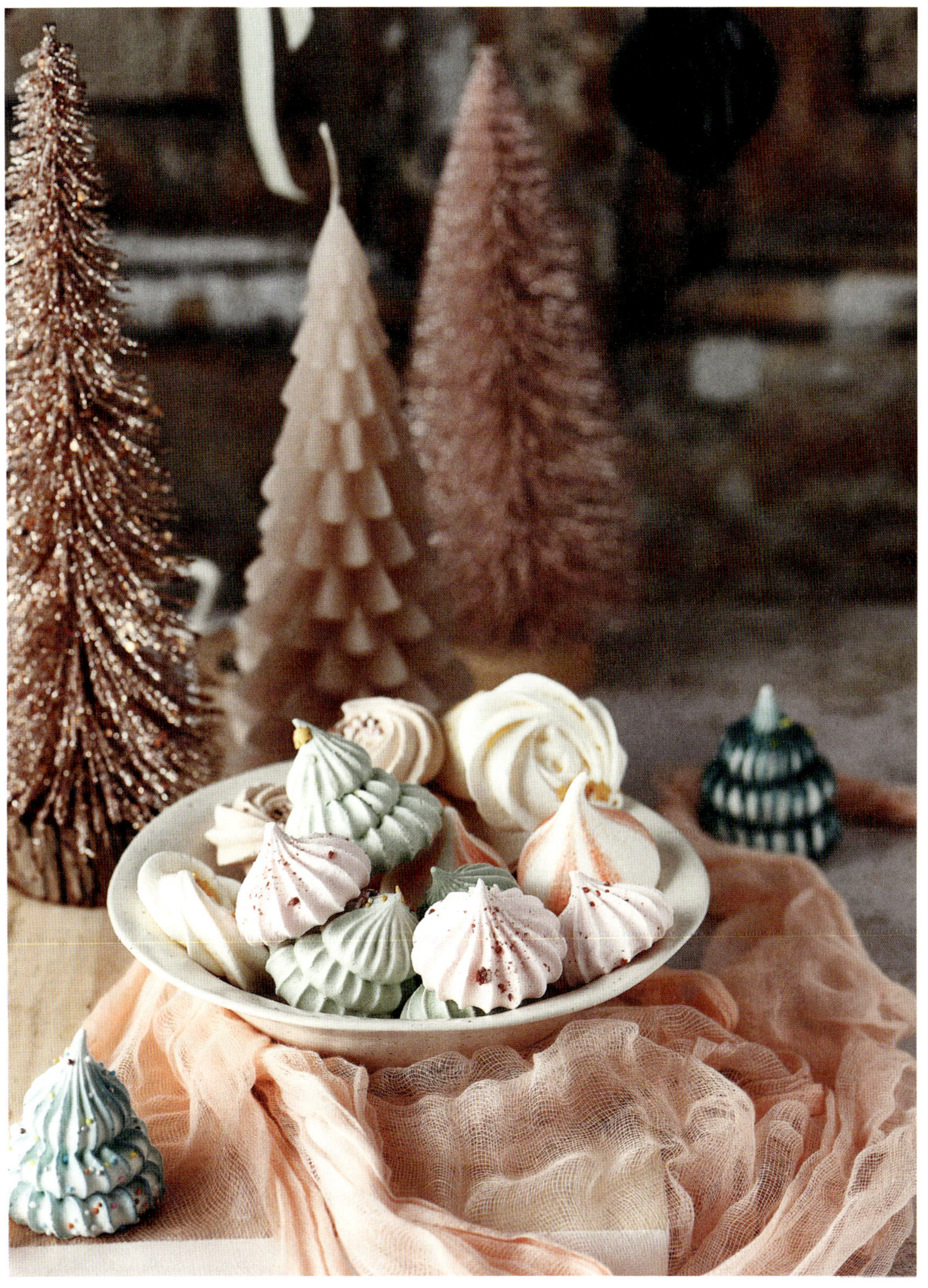

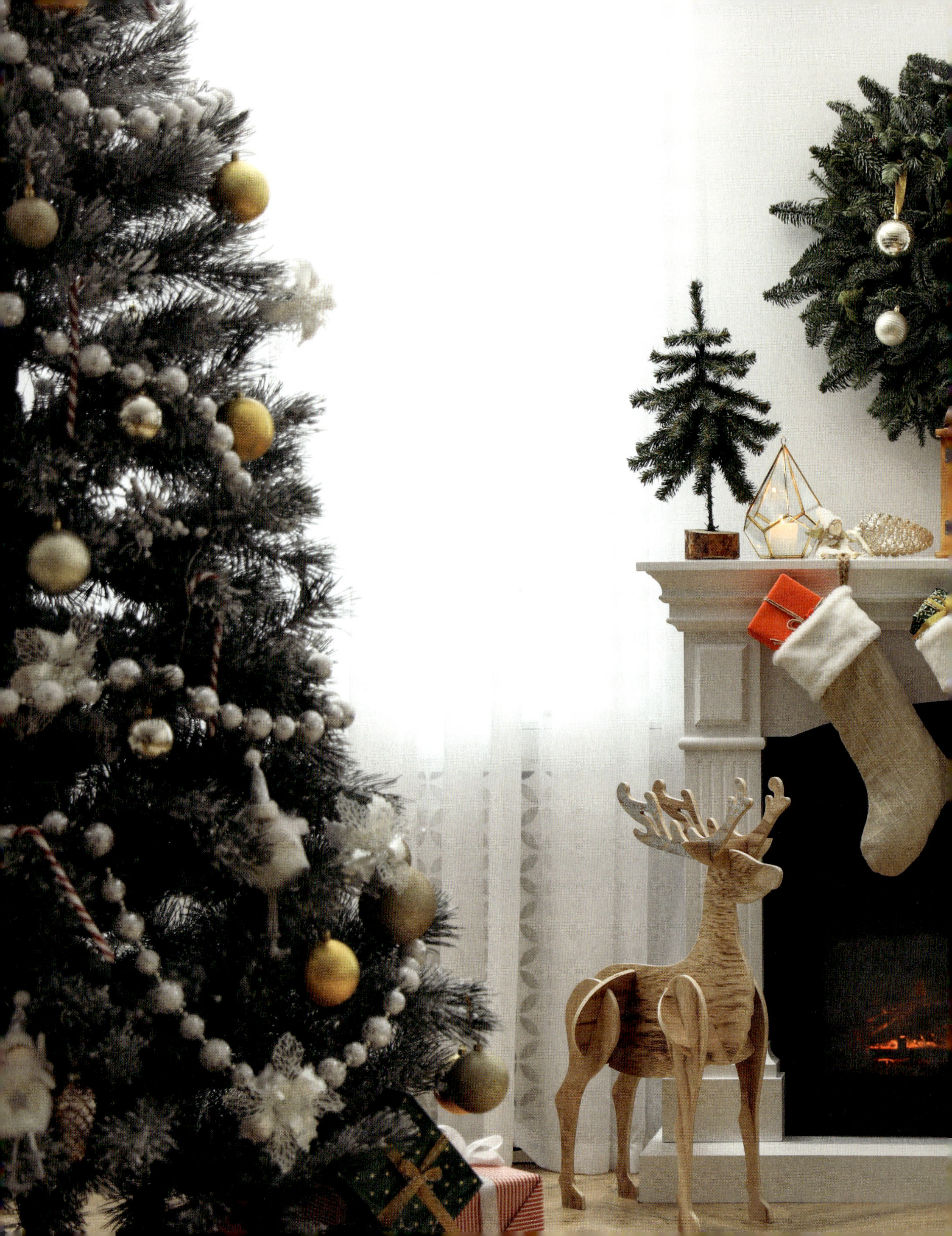

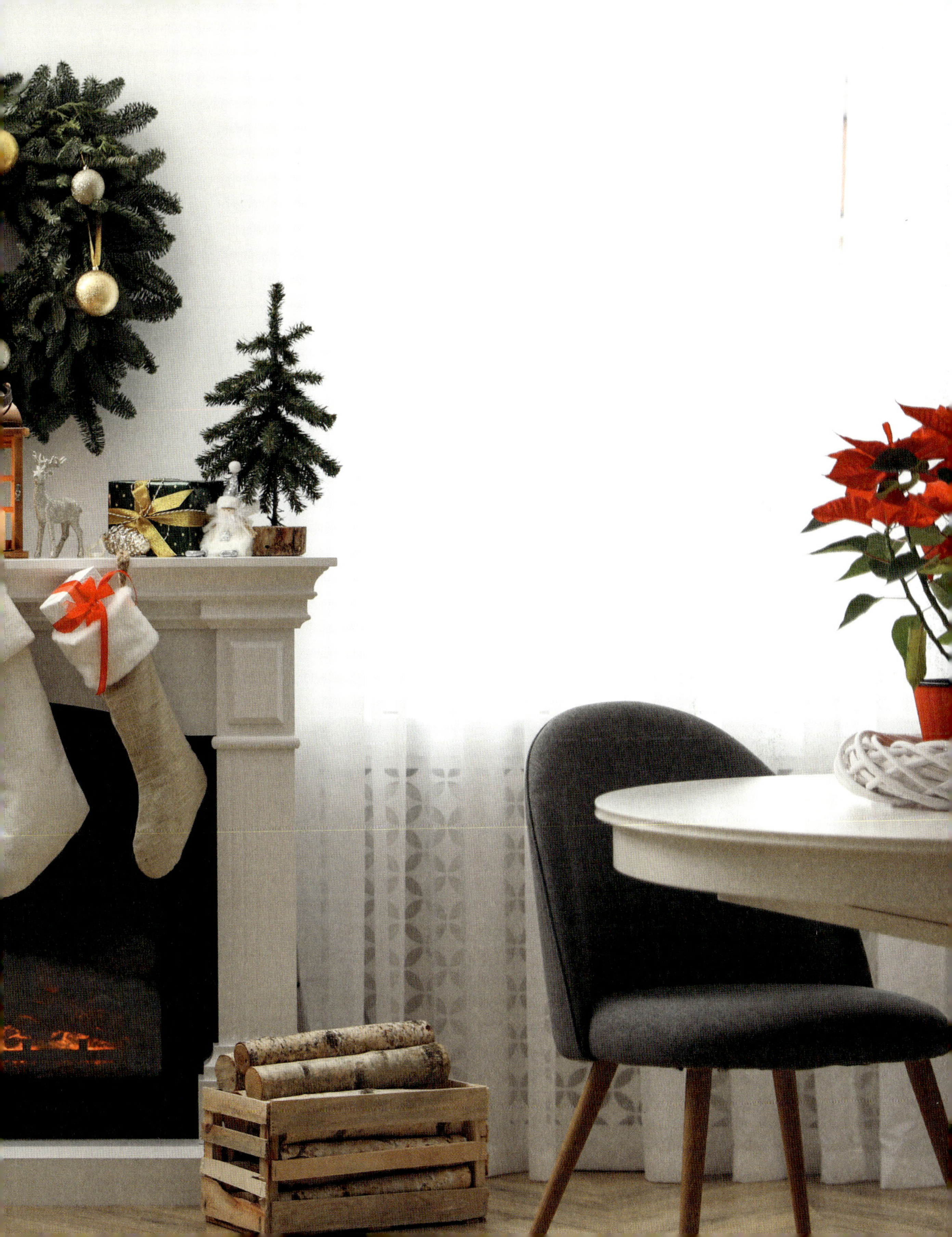

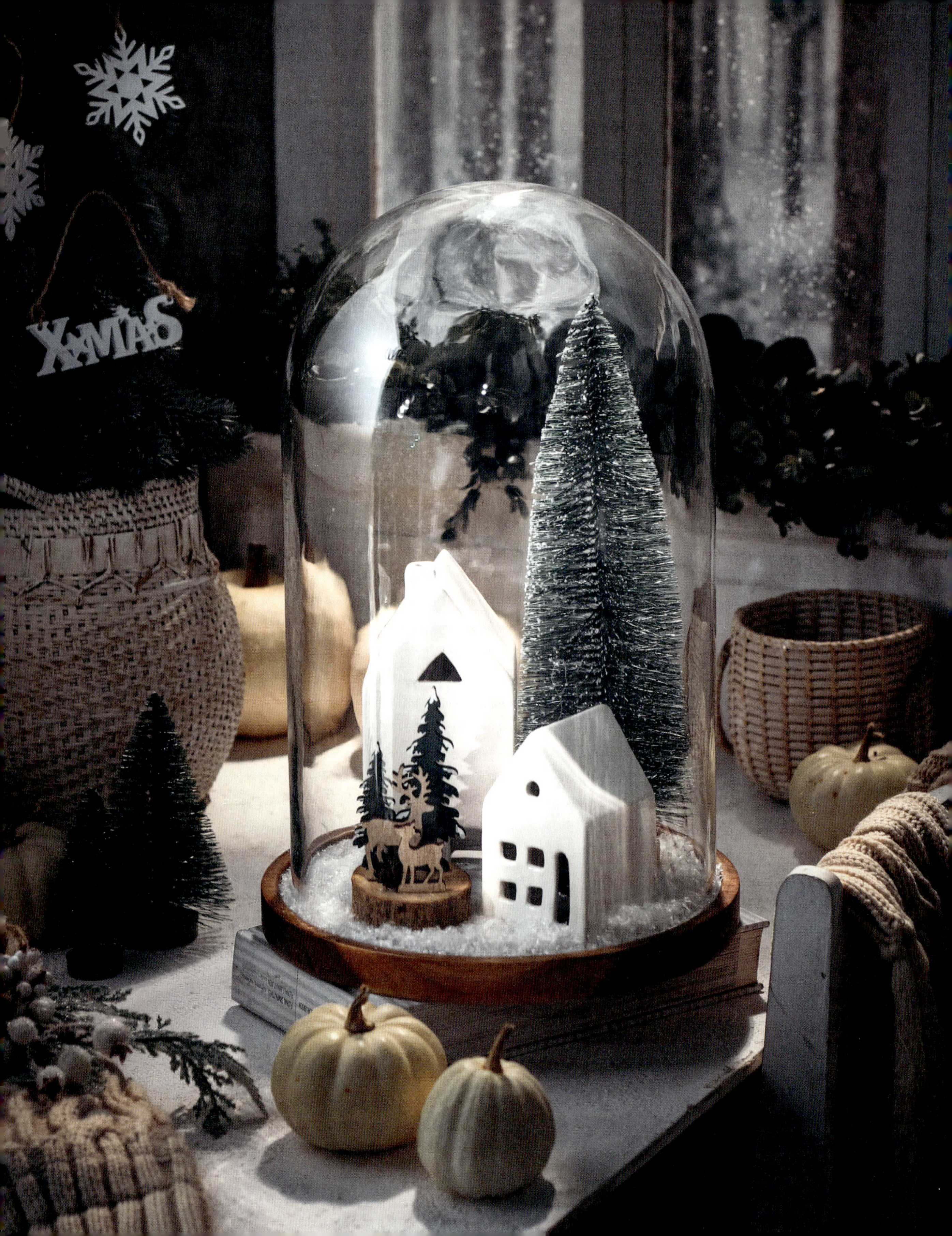
XMAS

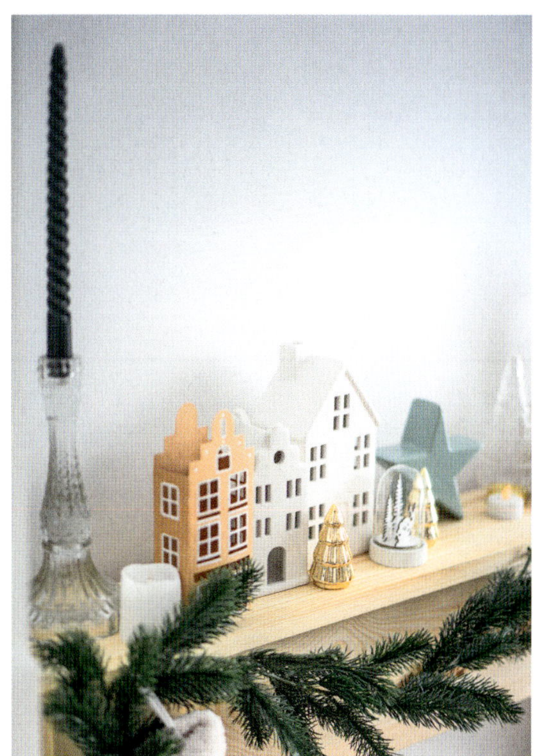

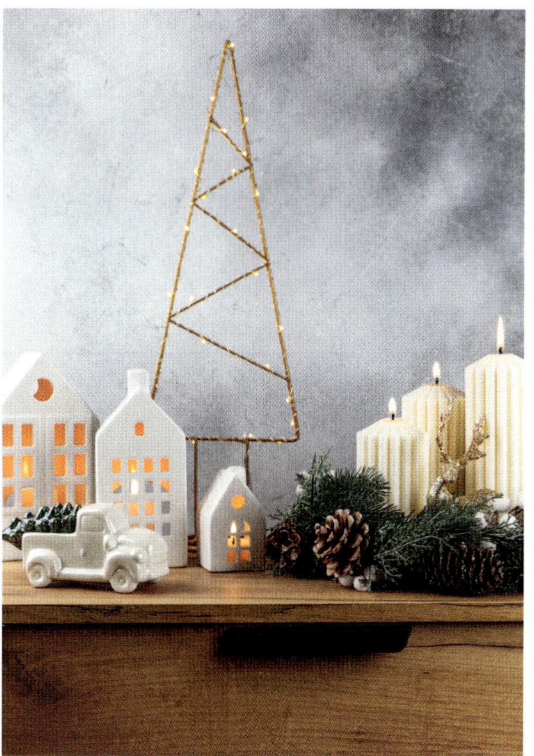

Miniature townscapes and little houses with a glowing candle at their windows always add a thrill and are lovely to bring out for Advent.

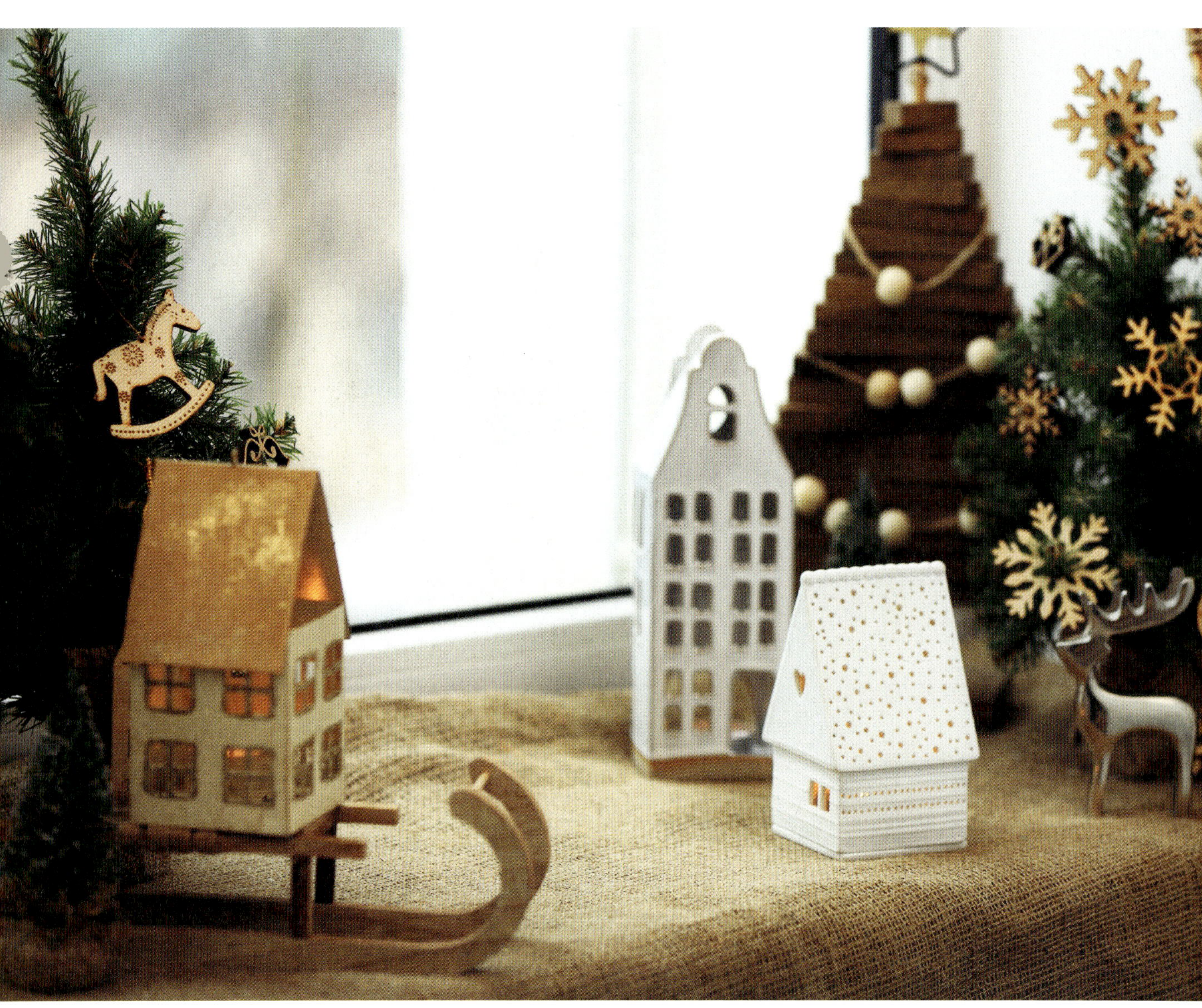

When you have an array of cute decorations, these always look better in groups. Cluster items together on a tray or windowsill, so they don't appear isolated.

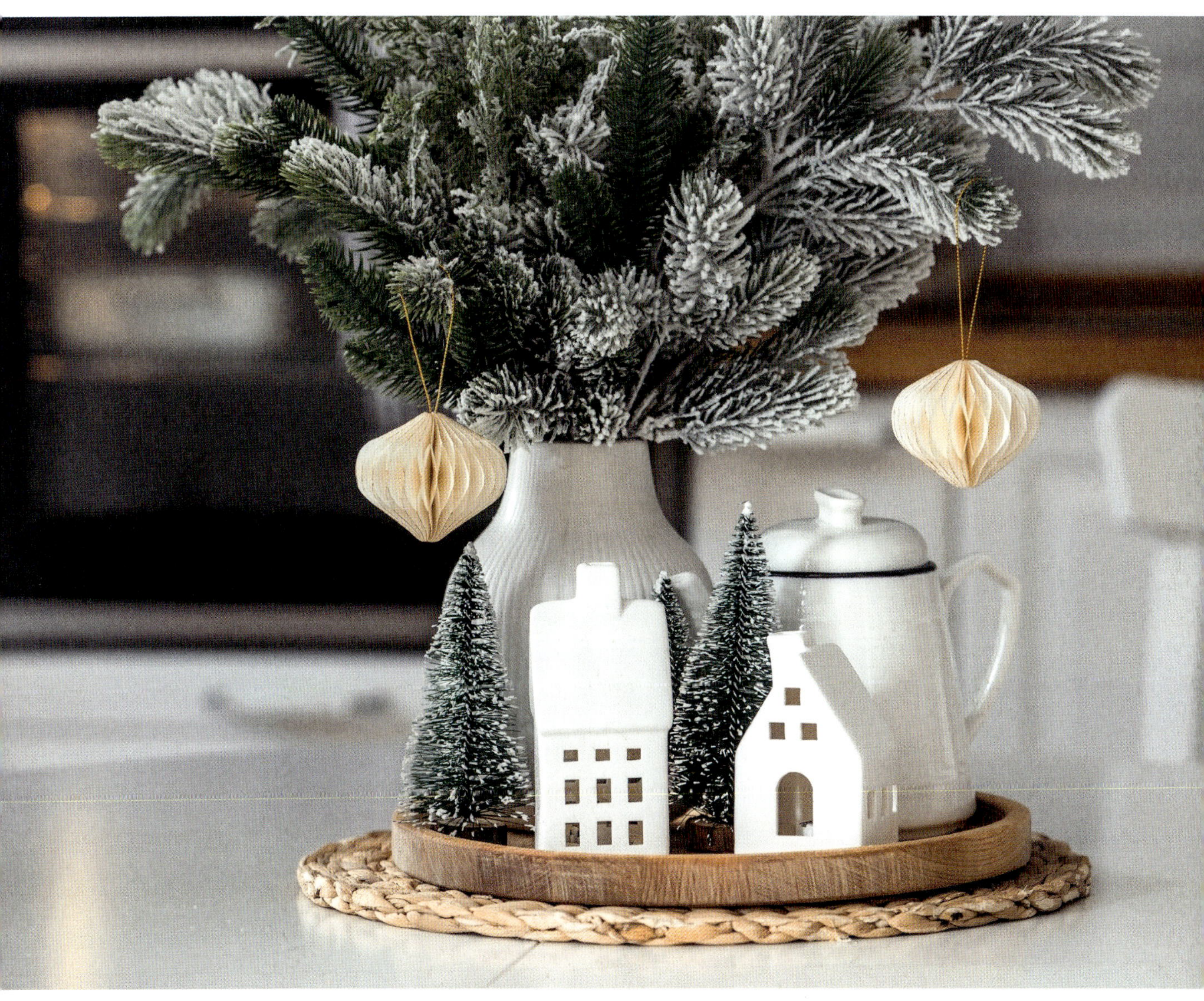

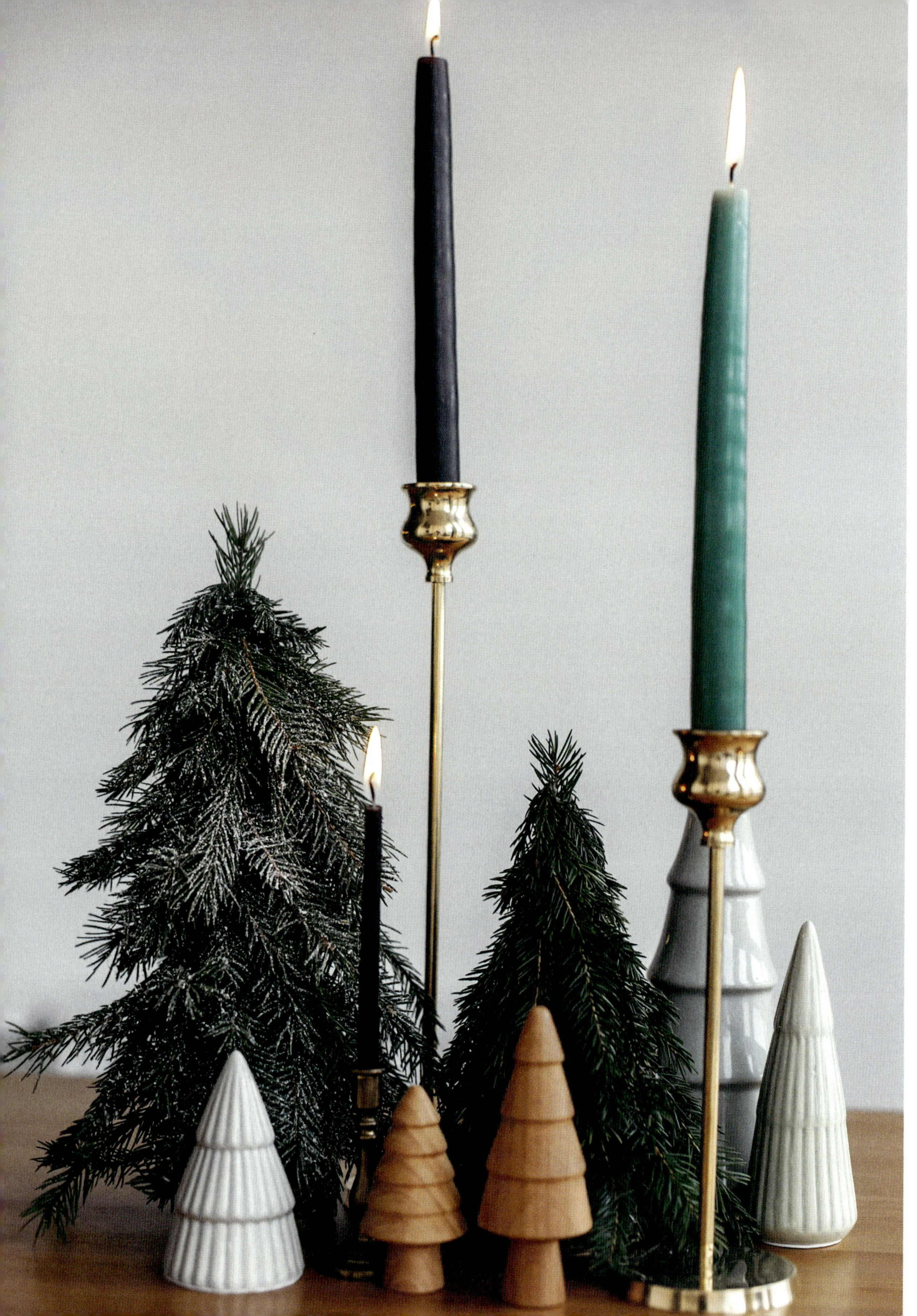

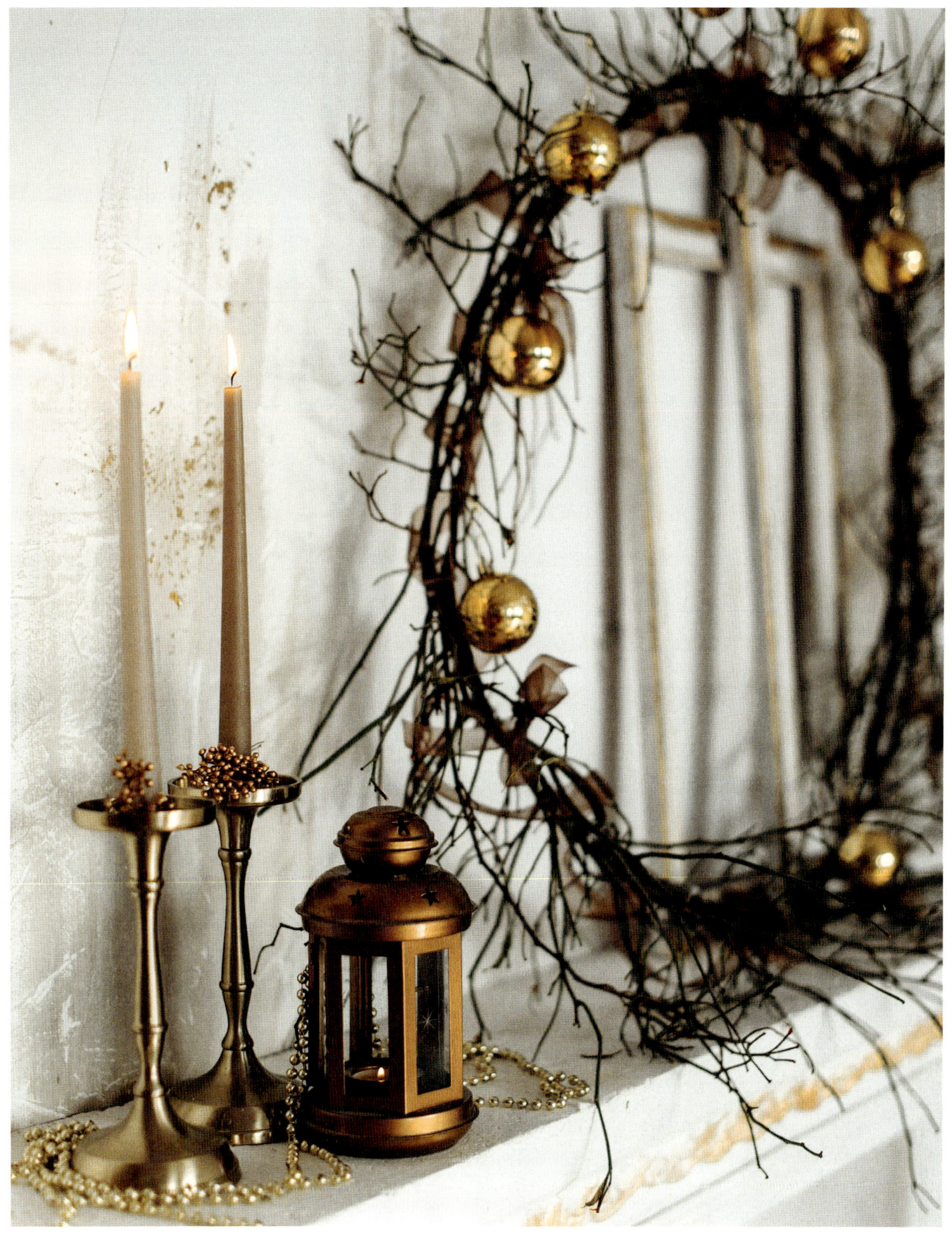

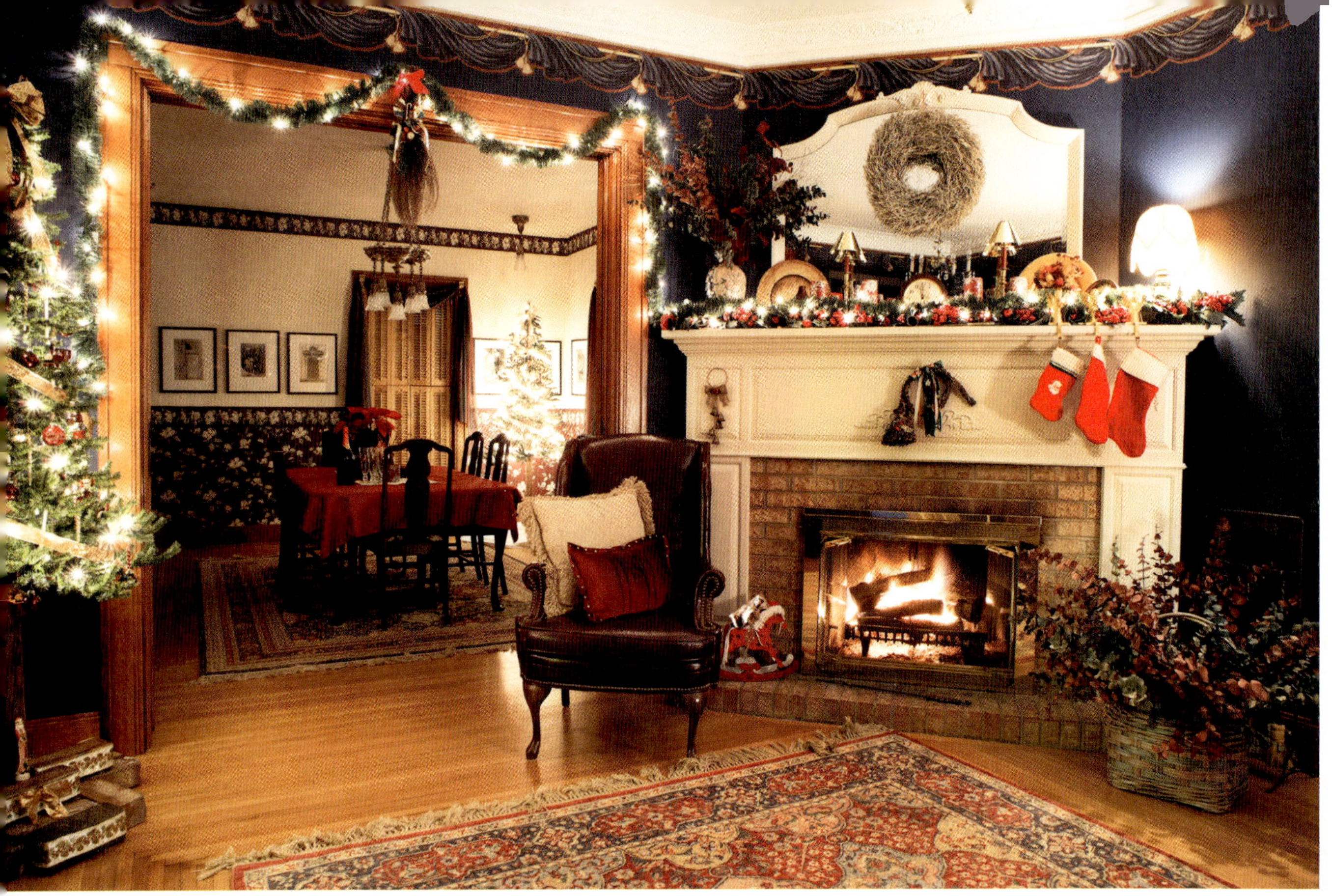

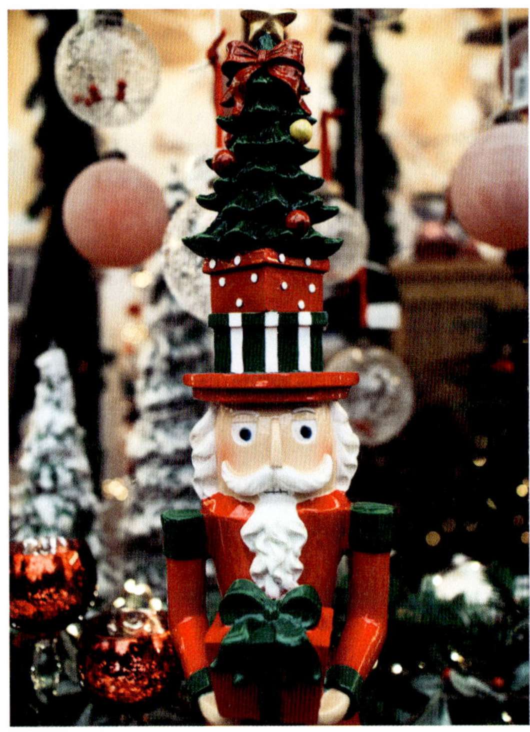

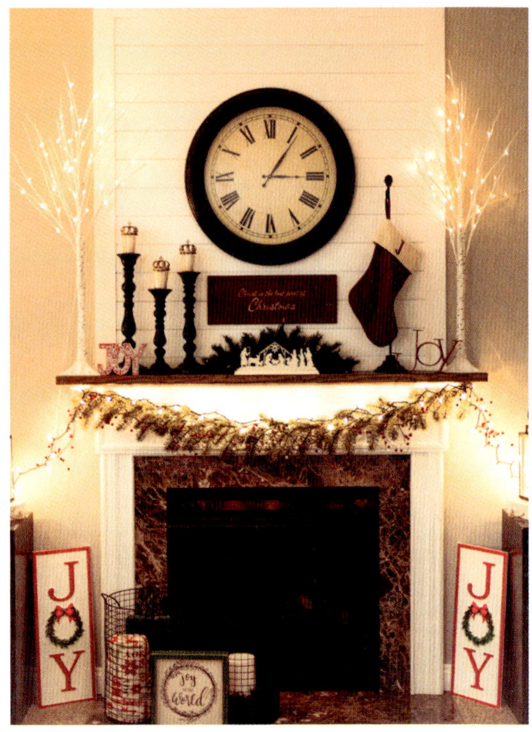

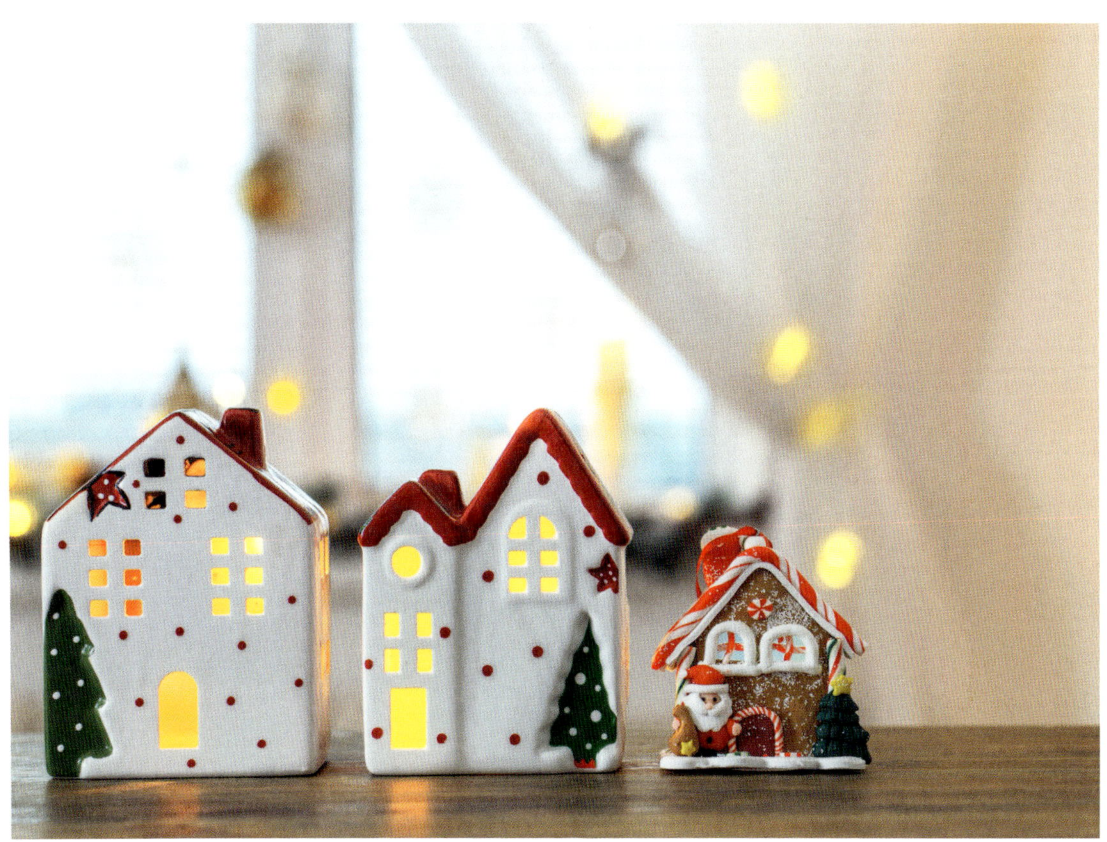

Even the most contemporary design lovers will agree that Christmas doesn't feel quite right without a nod to tradition. You can go all out with garlands and Nutcracker decorations, or opt for candy cane-inspired elements, which look charming on a table with their red and white stripes.

Sustainability

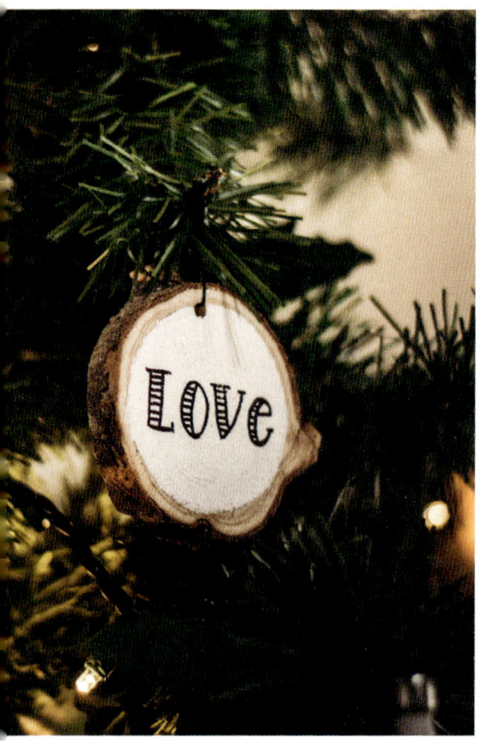

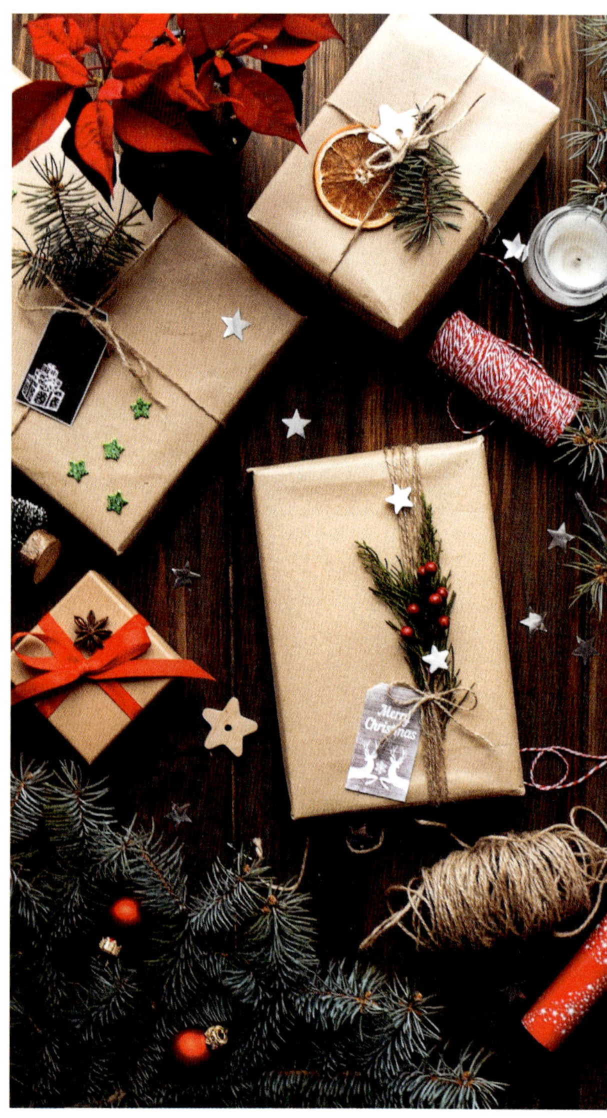

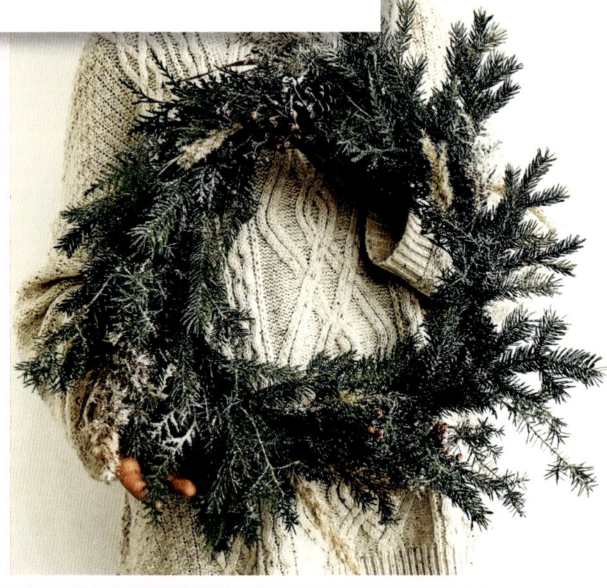

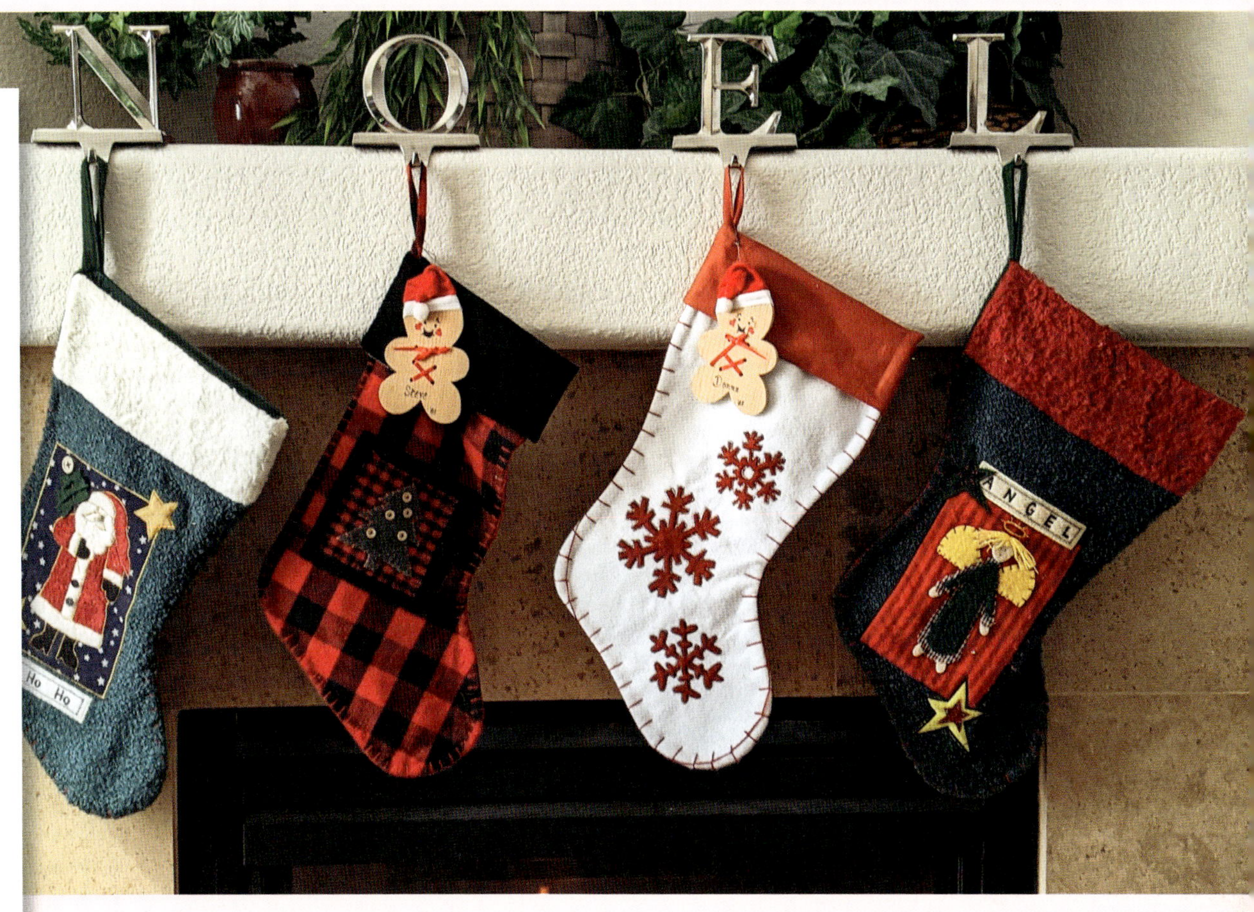

Sustainable Christmas

The season of goodwill is the perfect time to move towards a sustainable future. Gifting experiences and buying better but fewer gifts make a difference, as does the choice of materials, eating seasonally and avoiding surplus packaging and single-use items. Use LED lights on your Christmas tree, make decorations and buy a tree from a FSC-certified forest, taking care to dispose of your tree properly once the season is over.

Personalize presents with a sprig of fern, held in place by natural string. Stylish and easy to make, a wreath is easy to pull together using cuttings from the garden. Use ivy and evergreens as a base, securing with twine. Work in more foliage—large headed blooms, bright berries—and finish with a bow. Single-use Christmas crackers are on the eco-naughty list, so opt for sustainable alternatives that are made from fabric offcuts that can be reused every year. You can add your own gifts.

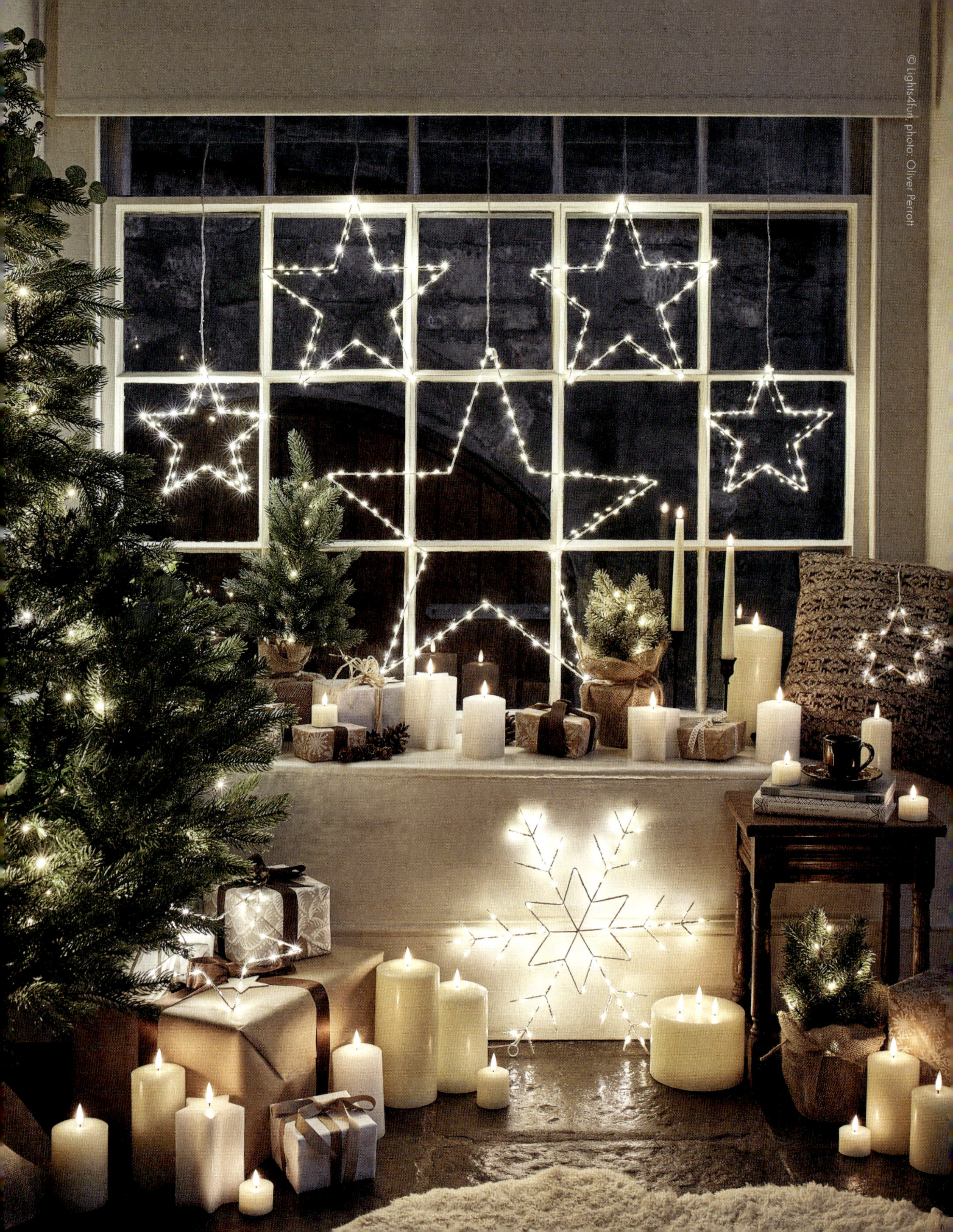

Bright and beautiful

There is something wonderfully enticing about twinkling lights and flickering flames. They catch the eye, create ambience, and bring a sense of contentment. From string lights, Christmas stars, and candles to LED deco objects, lighting can add the perfect festive atmosphere for your home.

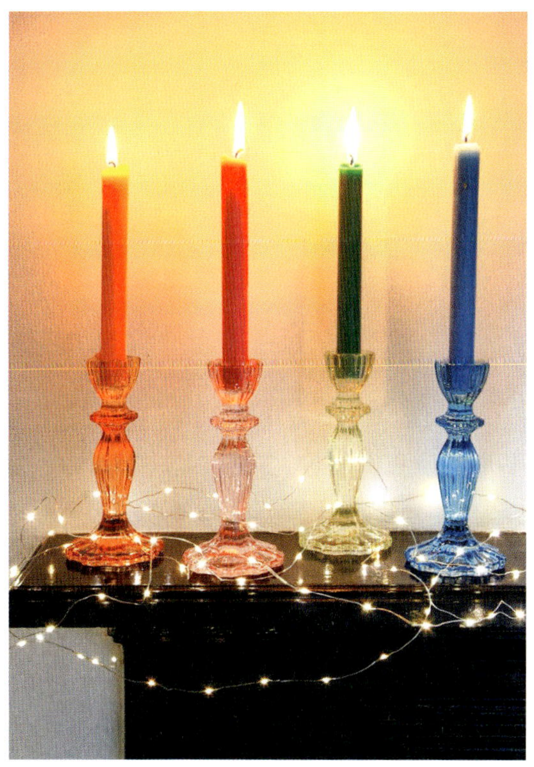

Candle holders from *Annabel James*

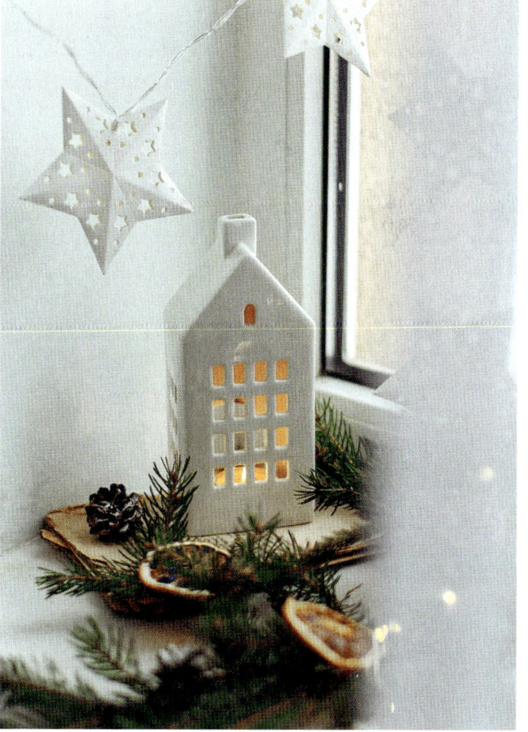

Christmas Window Decoration with Illuminating Stars by *Lights4fun*

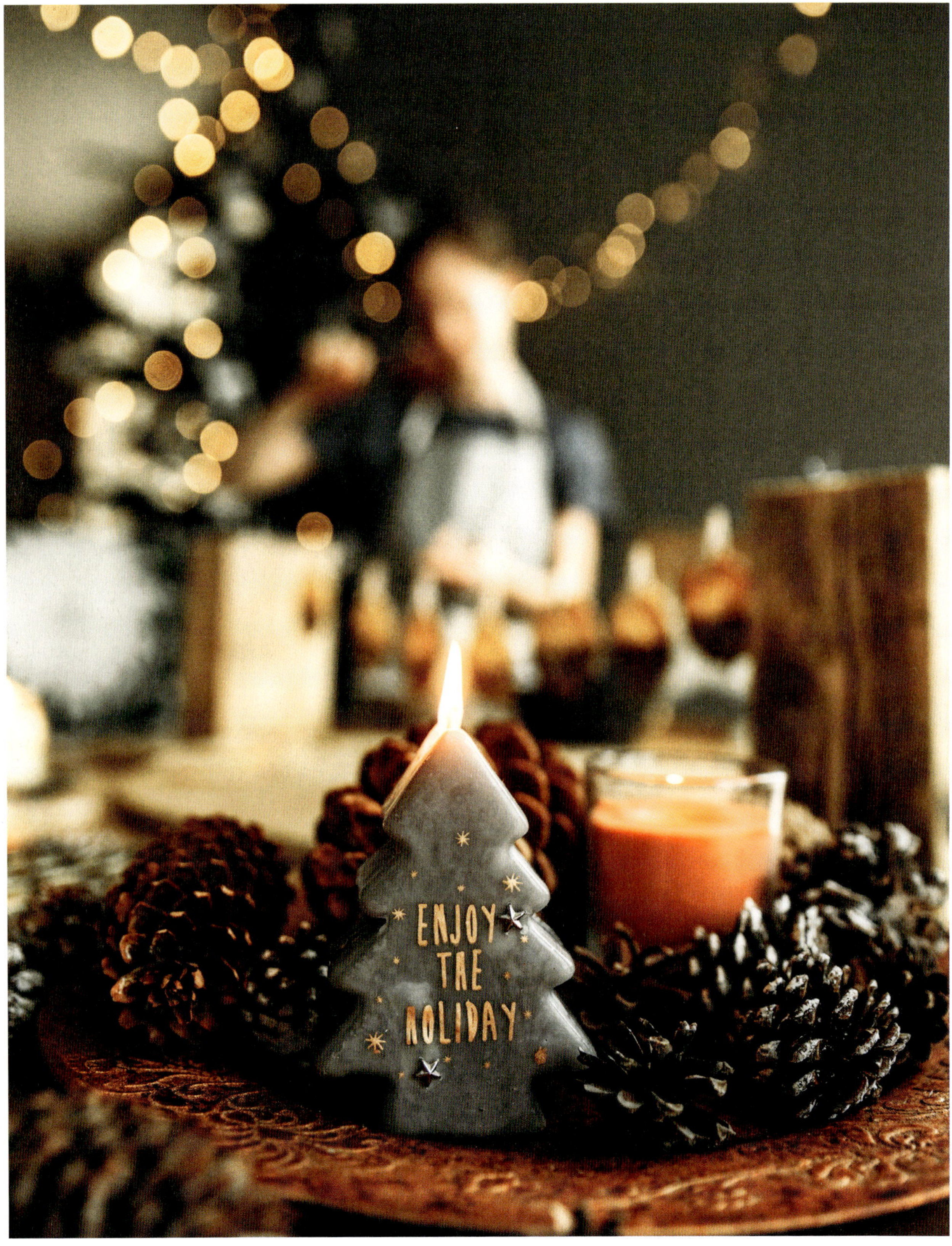
ENJOY
THE
HOLIDAY

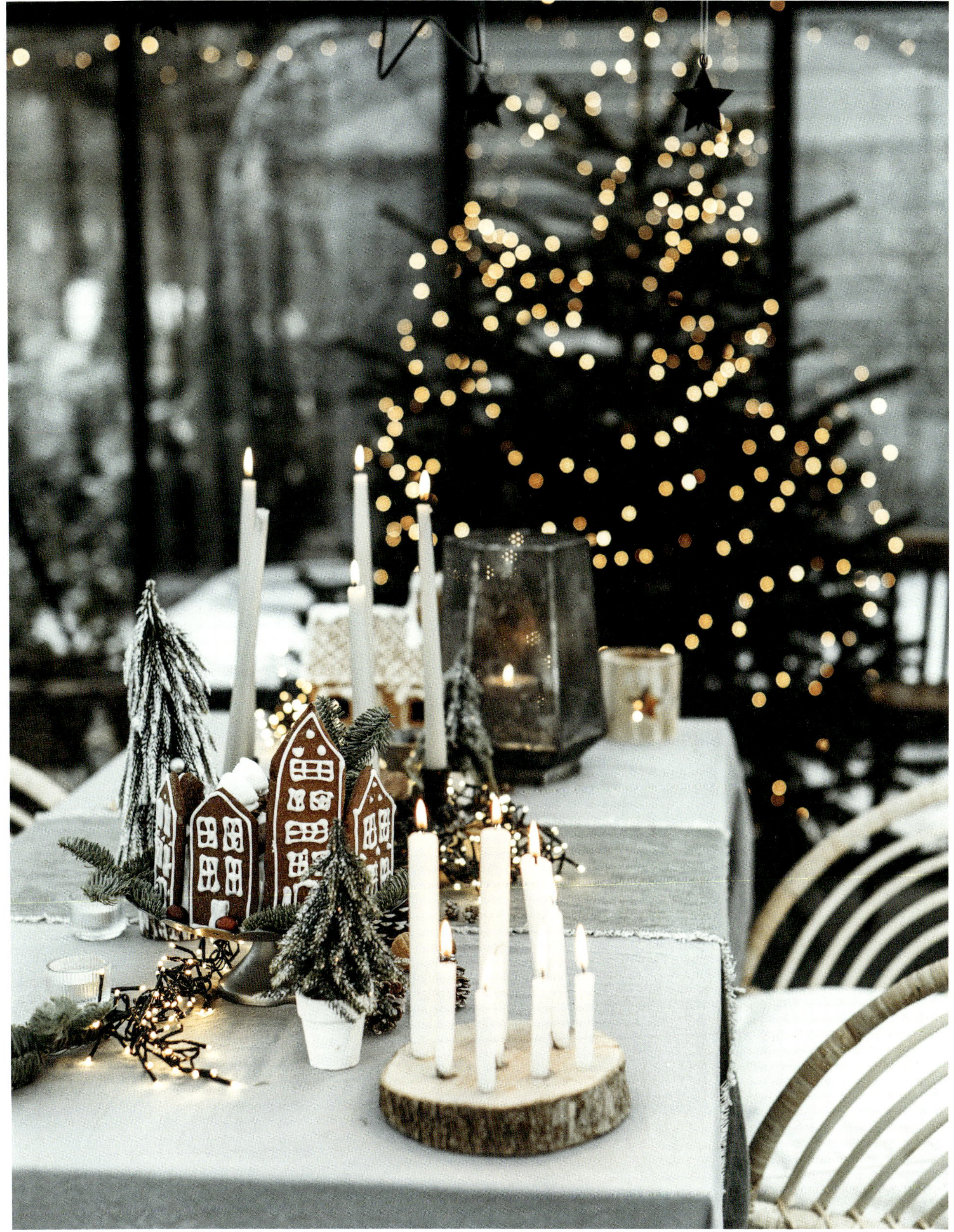

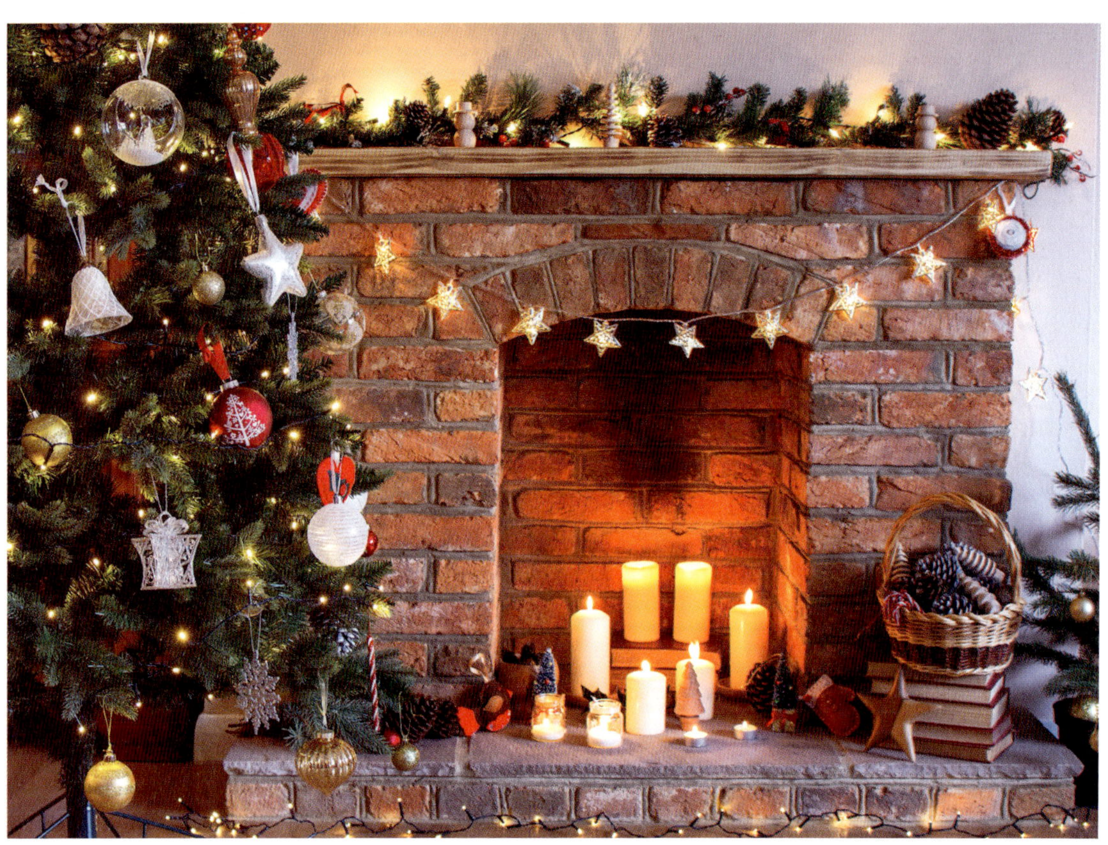

Creating a festive feel in the home starts with lighting. Choose bulbs with a warm glow that aren't too bright for an intimate effect. Festoon or string lighting is a great way to get a seasonal effect that can stay up all year round.

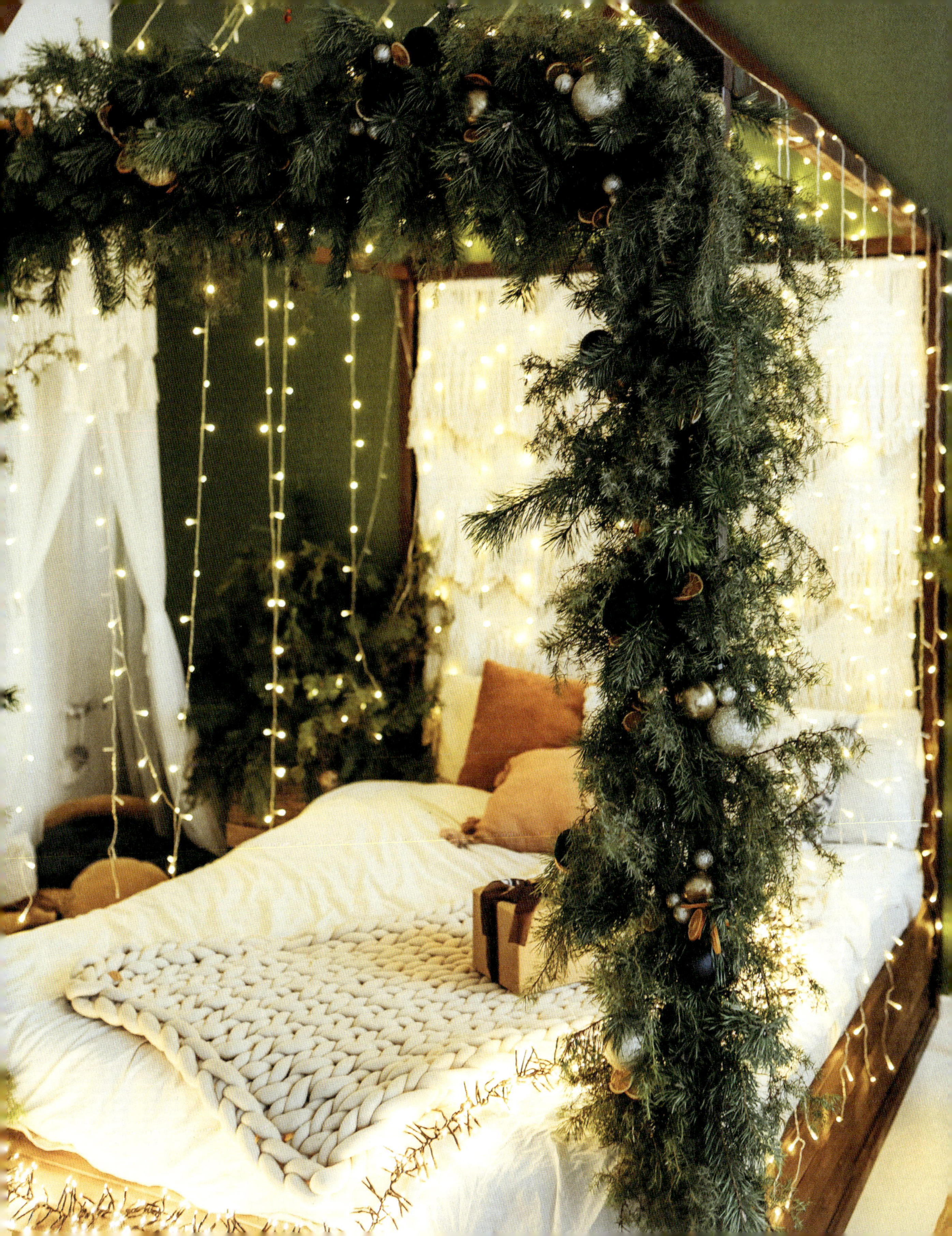

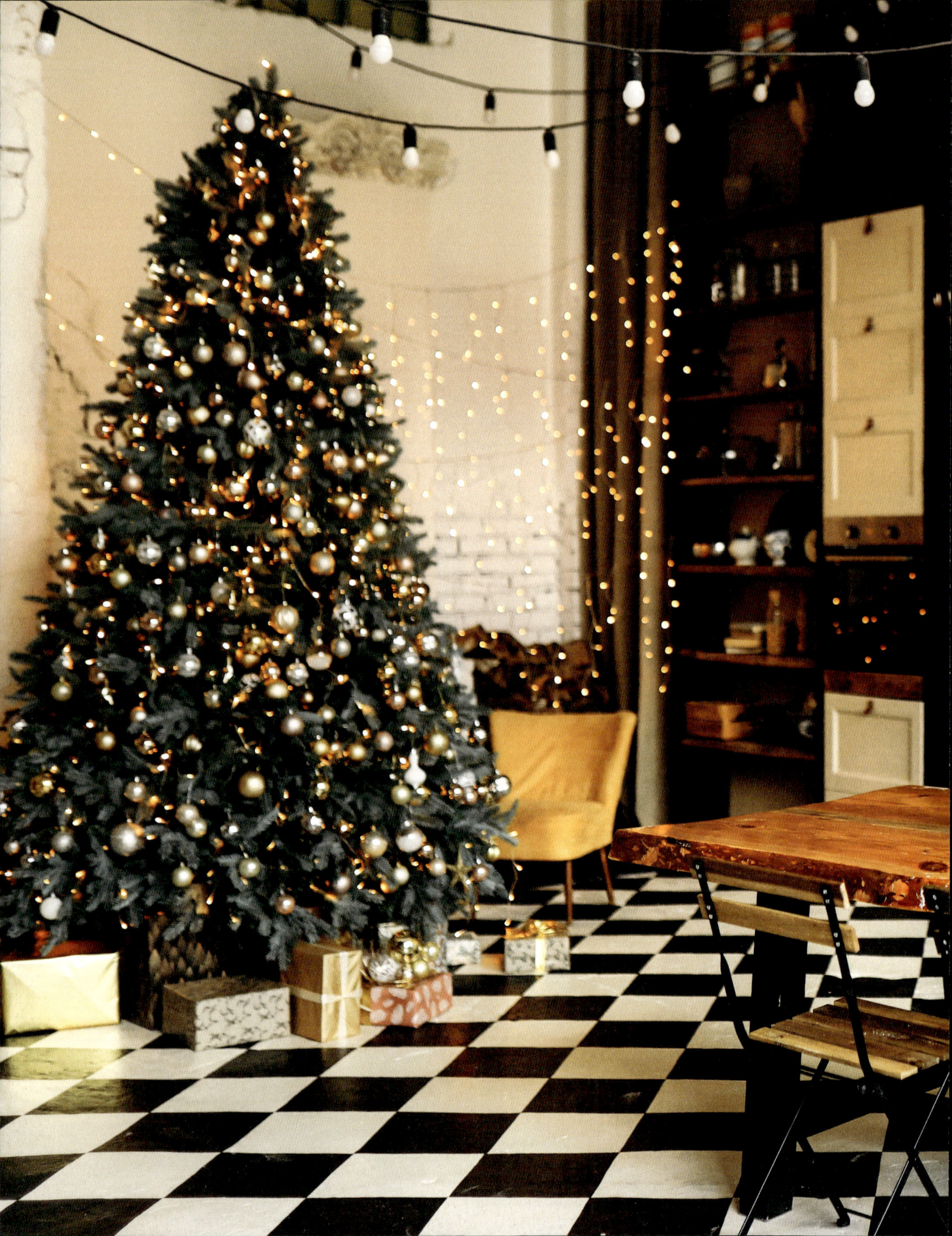

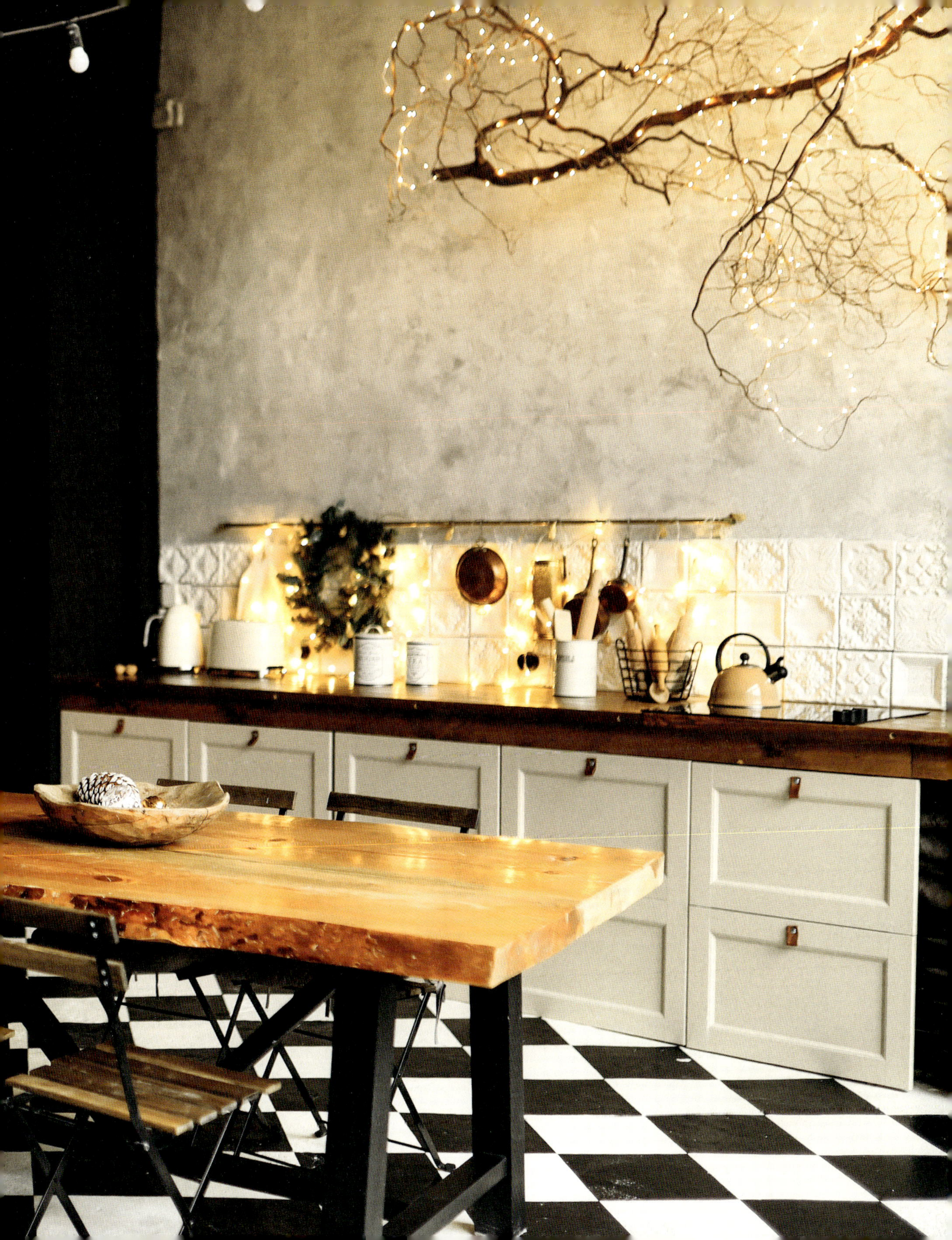

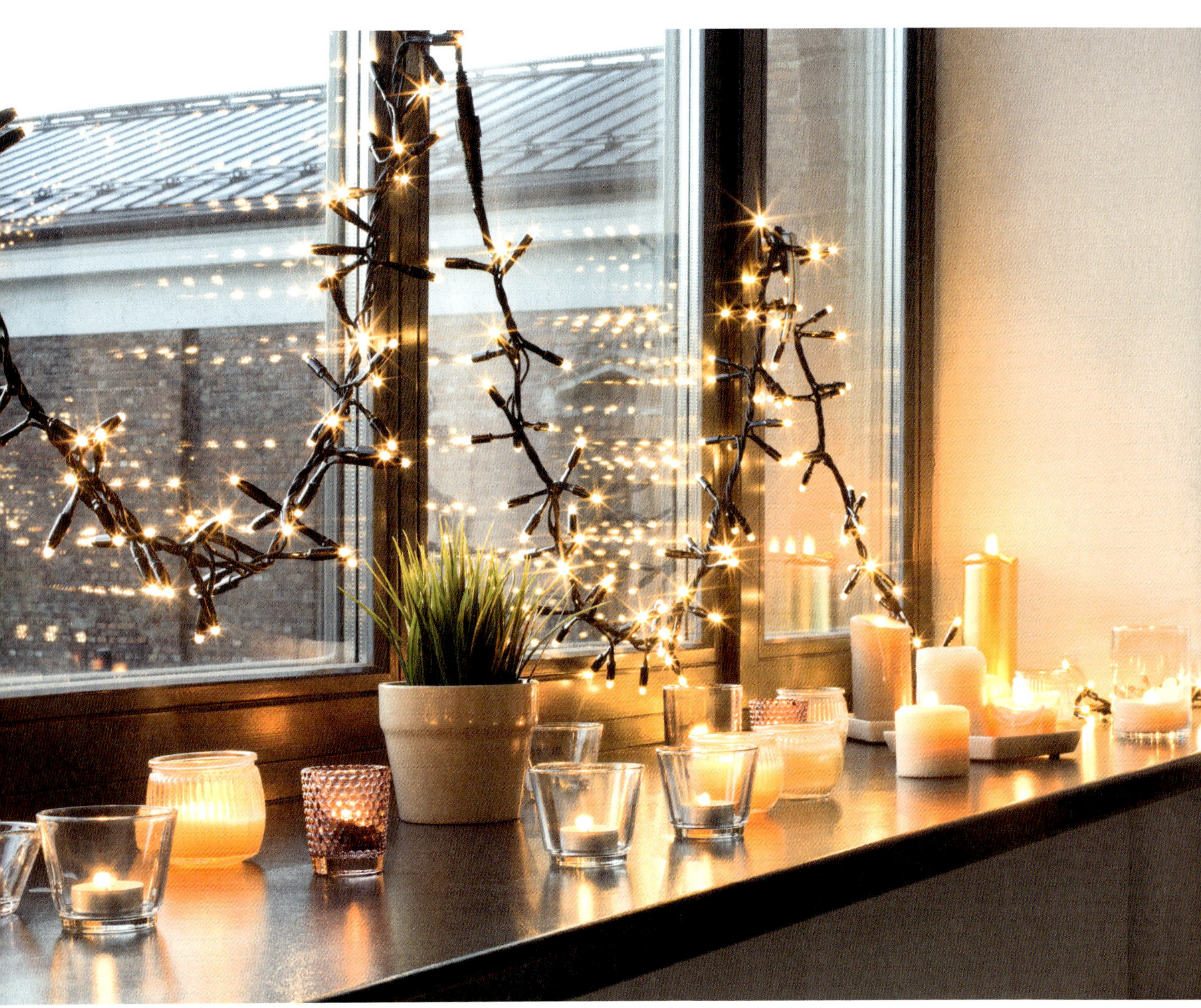

Consider where you need task lighting and what the desired atmosphere is for each area. A windowsill is a great spot for an array of candle and tea light details.

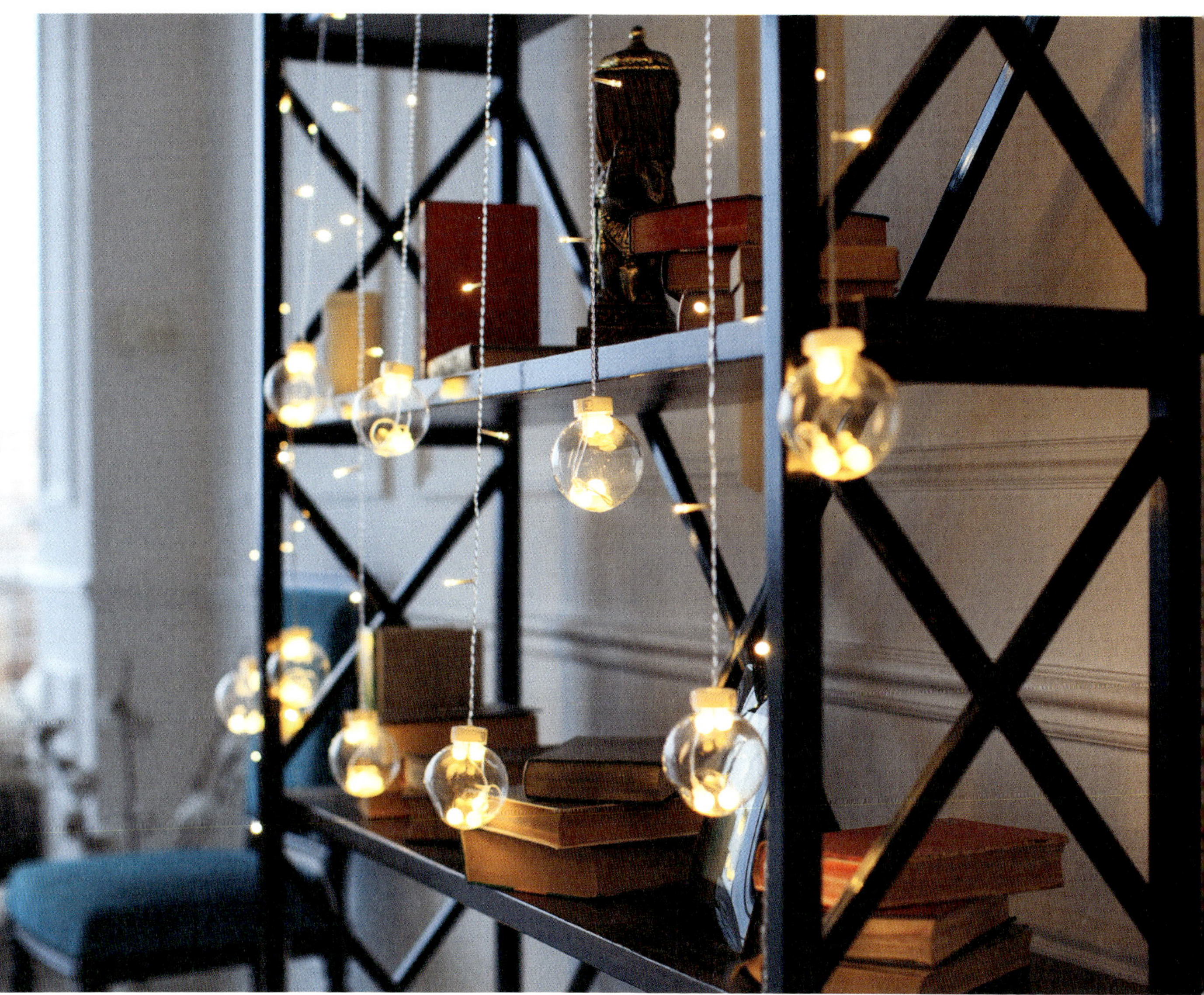

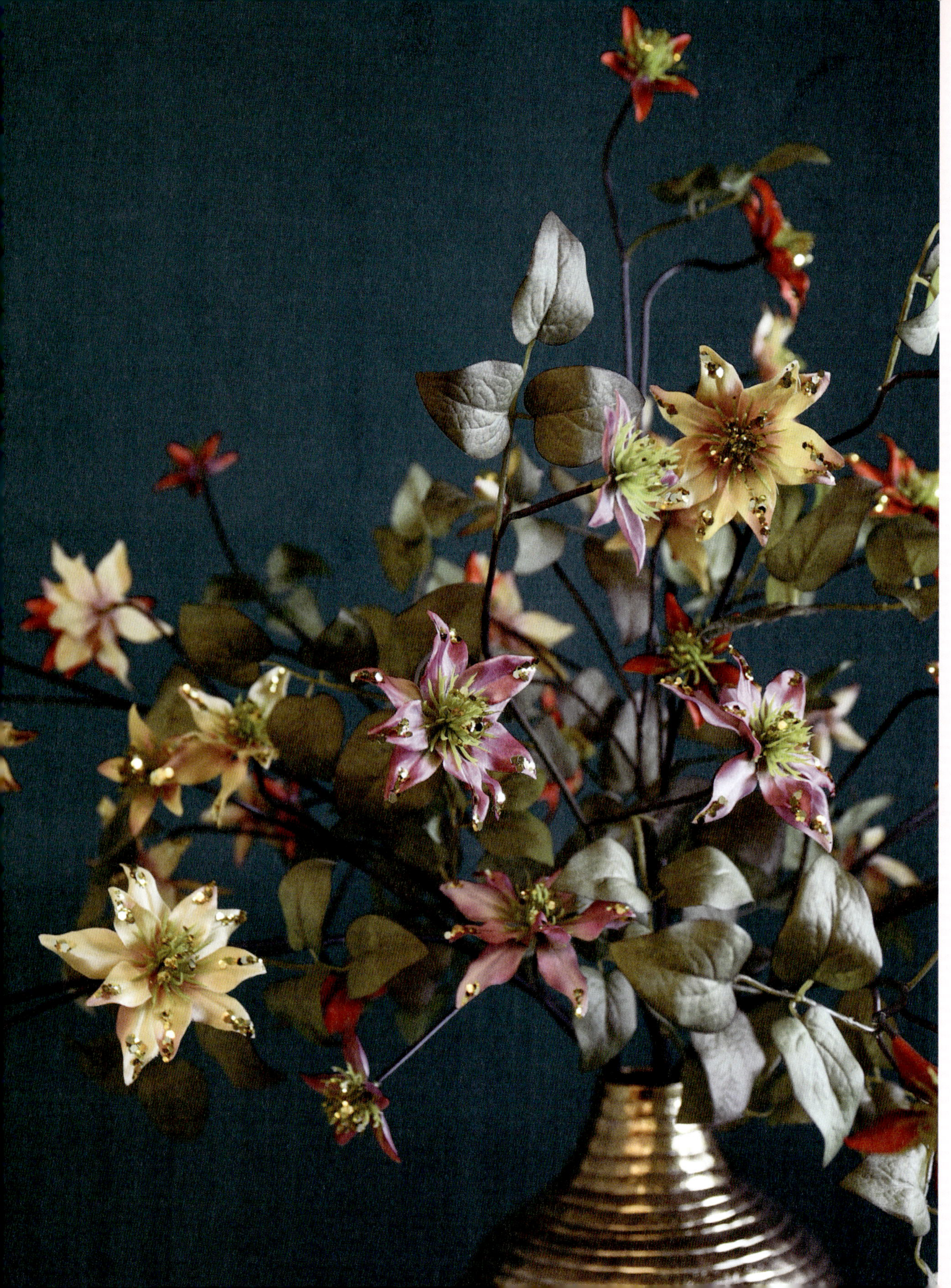

Festive florals

Ribbons, flowers, and foliage add a glamorous touch to a space and fill the room with scent. Grow a beautiful amaryllis or adorn petals with glitter for the full Christmas effect.

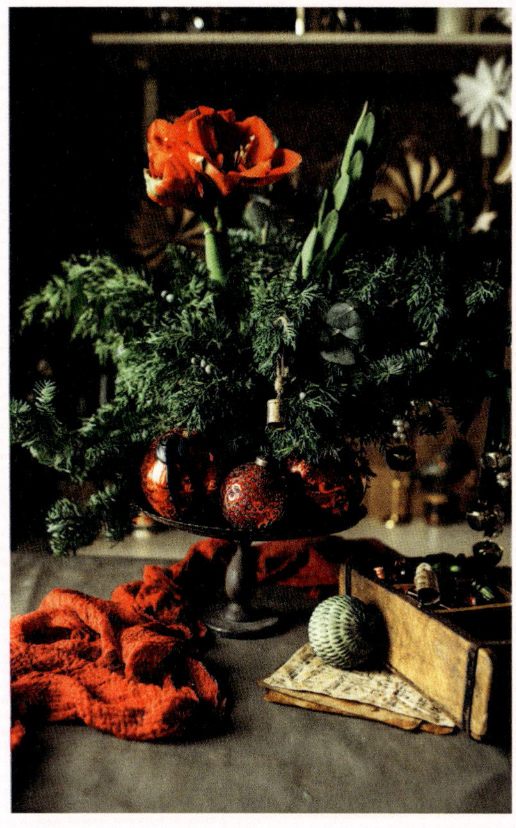

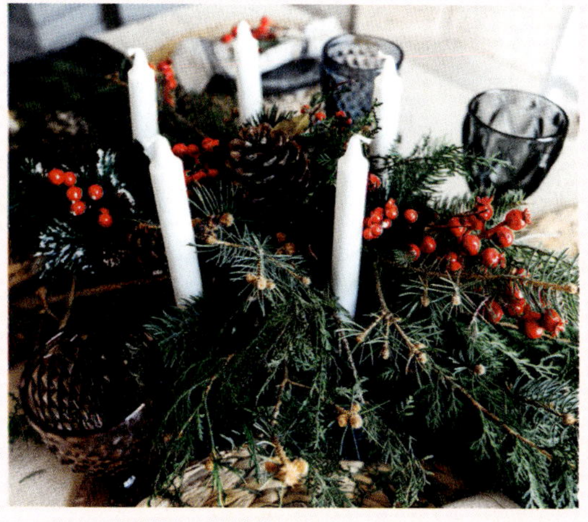

An evening centerpiece is a snap to make—just place candles in a pre-lit wreath—and it will create a lovely atmosphere.

< Assorted Christmas Flowers by *Gisela Graham London*

Fit for a feast

When we set the table, it's all about layering. A good place to start is by matching the colors with your dining room or other decorations. A simple tablecloth or table runner works well and creates a central focus point. Pair it with decorative plates or napkins that feel more festive before adding in glassware and foliage. Candlelight is always a winner. Pick candelabras or vases with narrow bases so you can still see across the table and have plenty of space for the food.

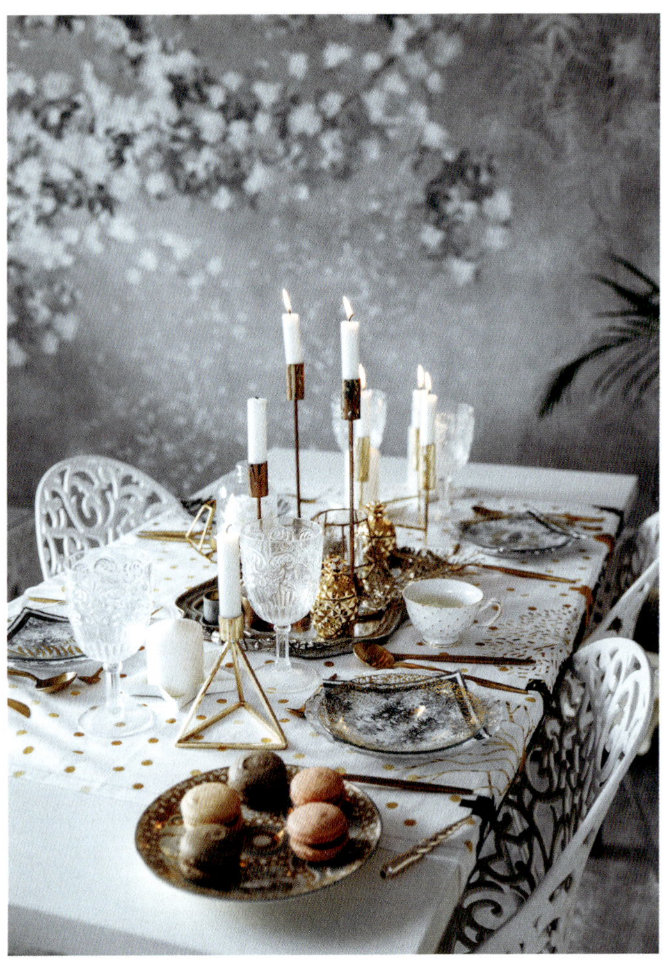

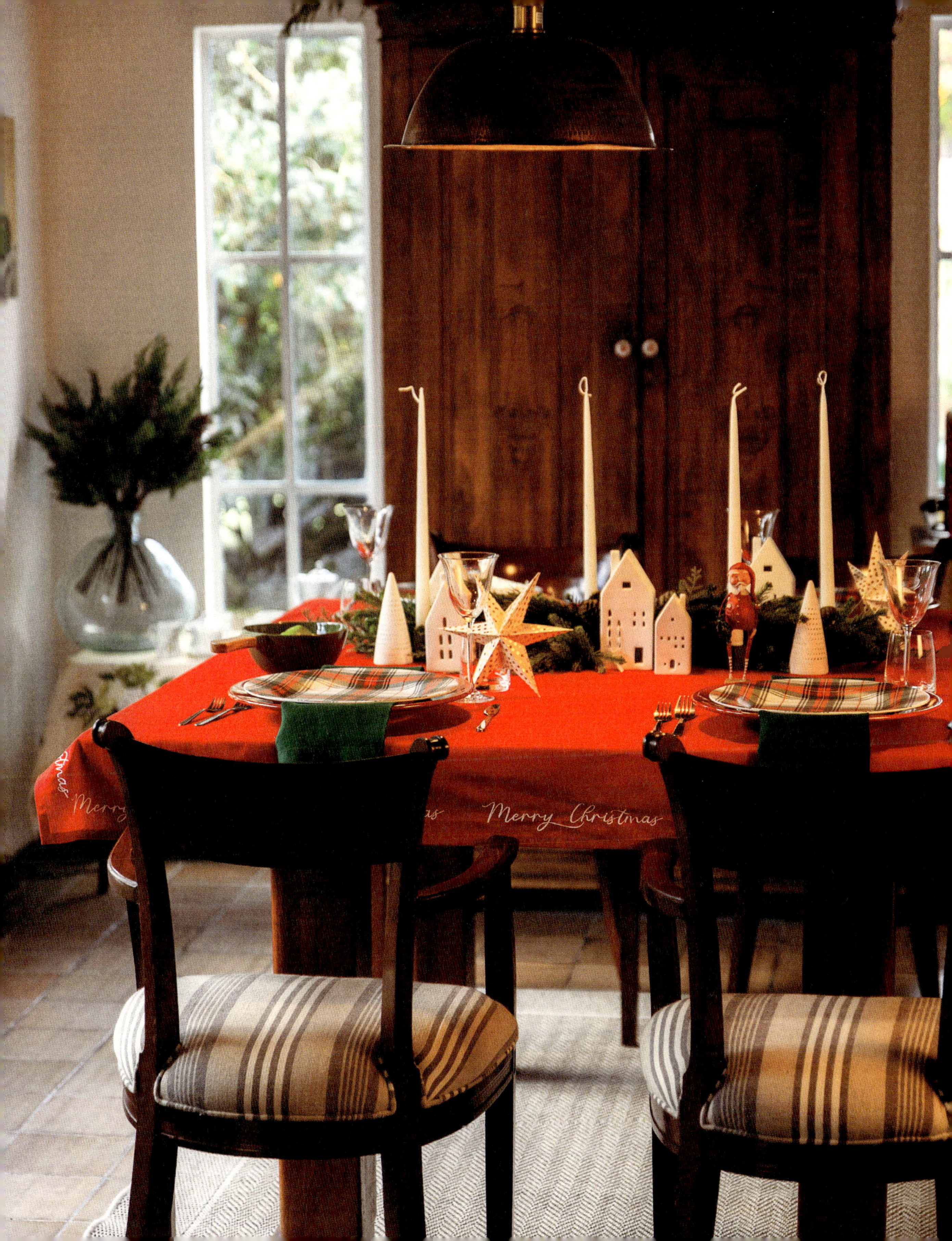
Merry Christmas

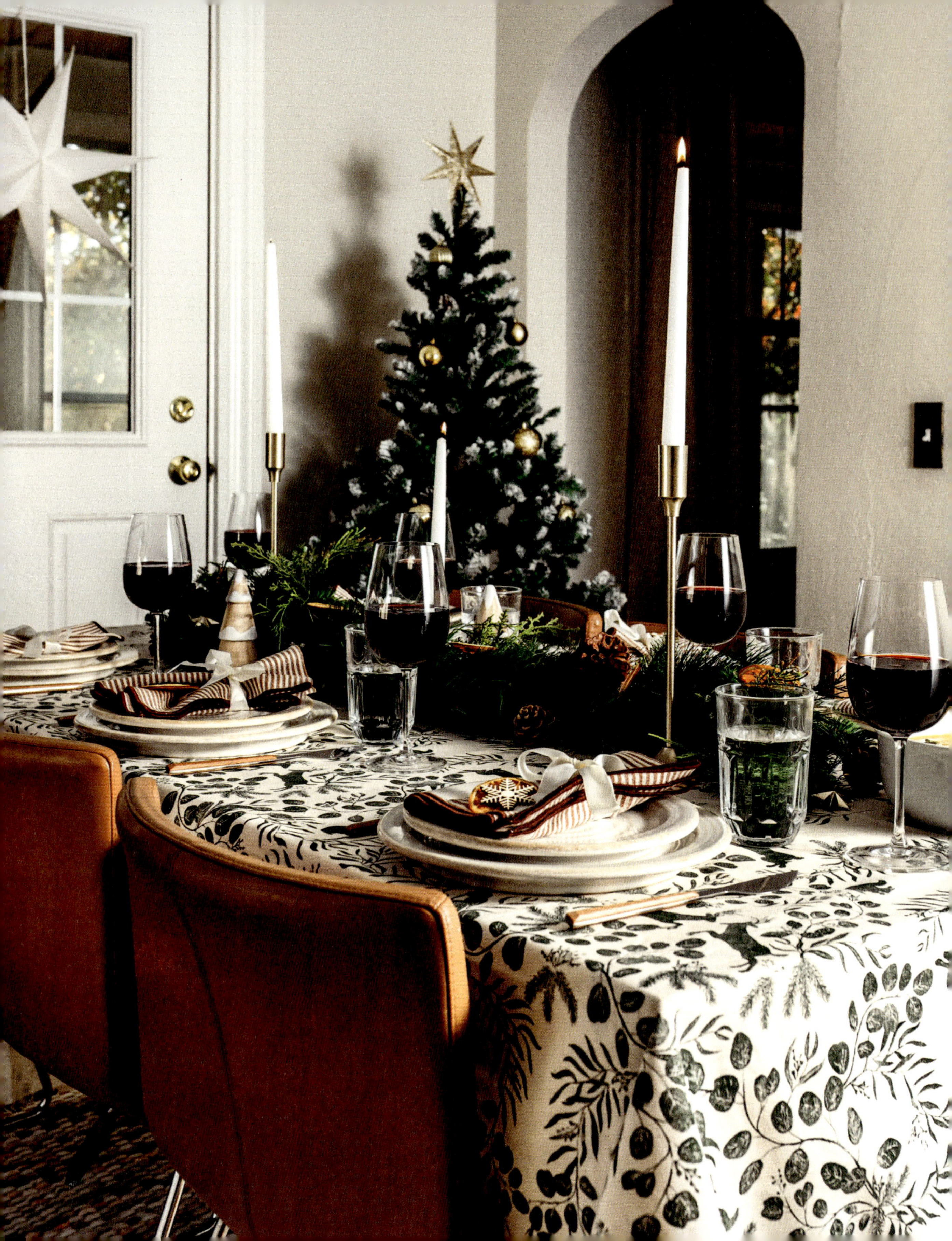

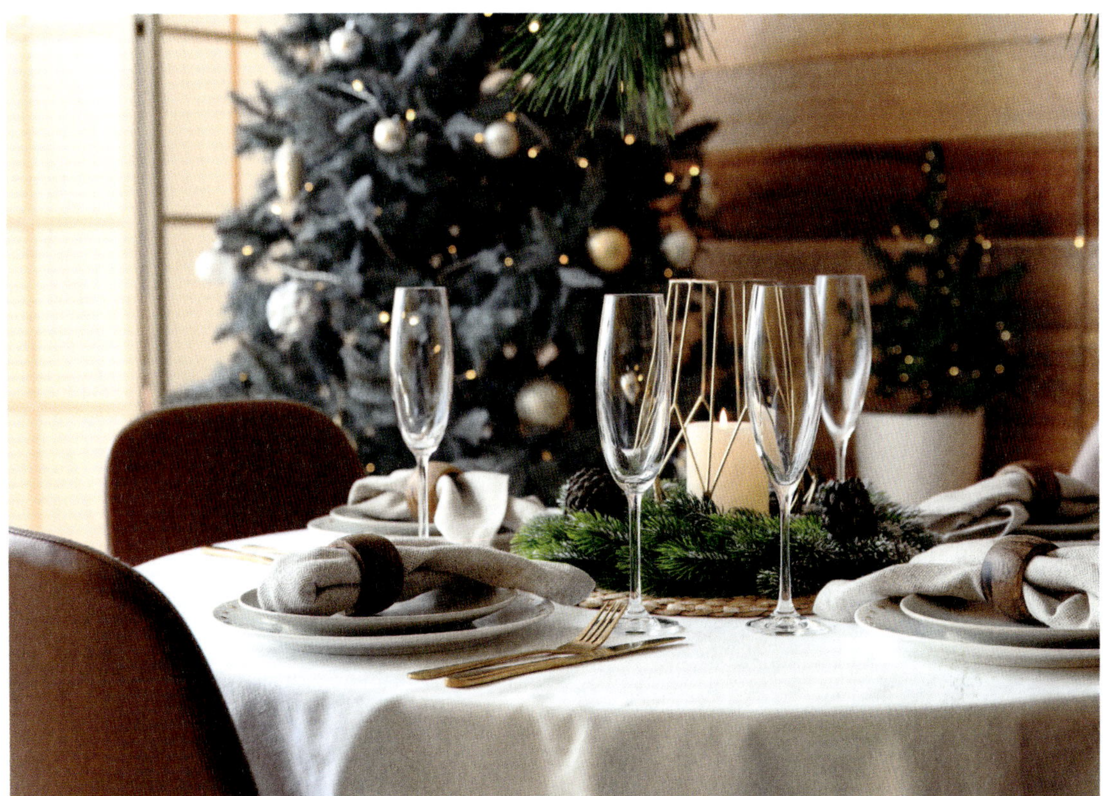

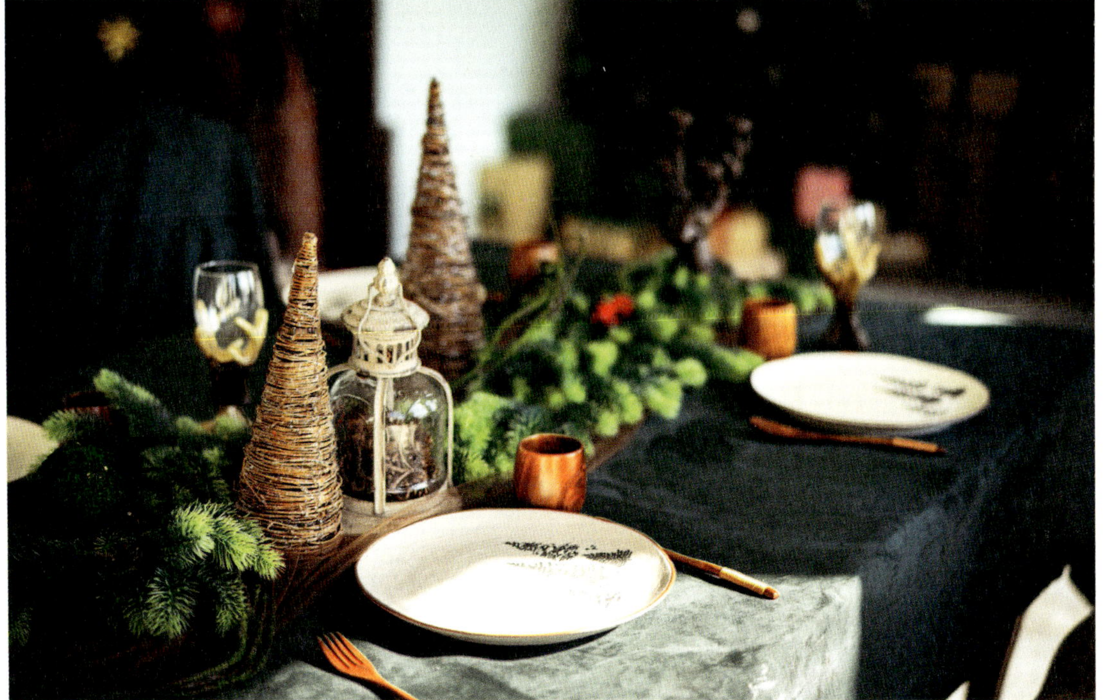

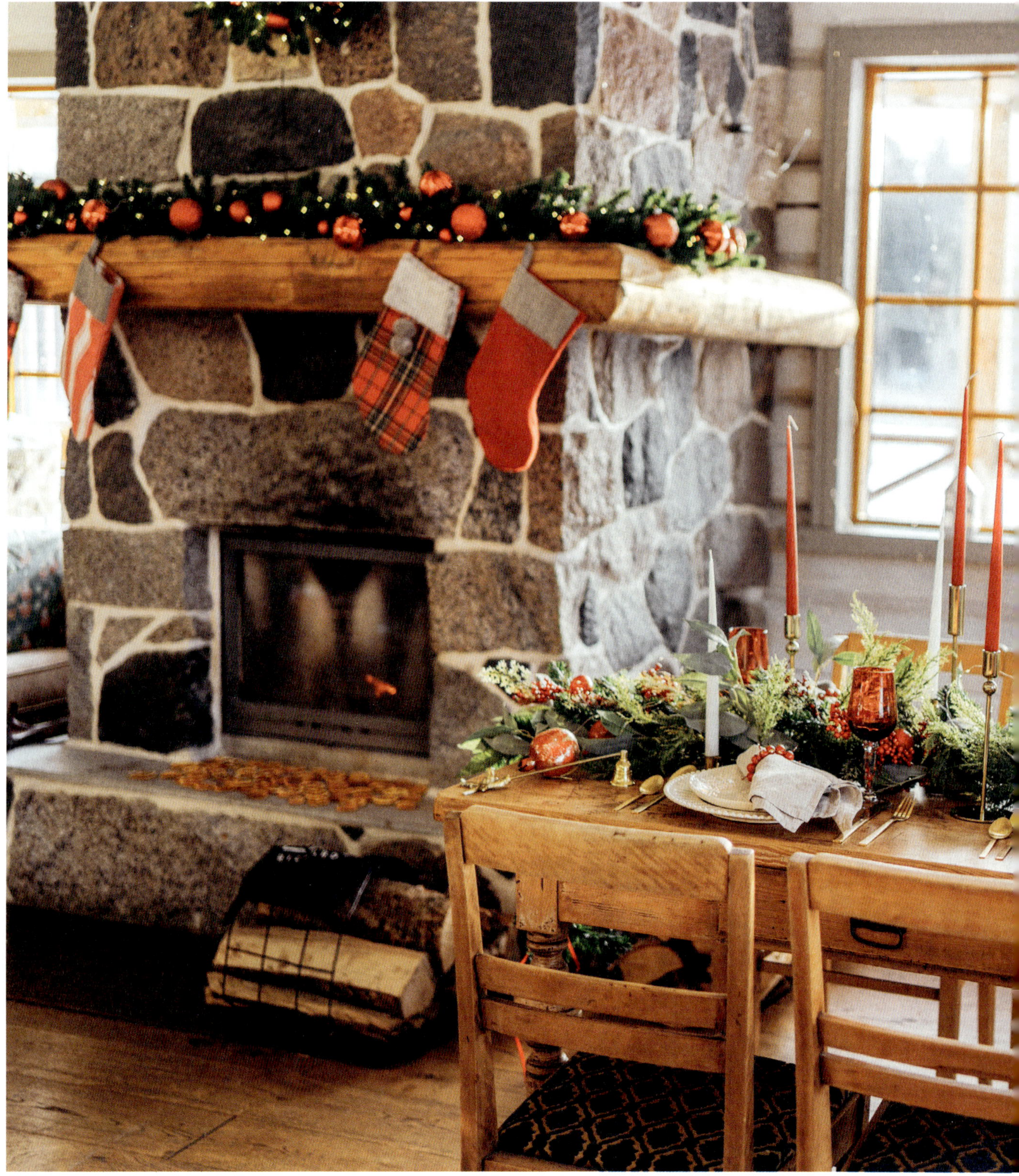

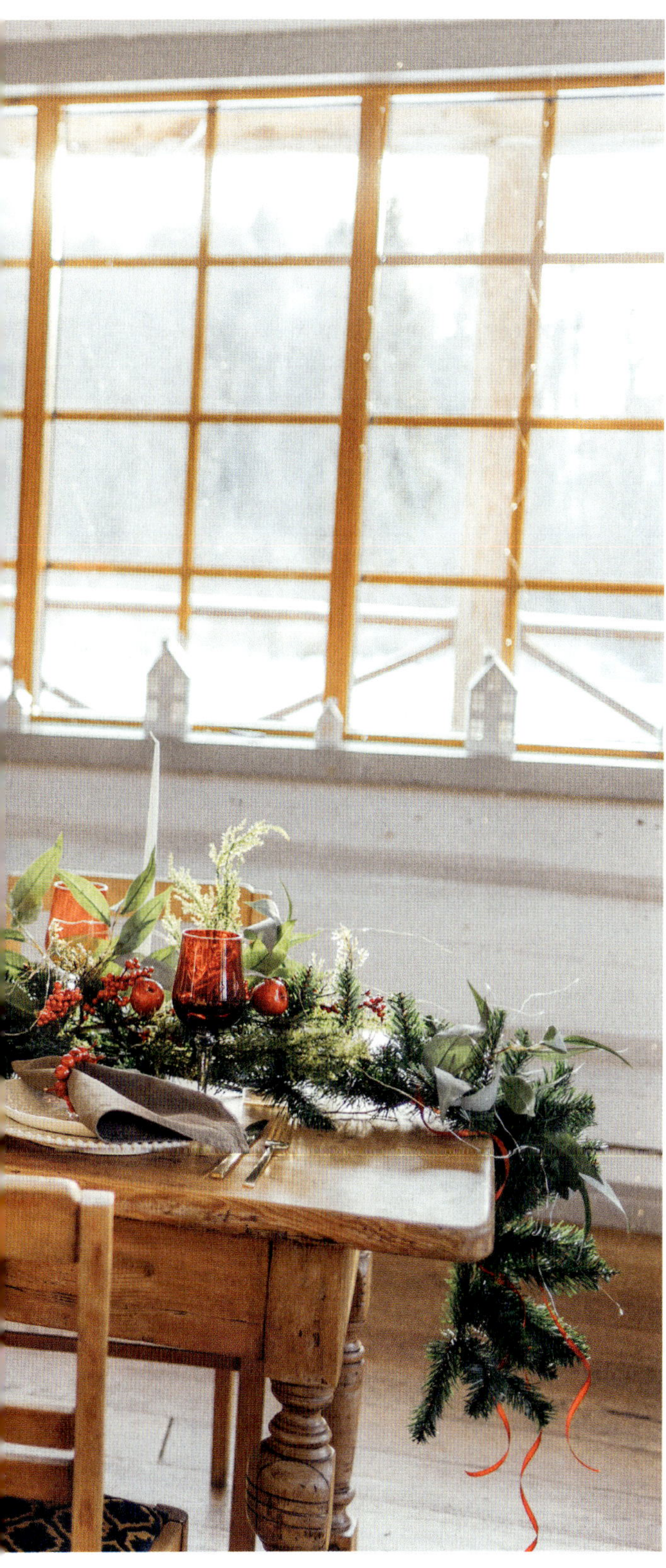

Red candlesticks, napkin rings and glassware go nicely with the rest of the decorations in this country home.

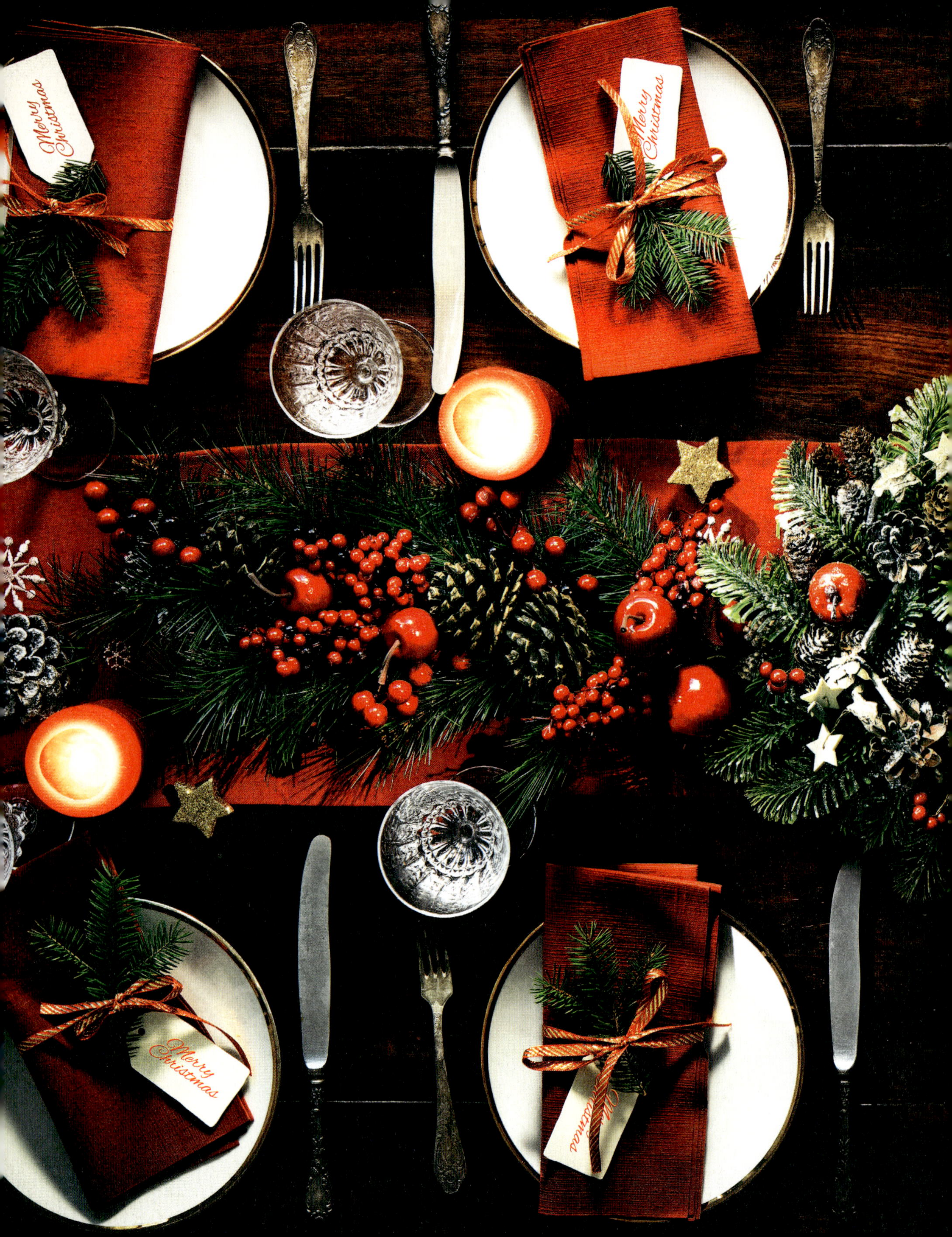
Merry Christmas
Merry Christmas
Merry Christmas

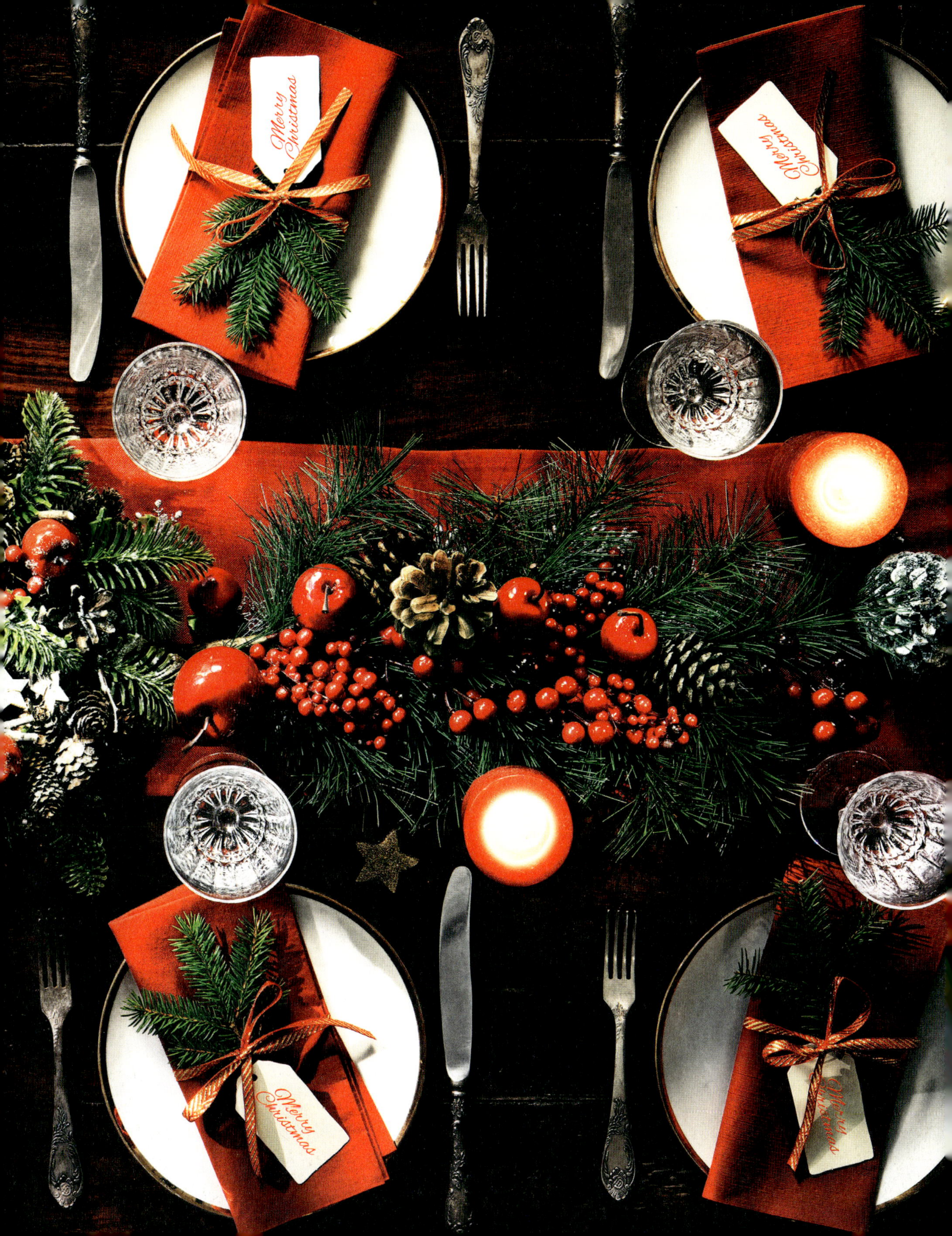
Merry Christmas
Merry Christmas
Merry Christmas
Merry Christmas

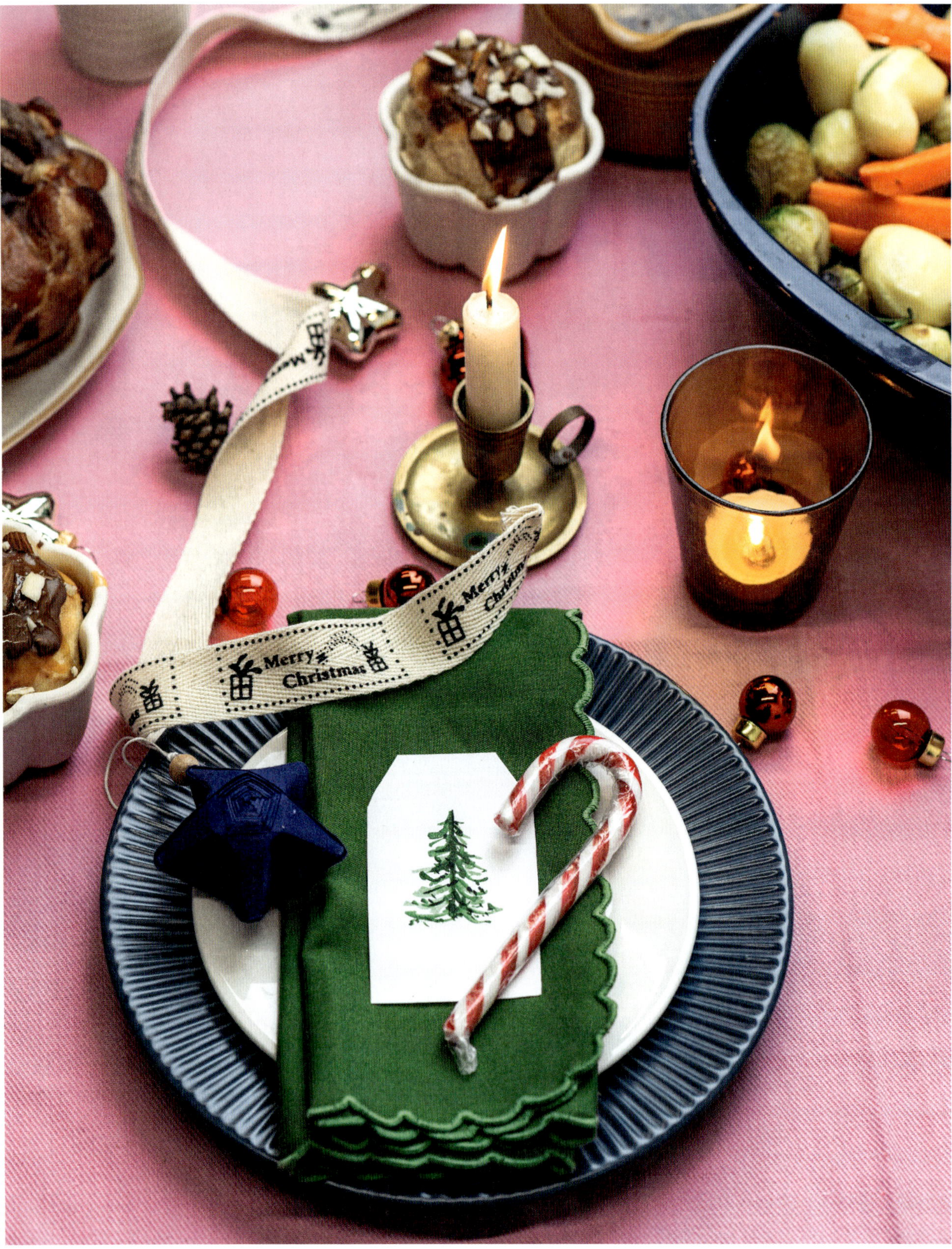
Merry Christmas
Merry Christmas

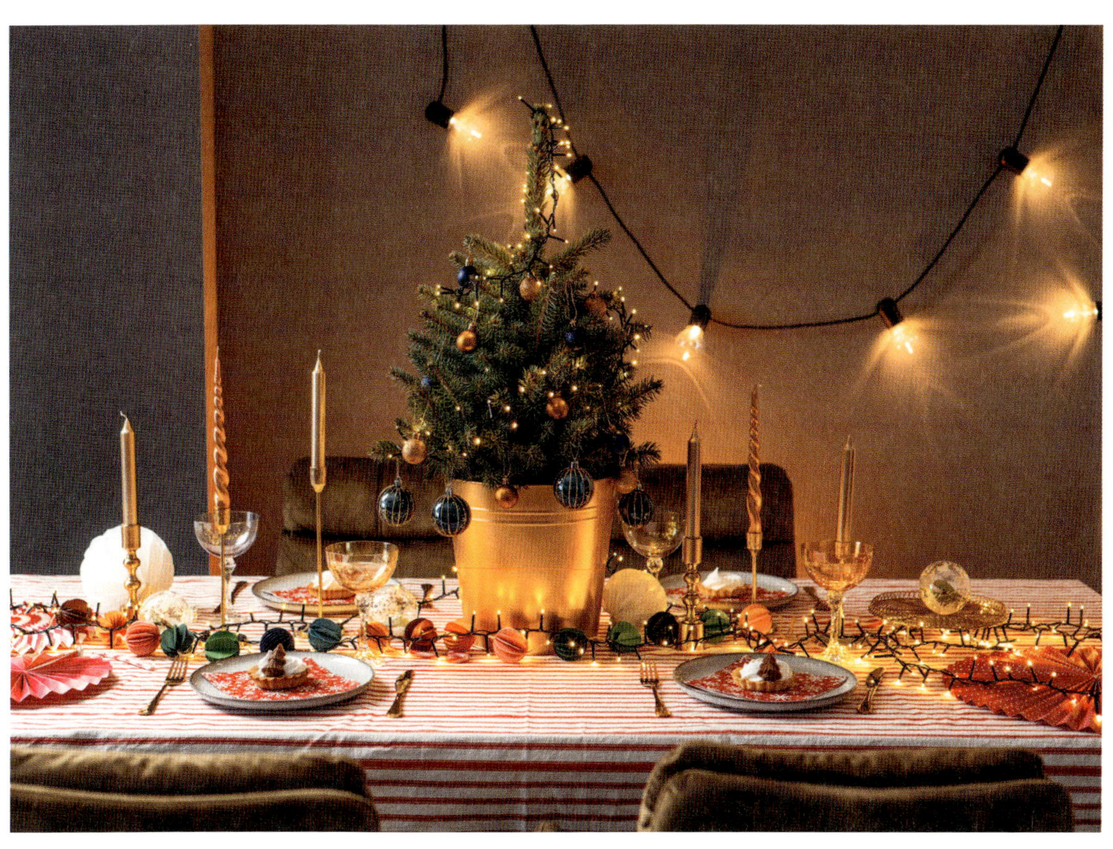

Layered textiles in berry tones of pink, red and cinnamon create an inviting backdrop for traditional decorations and trimmings.

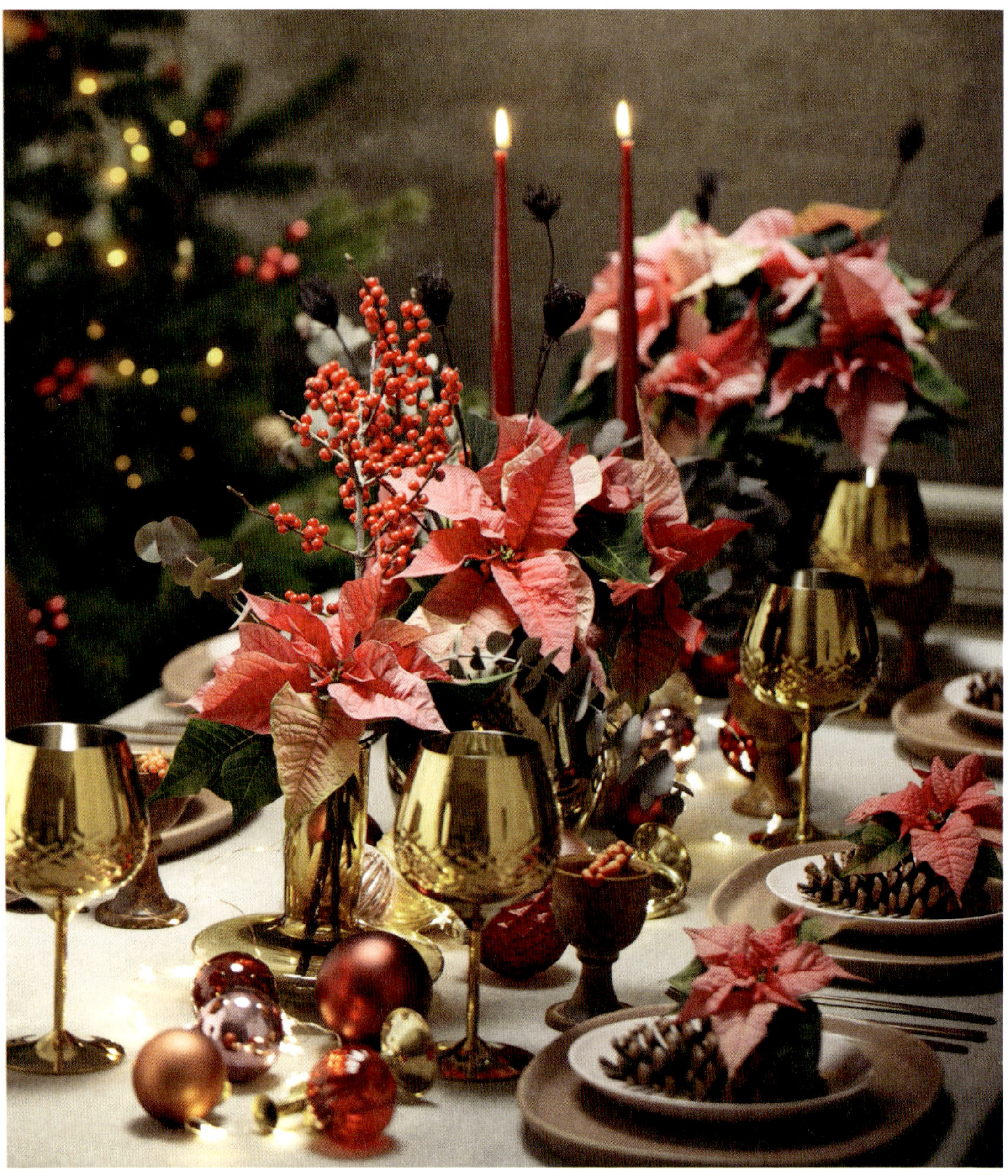

Thoughtful additions to a table make all the difference, from personalized place settings or a gift for each guest. Here, gold is used for glamour, with baubles used to fill spaces, and height is added with candles.

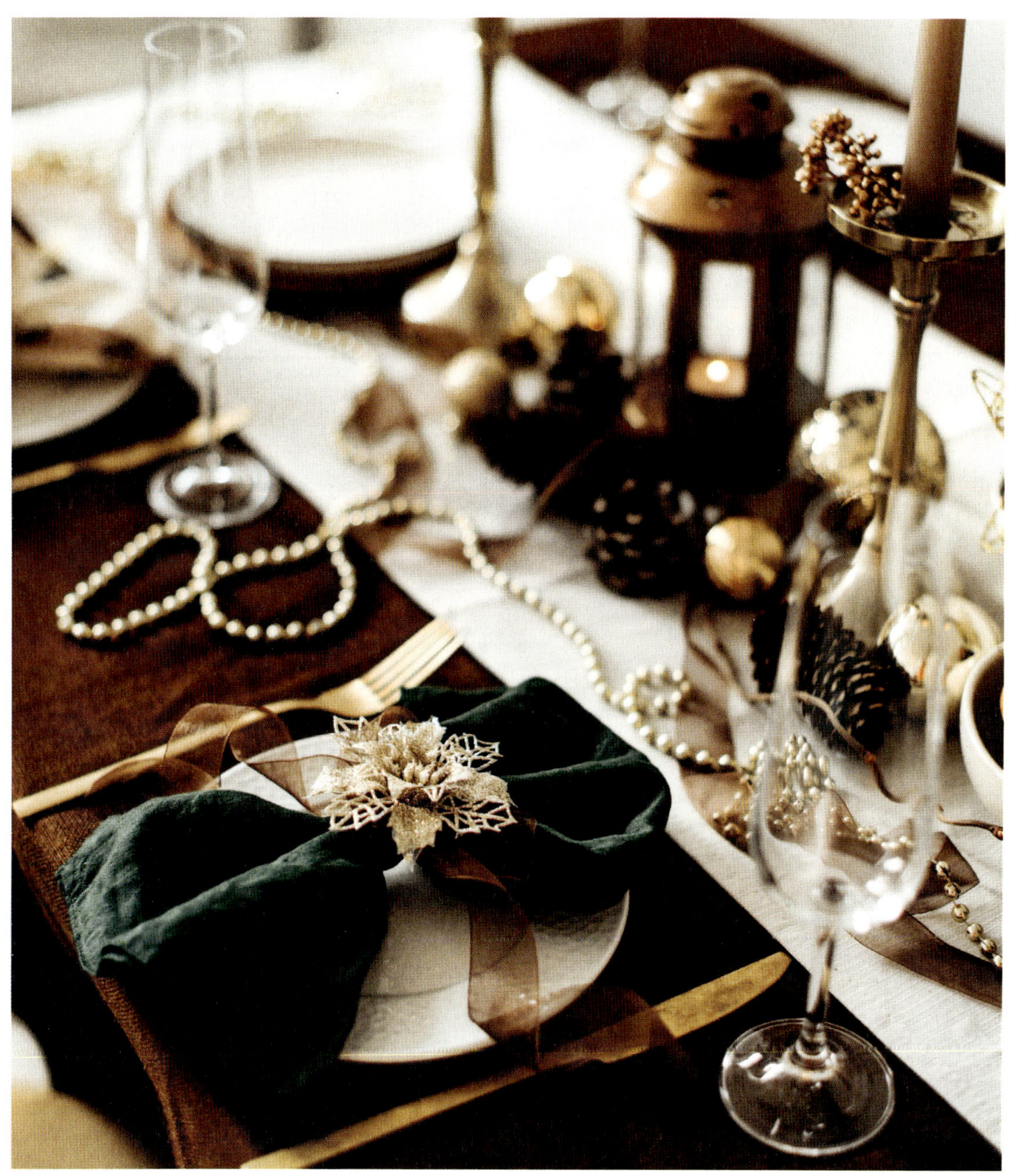

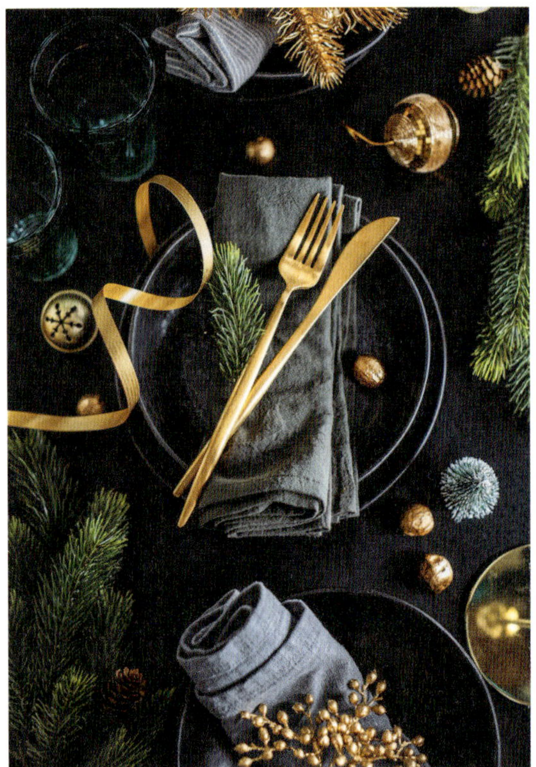

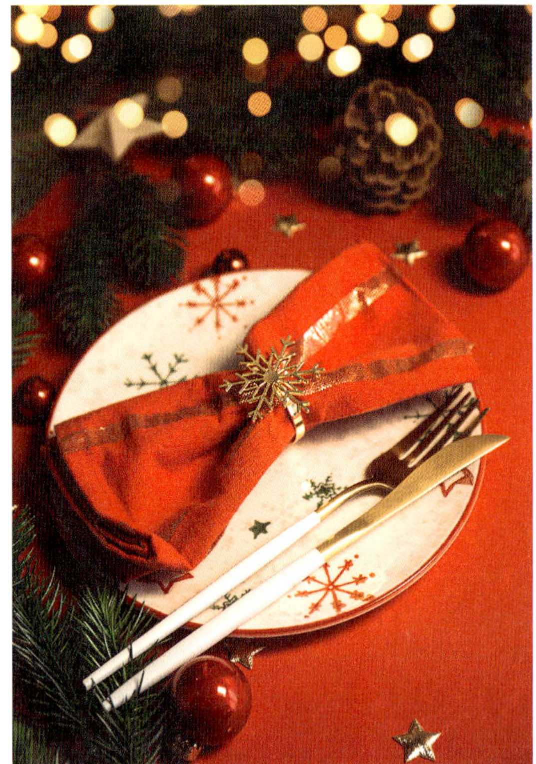

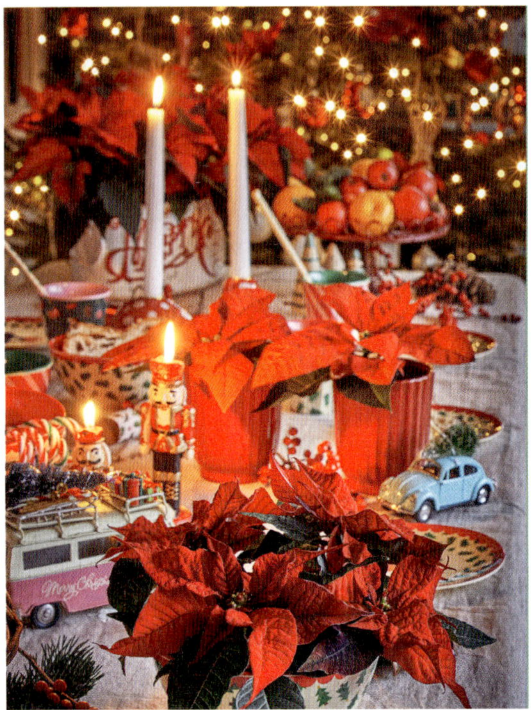

Layer up linens and crockery and create personalized place settings with decorative flourishes. Glass domes are dressed up with fairy lights and moss.

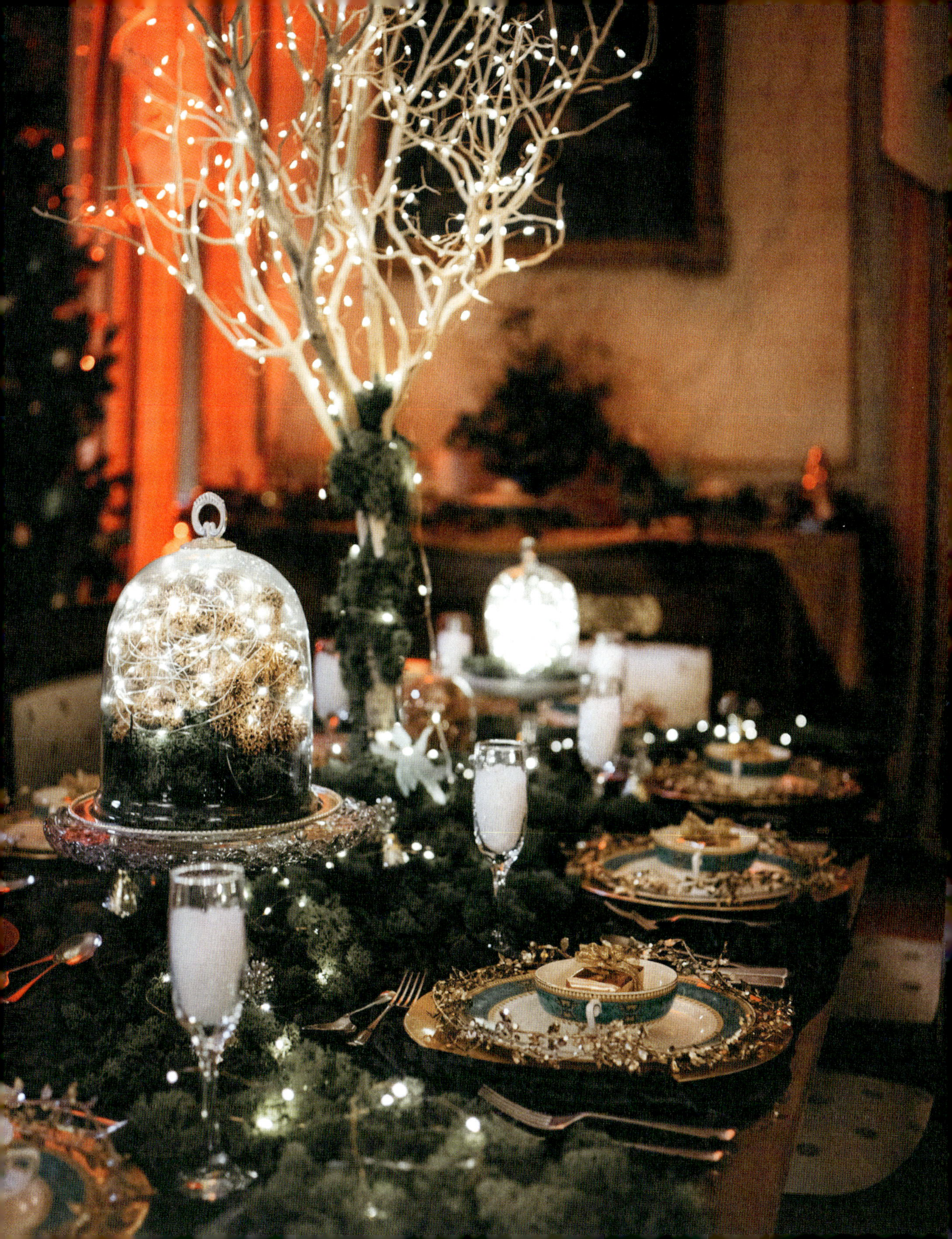

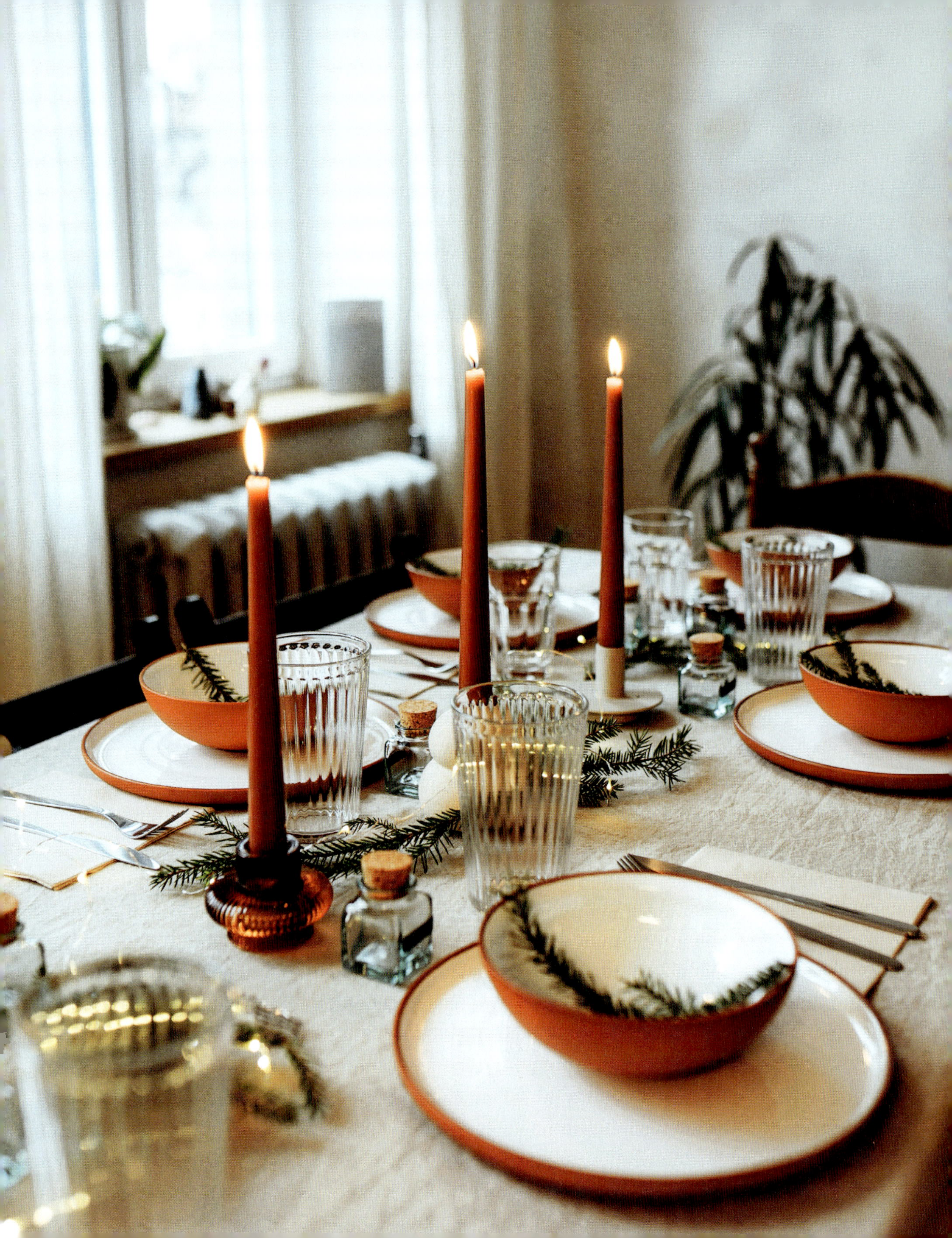

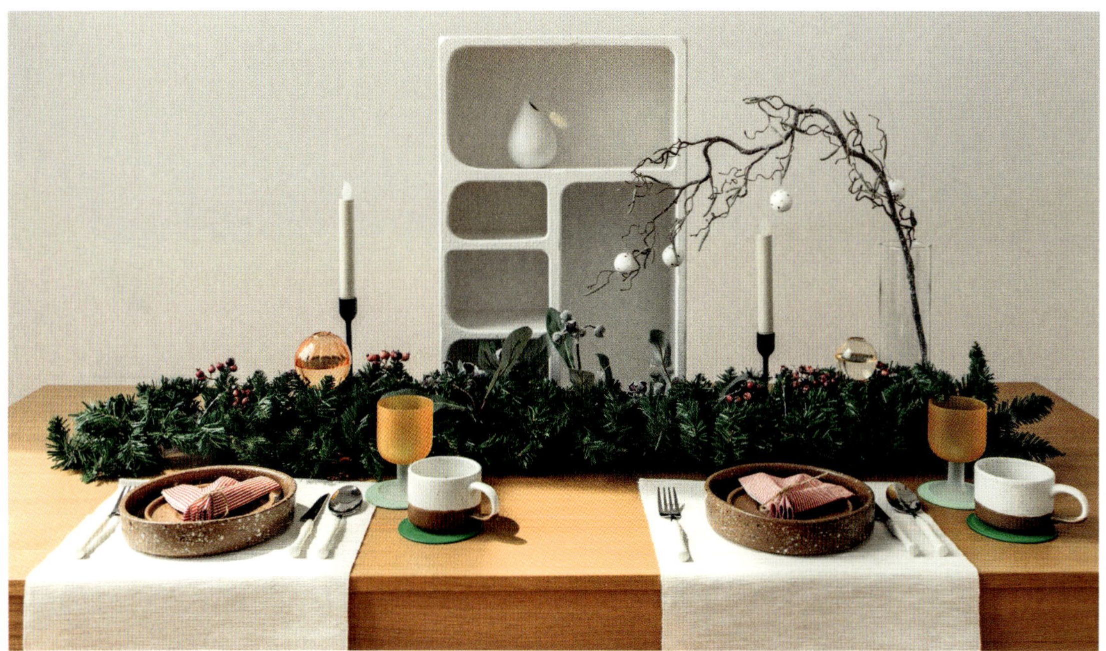

Simplicity is key to a Scandi look with beautiful earthenware bowls, matching terracotta candlesticks and a simple sprig of fir for decoration.

THE FINAL TOUCH

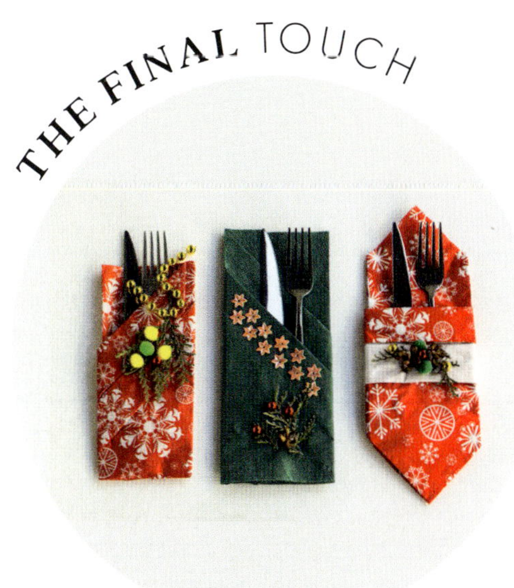

To make Scandinavian style holiday napkins, stamp patterns onto a plain napkin. A pattern of snowflakes and stars will add a handmade folk touch.

FEATURE

CHRISTMAS NOSTALGIA

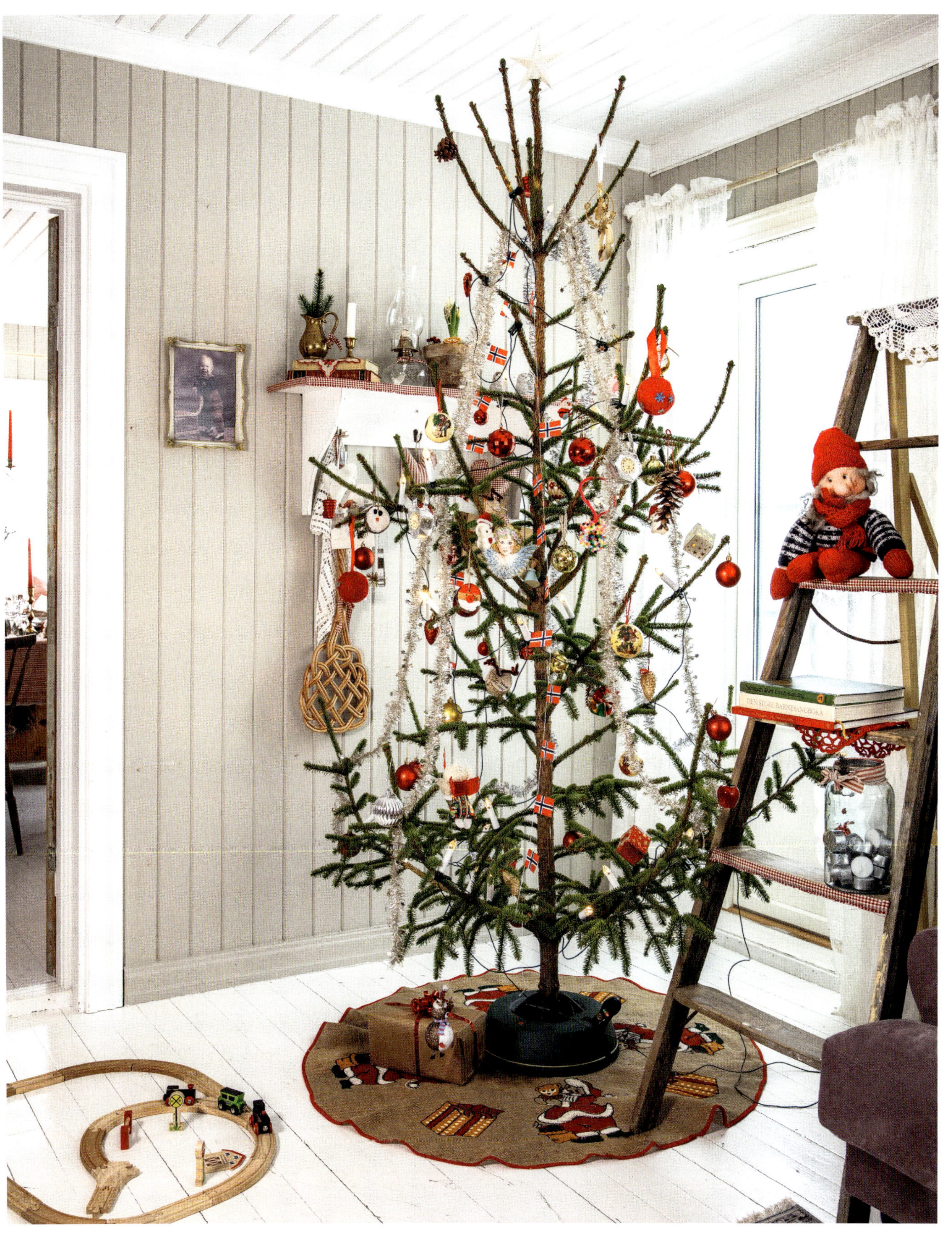
DEN STORE BARNESANGBOKA

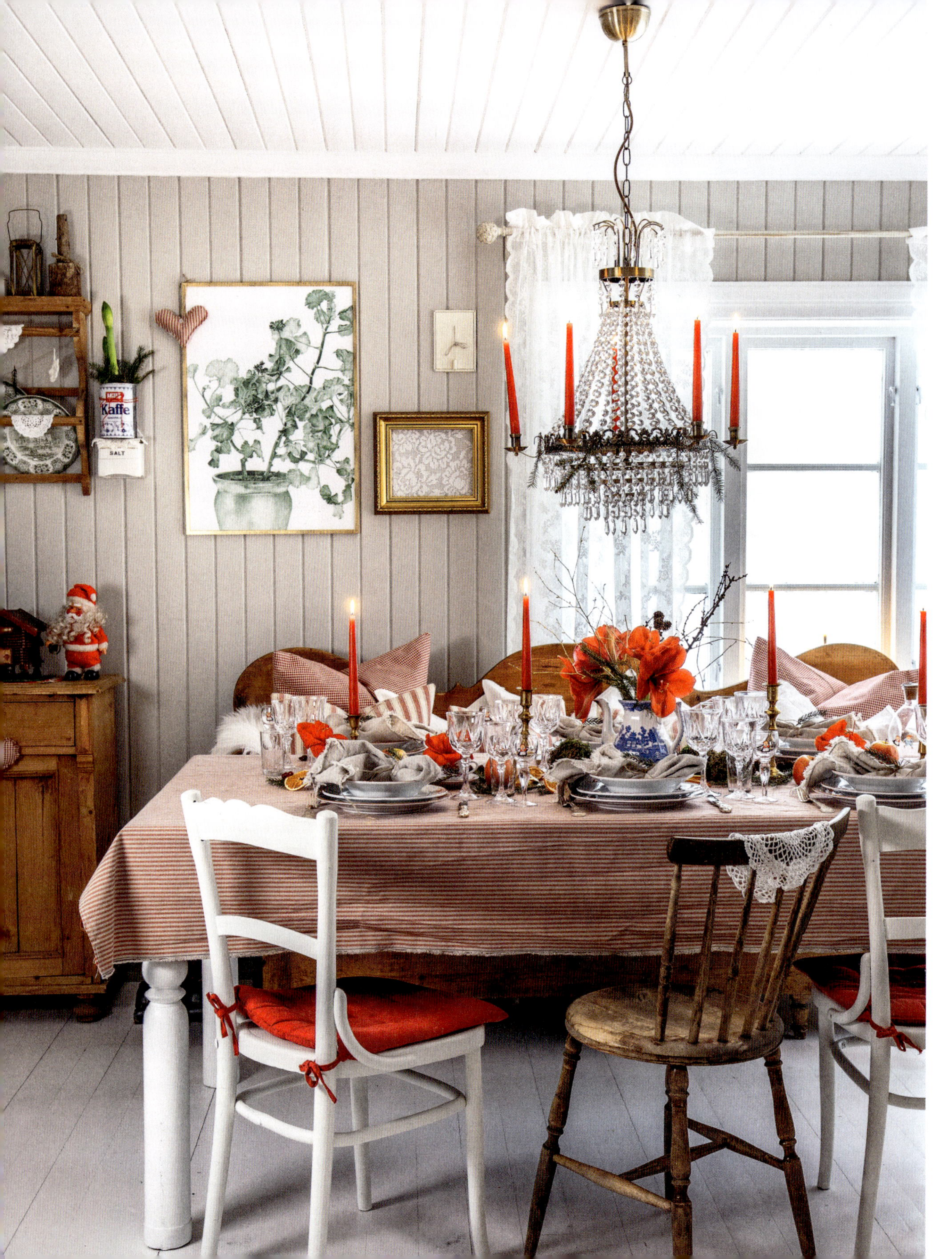
Kaffe
SALT

A Nostalgic Christmas at Presterud

At Ida Marie and Anders' home, they decorate for Christmas using heirlooms from both sides of the family. Everything from dinnerware to Santa figurines are treasured antiques, to which they add a sprinkle of new.

"Mummy, I want to bake!" little 3-year-old Thelma shouts from the kitchen. The family is enjoying gingerbread baking and advent comforts these days, and now Thelma has taken it upon herself to gather flour, sugar, and eggs. As Ida Marie sets the table for Christmas Eve, Thelma is allowed to make her own cookie dough. She stands for a long time at the counter, stirring in the bowl while humming a Christmas tune. Outside the window, large snowflakes gently fall, contributing to the warm atmosphere throughout the house.

"There's a lot of anticipation in the air these days," says Ida Marie with a smile. Both Thelma and her older sister, Thea, age eight, are excitedly waiting for Santa. But the anticipation of waiting is almost the best part, Ida Marie thinks. She begins decorating for Christmas in late November, with more decorations emerging as Christmas approaches. In the evenings, the family always gathers to watch Christmas specials on TV, with something warm to drink and some Christmas cookies.

"All the preparations leading up to Christmas are my definition of Christmas joy," she says. However, Ida Marie works at a hotel and feels the pressure of the busy runup to Christmas. Therefore, she always tries to be well-prepared, both in terms of Christmas gifts and decorating at home. When expecting guests, she always sets the festive table one or two days in advance. "I love setting beautiful tables, and we have many inherited sets of china," she shares. Cutlery, glasses, and china services have been passed down through generations, and Ida Marie and Anders cherish using these items. In this way, they carry the history and the family with them around the table. But Ida Marie has been saving up for the Santa dinner set from Porsgrund since she was a little girl. "I've always received a piece or two of it, for birthdays and Christmas," she says. "And now I have a complete Santa dinner service, which I take great care of!"

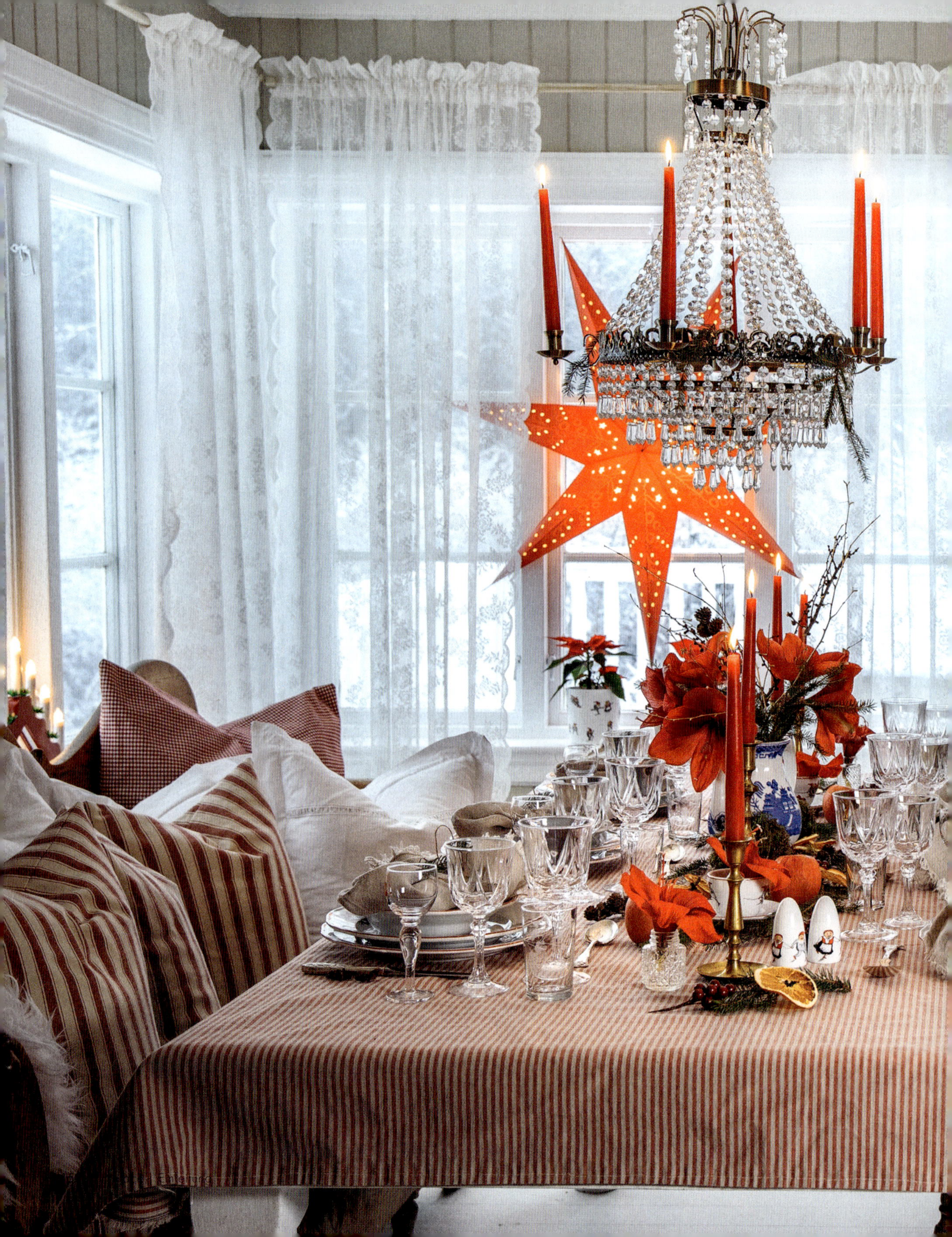

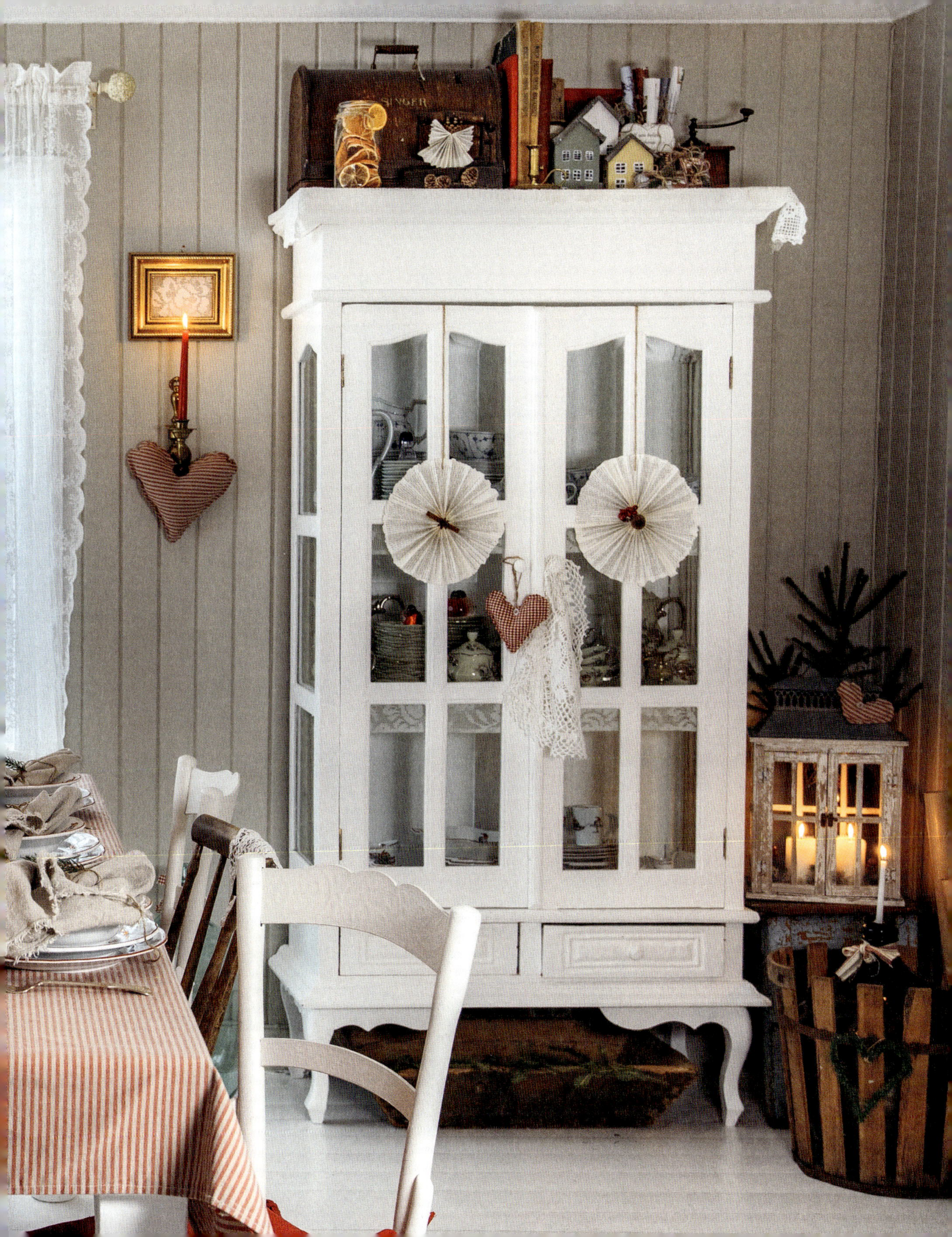
SINGER

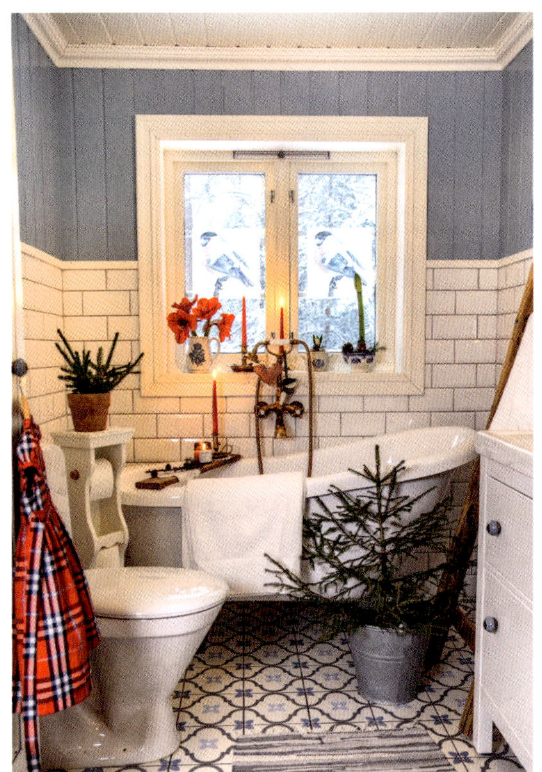

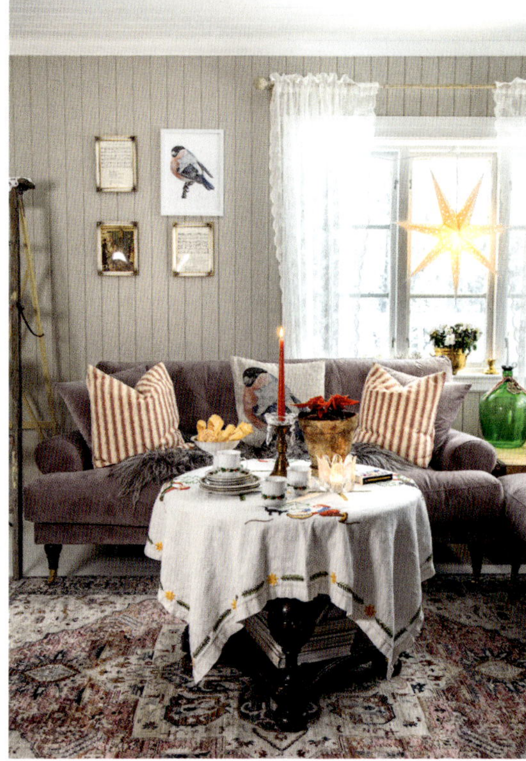

NOSTALGIC TREE

Ida Marie finds joy and inspiration on Instagram, and she eagerly shares her own interior design photos. When Anders went out to fetch the Christmas tree on his own, she was a bit worried when he came back. There was a terrible snowstorm that day, and he took the axe just outside their garden. They own several acres of woodland, and he figured it would be easy to find a tree. The trees were heavy with snow, making it difficult to see their true shapes. He found a large and beautiful one, which he showed to Ida Marie through the kitchen window. She gave a thumbs-up, and he brought it inside. The tree was about four meters tall, so he had to cut off the bottom part. Once the family got it into the living room, they noticed it was a bit sparse in terms of branches. "I've received many comments on that tree," says Ida Marie with a smile. "But most think it's very charming and nostalgic."

The children are allowed to decorate the tree as they wish, with a good mix of homemade, inherited, and new decorations. This way, the tree becomes just as cozy and nostalgic as the family likes it.

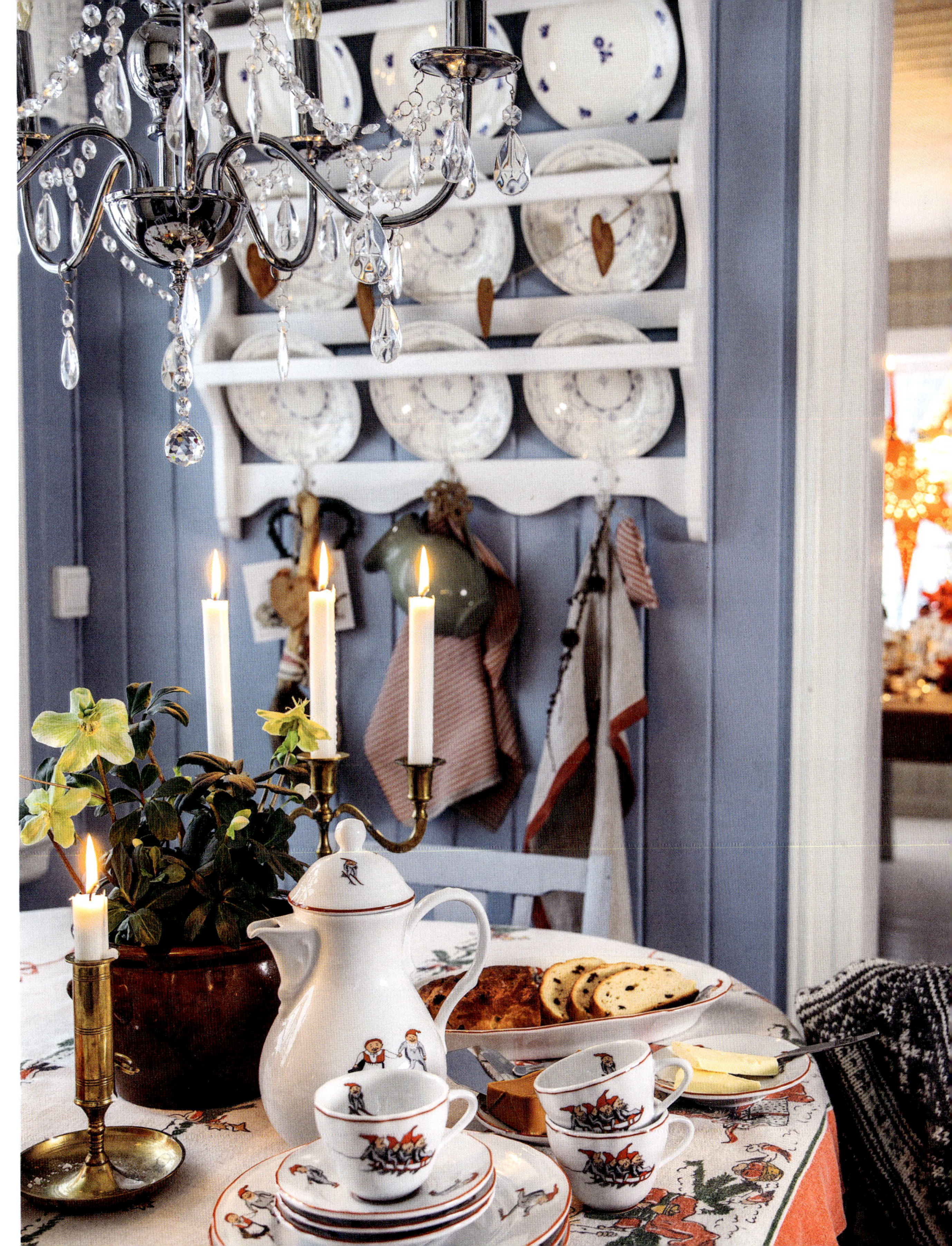

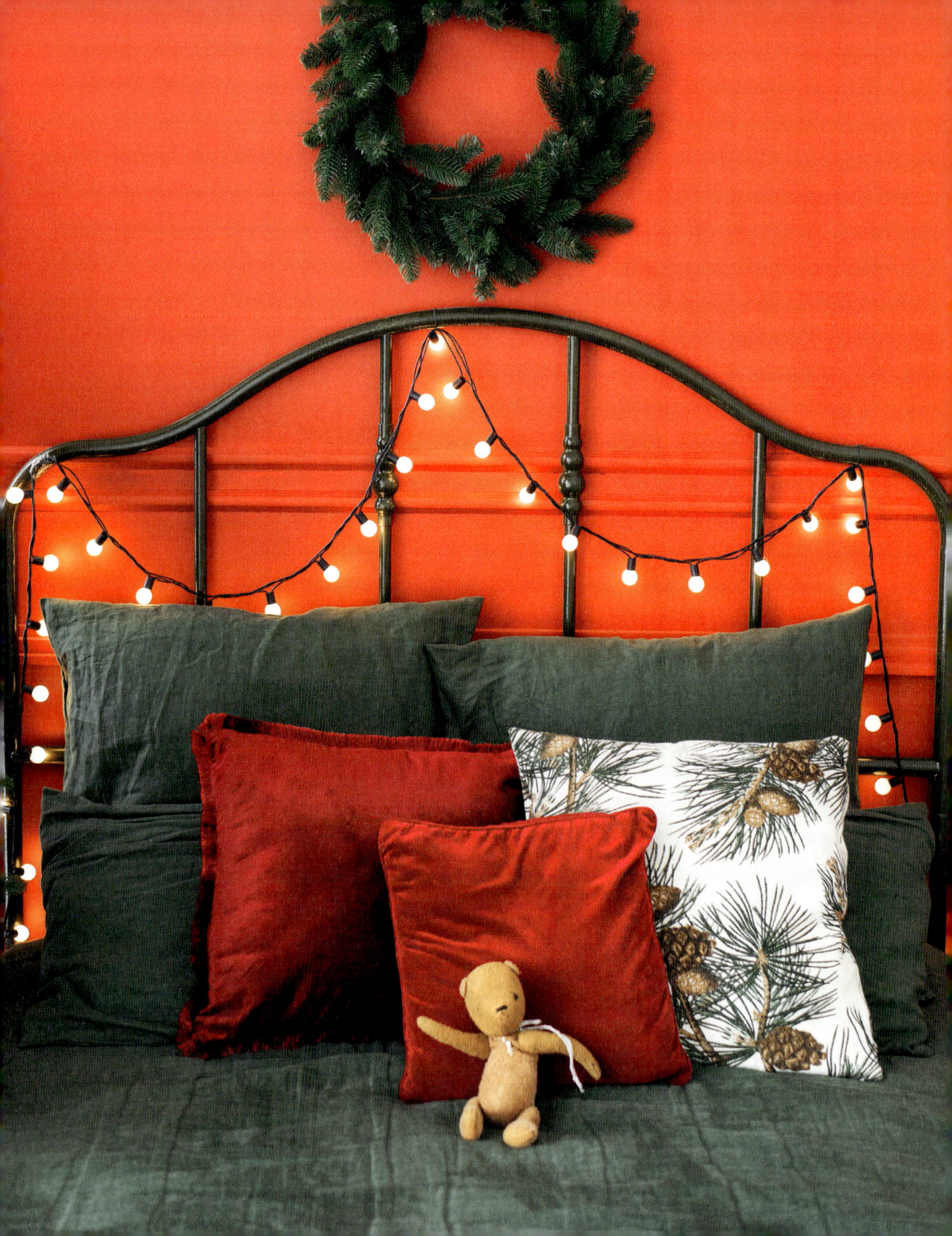

A cozy Christmas

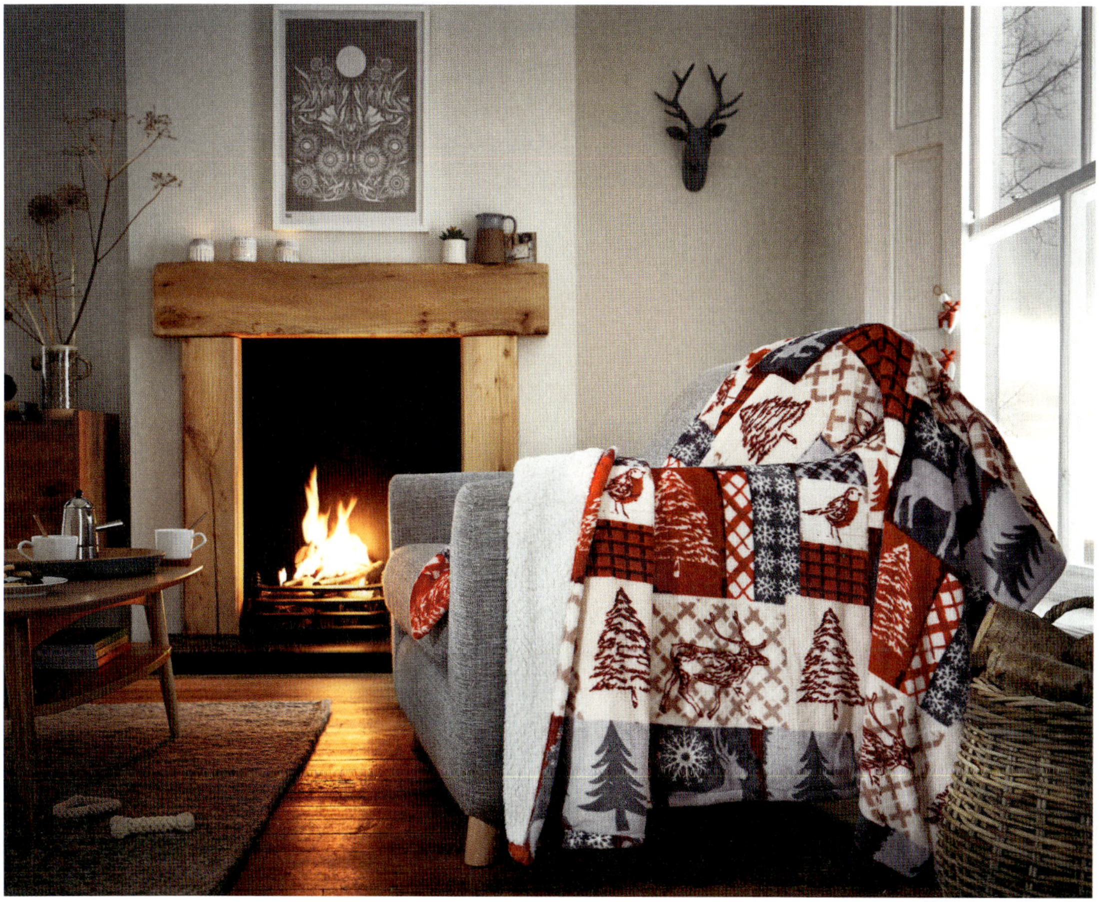

Comfortable and festive, Christmas Patchwork fleece throw by *Happy Linen Company.*

Bring in lots of soft textiles including fleece blankets, knitted stockings, velvet pillows and sheepskin rugs. Mixing rattan baskets with decorative elements such as a textured wall covering or wreath will create a warm and inviting space.

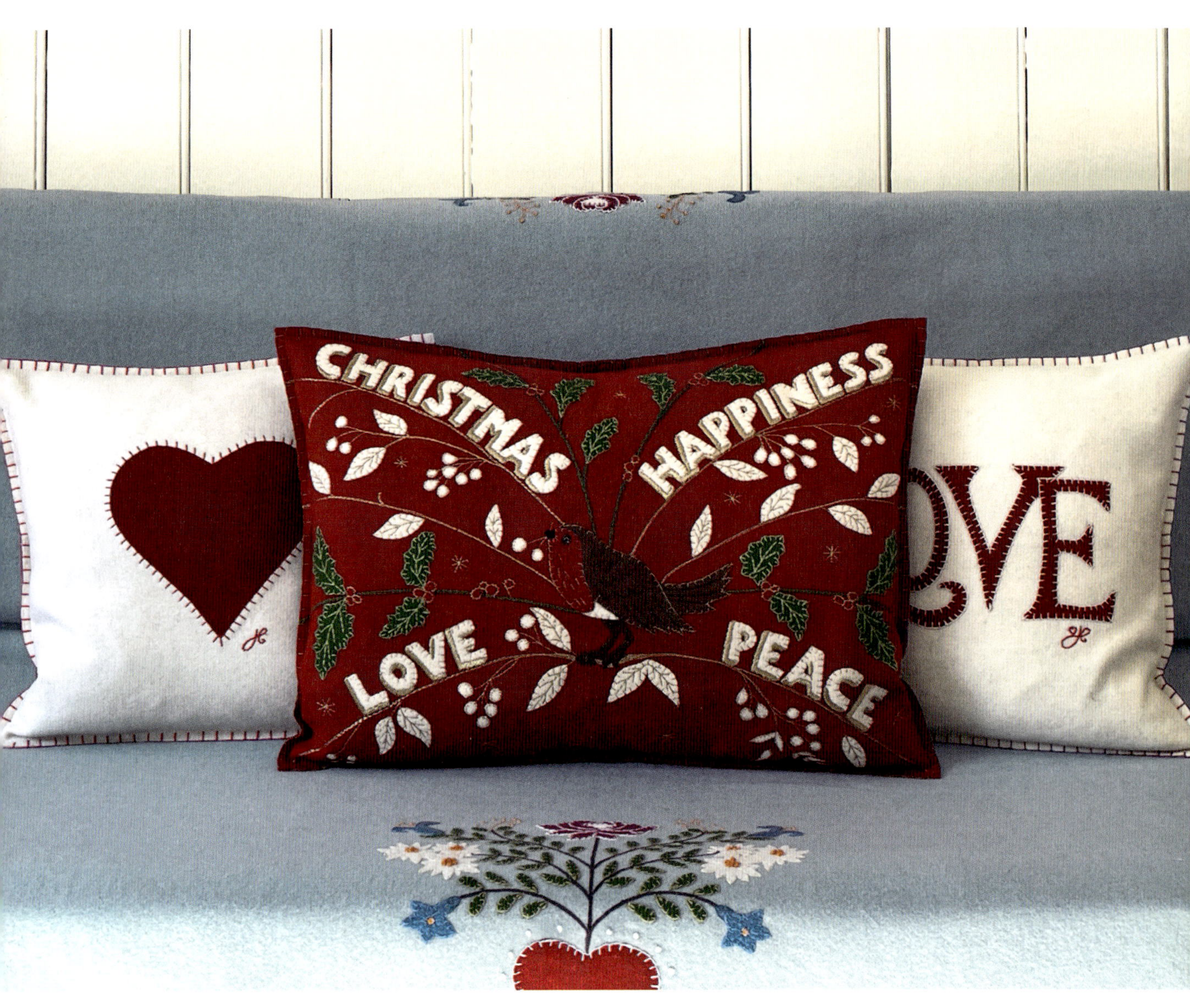

Brimming with Christmas cheer—these hand-embroidered cushions spread the perennial Christmas message. Designed by *Jan Constantine* and hand-stitched by artisans, they are destined to become beloved heirlooms.

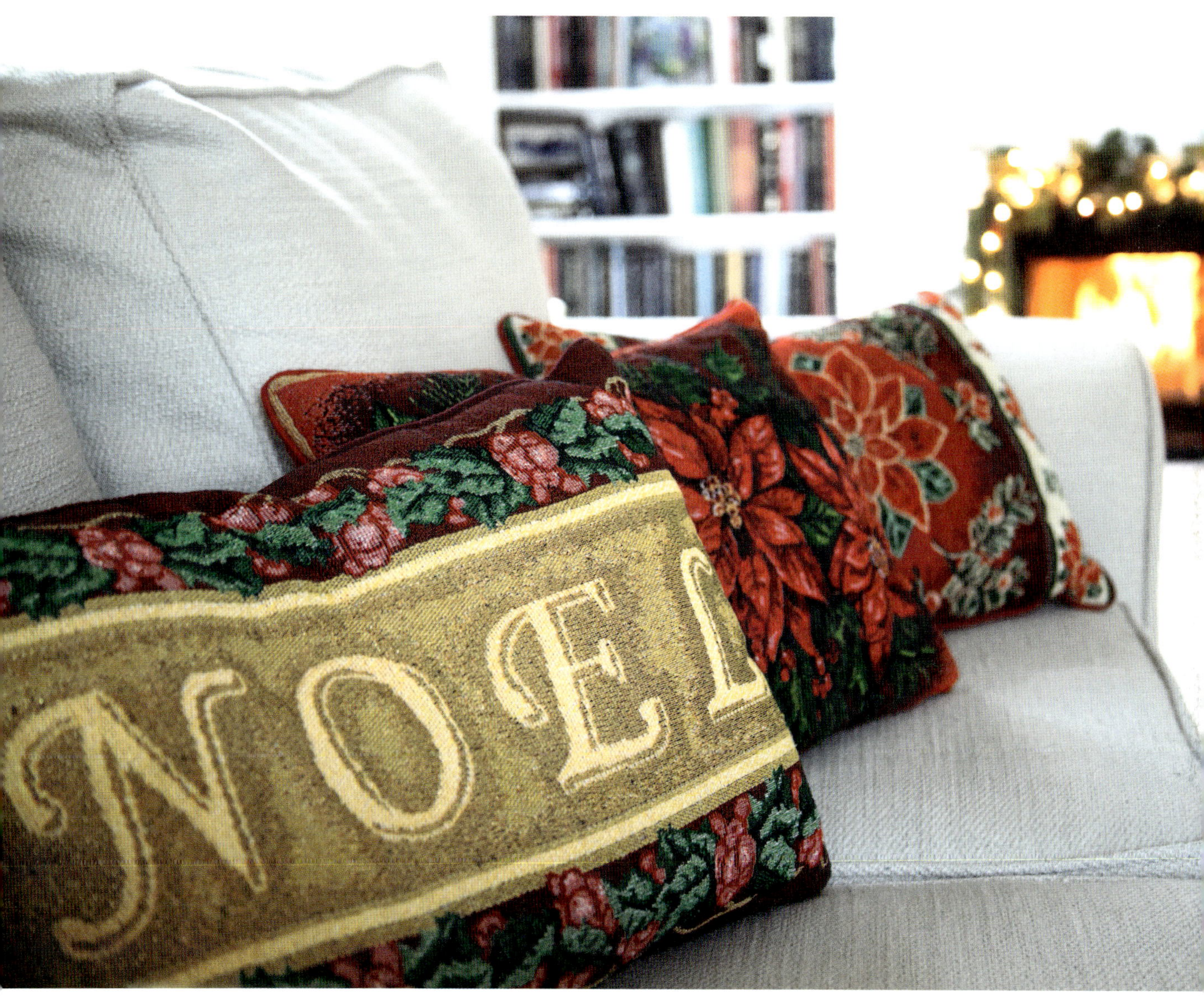
NOEL

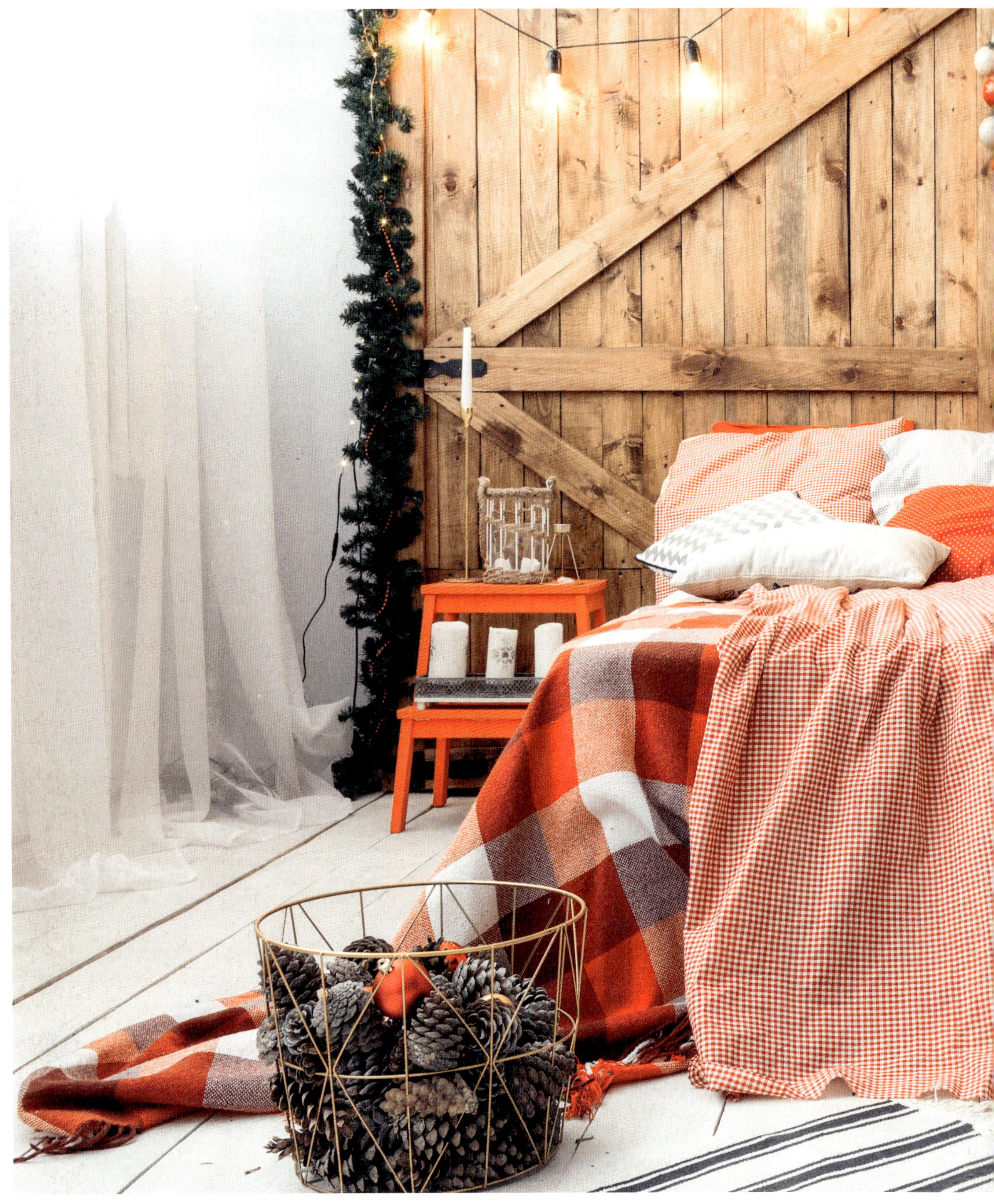

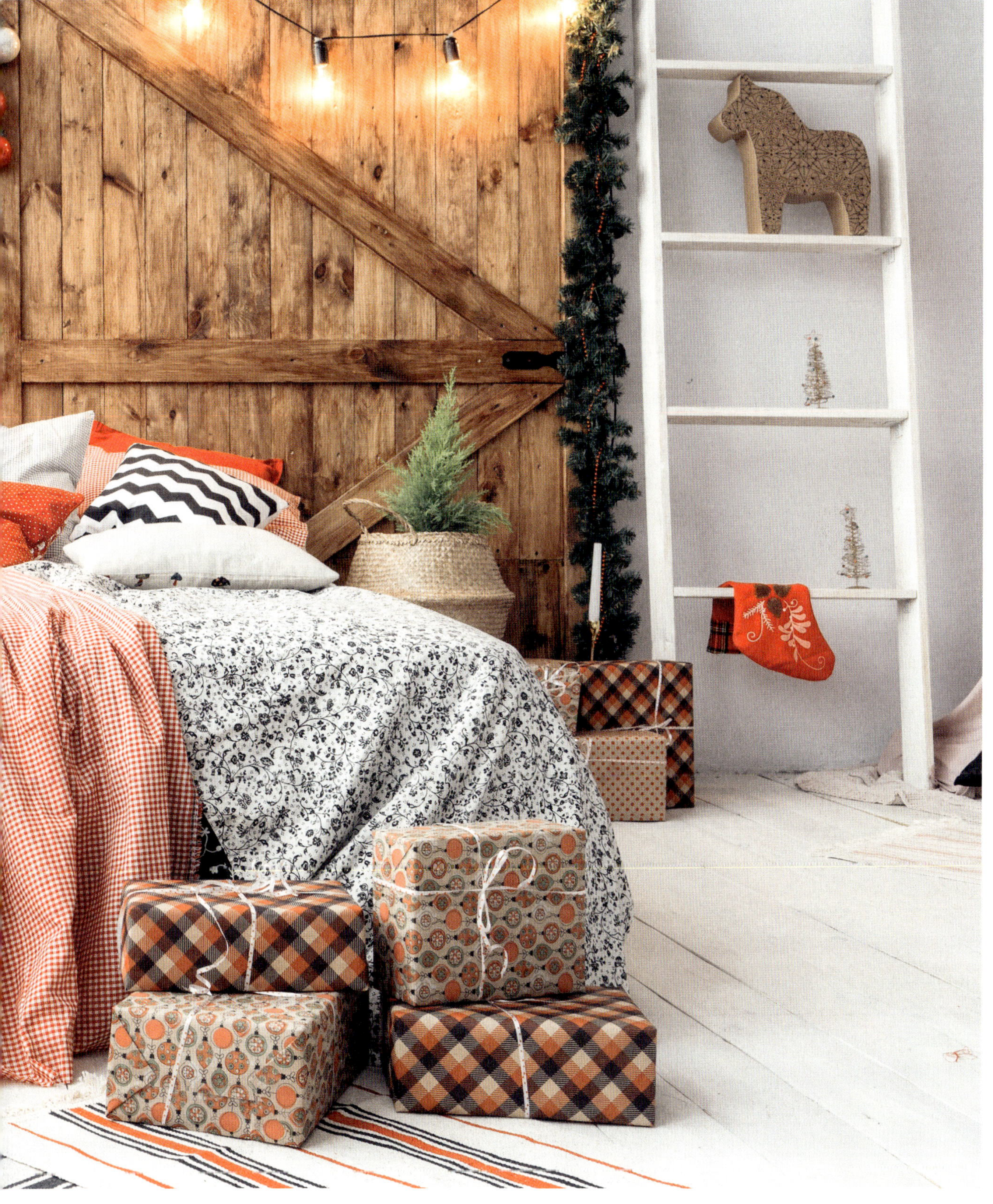

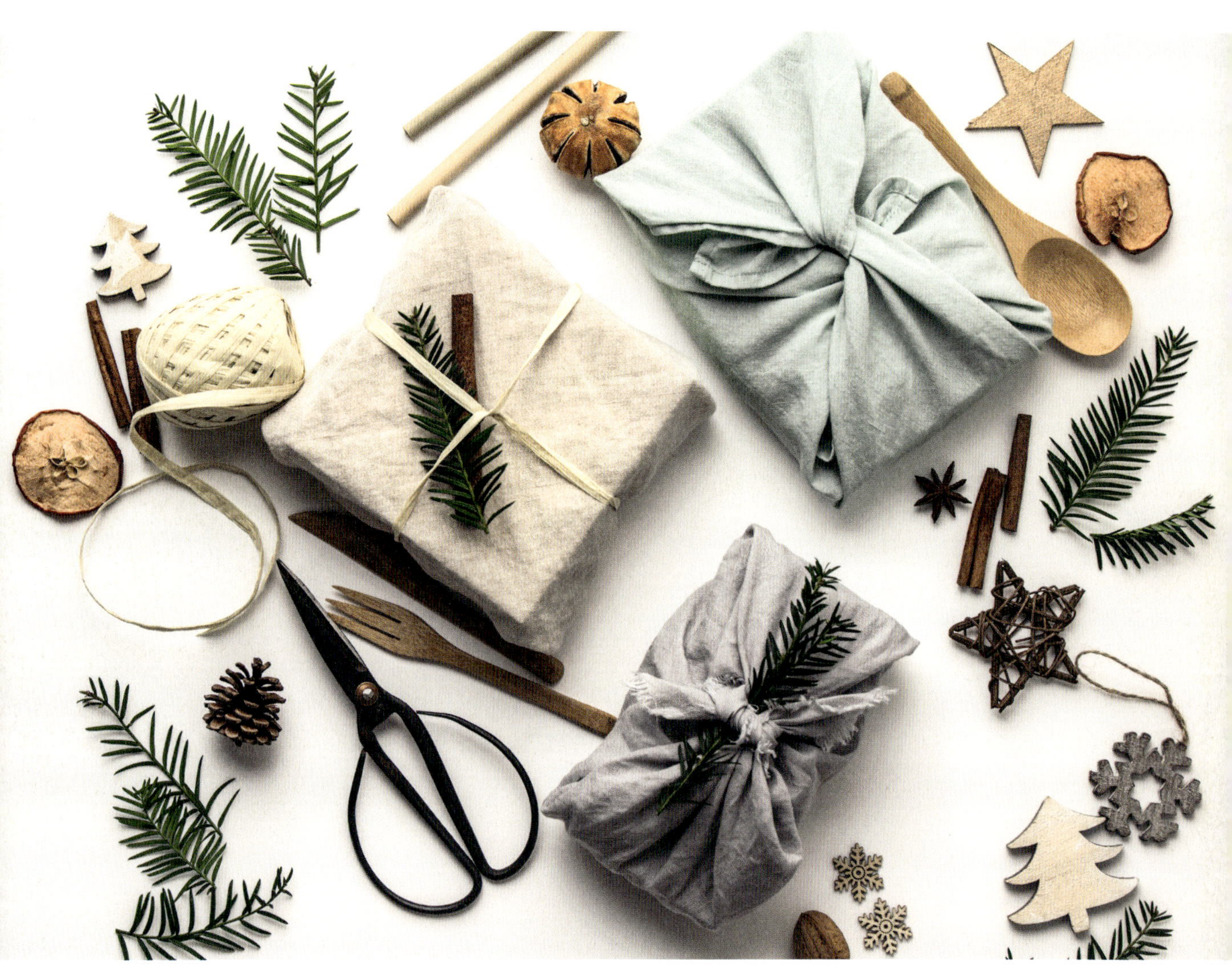

Reuse leftover scraps of fabric to make homemade stockings to hang from the mantel, or beautiful Japanese-style wrapped presents, tied at the top with a knot. A frayed hem adds to the rustic look; tuck in a sprig of rosemary or herb to complete.

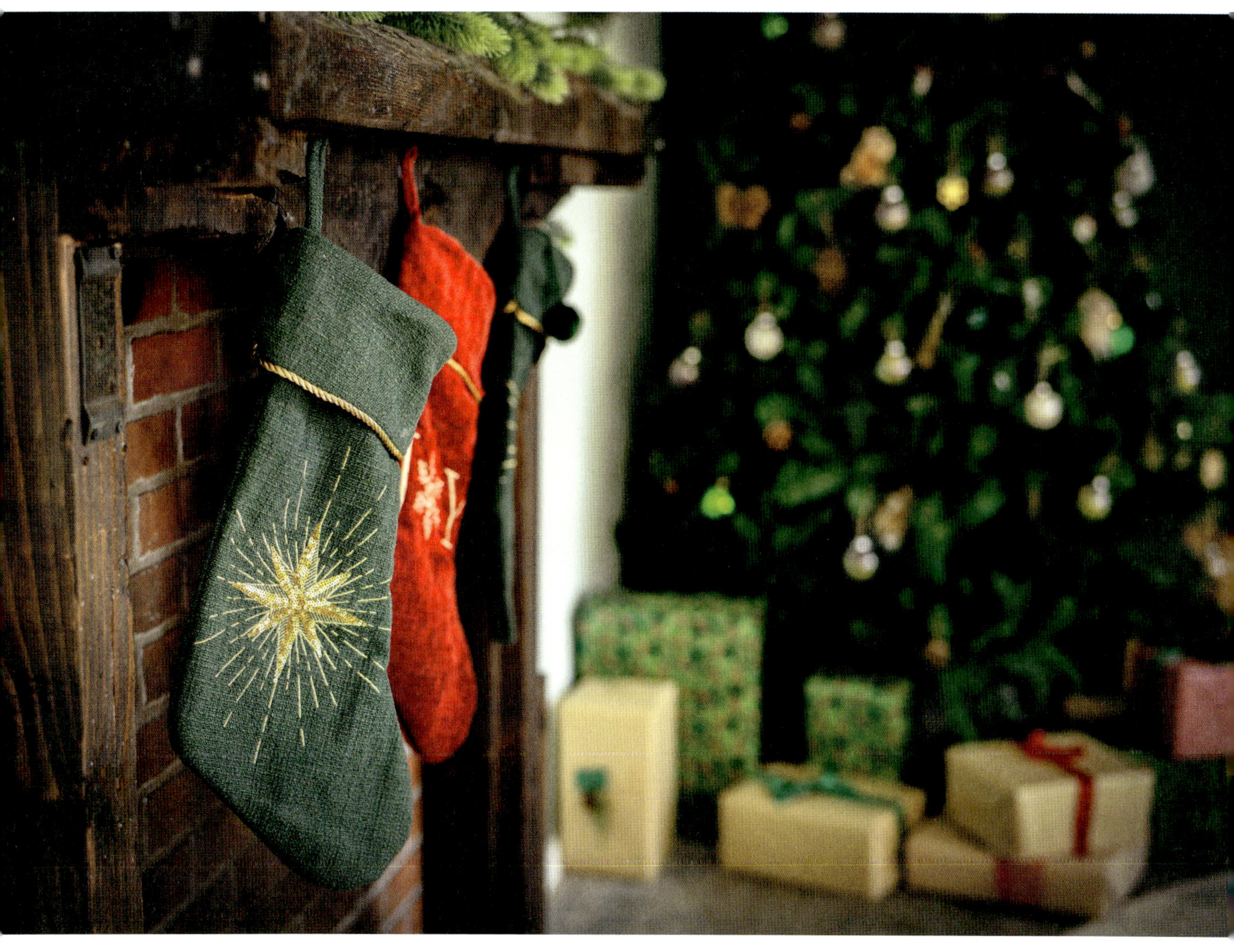

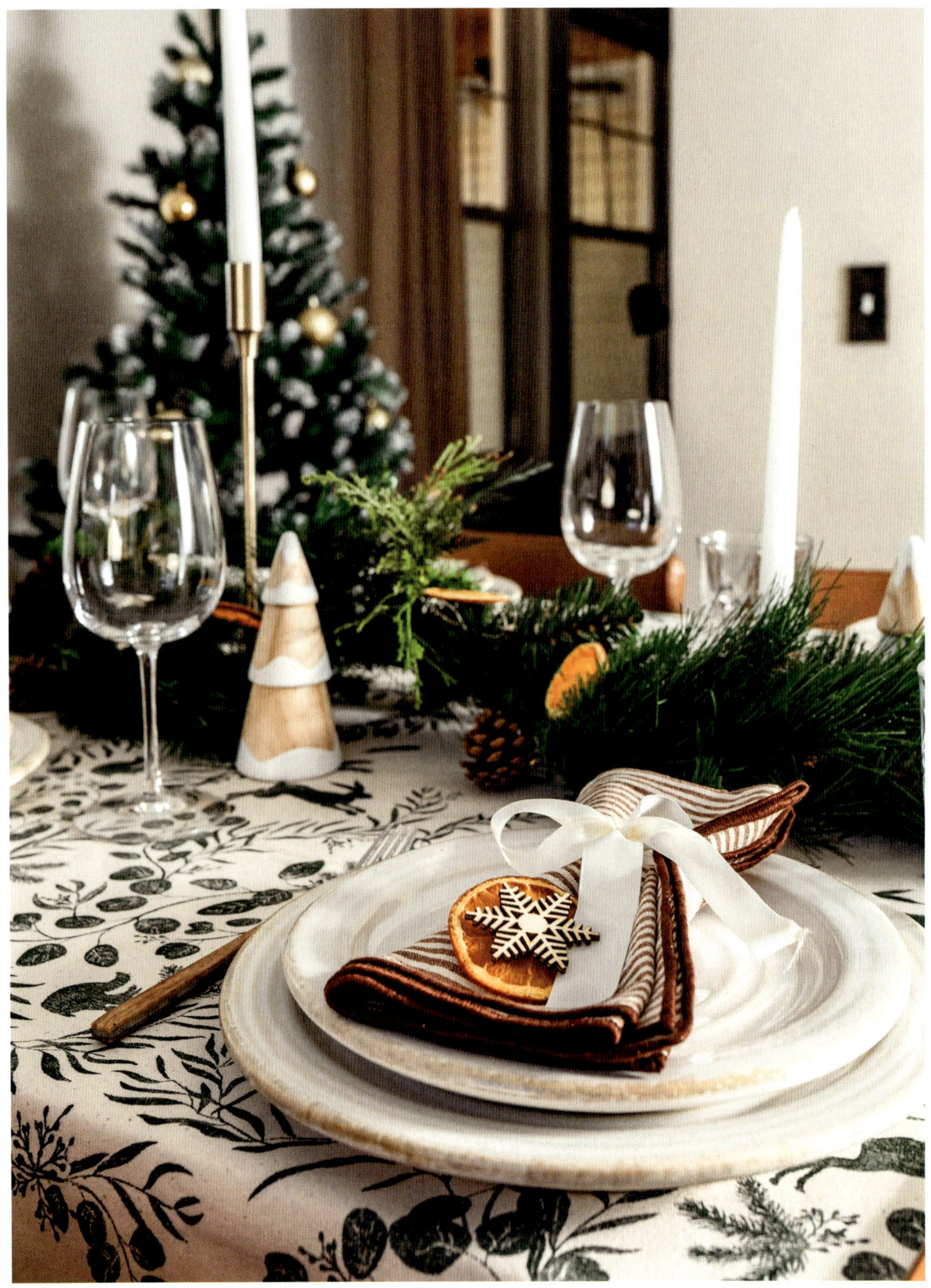

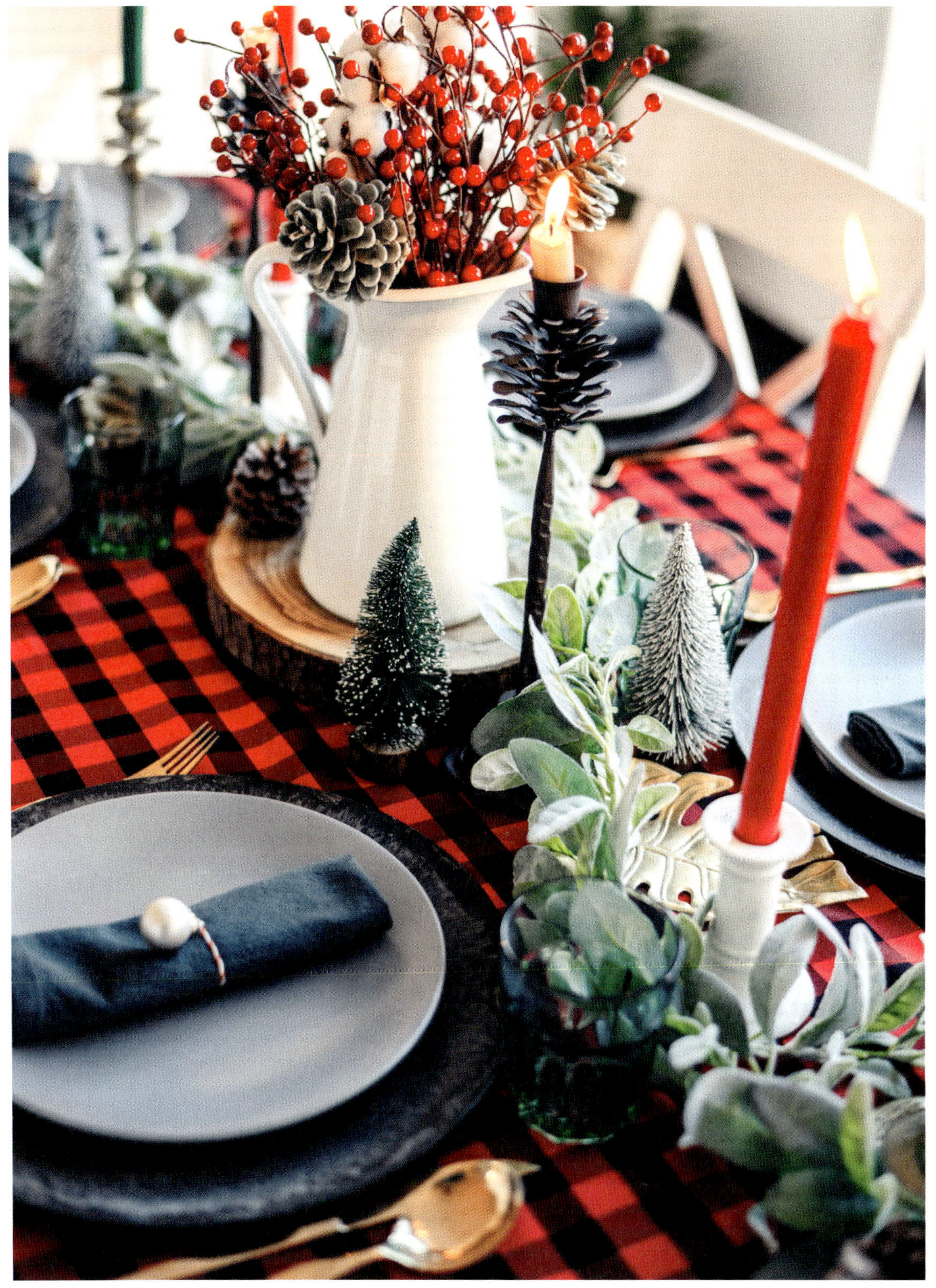

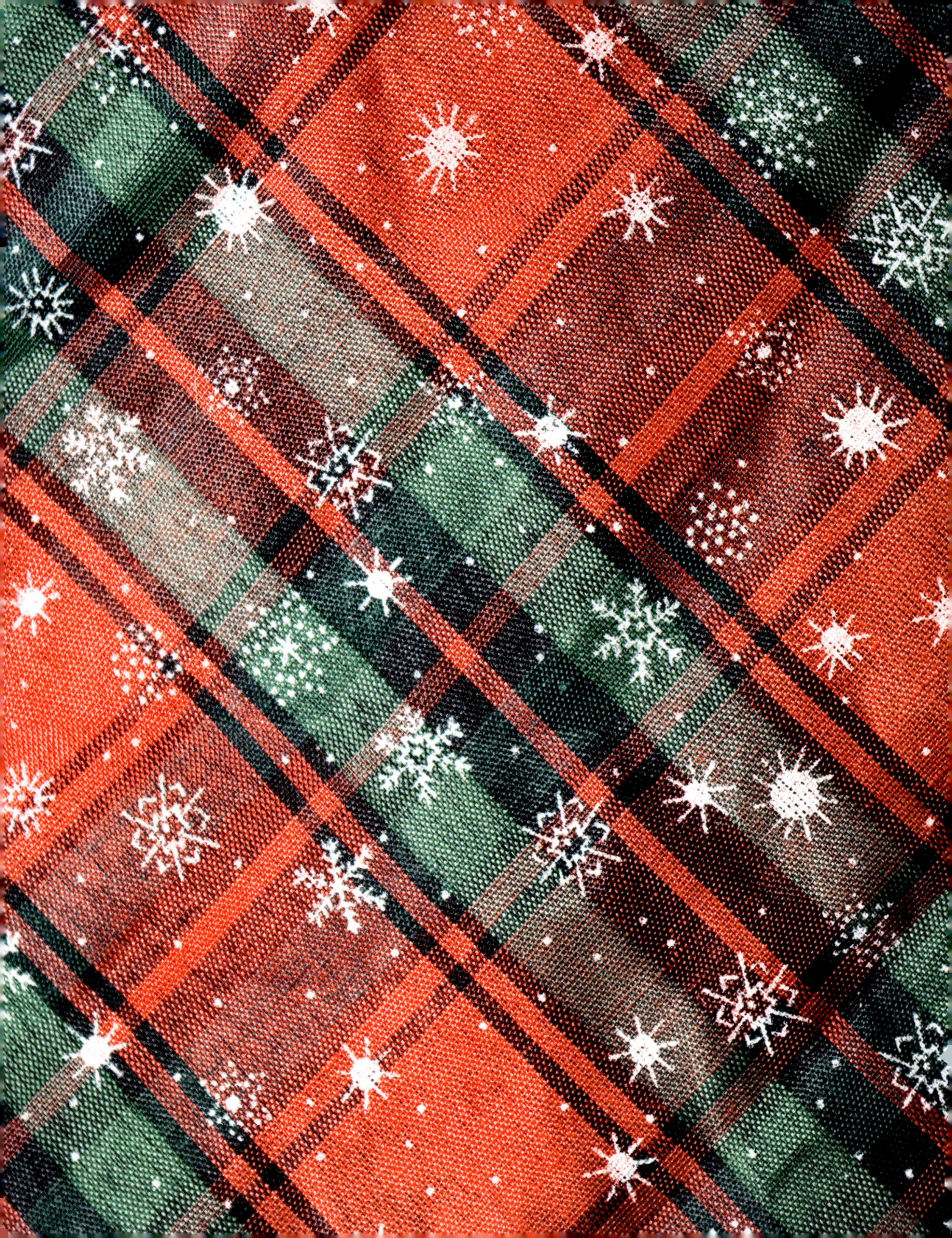

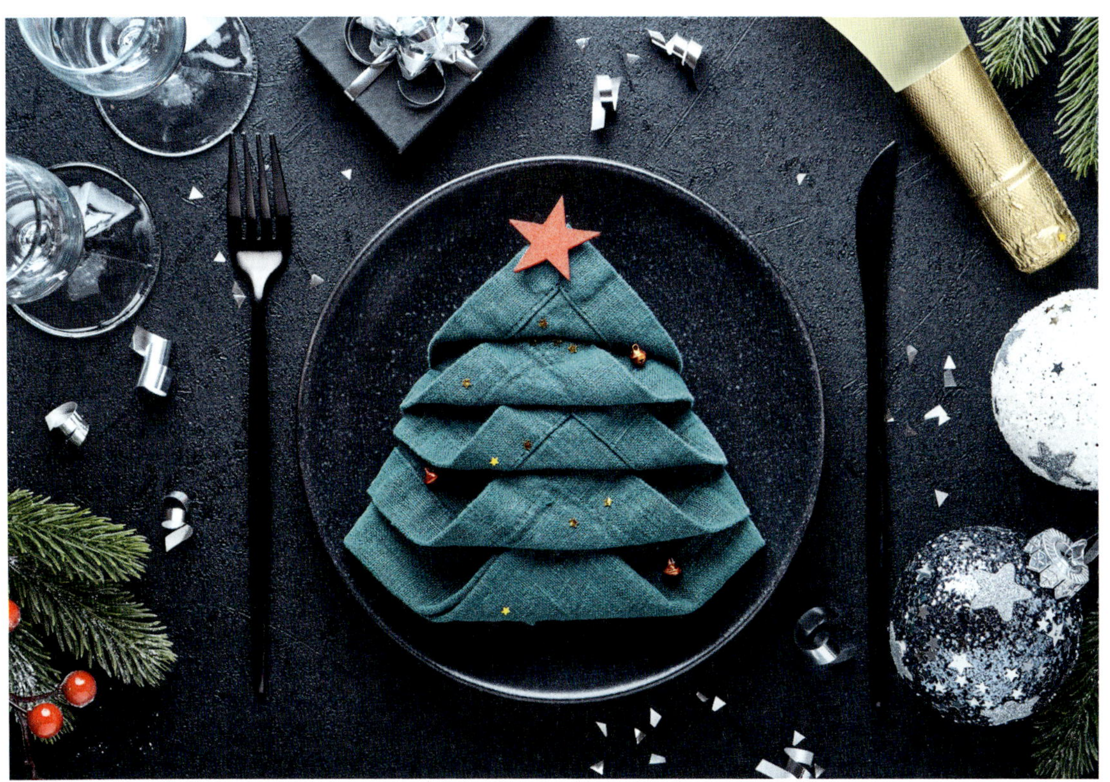

Tartan in red and green is the epitome of Christmas styling. You don't have to go with a full tablecloth. A napkin detail gives the same effect. Making the switch to linen napkins not only feels fancy—they are soft and pleasing to touch—but are also washable, so they hold up to constant use.

Deck the walls

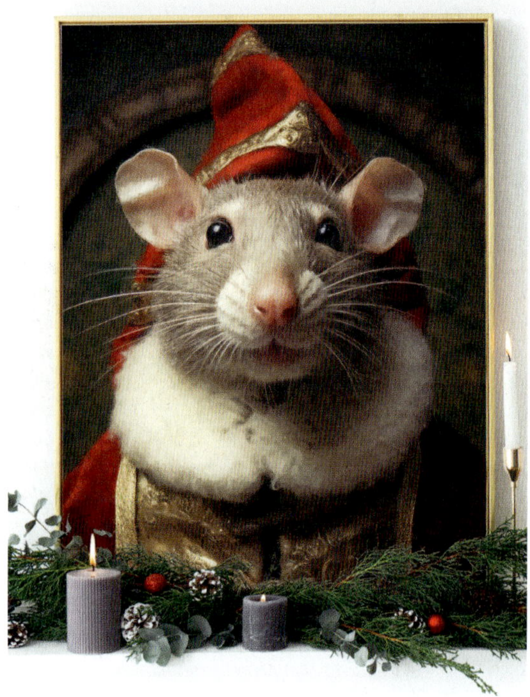

Festive wall art: Christmas Mouse poster print by *Ink & Drop*

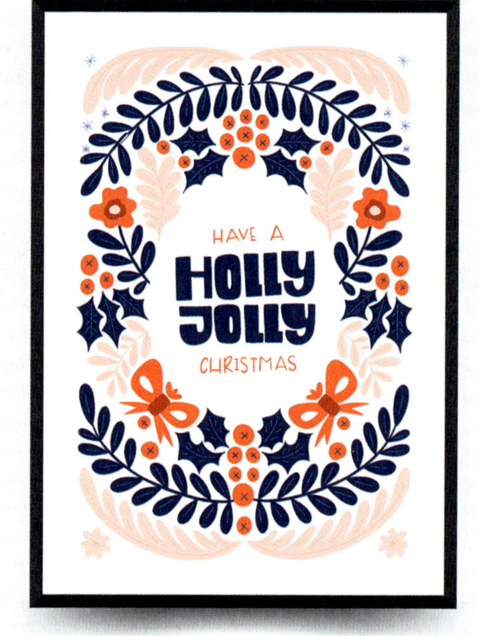

A blank wall is an opportunity to add festive personality in a room. Garlands, wreaths, and framed pictures are a final piece of eye candy that can upstage the tree.

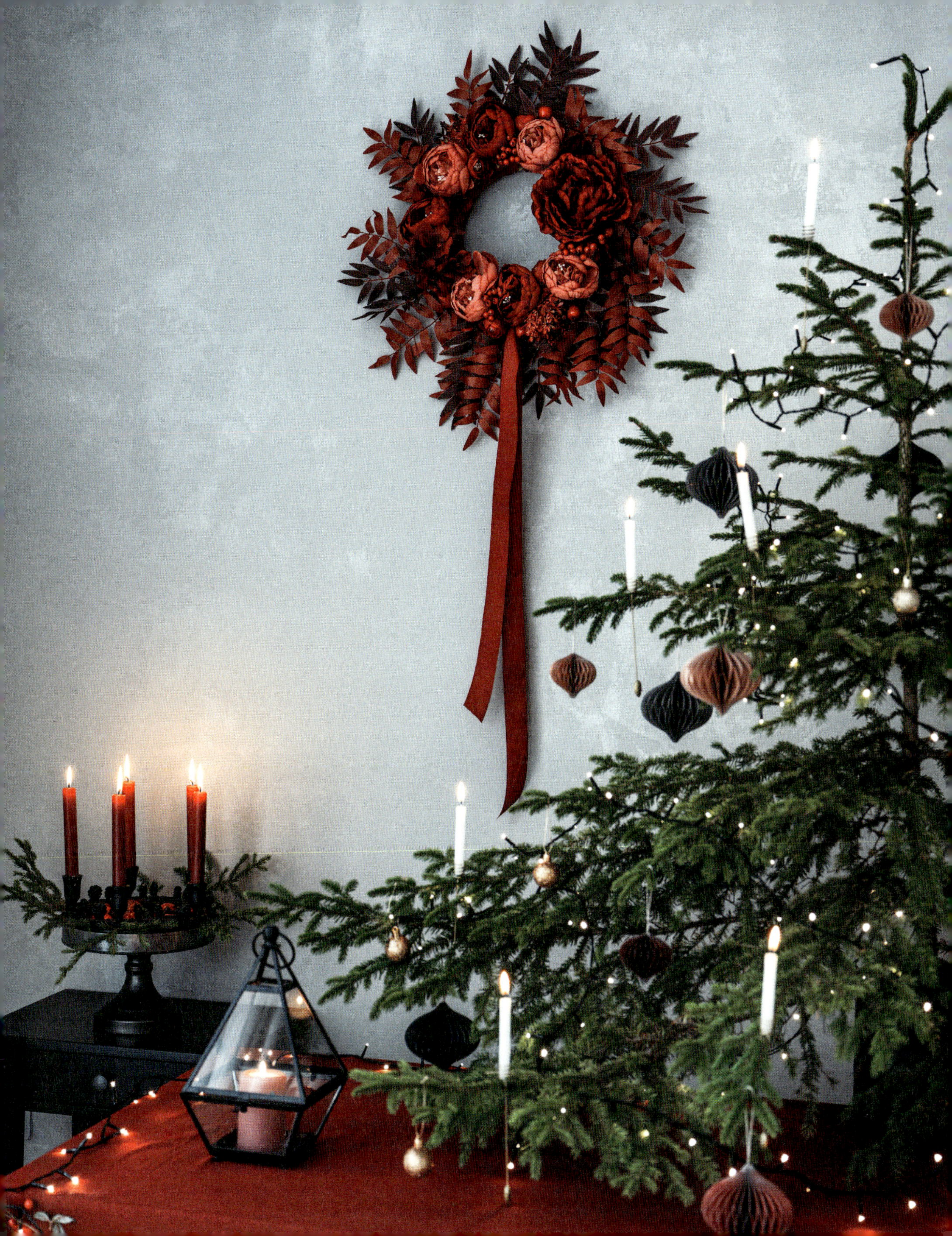

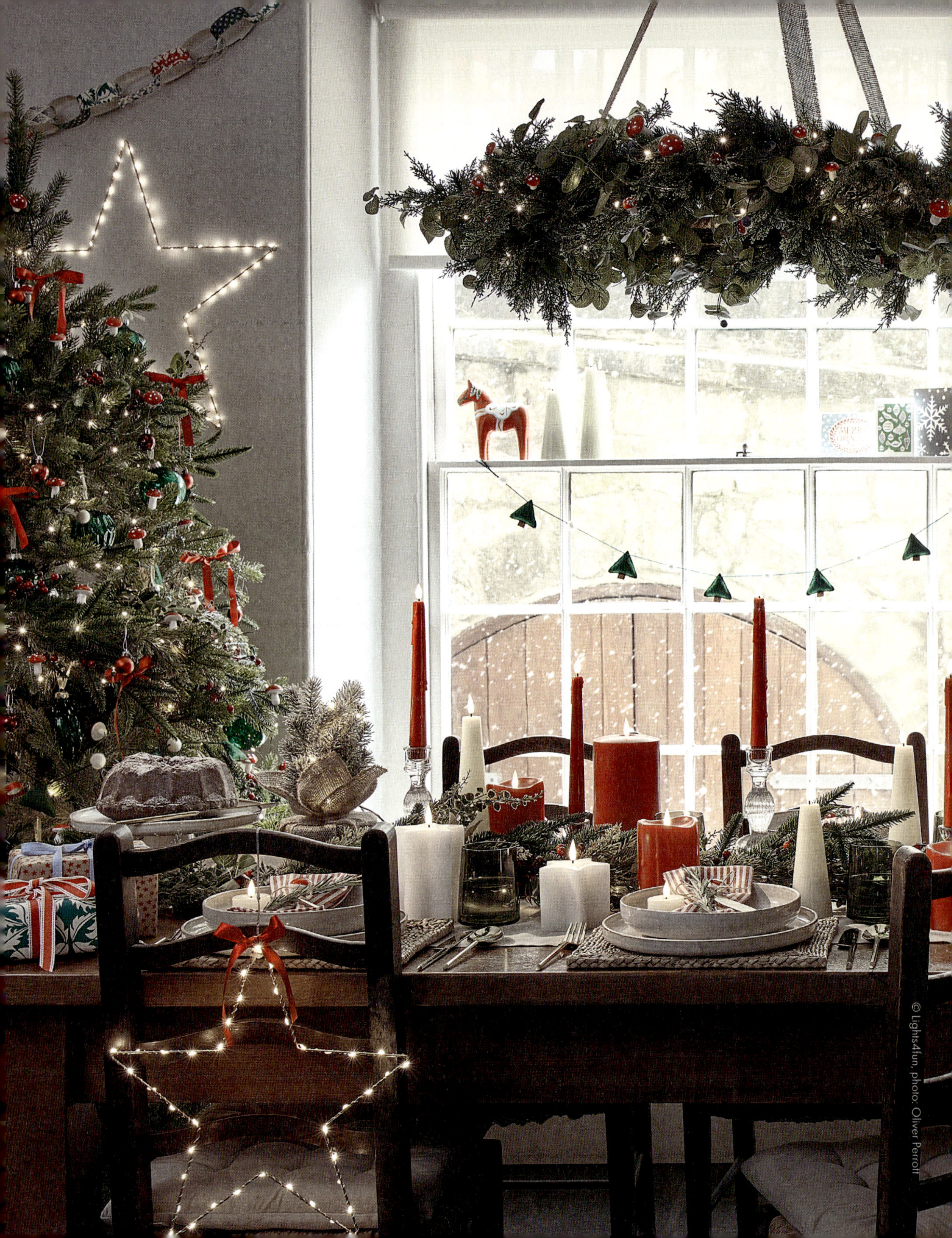

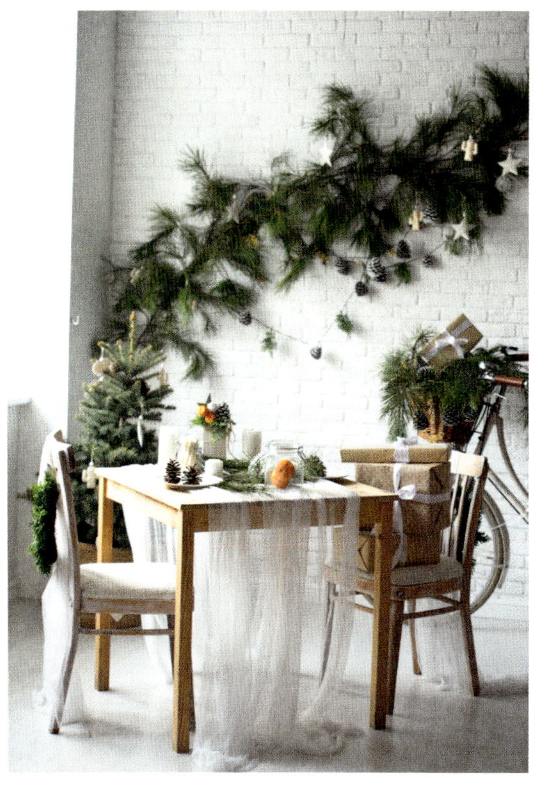

Fresh branches and garlands of pine draped over windows and mantels—and even light fixtures—will help fill a room with the scent of the season. A simple conifer branch can be used around a picture or mirror frame, or used to cover an entire wall, dotted with paper stars and silver bell garlands.

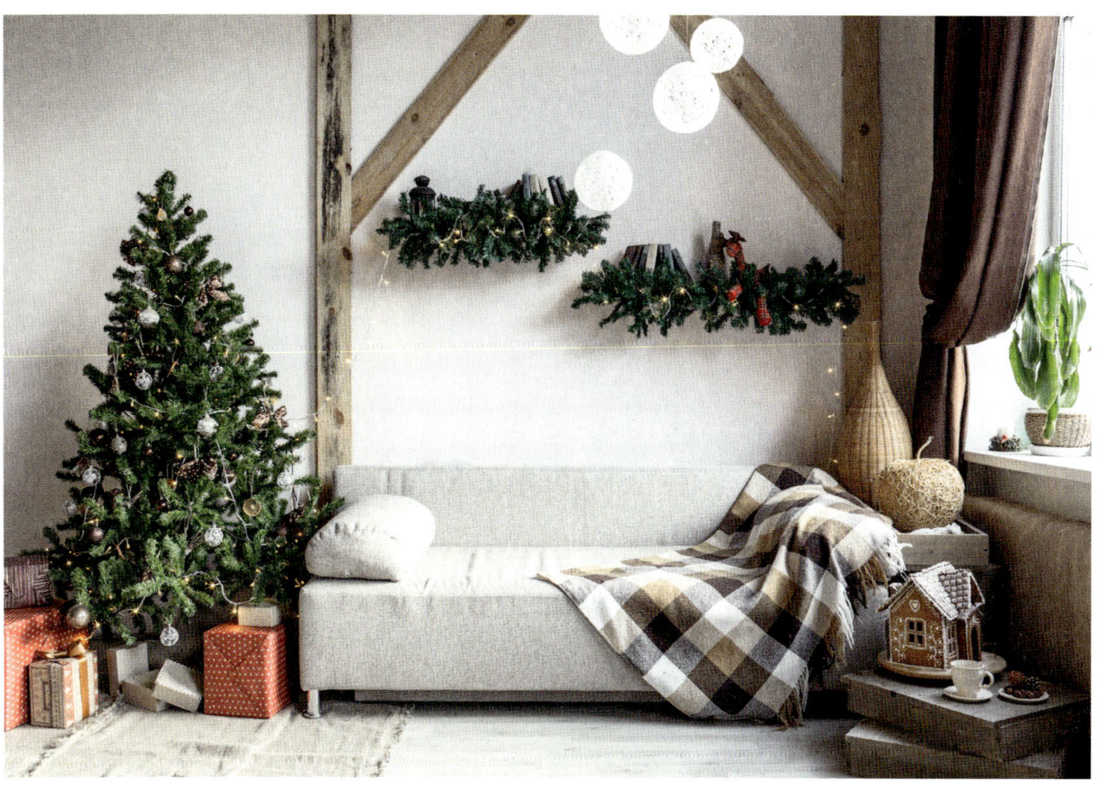

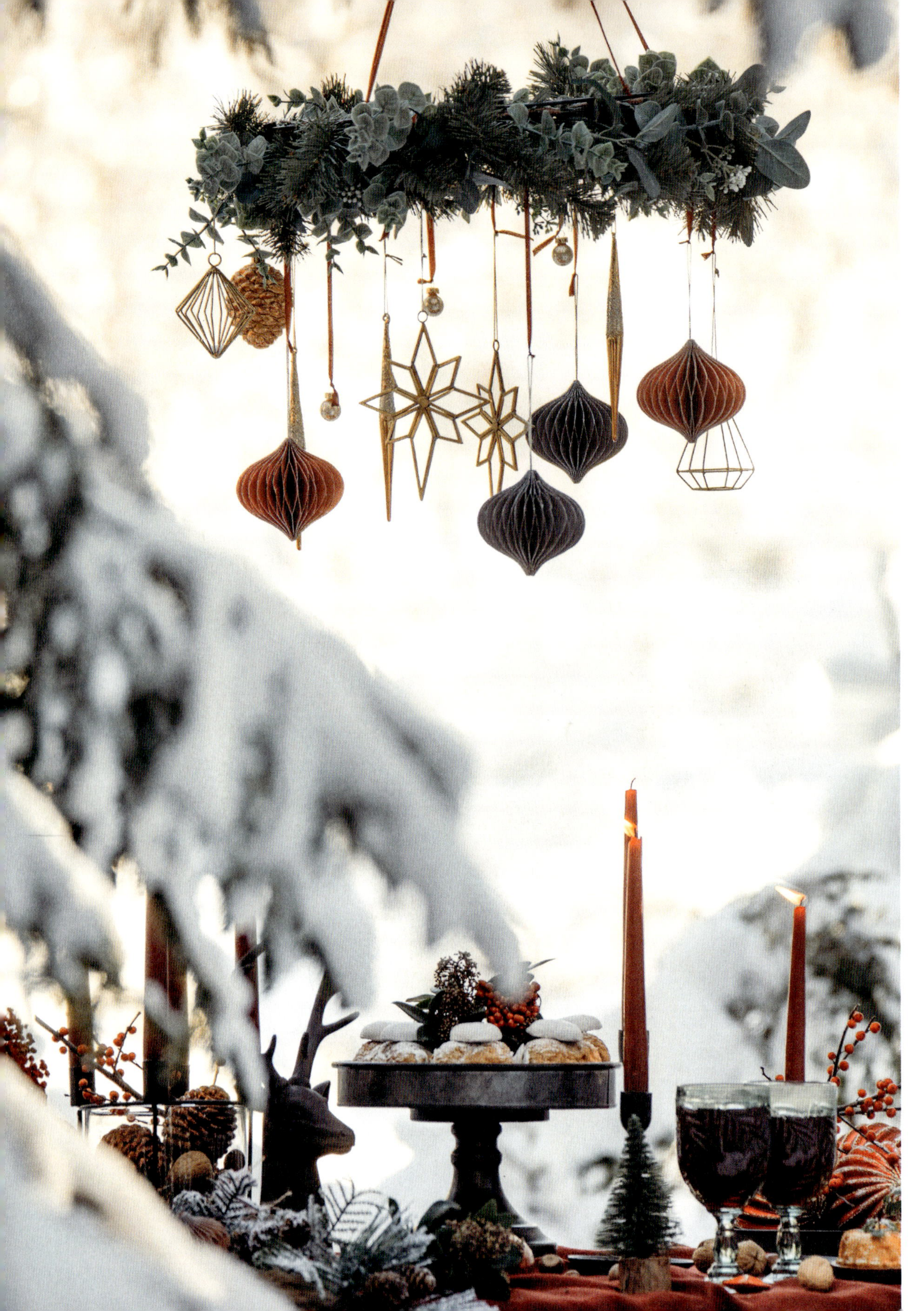

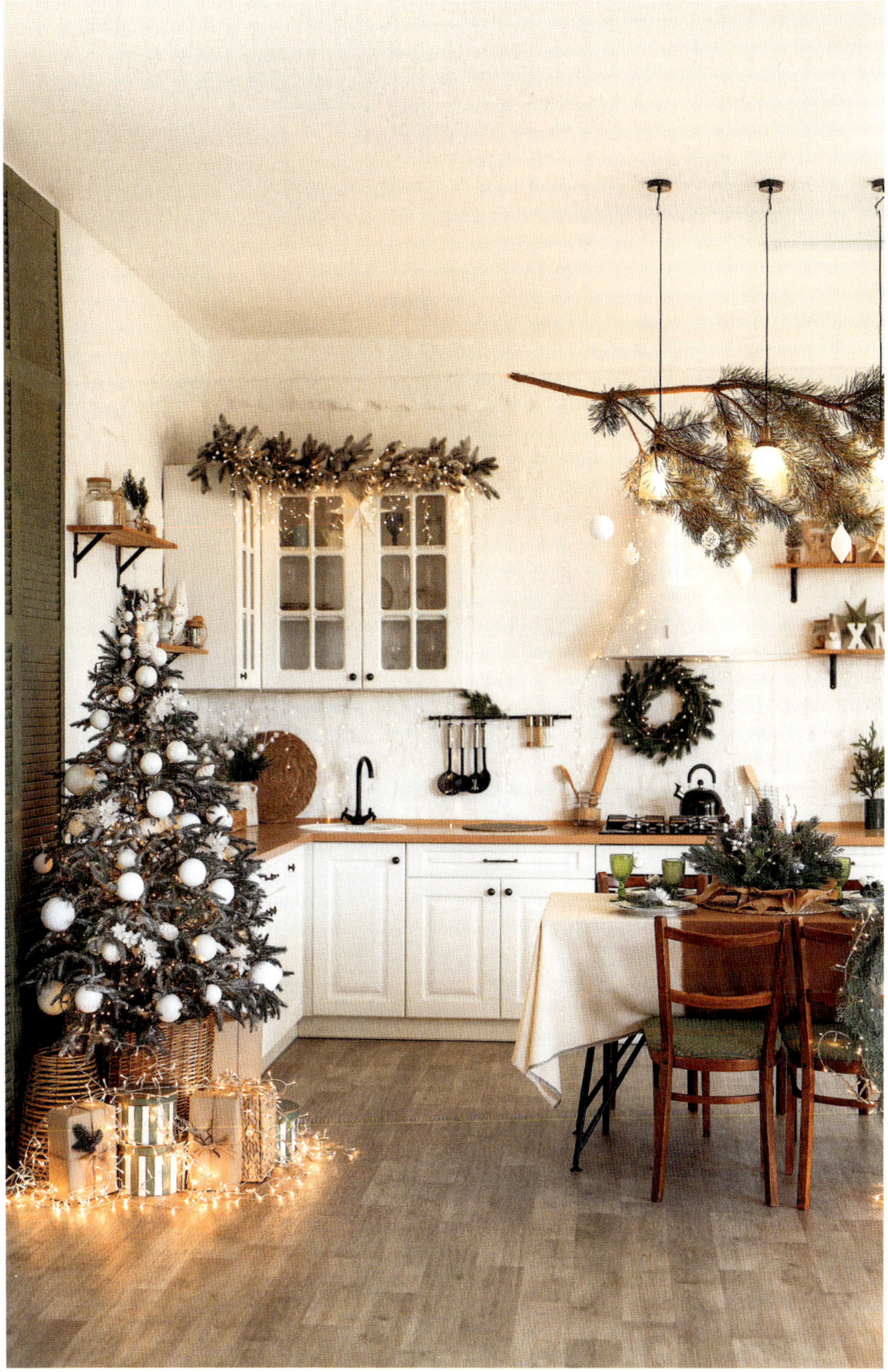

Spruce up a wire wreath or a tree branch with an assortment of baubles. Rather than hanging from the wall, hang the decorative pendant from the ceiling instead.

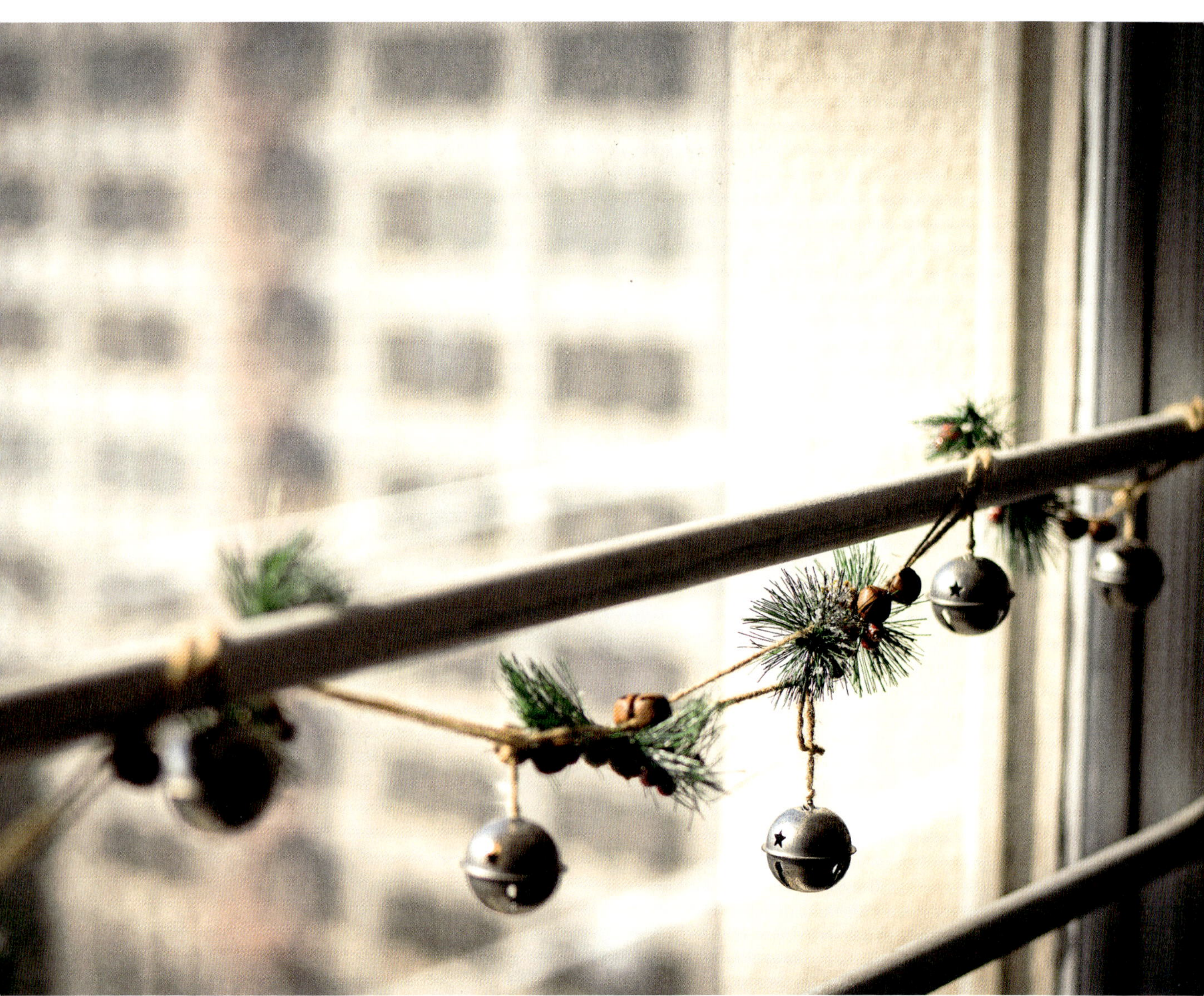

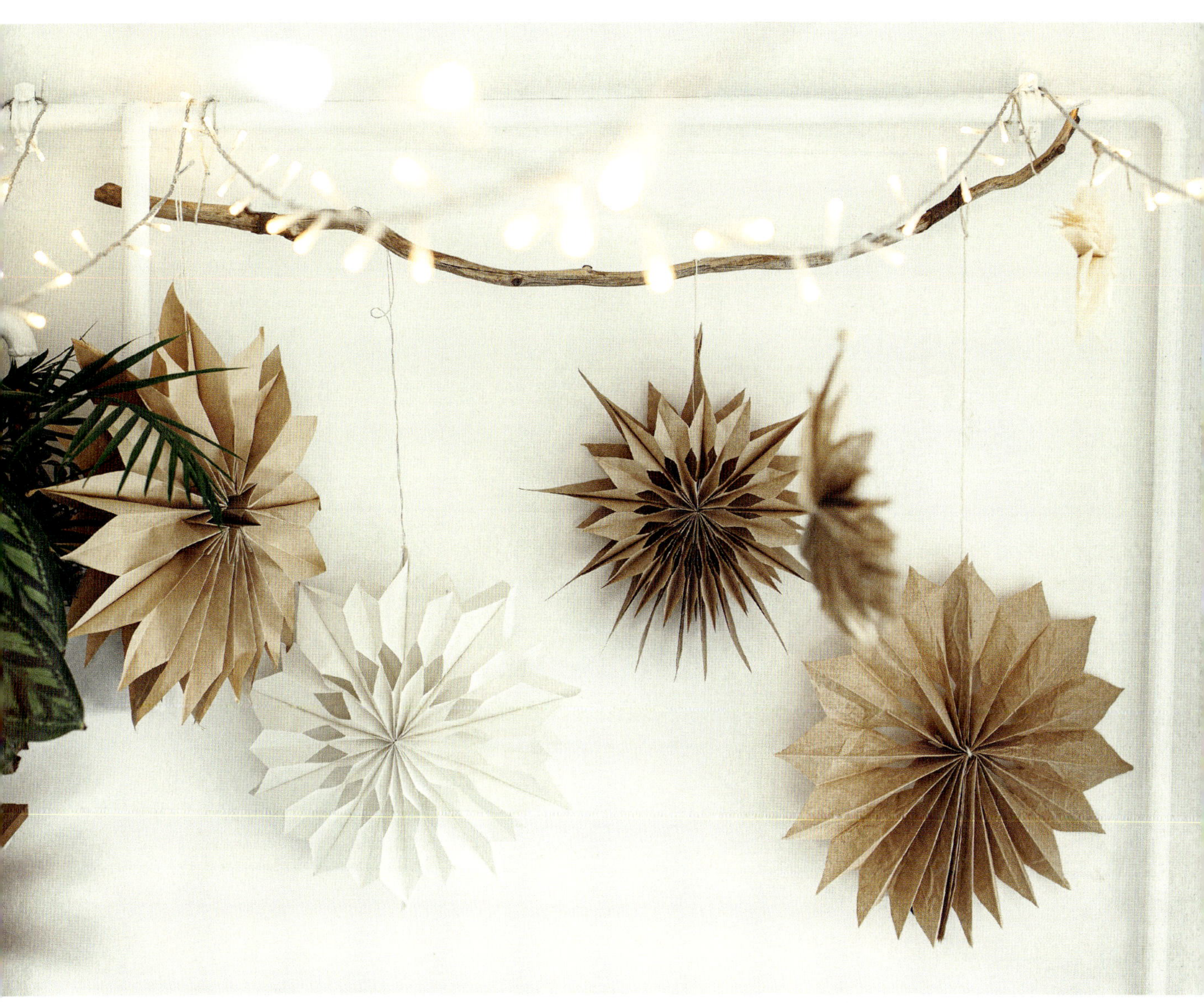

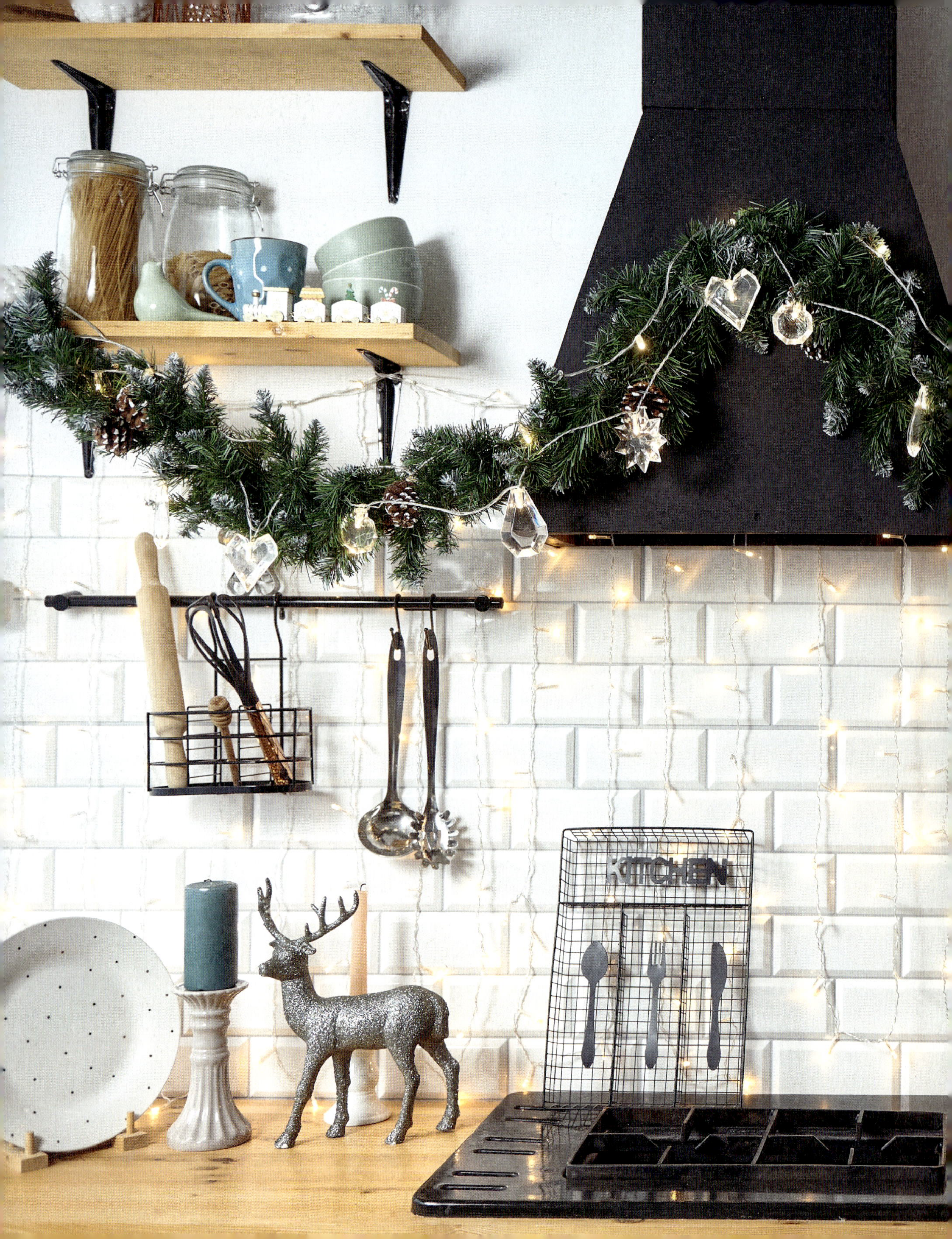
KITCHEN

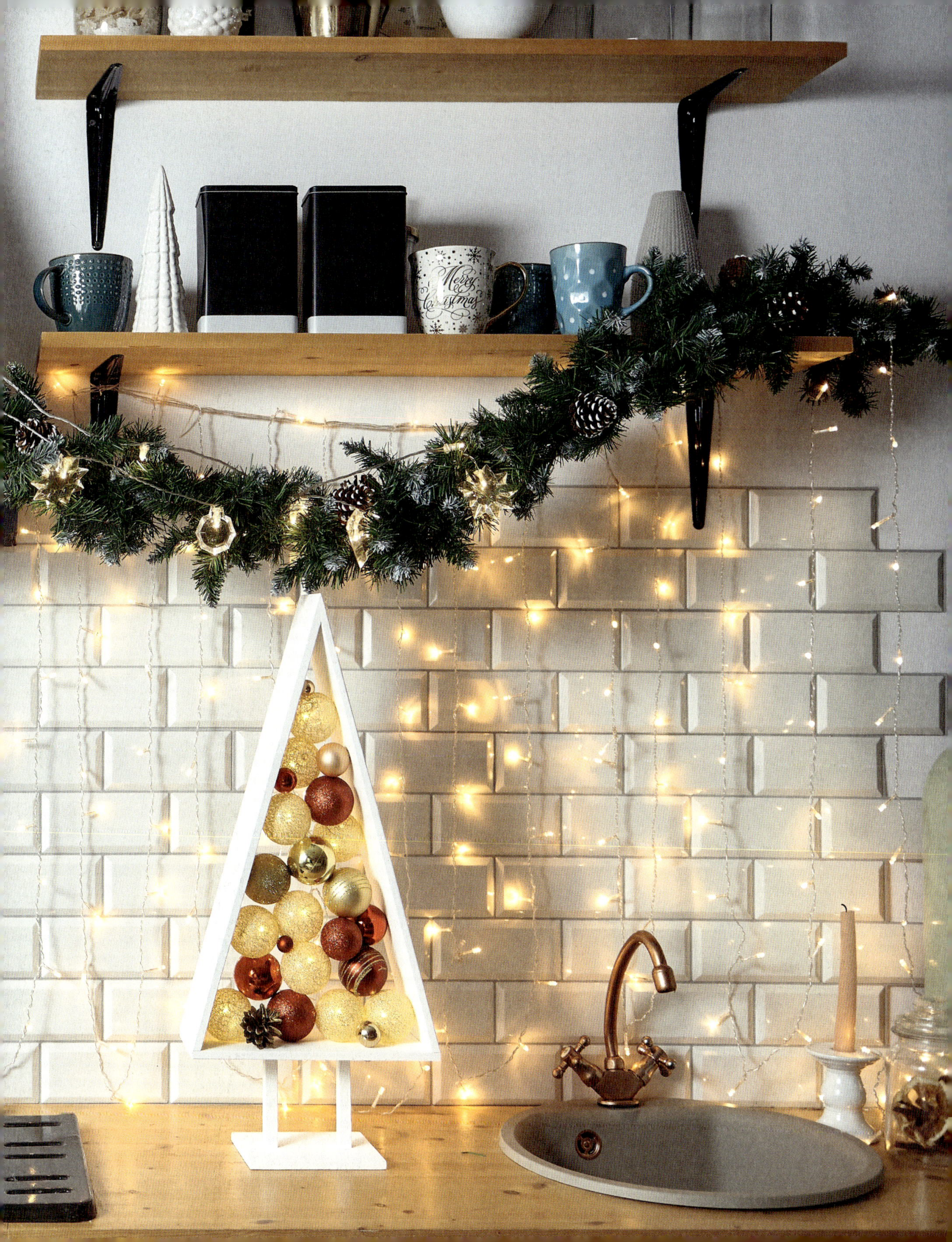
Merry Christmas

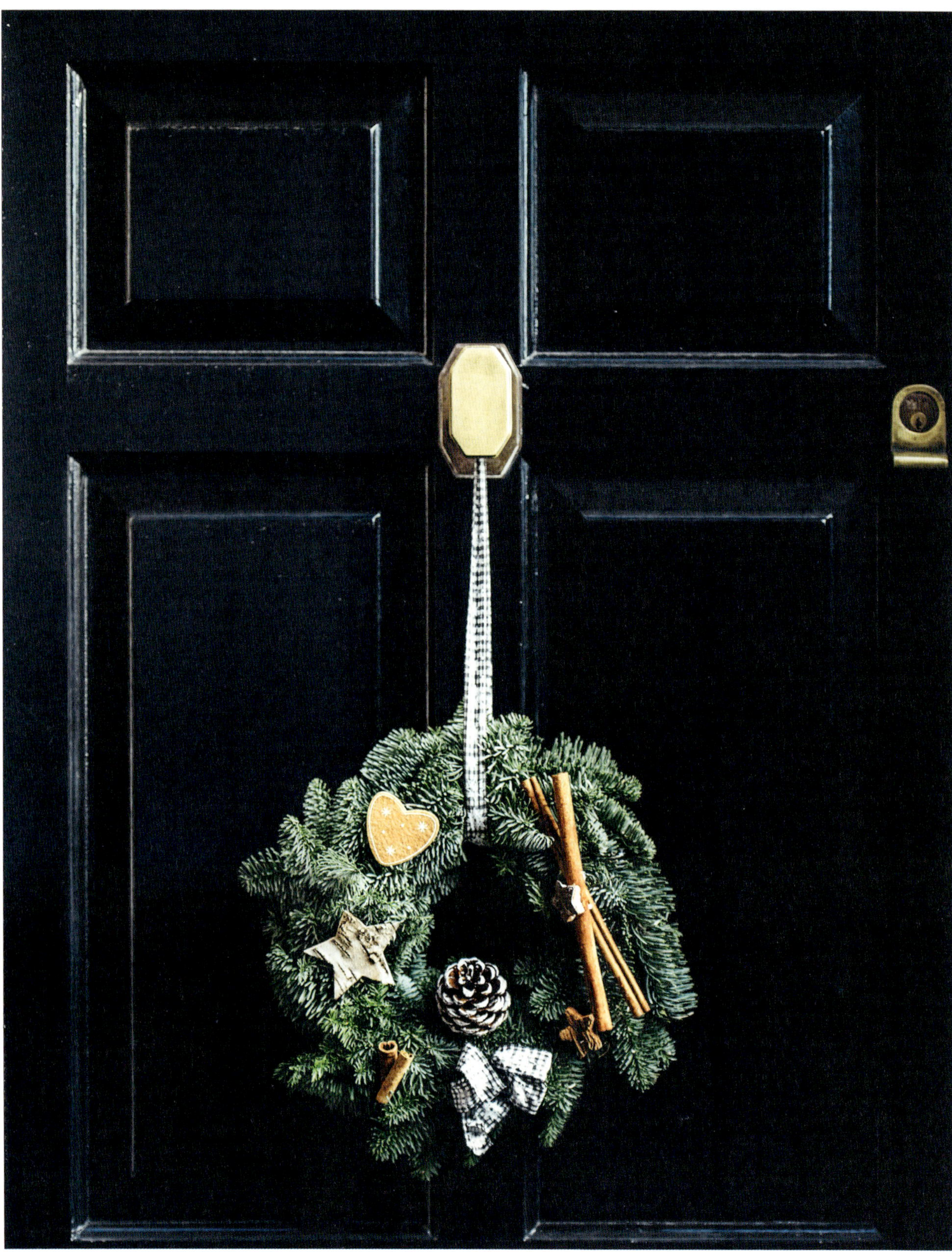

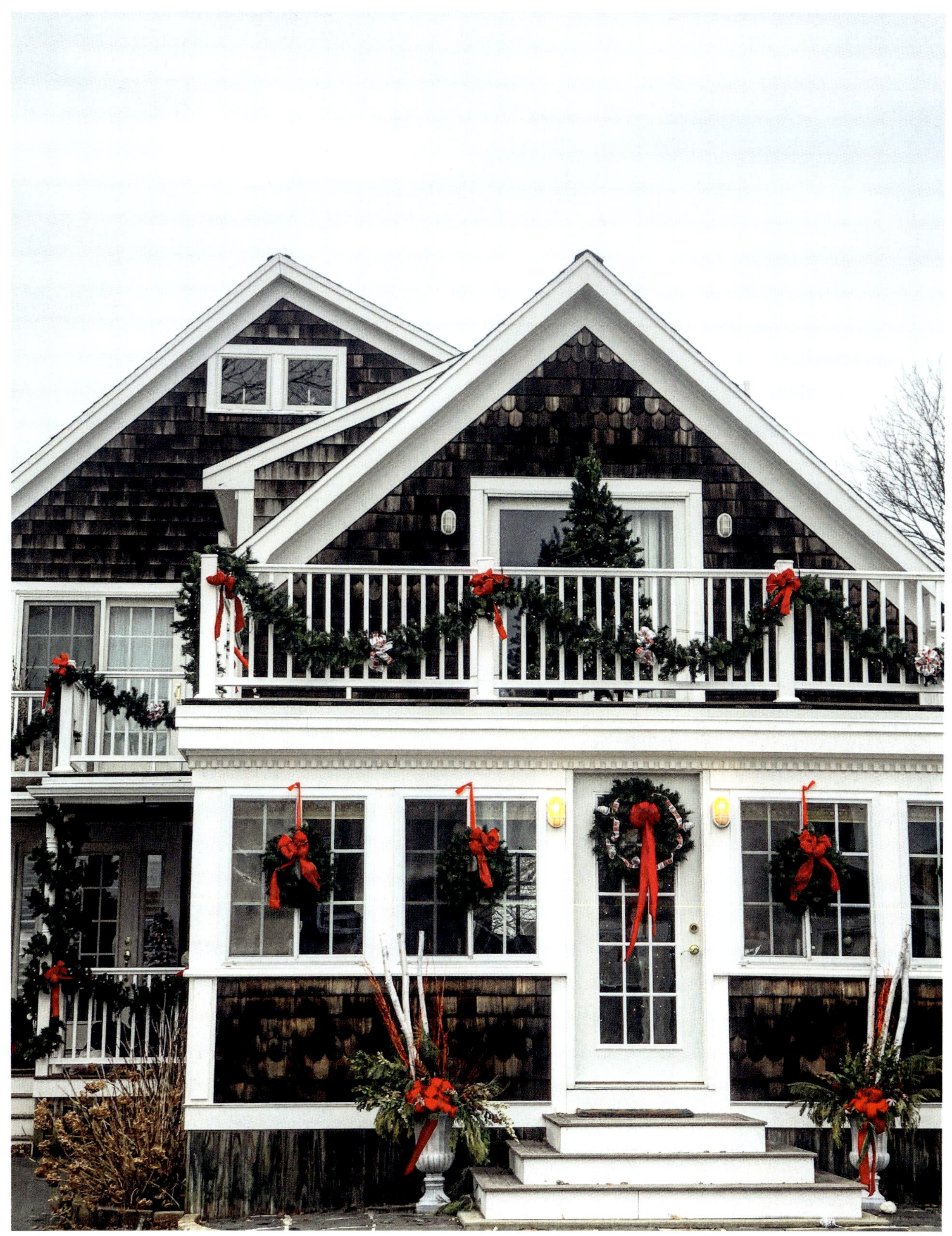

FEATURE

BOLD CHRISTMAS SPIRIT

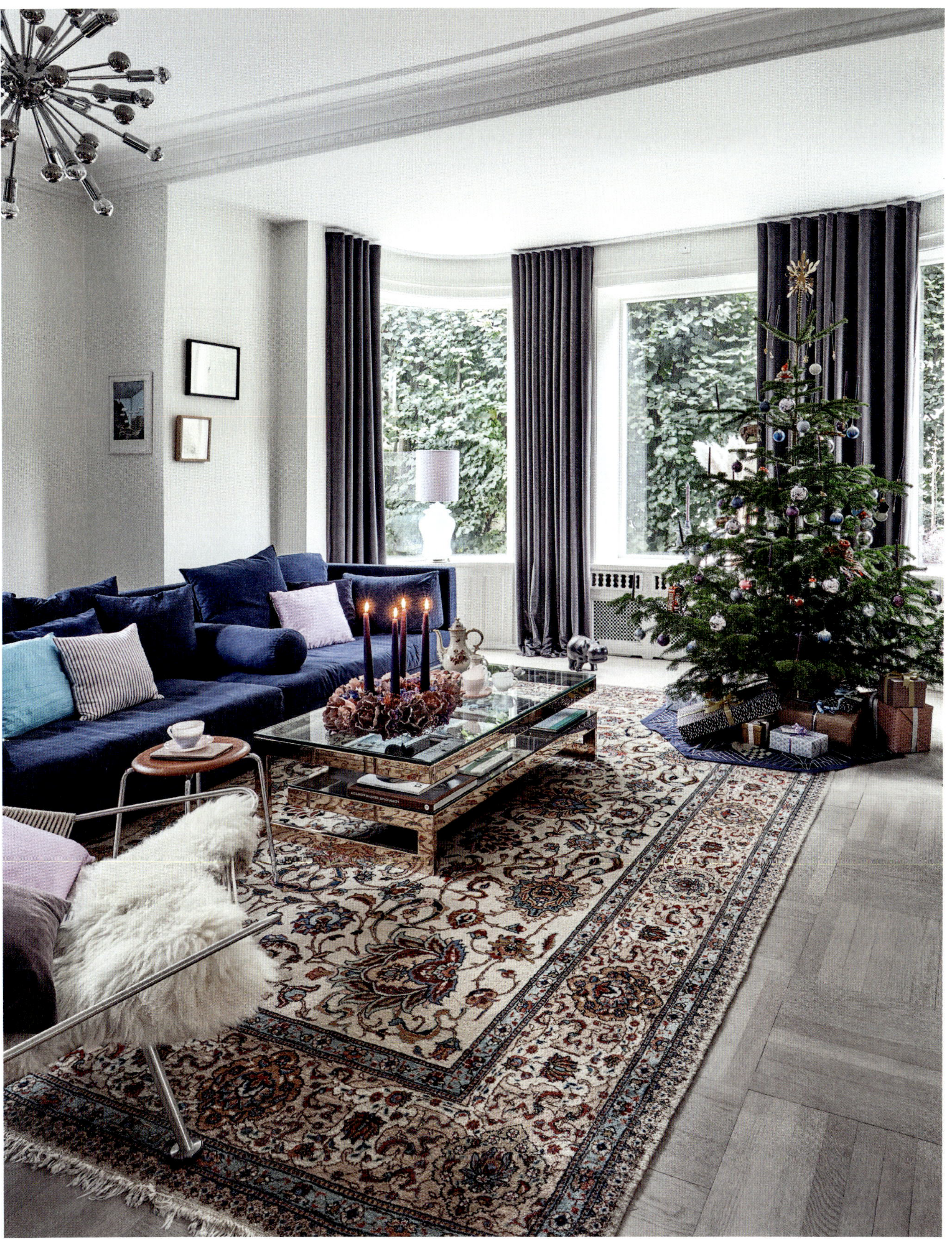

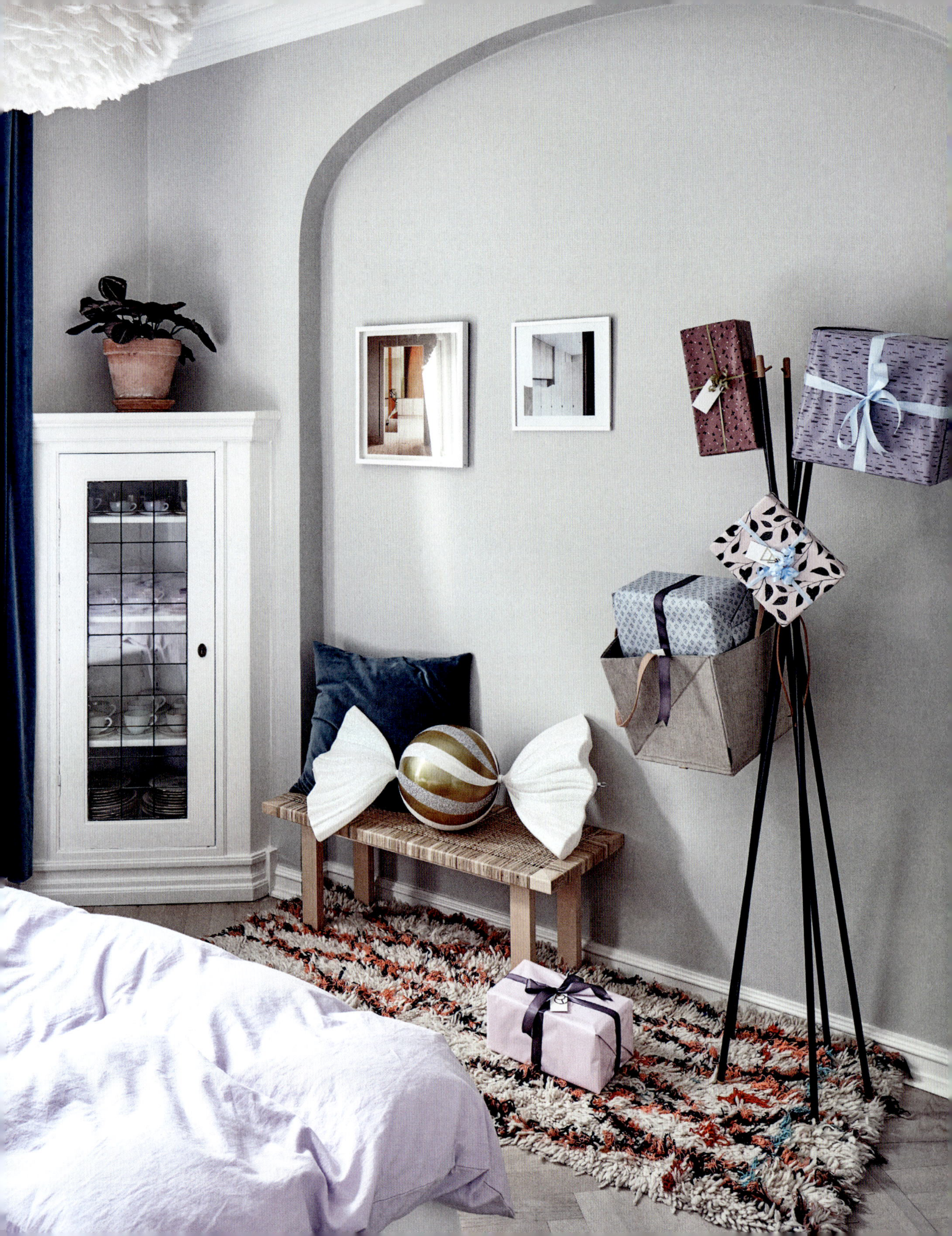

Cathrine has created an advent calendar with large presents hung on a coat rack.

A Fairy-tale Christmas

Christmas with Cathrine and Anders de Lichtenberg will likely remind you of your childhood dream Christmas. "I love the beautiful and traditional about Christmas, but it has to be lively, dynamic, and with a touch of humor," Cathrine summarizes her approach to Christmas decorating, as she hangs yet another glass zebra on the tree. "To me it has to be extravagant, and full of surprises, but at the same time, there should be room for change, and renewal, new decorations and new traditions."

The 1898 home, with its old marble sills, original built-in corner cabinets, stucco, high paneling, and parquet flooring, calls for with the playful use of classical elements, according to Cathrine. She continues: "We spent time stationed in Africa, and I incorporate a lot of African frivolity and joy in decoration within our Danish home. Christmas is my favorite time of the year, where it is possible to be bold, but also have room to add something childish and fairy-tale like." Cathrine's Christmases have always had a special touch. In particular, Christmas at her grandmother's made an indelible impression on Cathrine that still colors her view of how Christmas should be—not in terms of a precise look, necessarily, but more in the level of extravagance required "Christmas at my grandmother's with the whole family has, over the years, involved more than 500 Christmas gnomes and an overwhelming amount of Christmas decorations. Though my taste is different today, and Christmas gnomes are not part of my adult universe, that childish feeling of overabundance, particularly the idea that anything goes, has become part of my Christmas spirit."

The rooms within Catherine's and Anders apartment have been decorated in a way that allows design classics, complementary colors on the walls, pieces of art, and spectacular lighting to harmonize, creating a unique atmosphere. At Christmas, a spectacularly set dining table, a blue and violet color scheme, and oversize bonbons and caramels, together with pine garlands in the windows, create a magical and positively overwhelming mood.

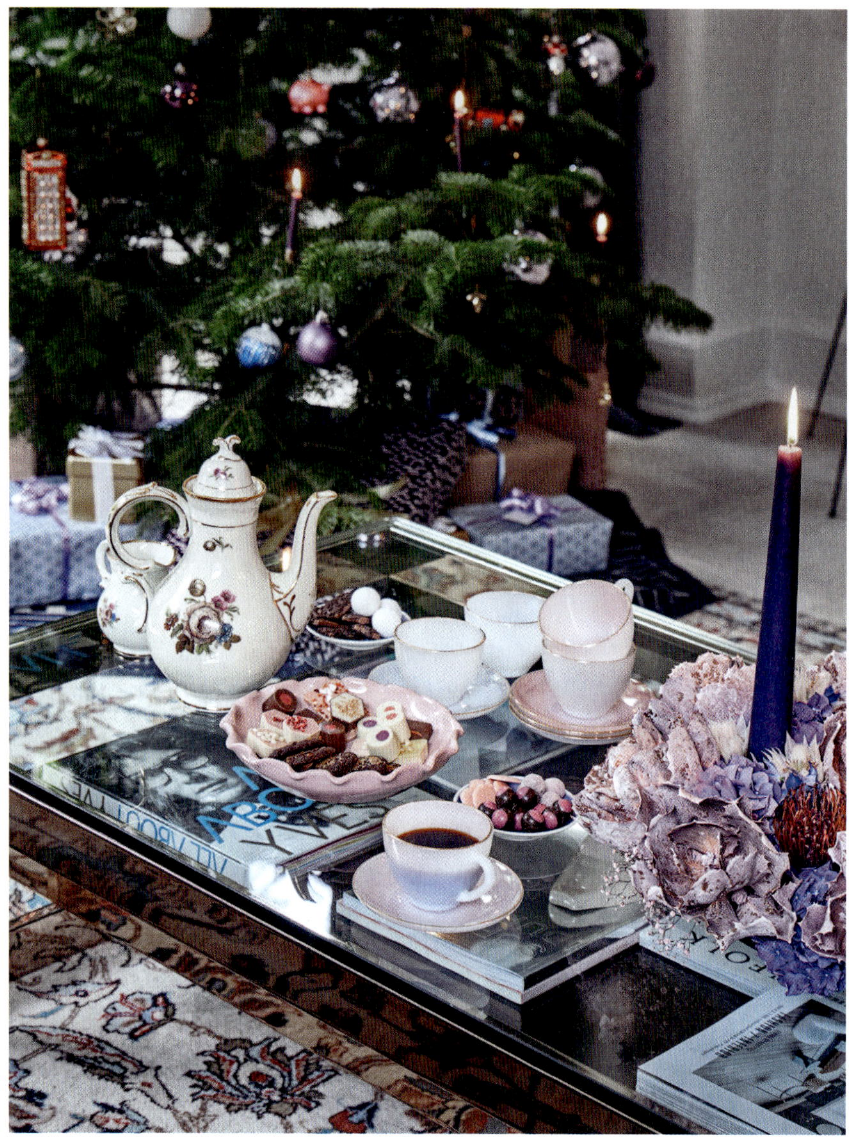

TRADITIONS

Traditions are important to Cathrine, especially when it comes to baking: "As children, we were all invited to bake Christmas cookies together with my grandmother. My grandfather was a baker, and this was our special tradition at Christmas. It was a wonderful day, and somehow my grandmother mastered the whole process with children and baking, so everything turned out delicious. When I want to bake for Christmas today, it has nothing to do with being a housewife, but more with receating something where wild and unfettered childhood joy was the most important order of the day."

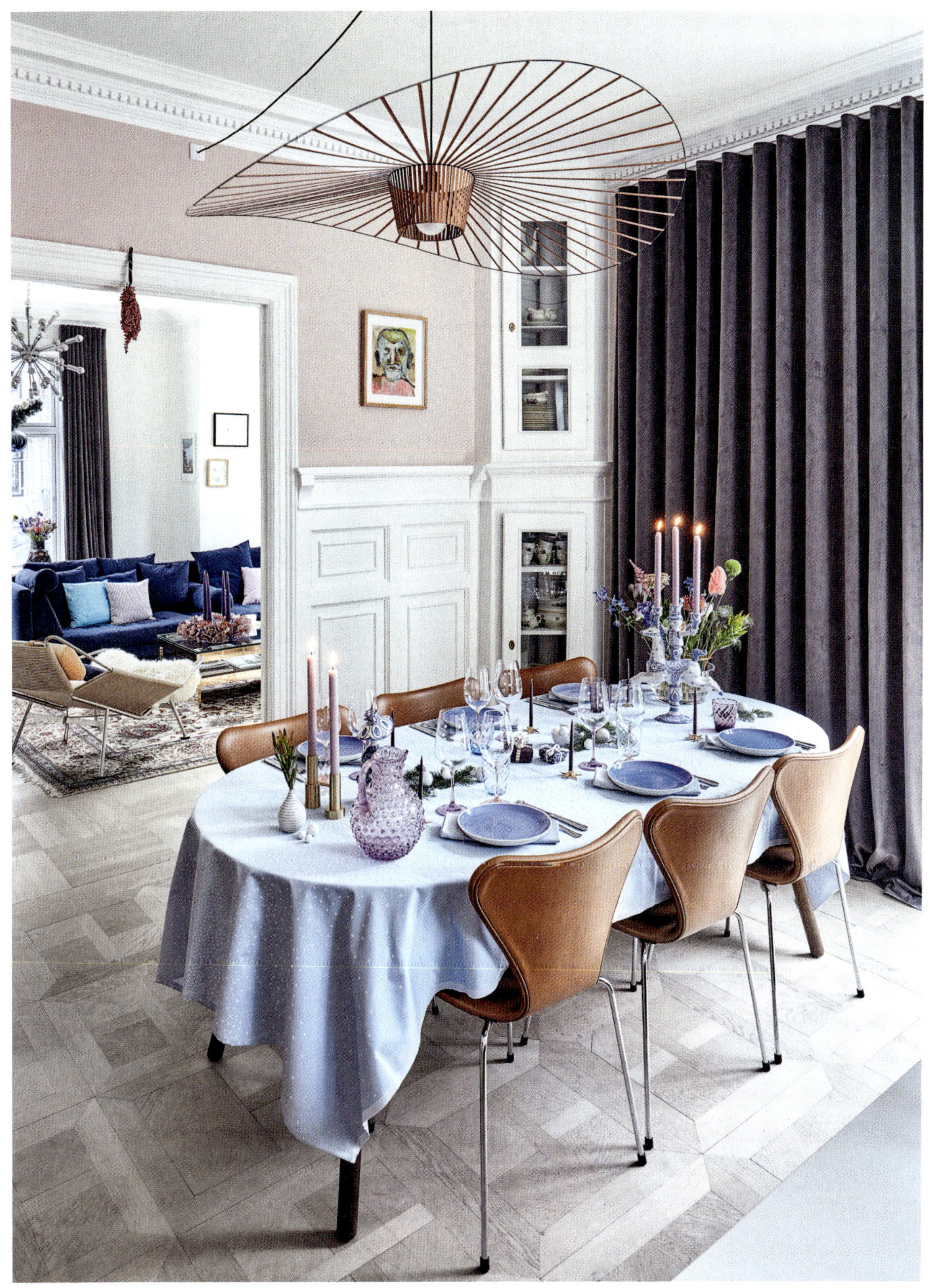

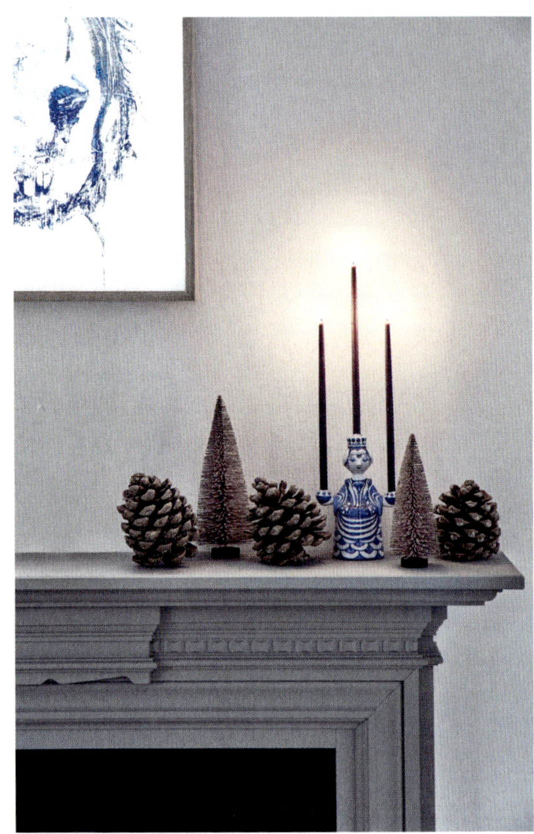

The weeks before Christmas are always a busy time. The family has special Advent customs they repeat every year, and luckily, Cathrine and Anders had no trouble blending their respective family traditions.

Cathrine says: "Traditions around Christmas are important to both our families, but Anders and I are not competitive. We delegate the various food courses for Christmas Eve to family members coming to celebrate with us. We like to take it easy and stay in our pyjamas throughout the day. It is important to relax and enjoy the time we spend together in our home."

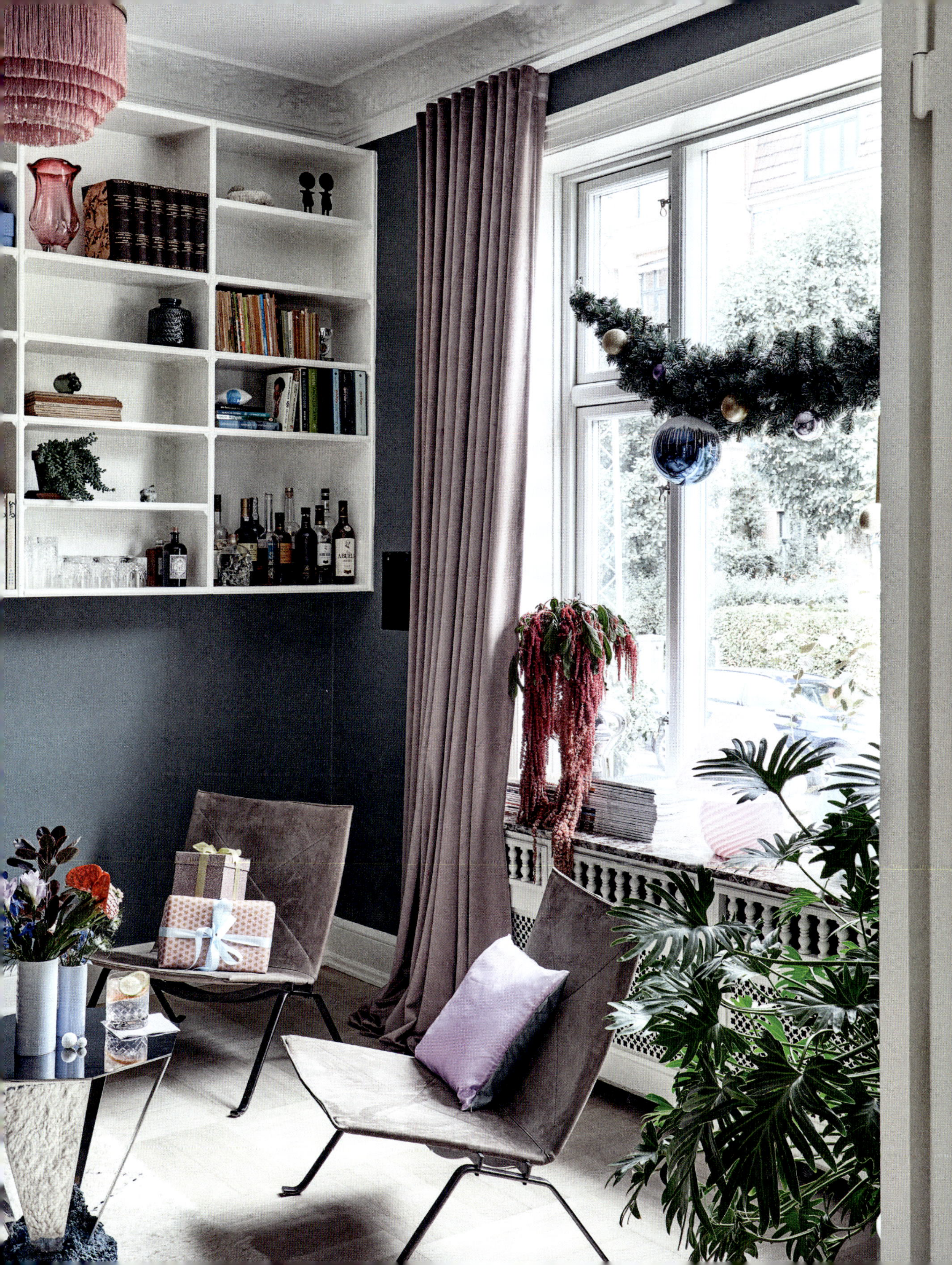

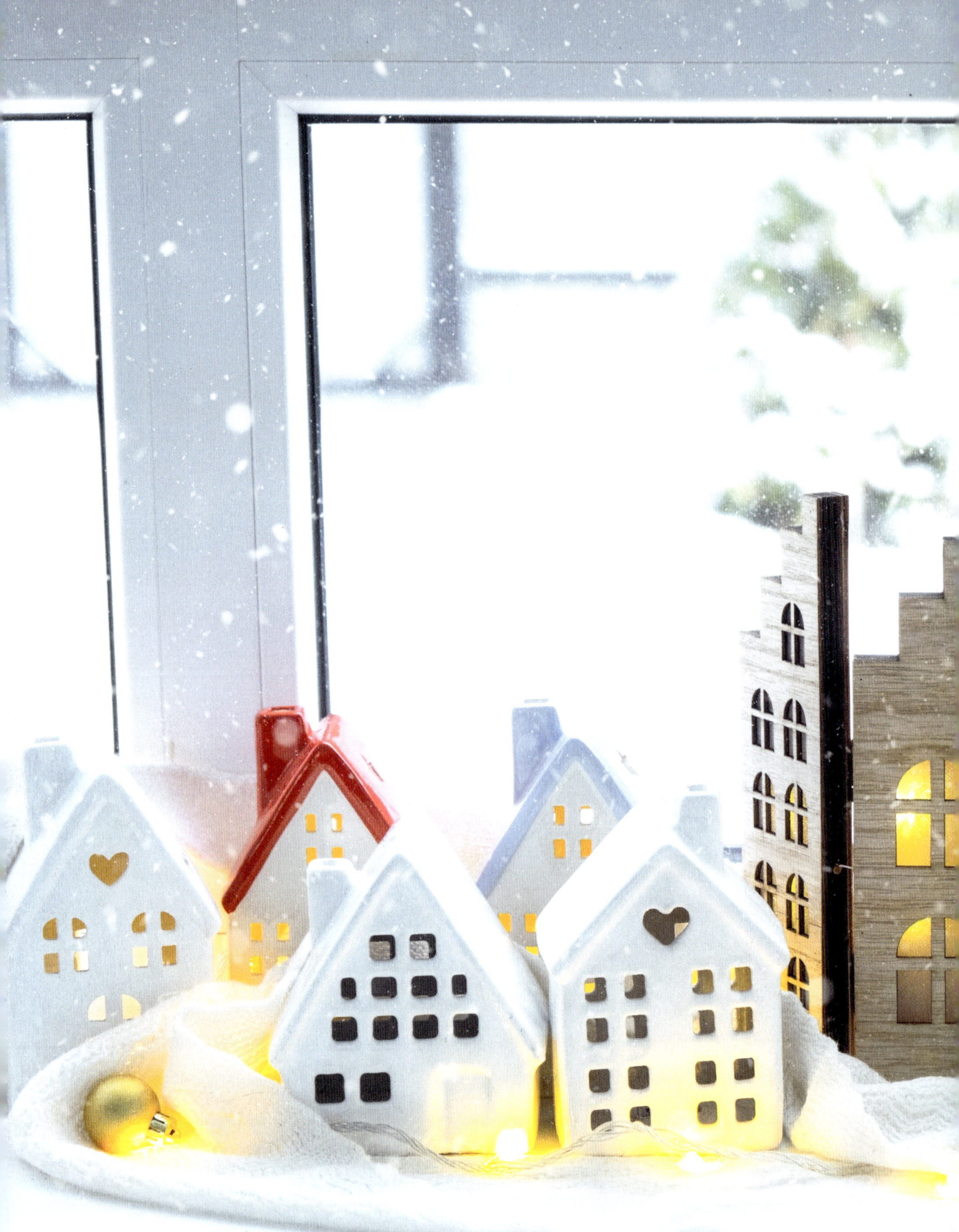

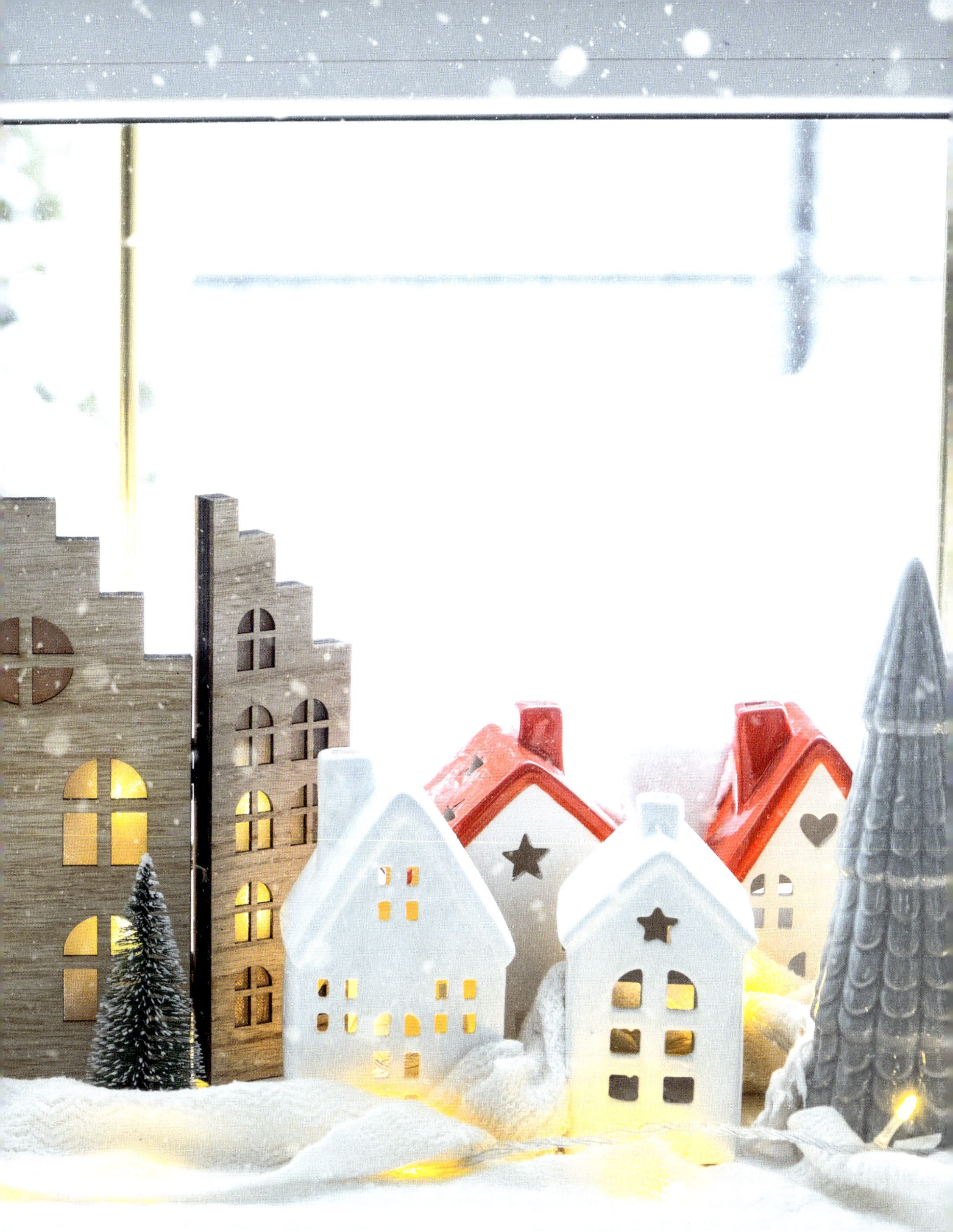

INDEX

MANUFACTURERS / DESIGNERS / SHOPS

FEATURES

PRODUCTS

p. 48/49: Bespoke buttoned footstool: Craft Upholstery | Sofa: Ilva at Redbrick Mill | Plumage rug: Wendy Morrison Design | Large arcing lamp: Bloom by Hiroshi Kawano, Urban Lux | Wall paint *De Nimes*, estate emulsion: Farrow & Ball

p. 51: Expona vinyl flooring by Polyflor: Floormart. Lou Lou Ghost armchairs and La Marie dining chairs by Kartell: Graham & Green

p. 52: Open edition prints: Circus dancer (left of Special), Circus Ringmaster (right of Special), and Circus Horse (below) by Florence Lee & Co. | Harlequin Blue candlestick from St Millies Living: Trouva

p. 53 top: Swan's Head decoration by Willa Arlo Interiors: Wayfair

p. 53 bottom: Allante Looped Purple Stair Runner: Rosalind Wheeler via Wayfair | Tiles: Bowood 50 LM-023: London Mosaic

p. 54/55: Paneling painted *Railings* by Farrow & Ball | Sideboard painted Rust-Oleum Bright Neon Pink: Sprayster | Sofa: Distinctive Chesterfields

p. 81: Cane outdoor setting: local Vinnie's | palm tree fabric: Escape to Paradise

p. 82: Rug: Spotlight | Table and Benches: Ikea | Timber board: Target

p. 84: Coffee table: Freedom

p. 87: Rug: Fab Habitat |Cushions: Ikea, Target, Design Twins and Citta

p. 120: Osby Snowflake Christmas Window Light |

INDEX

PRODUCTS | IMAGE CREDITS

53cm Pre Lit Frosted Mini Christmas Tree | 30cm Pre Lit Frosted Mini Christmas Tree | TruGlow® Ivory LED 3 Wick Candle | 15cm Gold Osby Star Light Duo | 8 Ivory TruGlow® Remote Control LED Taper Candles | 100 Warm White Outdoor Micro Fairy Lights Green Cable | 4 TruGlow® Ivory LED Votive Candles | 6 Ivory TruGlow® LED Mini Votive Candles with Remote Control | TruGlow® White Star Christmas Candle Duo | TruGlow® Ivory LED Pillar Candle Trio | TruGlow® Ivory Chapel Candle Trio | TruGlow® White LED Pillar Candle Trio | TruGlow® Ivory LED Slim Pillar Candle Trio | Dual Colour LED Osby Star Curtain Light | 23cm Osby Star Window Light: Lights4fun Ltd.

p. 121: Glass candlestick holders: Annabel James

p. 130: Dark Pink Flower/Leaf Branch | Yellow/Pink Flower/Leaf Branch | Red Flower/Leaf Branch: Gisela Graham London

p. 157: Christmas Patchwork Sherpa Fleece Throw: Happy Linen Company

p. 158: Christmas Robin Cushion (Red) | Heart Cushion (Cream) | Love Cushion (Cream) | Alpine Edelweiss Throw (Duck Egg Blue): Jan Constantine

p. 168: Christmas Mouse Animal Portrait Print: Ink & Drop

p. 171: 55 Mini Mushroom Decorations | 50 Warm White LED Micro Battery Outdoor Fairy Lights | 2m Frosted Berry and Pinecone Garland | Osby Star Window Light Bundle | TruGlow® White Star Real Wax Christmas Candle Duo | 6 Ivory TruGlow® Real Wax LED Mini Votive Candles | TruGlow® Ivory Real Wax Cone LED Pillar Candle Trio | Felt Tree Christmas Garland | TruGlow® Red Dripping Wax LED Pillar Candle Trio | 4 TruGlow® Red Dripping Wax LED Taper Candles | 30cm Pre Lit Frosted Mini Christmas Tree | TruGlow® Red Real Wax LED Chapel Candle 20cm | 300 Warm White LED Micro Christmas Tree Lights: Lights4fun Ltd.

p. 181: Sofa: Eilersen | Curtains: &Drape | Table by Belgo Chrome, purchased at Bukowski's auction house | Flagline chair by Wegner: DBA

p. 182: Clothes stand: OX Denmarq | Bench: Ikea | Deco object round candy gold: Hoffland's

p. 184: Vintage cups from Arcopal | Chocolate from Hotel Chocolat

185: Plates: Anne Black | Tablecloth: Georg Jensen Damask | Lilac glass jug: Antique Brocante Vintage | Pendant light *Vertigo Pendant*, designed by Constance Guisset: Petite Friture | Chairs designed by Arne Jacobsen: Fritz Hansen

p. 186: Sculpture by Bjørn Wiinblad | Two small Christmas trees: Søstrene Grene

p. 187: Curtains, Lavender Haze, a result of a collaboration between Cathrine and curtain makers &Drape | The Jubilee chairs PK 22 designed by Poul Kjærholm, found on DBA | Flowers in the window from Amarantus

Cover: © Мария Балчугова/AdobeStock
Front and end papers: Designed by coolvector/Freepik
Icons, Ornaments: Designed by Freepik

p. 2: Cameron Stewart/Unsplash; p. 5: © Andrea Barcelo/Shutterstock; pp. 6/7, 165: Libby Penner/Unsplash; pp. 8, 17, 27 (top left), 90, 97, 145, 178: Annie Spratt/Unsplash; p. 10: © Andrei Yarashevich/Shutterstock; pp. 11, 100/101, 159: © jan j. photography/Shutterstock; p. 12: Timothy James/Unsplash; p. 13: © Netrun78/Shutterstock; p. 14: SJ Objio/Unsplash; p. 15: Bruna Branco/Unsplash; p. 16: © Oksana Schmidt/Shutterstock; p. 18: © Agave Studio/Shutterstock; p. 19 (top): © kriina2000/AdobeStock; p. 19 (bottom): © Nastassia Kudzina/AdobeStock; p. 20 (top left): Uliana Kopanytsia/Unsplash; (bottom): © Netrun78/AdobeStock; (top right): Olivie Strauss/Unsplash; pp. 21 (top), 103, 116 (top): © Susan Law Cain/Shutterstock; (bottom): © sonyachny/AdobeStock; p. 22: © teressa/AdobeStock; pp. 24/25: © Evgeny Atamanenko/Shutterstock; pp. 26, 59, 122, 123, 141, 169, 172: Anita Austvika/Unsplash; p. 27 (top right): © Rawpixel.com/AdobeStock; (bottom): © Paul Maguire/Shutterstock; pp. 28/29: © Jason Lugo/LugoStock/AdobeStock; pp. 30–37: © Andreas von Einsiedel/living4media; pp. 38/39: © rangizzz/AdobeStock; p. 40: jsb co/Unsplash; pp. 41, 132: © Мария Балчугова/AdobeStock; p. 42: © Kolpakova Svetlana/Shutterstock; pp. 43, 114, 118 (bottom): Getty Images/Unsplash; pp. 44/45: © JasminkaM/Shutterstock; p. 46: © slavun/AdobeStock; p. 47: © Tatiana Skorina/AdobeStock; pp. 48–55: © Robert Sanderson/living4media; pp. 56/57, 160/161: © malkovkosta/AdobeStock; p. 58: © DigitalVisuals/AdobeStock; pp. 60, 128: © Ground Picture/Shutterstock; pp. 61, 62: Olena Bohovyk/Unsplash; p. 63: © AlexanderLipko/Shutterstock; pp. 64/65: © Verilux Photography/Shutterstock; p. 66: Hert Niks/Unsplash; p. 67: Kenny Eliason/Unsplash; pp. 68, 71 (right): © Floral Deco/Shutterstock; p. 69: © Anna Markina/Shutterstock; pp. 70, 156: © Sunshine/AdobeStock; pp. 71 (left), 108/109, 112: © New Africa/Shutterstock; pp. 72/73, 96: Sandra Seitamaa/Unsplash; p. 74 (left): Camylla Battani/Unsplash; (right): Genevieve Rusnac/Unsplash; p. 75: Sven Brandsma/Unsplash; p. 76: Veronika Jorjobert/Unsplash; p. 77: Melyna Cote/Unsplash; pp. 78, 135 (top): © Pixel-Shot/Shutterstock; p. 79: Jason Hawke/Unsplash; pp. 80–87: © Lynden Foss/Living Inside; p. 88: Sincerely Media/Unsplash; p. 91: © stenkovlad/AdobeStock; p. 92: Markus Spiske/Unsplash; p. 93: Maria Slama/Unsplash; p. 94: Taisiia Shestopal/Unsplash; p. 95: Valentin Petkov/Unsplash; p. 98: Liane May/Unsplash; p. 99: Switching Lanes/Unsplash; p. 102 (top left): © Fusionstudio/Shutterstock; (top right): Levi T/Unsplash; (bottom left): © fabrizio248/AdobeStock; (bottom right): © Maren Winter/Shutterstock; pp. 104/105: © Followtheflow/Shutterstock; p. 106 (top): Tyler Delgado/Unsplash; (bottom): © Jane_Mori/Shutterstock; p. 107: Olivie Strauss/Unsplash; p. 110: © ANDY DJATI/Shutterstock; p. 111 (left): © simplystocker/Shutterstock; (right): © Avocado_studio/Shutterstock; p. 113: © PhotoJuli86/Shutterstock; pp. 115, 143: Kateryna Hliznitsova/Unsplash; p. 116 (bottom left): Ripley Elisabeth Brown/Unsplash; (bottom right): Matthew Ball/Unsplash; p. 117: © Maya Kruchankova/Shutterstock; p. 118 (top left): Giselle Lazcano/Unsplash; (top right): Olesia Buyar/Unsplash; p. 119: Donna Spearman/Unsplash; pp. 120, 170: Lights4fun.co.uk © Lights4fun Ltd., Image Shot by Oliver Perrott; p. 121 (left): © Annabel James; (right): Olesia Hnatkevych/Unsplash; p. 124: © Lilly Trott/Shutterstock; pp. 125, 146: Daiga Ellaby/Unsplash, pp. 126/127: © Elizaveta Starkova/Shutterstock; p. 129: © flauma/Shutterstock; p. 130: © Gisela Graham London; p. 131 (left): © alekuwka/Shutterstock; (right): © AntonenkoS/Shutterstock; p. 133: Pablo Merchan Montes/Unsplash; pp. 134, 164: Natalie Behn/Unsplash; pp. 135 (bottom), 163, 174: Oxana Melis/Unsplash; pp. 136/137: © Maria Onoper/Shutterstock; pp. 138/139: © Alexander Raths/AdobeStock; p. 140: Margaret Jaszowska Unsplash; pp. 142, 144 (bottom): Charlotte Cowell/Unsplash; p. 144 (top left): © nerudol/AdobeStock; (top right): © Kseniya/AdobeStock; p. 147 (top): Levi T/Unsplash; (bottom): © Gulsen/AdobeStock; pp. 148–155: © Lise Mari Stang-Jacobsen/living4media; p. 157: © Happy Linen Company; p. 158: © Jan Constantine; p. 162: © Natalia Klenova; p. 166: © ibreakstock/AdobeStock; p. 167: © kasia2003/AdobeStock; p. 168 (left): © Ink & Drop; (right): © KozyPlace/AdobeStock; p. 171 (top): © darkfreya/AdobeStock; (bottom): © Fusionstudio/Shutterstock; p. 173: © sergiophoto/Shutterstock; p. 175: © Bogdan Sonjachnyj/Shutterstock; pp. 176/177: © Dmitrii Pridannikov/Shutterstock; p. 179: Lindsay Doyle/Unsplash; pp. 180–187: © Martin Sølyst/Living Inside; pp. 188/189: © Simol1407/Shutterstock

Imprint

Editorial Coordination and Book Composition by
Nadine Weinhold
Production by Sandra Jansen-Dorn
Cover Design by Eva Stadler
Design by Jens Grundei
Copyediting by Amanda Ennis
Proofreading by Nadine Weinhold
Color Separation and Prepress by Jens Grundei

Published by gestalten, Berlin 2025
ISBN: 978-3-96171-624-1
Library of Congress Number 2024935643

2nd printing, 2025

Printed in Slovakia by Neografia a.s.

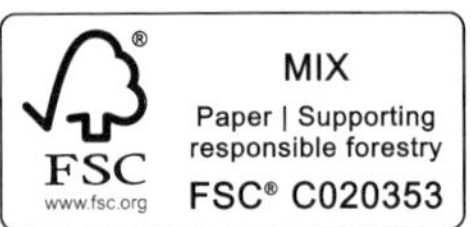

Bibliographic information published by the Deutsche Nationalbibliothek. The Deutsche Nationalbibliothek lists this publication in the Deutsche Nationalbibliografie; detailed bibliographic data is available online at www.dnb.de

For more information, and to order books, please visit www.teneues.com and www.gestalten.com

Die Gestalten Verlag GmbH & Co. KG
Mariannenstrasse 9–10
10999 Berlin, Germany
hello@gestalten.com

Düsseldorf Office
Waldenburger Straße 13
41564 Kaarst, Germany
verlag@teneues.com

teNeues Press Department
presse@gestalten.com

https://instagram.com/teneuespublishing

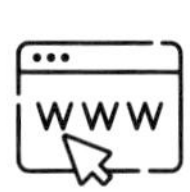

www.teneues.com

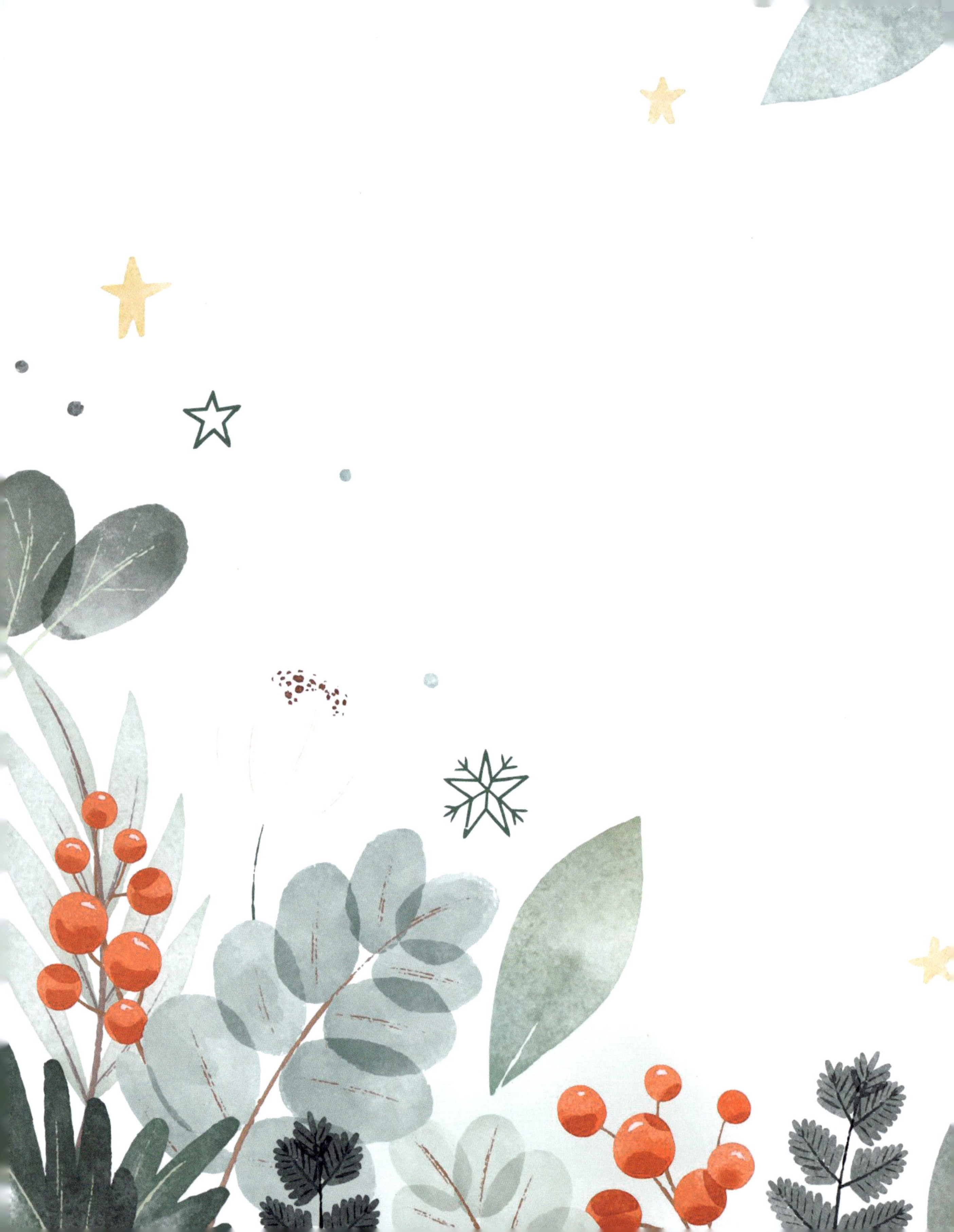